NINTH EDITION

MARKETING MISTAKES AND SUCCESSES

Robert F. Hartley
Cleveland State University

WILEY

www.wiley.com/college/hartley

11-06

Associate Publisher/Acquisitions Editor	Judith Joseph
Marketing Manager	David Woodbury
Editorial Assistant	Jessica Bartelt
Associate Production Manager	Kelly Tavares
Production Editor	Sarah Wolfman-Robichaud
Managing Editor	Lari Bishop
Illustration Editors	Gene Aiello, Benjamin Reece

This book was set in New Caledonia by Leyh Publishing LLC, and printed and bound by Courier Companies. The cover was printed by Lehigh Press.

This book is printed on acid-free paper.∞

ISBN 0-471-44638-6

Printed in the United States of America

10 9 8 7 6 5 4 3 2

PREFACE

Welcome to this ninth edition of *Marketing Mistakes and Successes.* The first edition was published more than twenty-five years ago. Who would have thought that interest in mistakes would have been so enduring.

I know of one person, Michael Pearson of Loyola University, New Orleans, who has used all of the editions. If anyone else has, going back to 1976, I would really like to hear from you—I might even splurge for a nice dinner. I know that many of you are past users though, and hope you will find this edition a worthy successor to earlier editions.

After so many years of analyzing mistakes, and more recently some successes as well, it might seem a monumental challenge to keep these new editions fresh and interesting and still provide good learning experiences. But the task of doing so, and the joy of the challenge, has made this an intriguing labor through the decades. It is always difficult to abandon interesting cases that have stimulated student discussions, but newer case possibilities are ever competing for inclusion. Examples of good and bad management of problems and opportunities are always emerging.

For new users, I hope the book will meet your full expectations and be an effective instructional tool. Although case books abound, you and your students may find this one somewhat unique and very readable, a book that can help transform dry and rather remote concepts into practical reality and lead to lively class discussions and debates in the arena of decision making.

NEW TO THIS EDITION

In contrast to the early editions, which examined only notable mistakes, and based on your favorable comments about recent editions, I have again included some well-known successes. While mistakes provide valuable learning insights, we can also learn from successes, and we can learn by comparing the unsuccessful with the successful.

We have continued the Marketing Wars section introduced in the eighth edition, in which the moves and countermoves of four pairs of direct competitors were examined. We have also continued the Crisis Management section, but expanded it a bit to include change management. Again, we have included cases dealing with great comebacks, the truly inspiring examples of firms coming back from adversity. We have tried to keep the cases as current as possible by adding Postscripts, Later Developments, and Updates where appropriate. Some of these updates were inserted just before the book went into the production process.

A number of you have asked that I identify which cases would be appropriate for the traditional coverage of topics as organized in most marketing texts. With many cases it is not possible to truly compartmentalize the mistake or success strictly according to one topic. The patterns of success or failure tend to be more pervasive.

Still, I think you will find the following classification of cases by subject matter to be helpful. I thank those of you who made this and other suggestions.

Classification of Cases by Major Marketing Topics

Topics	Most Relevant Cases
Marketing research and consumer analysis	Coca-Cola, Disney, McDonald's, Maytag
Product	Nike/Reebok, Coca-Cola/Pepsi, McDonald's, Maytag, Perrier, Boeing/Airbus, Southwest Air, Vanguard, Firestone/Ford, Dell/Gateway, Harley-Davidson, IBM
Distribution	Nike/Reebok, Coca-Cola/Pepsi, Borden, Wal-Mart, Dell/Gateway, Snapple, United Way, Newell Rubbermaid, Vanguard
Promotion	Dell/Gateway, Pepsi/Coca-Cola, Nike/Reebok, Harley-Davidson, Maytag, MetLife, Vanguard, Wal-Mart
Price	IBM, Borden, Disney, Dell/Gateway, Vanguard, Southwest, Wal-Mart, Airbus/Boeing, McDonald's, ADM, Continental, Perrier
International	Pepsi/Coca-Cola, Nike, Disney, Maytag, ADM, Airbus/Boeing, McDonald's, Wal-Mart, Nike, Harley-Davidson, Firestone/Ford
Customer relations	Newell Rubbermaid, Vanguard, Maytag, Southwest, Wal-Mart, Harley-Davidson, Firestone/Ford, MetLife, United Way
Change/crisis management	Scott Paper/Sunbeam, Perrier, MetLife, Maytag, United Way, ADM, Boeing, Firestone/Ford, Disney
Great comebacks	Continental Airlines, Harley-Davidson, IBM
Nonprofit/nonproduct	United Way, Disney, Airlines
Social and ethical	United Way, MetLife, ADM, Wal-Mart, Ford/Firestone

TARGETED COURSES

As a supplemental text, this book can be used in a variety of courses, both undergraduate and graduate, ranging from introduction to marketing to marketing management and strategic marketing. It can also be used in international marketing. Even retailing, entrepreneurship, and ethics courses could make use of a number of these cases and their learning insights. It certainly can be used in training programs and would even be interesting to nonprofessionals looking for a good read about well-known firms and personalities.

TEACHING AIDS

As in the previous editions, this edition contains a number of teaching aids within and at the end of each chapter. Some of these will be common to several cases, and illustrate that certain successful and unsuccessful practices tend to cross company lines.

Information Boxes and Issue Boxes are included within each chapter to highlight relevant concepts and issues, or related information. Learning Insights help students see how certain practices—both errors and successes—cross company lines and are prone to be either traps for the unwary or success modes. Discussion Questions and Hands-On Exercises encourage and stimulate student involvement. A recent pedagogical feature is the Team Debate Exercise, in which issues and options can be debated for each case. New in certain cases is the "Be a Devil's Advocate" exercise, in which students can argue against a proposed course of action to test its merits. Invitation to Research suggests ways students can take the case a step further, to investigate what has happened since the case was written. In the final chapter, the various learning insights are summarized and classified into general conclusions.

An Instructor's Manual written by the author accompanies the text to provide suggestions and considerations for the pedagogical material within and at the ends of chapters.

ACKNOWLEDGMENTS

It seems fitting to acknowledge all those who have provided encouragement, information, advice, and constructive criticism through the years since the first edition of this book. I hope you all are well and successful, and I truly appreciate your contributions. I apologize if I have missed anybody, and would be grateful to know so that I can rectify this in future editions. I welcome updates of present affiliations.

Beverlee Anderson, University of Cincinnati; Y.H. Furuhashi, Notre Dame; W. Jack Duncan, University of Alabama–Birmingham; Mike Farley, Del Mar College; Joseph W. Leonard, Miami University (OH); Abbas Nadim, University of New Haven; William O'Donnell, University of Phoenix; Howard Smith, University of New Mexico; James Wolter, University of Michigan–Flint; Vernon R. Stauble, California State Polytechnic University; Donna Giertz, Parkland College; Don Hantula, St. Joseph's University; Milton Alexander, Auburn University; James F. Cashman, University of Alabama; Douglas Wozniak, Ferris State University; Greg Bach, Bismark State College; Glenna Dod, Wesleyan College; Anthony McGann, University of Wyoming; Robert D. Nale, Coastal Carolina University; Robert H. Votaw, Amber University; Don Fagan, Daniel Webster University; Andrew J. Deile, Mercer University; Samuel Hazen, Tarleton State University; Michael B. McCormick, Jacksonville State University.

Also: Barnett Helzberg, Jr. of the Shirley and Barnett Helzberg Foundation. My colleagues from Cleveland State: Dean Ephraim Smith, Ram Rao, Sanford Jacobs, Andrew Gross, and Benoy Joseph. From John Wiley & Sons: Tim Kent, Ellen Ford, Brent Gordon, Jeff Marshall, and Jessica Bartelt.

Robert F. Hartley
Professor Emeritus
Cleveland State University
Cleveland, Ohio
RFHartley@aol.com

CONTENTS

CHAPTER ONE

Introduction

At this writing, *Marketing Mistakes* has passed its twenty-fifth anniversary. The first edition, back in 1976, was 147 pages and included such long-forgotten cases as Korvette, W. T. Grant, Edsel, Corfam, Gilbert, and the Midi.

In this ninth edition, seven cases from the eighth edition have been dropped, and seven were added, several of these being modified from earlier editions. Other cases have been updated and in some instances reclassified. The popular "Marketing Wars" Part I, introduced in the eighth edition, is again included and follows major competitors in their furious struggles. New to this section is the current PC war between Dell and Gateway, with Hewlett-Packard from its acquisition of Compaq also drawn into the fray. Some cases are as recent as today's headlines; a few still have not come to complete resolution. In response to your feedback, the section on notable successes has also been continued.

We continue to seek what can be learned—insights that are transferable to other firms, other times, other situations. What key factors brought monumental mistakes to some firms and resounding successes for others? Through such evaluations and studies of contrasts, we may learn to improve batting averages in the intriguing, ever-challenging art of decision making.

We will encounter organizational life cycles, with an organization growing and prospering, then failing (just as humans do), but occasionally resurging. Success rarely lasts forever, but even the most serious mistakes can be (but are not always) overcome.

As in previous editions, a variety of firms, industries, mistakes, and successes are presented. You will be familiar with most of the organizations, although probably not with the details of their situations.

We are always on the lookout for cases that can bring out certain points or caveats in the art of marketing decision making, and that give a balanced view of the spectrum of marketing problems. The goal is to present examples that provide somewhat different learning experiences, where at least some aspect of the mistake or success is unique. Still, we see similar mistakes occurring time and again. From the prevalence of such mistakes, it is hard to say how much decision making has really improved over the decades.

Let us then consider what learning insights we can gain, with the benefit of hindsight, from examining these examples of successful and unsuccessful marketing practices.

LEARNING INSIGHTS

Analyzing Mistakes

In looking at sick companies, or even healthy ones that have experienced difficulties with certain parts of their operations, it is tempting to be overly critical. It is easy to criticize with the benefit of hindsight. Mistakes are inevitable, given the present state of decision making and the dynamic environment facing organizations.

Mistakes can be categorized as errors of omission and of commission. *Mistakes of omission* are those in which no action was taken and the status quo was contentedly embraced amid a changing environment. Such errors, often characteristic of conservative or stodgy management, are not as obvious as the other category of mistakes. They seldom involve tumultuous upheaval; rather, the company's competitive position slowly fades, until management finally realizes that mistakes having monumental impact have been allowed to happen. Often, the firm's fortunes never regain their former luster. But sometimes they do, and this leads us to the intriguing Part II, "Great Comebacks," showing how Continental Airlines, IBM, and Harley-Davidson fought back successfully from adversity.

Mistakes of commission are more spectacular. They involve hasty decisions, poor support and follow-up, misdirected expansion, and the like. Although the costs of eroding competitive position due to errors of omission are difficult to calculate precisely, the costs of errors of commission are often fully evident. For example, the costs associated with the deceptive selling efforts of MetLife in fines and restitution totaled nearly two billion dollars. With Euro Disney, in 1993 alone the loss was $960 million; it improved in 1994 with only a $366 million loss. With Maytag's overseas Hoover Division, the costs of an incredibly bungled sales promotion were more than $200 million, and still counting. Then there was the reckless purchase of Snapple by Quaker Oats CEO, William Smithburg, for $1.7 billion; Quaker sold the product less than three years later for $300 million.

Although they may make mistakes, organizations with sharp managements follow certain patterns when confronting difficult situations:

1. Looming problems or present mistakes are quickly recognized.
2. The causes of the problem(s) are carefully determined.
3. Alternative corrective actions are evaluated in view of the company's resources and constraints.
4. Corrective action is prompt. Sometimes this requires a ruthless axing of the product, the division, or whatever is at fault.
5. Mistakes provide learning experiences. The same mistakes are not repeated, and future operations are consequently strengthened.

Slowness to recognize emerging problems leads us to think that management is incompetent or that controls have not been established to provide prompt feedback at strategic control points. For example, a declining competitive position in one or a few geographical areas should be a red flag that something is amiss. To wait months before investigating or taking action may mean a permanent loss of business. Admittedly, signals sometimes get mixed, and complete information may be lacking, but procrastination is not easily defended.

Just as problems should be quickly recognized, the causes of these problems—the "why" of the unexpected results—must be determined as quickly as possible. It is premature, and rash, to take action before knowing where the problems really lie. Returning to the previous example, the loss of competitive position in one or a few markets may reflect circumstances beyond the firm's immediate control, such as an aggressive new competitor who is drastically cutting prices to "buy sales." In this situation, all competing firms will likely lose market share, and little can be done except to stay as competitive as possible with prices and servicing. However, closer investigation may reveal that the erosion of business was due to unreliable deliveries, poor quality control, uncompetitive prices, or incompetent sales staff.

With the cause(s) of the problem defined, various alternatives for dealing with it should be identified and evaluated. This may require further research, such as obtaining feedback from customers and from field personnel. Finally, the decision to correct the situation should be made as objectively as possible. If drastic action is needed, there usually is little rationale for delaying. Serious problems do not go away by themselves: They tend to fester and become worse.

Finally, some learning experience should result from the misadventure. A vice president of one successful firm told me

> I try to give my subordinates as much decision-making experience as possible. Perhaps I err on the side of delegating too much. In any case, I expect some mistakes to be made, some decisions that were not for the best. I don't come down too hard usually. This is part of the learning experience. But God help them if they make the same mistake again. There has been no learning experience, and I question their competence for higher executive positions.

Analyzing Successes

Successes deserve as much analysis as mistakes, although admittedly the need to analyze them is less urgent than with an emerging problem that requires quick remedial action. Any analysis of success should seek answers to at least the following questions:

Why were such actions successful?
　Was it because of the environment, and if so, how?
　Was it because of particular research, and if so, what and how?
　Was it because of particular engineering and/or production efforts, and if so, can these be adapted to other operations?
　Was it because of any particular element of the strategy—such as service, promotional activities, or distribution methods—and if so, how?
　Was it because specific elements of the strategy meshed well together, and if so, how was this achieved?
Was the situation unique and unlikely to be encountered again?

If the situation was not unique, how can these successful techniques be used in the future or in other operations at the present time?

ORGANIZATION OF THIS BOOK

In this ninth edition, the classification of cases is modified somewhat from earlier editions. As mentioned earlier, Part I on "Marketing Wars" examines the actions and countermoves of archrivals in a hotly competitive arena. Part II continues a section introduced in the sixth edition that many readers approved of: "Great Comebacks." The learning insights revealing how great adversity was finally turned to success seemed too fertile to abandon. Another section, first appearing in the eighth edition, is "Change and Crisis Management," in which we examine four firms that faced major changes and crises and mishandled them. Next are grouped cases of traditional marketing mistakes, and then cases of notable marketing successes. Finally, we can hardly ignore social and ethical concerns in the closer scrutiny of business practices today. Let us briefly describe the cases that follow.

Marketing Wars

What made the marketing war between Dell Computer and Gateway and Hewlett-Packard all the more fascinating was that it took place in an economic downturn particularly hard on technology firms. Yet one firm prospered despite this adversity.

Pepsi and Coca-Cola for decades competed in the lucrative international arena. Usually Coca-Cola won out, but it could never let its guard down, and it recently did so in Europe.

Boeing had long dominated the worldwide commercial aircraft market, with the European Airbus only a minor player. But a series of Boeing blunders, coupled with an aggressive Airbus, brought market shares close to parity; though now the momentum was with Airbus.

Reebok and Nike are major competitors in the athletic footwear and apparel market. Nike was overtaken by Reebok in the late 1980s, but then Nike surged far ahead. How did this happen?

Great Comebacks

The comeback of Continental Airlines from extreme adversity and devastated employee morale to become one of the best airlines in the country is an achievement of no small moment. New CEO Gordon Bethune brought marketing and human relations skills to one of the most rapid turnarounds ever, overcoming a decade of raucous adversarial labor relations and a reputation in the pits.

In an earlier edition, IBM was classified as a prime example of a giant firm that had failed to cope with changing technology. Along with many other analysts, the author thought the behemoth could never rouse itself enough to regain its status as a major player. But we were wrong, and IBM once again became a premier growth company.

In the early 1960s, Harley-Davidson dominated a static motorcycle industry. Suddenly, Honda burst on the scene and Harley's market share dropped from 70 percent to 5 percent in only a few years. It took Harley nearly three decades to revive, but now it has created a mystique for its heavy motorcycles and gained a new customer.

Crisis Management

Albert Dunlap had a well-deserved reputation as the premier hatchet man, the one who would come into a sick organization and fire enough people to make it temporarily profitable—he was known as "Chainsaw Al." Somehow, with Sunbeam this seemingly proven downsizing strategy did not work, and Dunlap himself was fired by the board of directors. Later investigations brought fraud suits for accounting misdeeds.

Product safety lapses that result in injuries and even loss of life are among the worst abuses any company can make. Worse, however, is when such risks are allowed to continue for years. Ford Explorers equipped with Firestone tires were involved in more than two hundred deaths from tire failures and vehicle rollovers. After news of the accidents began surfacing, Ford and Firestone blamed each other for the deaths. Eventually, inept crisis management brought a host of lawsuits resulting in massive recalls and billions of dollars in damages.

Perrier, the bottled water firm, encountered adversity when traces of benzene were found in some of its product. Responsibly, it ordered a sweeping recall of all bottles in North America and, a few days later, in the rest of the world while it tried to correct the problem. For five months Perrier kept the product off the market, thereby allowing competitors an unparalleled windfall. Worse was the public realization that claims regarding the purity of its product were false.

The man who led United Way of America to prominence as the nation's largest charity came to perceive himself as virtually beyond authority. Exorbitant spending, favoritism, conflicts of interest—these went uncontrolled and uncriticized until investigative reporters from the *Washington Post* brought to light the scandalous conduct. Amid the hue and cry, contributions plummeted as the organization sought to rectify the situation and cope with image destruction.

Marketing Mistakes

The problems of Maytag's Hoover subsidiary in the United Kingdom almost defy reason. The subsidiary planned a promotional campaign so generous that the company was overwhelmed with takers; it could neither supply the products nor grant the prizes. In a miscue of multimillion-dollar consequences, Maytag had to foot the bill while trying to appease irate customers.

McDonald's dominated the hamburger fast-food market for four decades, leaving all rivals in the dust, and became the model for enduring success. Today, McDonald's seems more like a faltering old man. It has become so vulnerable that it is finally exploring changes designed to bring back domestic growth and fight off Burger King and other eager competitors. Some say the changes are not radical enough.

In April 1992, just outside Paris, Disney opened its first theme park in Europe. It had high expectations and supreme self-confidence (critics later called it arrogance). The earlier Disney parks in California and Florida, and more recently in Japan, were all spectacular successes. But rosy expectations became a delusion as marketing miscues finally showed Disney that Europeans, and particularly the French, were not carbon copies of visitors elsewhere.

Borden, with its enduring symbol of Elsie the Cow, was the country's largest producer of dairy products. On an acquisitions binge in the 1980s, it became a diversified food processor and marketer—and a $7 billion company. But Borden allowed consumer acceptance of its many brands to wither through unrealistic pricing, ineffective advertising, and an unwieldy organization.

Snapple, a marketer of noncarbonated fruit-flavored and ice tea drinks, was acquired by Quaker Oats in late 1994 for $1.7 billion. As sales declined and losses mounted, it soon became apparent to all but the president of Quaker that far too much had been paid for this acquisition. No strategy changes could turn Snapple around. In 1997, Quaker sold Snapple for $300 million—a loss of $1.4 billion in less than three years.

Rubbermaid also miscalculated in the staying power of its brand name, and let customer service slip in dealings with behemoth retail chains. In 1999 it was acquired by Newell, a successful consumer products marketer to these chains. But the problems of Rubbermaid were not easily corrected and had a negative impact on the fortunes of Newell as well.

Marketing Successes

Vanguard, the second largest mutual fund company, is rapidly closing on Fidelity, the largest. Vanguard's strategy is to downplay marketing, shunning the heavy advertising and overhead of its competitors. It provides investors with better returns through far lower expense ratios, relying mostly on word of mouth and unpaid publicity to gain new customers, while old customers continue to pour money in.

In somewhat similar fashion, Southwest Airlines found a strategic window of opportunity as the lowest-priced carrier between certain cities. And how it milked this opportunity! Now it threatens major airlines in many of their domestic routes.

Our last success in this section is also about a firm that dominates its industry through offering customers lowest prices. Wal-Mart now is by far the largest retailer in the world, and its invasion of Europe is traumatizing retailers there. Its founder, Sam Walton, believed in frugality and a lean but efficient organization. The story of one man's rise to the pinnacle of his chosen field in just a few decades is inspiring. Despite his wealth and prestige, Walton had the common touch.

Ethical and Social Pressures

The huge insurance firm MetLife, whether through loose controls or tacit approval, permitted an agent to use deceptive selling tactics on a grand scale, in the process enriching himself and the company. Investigations by several state attorneys general brought a crisis situation to the firm that it was slow to react to. Eventually, fines and lawsuits totaled almost $2 billion.

ADM presents a paradox: It was a highly successful firm, but its success was tarnished by unethical practices and even illegal price-fixing. A dictatorial CEO also fostered political cronyism. A whistleblower brought jail sentences to several company executives and himself as well.

GENERAL WRAP-UP

Where possible, the text depicts major personalities involved in these cases. Imagine yourself in their positions, confronting the problems and facing choices at their points of crisis or just-recognized opportunities. What would you have done differently, and why? We invite you to participate in the discussion questions, the hands-on exercises, the debates appearing at the ends of chapters, and the occasional devil's advocate invitation (a devil's advocate is one who argues an opposing position for the sake of testing the decision). There are also discussion questions for the various boxes within chapters.

While doing these activities, you may feel the excitement and challenge of decision making under conditions of uncertainty. Perhaps you may even become a better future executive and decision maker.

QUESTIONS

1. Do you agree that it is impossible for a firm to avoid mistakes? Why or why not?

2. How can a firm speed up its awareness of emerging problems so that it can take corrective action? Be as specific as you can.

3. Large firms tend to err on the side of conservatism and are slower to take corrective action than smaller ones. Why do you suppose this is?

4. Which do you think is likely to be more costly to a firm: errors of omission or errors of commission? Why?

5. So often, the successful firm eventually loses its pattern of success. Why is success not more enduring?

PART ONE

MARKETING WARS

CHAPTER TWO

PC Wars: Dell Computer vs. Gateway et al.

The mettle of a person, or a firm, is best tested and judged not in the euphoria of prosperity and boom conditions, but in the bleakness of adversity. The several years before and after the millennium provided the testing ground in the marketing wars among personal computer (PC) makers.

By 2002 the lower-price PC market had narrowed to two main adversaries, both the founders of their firms: Michael Dell of Dell Computer and Ted Waitt of Gateway. Both had started their ventures in the mid-1980s on a shoestring. One was nineteen years old, the other twenty-two. Both became billionaires. By 2002 the PC boom was over, spending for technology was stagnant, and the high-tech industry was in the vanguard of the stock market collapse. Once-mighty organizations with highly valued names—Lucent, Cisco Systems, and Compaq—were only grim reminders of lost chances to cash out in the heady days of 50 percent annual growth.

Some analysts saw the PC market as saturated; everyone who needed and could afford a desktop or laptop already had one. Technological advances had slowed, with the current generation of machines already fast enough for most uses, thus lessening incentive to replace or trade up. The economic downturn further caused tightened rather than extravagant spending. As the product life cycle for PCs lengthened, long-term growth prospects dimmed for computer makers. The high stock multiples of only a few years before were hardly sustainable in a low-growth era. Furthermore, as the market became saturated, not all firms were likely to survive.

DELL COMPUTER

The Start

Michael Dell, a tall curly-haired youth of nineteen, started Dell Computer in a dorm room at the University of Texas in 1984 with $1,000. He had an idea that computer systems could be sold directly to customers rather than going through middlemen. He thought the manufacturer could better understand the needs of customers and provide them the most effective computing systems at lower prices. This direct marketing would also do away with retailers and their high margins.

Three years later, in 1987, Dell began its international expansion by opening a subsidiary in the United Kingdom. The next year, Dell took his enterprise public, with an initial offering of 3.5 million shares at $8.50 each, and became an instant multimillionaire. By 1992 Dell was included in the *Fortune* 500 roster of largest companies. In 1997 the presplit price per share of the common stock reached $1,000, and Michael Dell was a multibillionaire.

With the bruising industry downturn, Dell's stock price fell along with all the rest, its shares by mid-2002 down 55 percent from the early 2001 peak of $59. Michael Dell bought 8.5 million shares of his company to add to the 300 million he already owned.

Competition in 2002

In this troubled environment, Dell's revenue in 2001 grew 2.6 percent while that of the PC industry fell 14 percent. For the quarter ended May 3, 2002, Dell reported $457 million in earnings on sales of $8 billion. These figures were flat from the year-earlier figures, but far better than those of Dell's competitors.

Compaq, once the master of the PC business, found its stock collapsing from $50 to below $10, and was forced into a merger with Hewlett-Packard (H-P) since it could not compete profitably with Dell. Gateway was on the ropes, and even high-end manufacturers like Silicon Graphics (SGI) and Sun Microsystems were losing sales to Dell. Only IBM seemed insulated from Dell's competitive strength, due to its huge mainframe and services businesses that were not directly competitive.

Dell's Market Share Inroads

The economic downturn provided Dell a golden opportunity to grab market share.

It almost doubled its share of the worldwide PC market, going from 8 percent to 15 percent in just four years.[1] Much of this came when Dell cut prices as the downturn began, thus pressuring rivals with higher cost structures. Wall Street initially criticized this move as bound to destroy Dell's profits. But the consequent boost in market share instead led to increased profits.

When Hewlett-Packard acquired Compaq Computer for $19 billion in May 2002, it leapfrogged Dell to become the biggest PC maker in the world. But the dominance was short-lived. Next quarter, Dell's share of the PC market grew to 14.9 percent from 13.1 percent a year earlier, while H-P's combined share with Compaq fell to 15.5 percent from 18.3 percent before the merger.[2] By fall 2002, Dell regained its No. 1 worldwide ranking, shipping 5.2 million PCs to H-P's 5.0 million.[3]

Dell was also engaged in a major marketing battle with H-P in the printer arena. H-P had long dominated this market of printers and related gear, and with it the very

[1] "Muscling into New Markets," *Money*, November 2002, p. 49.

[2] Pui-Wing Tam, Gary McWilliams, and Scott Thurm, "As Alliances Fade, Computer Firms Toss Out Playbook," *Wall Street Journal*, 15 October 2002, pp. A1 and A8.

[3] Gary McWilliams, "Gateway's Loss Shrinks, But It Sees Gloomy Year," *Wall Street Journal*, 18 October 2002, p. A7.

lucrative ink refills market. These ink and toner refills brought H-P some $10 billion annually, this being 15 percent of its combined annual revenues.[4] See the Information Box: Vulnerability of Cash Cows. Dell's entry into this market through an alliance with No. 2 printer maker Lexmark struck at the vital organs of H-P. If Dell could pressure H-P's highly profitable printer business, H-P would be less able to subsidize its money-losing PC sector, thus adding to Dell's mastery of its core PC operation.

Dell also pursued a potential vulnerability of the H-P/Compaq merger. Longtime H-P and Compaq customers were justifiably apprehensive about the proposed acquisition and how it would turn out. Dell aggressively wooed these corporate customers, especially those buying PCs and the larger computer systems called servers. Dell believed it could offer them lower prices and better customer service.

Gateway was Dell's most direct competitor. Both firms sell PCs directly to customers by phone or on the Internet, thereby bypassing dealers and allowing customers to design the specifications to their individual needs.

A point of difference was the several hundred "Gateway Country" stores, in which customers could evaluate PCs in the store. Both companies geared their offerings to the low end of the price range, but Gateway was having serious problems competing with Dell on price. Gateway had lost $1 billion on $6 billion in revenues in 2001, and the company was on the ropes. See Table 2.1 for the trend in operating results from 1994 through 2001 for Dell, Gateway, and Hewlett-Packard, and the relative shifts in market shares for these three major PC competitors. Table 2.2 shows net income comparisons and the trends for these same three competitors.

INFORMATION BOX

VULNERABILITY OF CASH COWS

A cash cow is a product or division that is well entrenched with good profits in a low-growth market. Potential competitors seldom are attracted to such a market or willing to make the investment needed to go against a dominant firm. With no competitive threat, this firm has little incentive to invest more, and is content to "milk" the profits of the cash cow, especially if the cow is as essential as ink is to a printer.

However, danger can lurk in this complacent mind-set. If the product is profitable enough, and if entry into the industry is not prohibitive, then interlopers may still be attracted. Or in Dell's case, with H-P's cash cow subsidizing the money-losing PC sector in direct competition with Dell, it seemed worth attacking.

Therein lies the danger of being greedy with cash cow profitability. Any attempt to enter the market will bring prices and profits tumbling down. A more defensible strategy for the dominant firm is to be content with more modest profits and minimize competitive threats.

Do you think Dell will be successful in its "invasion" of the printer and ink refill market? What circumstances might affect its successful entry?

---

[4] Ibid., A8.

TABLE 2.1. Market Shares of Top Three Competitors (Million $), 1994–2001

	2001	2000	1999	1998	1996	1994
Dell						
Revenue[a]	31,168	31,888	25,265	18,243	7,759	3,475
Mkt. Share[b]	37.8%	35.3	33.1	25.1	15.2	11.2
Gateway						
Revenue	6,080	9,601	8,646	7,468	5,035	2,701
Mkt. Share	7.4%	10.6	11.3	10.3	9.8	8.7
Hewlett-Packard						
Revenue	45,226	48,782	42,370	47,061	38,420	24,991
Mkt. Share	54.8%	54.1	55.6	64.6	75.0	80.1

[a] The three competitors had slightly different fiscal years. They have all been adjusted to the same calendar years.

[b] The market shares are computed as the relative revenue to the total of these three leading competitors. For example, in 2001 the total revenues of Dell, Gateway, and H-P were $82,474 million. Dell's market share, then, was its own revenues divided by the total revenues for the year: 31,168 ÷ 82,474 = 37.8 percent

Commentary: The trend information of these statistics is of major significance. It shows that over these seven years, Dell has increased its market share relative to its major competitors from 11.2 percent to 37.8 percent, a major feat in a competitive market. In the same years, H-P has had a steady decline in market share from 80.1 percent to 54.8 percent. Gateway, after gaining market share steadily up to 1999, had a precipitous decline in its competitive position.

Sources: Company annual reports.

TABLE 2.2. Net Income Comparisons of Dell and Its Major Competitors (Million $), 1994–2001

	2001	2000	1999	1998	1996	1994
Dell						
Net income[a]	$1,246	2,236	1,666	1,460	531	149
% of three competitors[b]	66.6%	37.0	32.1	30.9	15.8	8.1
Gateway						
Net income	(1,014)	253	426	346	251	96
% of comp.	NM	4.2	8.2	7.3	7.5	5.2
H-P						
Net income	624	3,561	3,104	2,946	2,586	1,589
% of comp.	33.4	58.8	59.7	61.8	76.7	86.7

[a] The net income percentage of competition is computed similarly to note b in Table 2.1. Instead of relative market share based on revenues, this table compares net income.

[b] See note a in Table 2.1. NM means "not meaningful," in this case because of the net loss.

Commentary: Here again, trend information is very revealing of the shifting competitive strengths in this market. Dell's profitability compared to its two main rivals shows steady gains, with a huge jump in 2001. H-P's relative profitability has been steadily declining since 1994, and it took a real hit in 2001. Gateway's profitability, which had a nice trend during the industry's boom days, suffered badly in the industry downturn. With the huge loss in 2001 (a loss that continued in 2002, and into the first quarter of 2003, the ninth loss in the last 10 quarters) the company's viability as a separate entity may even be in doubt.

Sources: Company annual reports.

TED WAITT OF GATEWAY

In the fall of 2002, Ted Waitt (chairman and CEO of Gateway) had to be concerned. It would be bad enough if the computer collapse was affecting all firms equally, with market shares staying about the same. But that was not happening. While Gateway and most others were suffering, one firm—Dell—seemed somehow to be profiting and picking up great chunks of market share, much of it at Gateway's expense.

Waitt's thoughts went back to the beginning, to the farmhouse where in 1985 he and friend Mike Hammond had put their dreams to the test with a used computer, a three-page business plan, and a loan of $10,000 guaranteed by his grandmother. He had dropped out of the University of Iowa to devote full time to this fledgling endeavor, to this dream. The business plan was simple and had not changed much even in 2002: Offer products directly to customers and build them to their specifications, with the goal of providing the best value for the money. The enterprise grossed $100,000 the first year, and was on its way to becoming a multibillion-dollar company.

Now his thoughts turned to the heady years of growth and unbelievable promise. In 1989 he began selling computers online, taking pride in being the first in the industry to do so. Even mighty Dell did not use the Internet for sales until 1996. In 1991 Waitt got the idea of introducing the cow-spotted boxes, which brought wide acclaim for Gateway and made its products distinctive. He was then on a roll, and in 1992 began offering customers a choice of software at no additional cost. It was with a great sense of achievement that he learned in 1993 that Gateway had become one of the *Fortune* 500 biggest firms, one year after Dell had joined these prestigious ranks. Not bad for an Iowa farm boy. But that same year, something even more momentous happened. Waitt took the firm public, and investor enthusiasm was so great that he became an instant multimillionaire, and not long after, a multibillionaire. A person can get used to these accomplishments. In 1996 Waitt introduced a nationwide network of what he called Gateway Country stores—after all, he was a country boy—where customers could try out his products, get advice from technical experts, and learn more about technology in high-tech classrooms.

He shrugged his shoulders in disgust. In 1999 his one-third share of the business was worth $9 billion. In 2002 it was worth $400 million and still falling, an unbelievable personal loss of over $8.5 billion. He probably felt flummoxed.

At first Waitt blamed his handpicked successor, who was ousted when he returned as CEO. But his magic touch now seemed to elude him. He faced a battle for market share in a down market and a price war to boot with Dell, his nemesis. Michael Dell had somehow gotten his costs so low that he could undersell all competitors and still make money. In desperation, Waitt slashed Gateway's workforce by 10 percent. But it was not enough. Then he scaled back the company's international ambitions by exiting Europe and Asia, and reduced the workforce by another 25 percent. But Gateway's U.S. market share dropped from 7.4 percent in 2001 to 5.6 percent in 2002.

Waitt turned his attention to Apple Computer. If he couldn't match Dell on price, maybe he could attack Apple. On August 26, 2002, he launched a nationwide TV brand battle against Apple with a new computer—the Profile 4, which resembled Apple's iMacs but was $400 cheaper (albeit with fewer features). For years Waitt had struggled to establish Gateway as a cult brand (hoping his rural Holstein theme with the black-and-white cow spots would convey an image of heartland honesty and dependability), one that would appeal to Apple's cult-like followers as well as others. But that had not happened, and he was thinking of putting the cow to rest. Apple had nourished its cult with magazines, chat groups, and a storied twenty-year battle against the standard PC. But could Gateway gain some of this following? Critics were not very complimentary, citing Profile 4's lack of a rewriteable DVD drive and upgraded graphics, its boxiness compared with Apple, and a screen that did not swivel as smoothly. Well, critics be d----d; his model was still $400 cheaper.

But the price war with Dell could not be ignored. Trying to reduce costs was cutting into muscle, hurting market share, and still not yielding profits. The loss in the quarter ending June 30, 2002, tripled to $61 million on revenues of $1 billion. By contrast, Dell was prospering with a $501 million profit on sales of $9.5 billion, up 11 percent from the previous year. To add salt to the wounds, a Dell executive gloated in a prominent business journal: "It hasn't been a tough market for us."[5]

Now analysts were picking at Gateway's bones, like jackals on the prowl. They were speculating that many of the company's 274 stores would have to be closed, and more production outsourced to foreign manufacturers, if there was any hope of returning to profitability.[6]

Doggedly, Waitt predicted as 2002 drew to a close that Gateway would show a quarterly profit at some point during 2003. But he was disconcerted to learn that both the Council of Institutional Investors and the huge California Public Employees Retirement System had added Gateway to their lists of underperformers.[7]

COMPETITIVE STRENGTH OF DELL

Low Cost Structure

Dell depended heavily on technology developed by others. Essentially, Dell had turned low-end computers into a commodity, so that they could supplant high-priced brands. In the process, once high-flying firms such as Digital Equipment, Apollo Computer, and Data General were now in the graveyard. No one seemed able to match Dell's low prices and still be profitable.

Dell's operating costs, and this included research and development, were around 10 percent in 2001, compared with 20 percent at Compaq, 21 percent at Gateway, 22 percent at H-P, and 45 percent at Cisco. Trying to match the costs of Dell was no simple matter. Compaq and H-P in their merger hoped to cut $2.5 billion out of their combined costs. Dell, half the size of the two companies after their merger, actually cut $1 billion in operating and manufacturing costs in 2001, and planned to do so again in 2002.[8] See the Information Box: Dell Production Efficiencies.

[5] Arlene Weintraub, "Gateway: Picking Fights It Just Might Lose," *Business Week*, 9 September 2002, p. 52.
[6] Ibid.
[7] McWilliams, "Gateway's Loss," A7.
[8] Daniel Fisher, "Pulled in a New Direction," *Forbes*, 10 June 2002, p. 104.

INFORMATION BOX

DELL'S PRODUCTION EFFICIENCIES

In 2001, Dell wrung $1 billion out of its costs, half of that coming from manufacturing. Other areas of cost savings included product design, logistics, and warranty costs. The company vowed to cut another $1 billion in 2002.

Dell reduced manufacturing costs with a more efficient factory layout, computer-directed conveyor systems, robots, and constant attention to simplifying assembly and reducing the number of people needed to complete a product. Purchasing managers worked with suppliers to watch parts inventories hourly, ensuring there were just enough parts to meet expected demand without excess inventory. Its constant attention to improving efficiency enabled Dell to increase production by a third in two years while cutting manufacturing space in half.

Do you see a downside to constantly trying to improve efficiency and cost-cutting?

Source: Fisher, "Pulled in a New Direction," 110.

Dell typically entered a market only after the technology had become standardized and cheap. In the process, it saved on R&D. Cisco, for example, spent 18 percent of its revenue on R&D, while Dell spent a puny 1.5 percent. This allowed Dell to capitalize on its leaner operations and undercut rivals. Seemingly, the march toward standardization had been unstoppable. For example, Lotus Notes had been largely supplanted by Internet browsers. But standardization might not make such inroads against the proprietary bastions of storage—mainframe computers, switches, and networking equipment.

Marketing Efforts

In 2000, Dell introduced a blond character named Steven into its PC commercials. Steven—played by actor Ben Curtis, a 21-year-old college student—soon blanketed the pop culture landscape as he shilled for Dell. In the commercials, Steve practically grew up before our eyes, moving from high school to an undisclosed college campus. The original commercial spots had Steven trying to harangue parents into buying their high school offspring a Dell. Three months later, Steven's famous tag line was added: "Dude, you're getting a Dell." (In his portrayal of Steve, Ben earned $100,000 a year.) How much this ad campaign contributed to Dell's increasing popularity, especially among younger PC users, is impossible to determine—a deficiency of most advertising—but the company spent one-third of its $226.8 million budget on ads of Steven. Most of the remainder was aimed at business customers interested in servers and corporate personal computers.

In late 2002, however, Dell's commercials began downplaying Steven, replacing him with young "Dell interns." Although the emphasis was still directed at the youth market, it looked like Steven's $100,000 contract was in jeopardy. [9]

In late 2002, Dell began opening kiosks in major malls across the country. These booths in heavily trafficked areas gave consumers the chance to touch and play with Dell computers instead of just seeing them in pictures. The rent was far less than for a store in the mall, while visibility was greatly increased.

New Horizons for Dell

In 1997 Dell made a strategic decision to expand beyond PCs into the market for servers, those high-end computers with multiple microprocessors to run complex software. By 2002, servers and other so-called enterprise systems accounted for 20 percent of revenues.

Michael Dell's expanded target list began encompassing the entire $1 trillion information technology (IT) market, going beyond desktop PCs and servers to storage devices, switches, even mainframe-like systems—"enterprise computing," which is technobabble for assembling and running computer networks. Estimates were that Dell could double revenues to $60 billion in four or five years if it could gain a strong foothold in these expanded markets.[10]

The problems with this ambitious goal were that Dell would be forced to change from assembling boxes depending on technology developed by others to spending billions developing its own engineering service and support talent. At the least, in such expansion of horizons Dell's puny R&D expenditures would have to be significantly increased. There was always the possibility of acquisitions. After all, Dell had a hefty $4 billion in cash at the end of 2002, and its stock was commanding a multiple of twenty-five times its 2003 estimated earnings, while its peers traded for 15 times their earnings.[11]

The PC market, though growing only slowly, still offered Dell great potential as it gained ever more dominance in this market. In an interview with *Money* magazine in November 2002, Michael Dell noted that 30 million computers had been sold in the United States in the previous quarter, most of them upgrades and replacements. He noted that 180 million computers out there were probably over three years old, and 50 million of those were in large corporations: "A personal computer is like a rubber band: You can stretch it and it works. But eventually you can stretch it too hard and it breaks. ... The 'maybe we don't need to upgrade' idea won't last long."[12] With just 15 percent of the worldwide PC market, Dell had plenty of market share to grab.

---

[9] Suzanne Vranica, "Dell, Starting New Campaign, Plans for Life without Steven," *Wall Street Journal*, 16 October 2002, p. B3; Brian Steinberg of Dow Jones, "Dell Dude's Getting Benched for Interns," reported in *Cleveland Plain Dealer*, 15 October 2002, p. C2.

[10] Fisher, "Pulled in a New Direction," 104 ff.

[11] "Muscling into New Markets."

[12] Ibid.

Industry Frenetic Price Competition

In fall 2002, with the Christmas season looming, PC makers dropped prices to new lows. Big names like IBM and H-P, which usually catered to the higher-end market, went squarely after low-price leader Dell. Other makers dropped their already-low prices even lower. For example:

- H-P and eMachines had models starting at $399.
- Gateway announced its own $399 desktop.
- Microtel Computer Systems brought out a bare-bones machine for $199.
- H-P cut prices for its new H-P Compaq Evo to $899, from $1,100 a few months before.
- Even laptop prices plummeted: for example, IBM's Think-Pad notebooks were reduced to $950.

The severe industry price-cutting soon extended beyond PCs. H-P reduced operating costs by $800 million by consolidating suppliers and shutting factories. It sought to increase selling efforts direct to customers, thus bypassing middlemen, and expected such direct efforts to reach one-third of all sales by November 2003. To be competitive, H-P cut prices on computers aimed at business buyers by 10 percent to 15 percent. Dell entered the switch market (the technology linking computer networks) with prices one-half to two-thirds those of comparable models from 3Com and Cisco. 3Com promised "aggressive discounts to meet Dell pricing."[13]

To counter the severe price-cutting of rivals, Dell started selling unbranded PCs through computer dealers that it had traditionally shunned. This program was aimed at small- and medium-size businesses.

ANALYSIS

In the PC industry, Dell reigned supreme with its lowest-cost business model. Competitors with higher operating costs usually could not match Dell's prices without losing money. The PC price war in late 2002 taxed industry profits, but hardly hurt Dell. Still, this market was becoming saturated. To justify its high stock valuations, Dell sought to expand beyond PCs and even beyond servers and storage devices—the larger computers—to designing whole computer systems. Compaq had tried this approach a few years before, buying Digital Equipment in a futile effort to double revenues from entrenched competitors like Cisco Systems and IBM. Dell's success in these expansion efforts remains to be seen, but the Gateways and Compaqs seem vulnerable.

Can Gateway survive? During the writing of this text in late 2002, the issue was in doubt. A severe price war could be the final blow, although Gateway may be able to prune its costs enough to be reasonably competitive and still be profitable as a

---

[13] Tam et al., "As Alliances Fade," A8.

niche player. A judicious merger is always possible, or an innovative breakthrough a remote possibility. It seems unlikely that Gateway can develop the cult following that Apple enjoys, and given nothing particularly distinctive about its products, Gateway is vulnerable to price competition.

A major marketing strategy involves product differentiation, that is, making your product or service unique in some way. The more a firm can attain such distinction, the more latitude it has in pricing. One would think with a product as complex as a computer that differentiation should be easily achieved in the various product features, in the servicing, in customer relations. But increasingly most computers—particularly PCs—have become more standardized, with similar features and peripherals, similar warranties, and similar customer service (or lack thereof).

Another marketing phenomenon that should be affecting the PC market is perception of the price/quality relationship: the common notion that the higher the price, the higher the quality; and conversely, the lower the price, the lower the quality. While this perception held sway in the early years of computer technology, it is far less the case today with many customers. Dell, the lowest-cost producer, still has one of the best reputations for service.

UPDATE—2003

By the end of Christmas season 2002, Ted Waitt's hopes that this might be a turn-around year were dashed. He had stocked his 274 retail stores with cash-and-carry PCs, he had broadened the merchandise assortment to include hot sellers such as digital cameras and plasma TVs, and he had spent dearly for advertising. He tried to build PC sales by price-matching, everyday low prices, and even daily specials; but all these efforts only added to Gateway's losses. Now he had to contemplate restructuring again, with the retail chain foolishly created in the heady days of 1996 coming under close scrutiny for new cost cuts. *Wall Street Journal* noted, however, that Waitt was in no danger of losing his job since he was the largest stockholder.[14]

WHAT CAN BE LEARNED?

A Price War Can Be Disastrous

A price war developed toward the end of 2002. An economic downturn and disinterested customers were background factors, but Dell initiated it. Generally a price war is detrimental to all participants, because of its effect on profitability, and is shunned by mature industries (though gasoline wars do flare up from time to time). Most firms in a mature industry have similar costs, and innovations are scarce; so all firms suffer from such price wars, even though revenue may increase somewhat because of the lower prices.

[14] Gary McWilliams, "Under Gateway's Tree, Another Shake-up," *Wall Street Journal*, 6 January 2003, pp. A13 and A15; and "Slaughterhouse," *Forbes*, 20 January 2003, p. 34.

For new industries, price wars are more common, as technology advances and production economies develop and as inefficient firms are weeded out. But the computer industry has matured, and most marginal firms are long gone. Dell, alone among its competitors, stood to gain from a price war, and Michael Dell had no qualms about starting one.

Survival of the Fittest—Power of Lower Costs

If a firm has managed to reduce its operating costs and overhead significantly below its competitors, and if the competitors are not able to quickly match these cost reductions, then a price war can be a shrewd marketing strategy. While it may reduce profits somewhat, market-share gains could be significant, and such gains may be lasting. In two later cases, Southwest Airlines and Vanguard, we find similar instances of firms having significantly lower costs than the rest of the industry; their advantage has not been matched since few firms could cut costs sufficiently to meet their prices and still be profitable. The power of lower costs can make for a survival-of-the-fittest environment and result in greater efficiency and price benefits to customers.

Is It Possible to Develop a Cult Following?

A cult following usually depends on a company or brand developing (or acquiring) a sort of mystique. Few brands have been able to do this. Coors Brewing Company did back in the 1960s when it became the beer of celebrities and the emblem of the purity and freshness of the West. Marlboro rose to become the top seller using a somewhat similar image, the Marlboro man. The Ford Mustang had a mystique at one time, and Apple also had its devoted followers. But no one has beat Harley-Davidson in capitalizing on the mystique of its big motorcycles, and we will describe this feat in a later case.

How does a firm develop a mystique? There is no simple answer, no guarantee. Certainly a company's product has to be distinctive, even if only psychologically. But it takes more than a distinctive product—many firms strive for this, and few achieve a mystique. Image-building advertising, focusing on the type of person the firm is targeting, may help. Even better is image-building advertising of people who customers might wish to emulate—like Nike did so well with athletes.

Perhaps, in the final analysis, acquiring a mystique is more fortuitous than deliberate. Two lessons, however, can be learned about mystiques. First, they seldom last forever. Second, once they are gained, the company may be able to exploit them by extending the name or logo to other goods, even unrelated ones, through licensing (more about this in the Harley-Davidson case). See the Information Box: Trying to Upgrade an Image, Maybe to a Mystique for a report on Gateway's efforts to change its image, hopefully to one that might have more potential for a cult following than its black cow spots.

The Prescription for Great Wealth

Great wealth can come from going public with a successful format. We saw in this case how Michael Dell and Ted Waitt both became not only millionaires, but

---

INFORMATION BOX

TRYING TO UPGRADE AN IMAGE, MAYBE TO A MYSTIQUE

For years the Gateway brand has been symbolized by a Holstein cow—the white boxes speckled with black cow spots—and the company carried over this theme in its Gateway Country stores. CEO Ted Waitt even appeared in television commercials with a bovine co-star. He had hoped such a homespun flavor might appeal to many buyers, perhaps conveying an image of integrity and frugality. But as the computer war intensified, with Gateway steadily losing market share, Waitt thought an upgrade was needed, and he killed his beloved cow. "I'm calling it the de-prairiefication" of the company, he said. The change to sleek black-and-silver PCs and laptops goes beyond the product to the stores and advertisements.

Analysts were divided in their endorsement of the shifting strategy. "I don't think consumers will hold it against them that they don't have the cow. Any campaign gets old after a while," said one.

Others disagreed: "The cow motif was one of those odd, quirky, counterintuitive trademarks that succeeded in spite of themselves."

"Odd and quirky" sounds like getting close to a mystique. Do you think Ted Waitt made a good decision in de-prairiefication? Why or why not?

Source: Adapted from Frank Ahrens, "Gateway Changing Its Spots to Create an Upscale Image," *Washington Post,* as reported in *Cleveland Plain Dealer,* 10 November 2002, p. G3.

---

billionaires, when they took their enterprises public. They had prior examples and inspirers: Bill Gates of Microsoft and Steve Jobs of Apple.

While these are extraordinary success stories, on smaller scales many small businesses can find themselves attractive to investors seeking growth companies that may offer better potential than existing firms. If the founder of the business keeps a substantial block of the company's stock, the payoff in investors' appraisal of the enterprise can be mind-boggling.

CONSIDER

Can you identify additional learning insights that could be applicable to other firms in other situations?

QUESTIONS

1. "Tradition has no place in corporate thinking today." Discuss this statement.
2. Discuss the pros and cons involved in Dell's decision to start a price war as the downturn worsened in 2000.

3. Do you think Dell should have phased out Steven in its commercials? Why or why not?

4. "The computer industry—and most high tech as well—is saturated. This is no longer a growth area, and investors should look elsewhere for growth." Evaluate this statement.

5. "Gateway, with its Holstein cow image, was on the verge of developing a cult following. Now they're doing away with it. I'm selling my Gateway stock." Evaluate this attitude.

6. "I see no one in this foreseeable market who can compete with Dell." Evaluate.

7. How do you judge the quality of a product, computer or otherwise? Do you base it mostly on price? Discuss your perception of price and quality, as well as any ramifications.

HANDS-ON EXERCISES

1. *Be a Devil's Advocate* (one who argues against a proposed decision to test its merits). Argue against Ted Waitt's decision to abandon the cow. Be as persuasive as you can.

Before

2. You are Ted Waitt of Gateway just before the slide of the high-tech industry. What might you have done to prevent the profit collapse and market-share erosion that occurred? Defend your position.

After

3. You are Ted Waitt of Gateway near the end of 2002, with your firm on the ropes. What restorative program do you propose? Defend your ideas.

TEAM DEBATE EXERCISES

1. Debate Dell's ambitious plan to move ahead into other areas, such as servers, storage devices, switches, even mainframe-like systems—enterprise computing. Is the company likely to overextend itself in its search for the ultimate growth?

   The class may want to divide into two groups, with one arguing as persuasively as possible for the greatest growth. The other group will strongly contest this strategy, proposing a more conservative approach to growth. Each group should be prepared to attack the opponents' arguments as well as defend its own position.

2. "There is no need to be unduly concerned with Dell's price war. Our products are higher quality than Dell's and consumers and business customers alike will quickly recognize that they get what they pay for." Debate this

statement by a Hewlett-Packard executive, having one group support it and the other contest it.

INVITATION TO RESEARCH

1. Do some research on the controversial merger of Compaq and Hewlett-Packard. What potential difficulties do you see? Do you think on balance the merger was desirable?

2. What is the situation in the PC industry today? Is the price war still on? Has Gateway survived? Has Dell's market share continued to increase? Has Dell been able to invade H-P's printer and ink refill domain?

CHAPTER THREE

Cola Wars:
Pepsi vs. Coca-Cola

*I*ntense competition between Pepsi and Coca-Cola has characterized the soft-drink industry for decades. If anything could be called "war" outside of actual bloodshed, this was it. Despite strong challenges from Pepsi, however, Coca-Cola ruled the soft-drink market throughout the 1950s, 1960s, and early 1970s. It outsold Pepsi by two to one. But this was to change. Then the "war" switched to the international arena, and it became a "world war."

EARLY BATTLES, LEADING TO NEW COKE FIASCO

Pepsi Inroads, 1970s and 1980s

By the mid-1970s, the Coca-Cola Company was a lumbering giant. Performance reflected this. Between 1976 and 1978, the growth rate of Coca-Cola soft drinks dropped from 13 percent annually to a meager 2 percent. As the giant stumbled, Pepsi Cola was finding heady triumphs. First came the "Pepsi Generation." This advertising campaign captured the imagination of the baby boomers with its idealism and youth. This association with youth and vitality greatly enhanced the image of Pepsi and firmly associated it with the largest consumer market for soft drinks.

Then came another management coup, the "Pepsi Challenge," in which comparative taste tests with consumers showed a clear preference for Pepsi. This campaign led to a rapid increase in Pepsi's market share, from 6 to 14 percent of total U.S. soft-drink sales.

Coca-Cola, in defense, conducted its own taste tests. Alas, these tests had the same result—people liked the taste of Pepsi better, and market-share changes reflected this. As Table 3.1 shows, by 1979 Pepsi had closed the gap on Coca-Cola, with 17.9 percent of the soft-drink market to Coke's 23.9 percent. By the end of 1984, Coke had only a 2.9 percent lead, while in the grocery store market it was trailing by 1.7 percent. Further indication of the diminishing position of Coke relative to Pepsi was a study done by Coca-Cola's own marketing research department. The study

TABLE 3.1.   Coke and Pepsi Shares of Total Soft-Drink Market, 1950s–1984

		1975		1979		1984	
	Mid-1950s Lead	% of Market	Lead	% of Market	Lead	% of Market	Lead
Coke	Better than 2 to 1	24.2	6.8	23.9	6.0	21.7	2.9
Pepsi		17.4		17.9		18.8	

Source: Thomas Oliver, *The Real Coke, The Real Story* (New York: Random House, 1986), pp. 21, 50; "Two Cokes Really Are Better Than One—For Now," *Business Week,* 9 September 1985, p. 38.

showed that in 1972, 18 percent of soft-drink users drank Coke exclusively, while only 4 percent drank only Pepsi. In ten years the picture had changed greatly: Only 12 percent now claimed loyalty to Coke, while the number of exclusive Pepsi drinkers almost matched, with 11 percent. Figure 3.1 shows this change graphically.

What made the deteriorating comparative performance of Coke all the more worrisome and frustrating to Coca-Cola was that it was outspending Pepsi in advertising by $100 million. It had twice as many vending machines, dominated fountains, had more shelf space, and was competitively priced. Why was it losing market share? The advertising undoubtedly was not as effective as that of Pepsi, despite vastly more money spent. And this raises the question: How can we measure the effectiveness of advertising? See the Information Box: How Do We Measure the Effectiveness of Advertising? for a discussion.

Coca-Cola Tries to Battle Back

The Changing of the Guard at Coke

J. Paul Austin, chairman of Coca-Cola, was nearing retirement in 1980. Donald Keough, president for the American group, was expected to succeed him. But a new name, Roberto Goizueta, suddenly emerged.

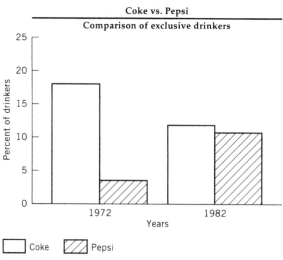

Figure 3.1.   Coke versus Pepsi: Comparison of exclusive drinkers, 1972 and 1982.

INFORMATION BOX

HOW DO WE MEASURE THE EFFECTIVENESS OF ADVERTISING?

A firm can spend millions of dollars for advertising, and it is only natural to want some feedback on the results of such an expenditure: To what extent did the advertising really pay off? Yet, many problems confront the firm trying to measure this payoff.

Most methods for measuring effectiveness focus not on sales changes but on how well the communication is remembered, recognized, or recalled. Most evaluative methods simply tell which ad is the best among those being appraised. But even though one ad may be found to be more memorable or to create more attention than another, that fact alone gives no assurance of relationship to sales success. A classic example of the dire consequences that can befall advertising people as a result of the inability to directly measure the impact of ads on sales occurred in December 1970.

In 1970, the Doyle Dane Bernbach advertising agency created memorable TV commercials for Alka-Seltzer, such as the "spicy meatball man," and the "poached oyster bride." These won professional awards as the best commercials of the year and received high marks for humor and audience recall. But in December, the $22 million account was abruptly switched to another agency. The reason? Alka-Seltzer's sales had dropped somewhat. Of course, no one will ever know whether the drop might have been much worse without these notable commercials.

So, how do we measure the value of millions of dollars spent for advertising? Not well; nor can we determine what is the right amount to spend, what is too much or too little.

Can a business succeed without advertising? Why or why not?

Goizueta's background was far different from that of the typical Coca-Cola executive. He was not from Georgia, was not even southern. Rather, he was the son of a wealthy Havana sugar plantation owner. He came to the United States at age sixteen, speaking virtually no English. By using the dictionary and watching movies, he quickly learned the language and graduated from Yale in 1955 with a degree in chemical engineering. Returning to Cuba, he went to work in Coke's Cuban research lab.

In 1959 when Fidel Castro seized power, Goizueta's complacent life was to change. With his wife and three children he fled to the United States, arriving with $20. At Coca-Cola he became known as a brilliant administrator, and in 1968 was brought to company headquarters; he became chairman of the board thirteen years later, in 1981. Donald Keough had to settle for being president.

In the new era of change, the sacredness of the commitment to the original Coke formula became tenuous. The ground was laid for the first flavor change in ninety-nine years.

Introducing a New Flavor for Coke

With the market-share erosion of the late 1970s and early 1980s, despite strong advertising and superior distribution, the company began to look at the soft-drink product itself. Taste was suspected as the chief culprit in Coke's decline, and marketing research seemed to confirm this. In September 1984 the technical division developed a sweeter flavor. In perhaps the biggest taste test ever—at a cost of $4 million—191,000 people approved the new flavor by 55 percent over the original formulas of both Coke and Pepsi. Top executives unanimously agreed to change the taste and take the old Coke off the market.

But the results flabbergasted company executives. While some protests were expected, they quickly mushroomed; by mid-May 1985, calls were coming in at the rate of five thousand a day, in addition to a barrage of angry letters. People were speaking of Coke as an American symbol and as a long-time friend who had suddenly betrayed them.

Anger spread across the country, fueled by media publicity. Fiddling with the formula for the ninety-nine-year-old beverage became an affront to patriotic pride. Even Goizueta's father spoke out against the switch and jokingly threatened to disown his son. By then the company was beginning to worry about a consumer boycott against the product.

On July 11 company officials capitulated to the outcry. They apologized to the public and brought back the original taste of Coke.

Roger Enrico, president of Pepsi-Cola, USA, gloated, "Clearly this is the Edsel of the '80s. This was a terrible mistake. Coke's got a lemon on its hands and now they're trying to make lemonade." Other critics labeled it the "marketing blunder of the decade."[1]

Unfortunately for Pepsi, the euphoria of a major blunder by Coca-Cola was short-lived. The two-cola strategy of Coca-Cola—it still kept the new flavor in addition to bringing back the old classic—seemed to be stimulating sales far more than ever expected. While Coke Classic was outselling New Coke by better than two to one nationwide, for the full year of 1985, sales from all operations rose 10 percent and profits 9 percent. Coca-Cola's fortunes continued to improve steadily. By 1988 it was producing five of the ten top-selling soft drinks in the country, and had a total 40 percent of the domestic market compared to 31 percent for Pepsi.[2]

BATTLE SHIFTS TO INTERNATIONAL ARENA

Pepsi's Troubles in Brazil

Early in 1994, PepsiCo began an ambitious assault on the soft-drink market in Brazil. Making this invasion even more tempting was the opportunity to combat archrival Coca-Cola, already entrenched in this third largest soft-drink market in the world—behind only the United States and Mexico.

The robust market of Brazil had attracted Pepsi before. Its hot weather and a growing teen population positioned Brazil to become one of the world's fastest-growing soft-drink markets, along with China, India, and Southeast Asia. But the

[1] John Greenwald, "Coca-Cola's Big Fizzle," *Time*, 22 July 1985, pp. 48–49.
[2] "Some Things Don't Go Better with Coke," *Forbes*, 21 March 1988, pp. 34–35.

potential still had barely been tapped. Brazilian consumers averaged only 264 eight-ounce servings of soft drinks a year, far below the U.S. average of about 800.[3]

Three times before over the previous twenty-five years, Pepsi had attempted to enter the Brazilian market with splashy promotional campaigns and different bottlers. Each of these efforts proved disappointing, and Pepsi had quickly dropped them. In 1994 it was planning a much more aggressive and enduring push.

A Superbottler, Baesa, and Charles Beach

Buenos Aires Embotelladora SA, or Baesa, was to be the key to Pepsi's rejuvenated entry into Brazil. Baesa would be Pepsi's "superbottler," one that would buy small bottlers across Latin America, expand their marketing and distribution, and be the fulcrum in the drive against Coca-Cola. Charles Beach, the CEO of Baesa, was the person around whom Pepsi planned its strategy.

Beach, 61, was a passionate, driven man and a veteran of the cola wars, but his was a checkered past. He had been manager for a Carolina Coca-Cola bottler, but left to buy Pepsi's small Puerto Rican franchise in 1987. He was indicted by a federal grand jury on charges of price fixing and received a $100,000 fine and a suspended prison sentence.

Then, in 1989, Beach acquired the exclusive Pepsi franchise for Buenos Aires, Argentina—one of the most important bottling franchises outside the United States. By discounting and launching new products and packages, he caught Coke by surprise. In only three years he had increased Pepsi's market share in the Buenos Aires metro area from almost zero to 34 percent.[4]

With Pepsi's blessing, Beach expanded vigorously, borrowing heavily to do so. He bought major Pepsi franchises in Chile, Uruguay, and most importantly, Brazil, where he built four giant bottling plants. Pepsi worked closely with Baesa's expansion, providing funds to facilitate it.

However, they underestimated the aggressiveness of Coca-Cola. Their rival spent heavily on marketing and cold-drink equipment for its choice customers. As a result, Baesa was shut out of small retail outlets, those most profitable for bottlers. Goizueta, CEO of Coca-Cola, used his Latin American background to influence the Argentine president to reduce an onerous 24 percent tax on cola to 4 percent. This move strengthened Coke's position against Baesa, which was earning most of its profits from non-cola drinks in contrast to Coca-Cola.

By early 1996, Baesa's expansion plans—and Pepsi's dream—were floundering. The new Brazilian plants were running at only a third of capacity. Baesa lost $300 million for the first half of 1996, and PepsiCo injected another $40 million into Baesa.

On May 9, Beach was relieved of his position. Allegations were surfacing that Beach might have tampered with Baesa's books.[5] But PepsiCo's troubles did not end with the debacle in Brazil.

[3] Robert Frank and Jonathan Friedland, "How Pepsi's Charge into Brazil Fell Short of Its Ambitious Goals," *Wall Street Journal*, 30 August 1996, p. A1.

[4] Patricia Sellers, "How Coke Is Kicking Pepsi's Can," *Fortune*, 28 October 1996, p. 78.

[5] Ibid., p. 79.

Intrigue in Venezuela

Brazil was only symptomatic of other overseas problems for Pepsi. Roger Enrico, Pepsi CEO, had reasons to shake his head and wonder at how the gods seemed against him. But it was not the gods, it was Coca-Cola. Enrico had been on Coke's blacklist since he had gloated a decade before about the New Coke debacle in his memoir, *The Other Guy Blinked; How Pepsi Won the Cola Wars.* Goizueta was soon to gloat, "It appears that the company that claimed to have won the cola wars is now raising the white flag."[6]

The person Enrico thought was his close friend, Oswaldo Cisneros, head of one of Pepsi's oldest and largest foreign bottling franchises, suddenly abandoned Pepsi for Coca-Cola. Essentially, this took Pepsi out of the Venezuelan market.

Despite close ties between the Cisneroses and the Enricos, little things led to the chasm. The closeness had developed when Enrico headed the international operations of PepsiCo. After Enrico left this position for higher offices at corporate headquarters, Oswaldo Cisneros felt that Pepsi management paid scant attention to Venezuela: "That showed I wasn't an important player in their future," he said.[7] Because Cisneros was growing older, he wanted to sell the bottling operation; but Pepsi was willing to acquire only 10 percent.

Coca-Cola wooed the Cisneroses with red-carpet treatment and frequent meetings with its highest executives. Eventually, Coca-Cola agreed to pay an estimated $500 million to buy 50 percent of the business.

Pepsi's Problems Elsewhere in the International Arena

Pepsi's problems in South America mirrored its problems worldwide. It had lost its initial lead in Russia, Eastern Europe, and parts of Southeast Asia. While it had a head start in India, this was being eroded by a hard-driving Coca-Cola. Even in Mexico, Pepsi's main bottler reported a loss of $15 million in 1995.

The contrast with Coca-Cola was significant. Pepsi still generated more than 70 percent of its beverage profits from the United States; Coca-Cola got 80 percent from overseas.[8]

Table 3.2 shows the top ten markets for Coke and Pepsi in 1996 in the total world market. Coke had a 49 percent market share while Pepsi had only 17 percent, despite its investment of more than $2 billion since 1990 to straighten out its overseas bottling operations and improve its image.[9] With its careful investment in bottlers and increased financial resources to plow into marketing, Coke continued to gain greater control of the global soft-drink industry.

If there was any consolation for PepsiCo, it was that it depended on its overseas business far less than Coca-Cola did; but this was slim comfort in view of the huge potential this market represented. Most of Pepsi's revenues were in the U.S. beverage,

---

[6] Ibid., p. 72.

[7] Ibid., p. 75.

[8] Frank and Friedland, "Pepsi's Charge into Brazil," p. A1.

[9] Robert Frank, "Pepsi Losing Overseas Fizz to Coca-Cola," *Wall Street Journal,* 22 August 1996, p. C2.

TABLE 3.2. Coke and Pepsi Shares of Total Soft-Drink Sales, Top 10 Markets, 1996

Markets	*Market Shares*	
	Coke	Pepsi
United States	42%	31%
Mexico	61	21
Japan	34	5
Brazil	51	10
East-Central Europe	40	21
Germany	56	5
Canada	37	34
Middle East	23	38
China	20	10
Britain	32	12

Source: Company annual reports, and Patricia Sellers, "How Coke Is Kicking Pepsi's Can," *Fortune,* 28 October 1996, p. 82.

Commentary: These market share comparisons show the extent of Pepsi's ineptitude in its international markets. In only one of these top 10 overseas markets is it ahead of Coke, and in some, such as Japan, Germany, and Brazil, it is practically a nonplayer.

snack food, and restaurant businesses, with such well-known brands as Frito-Lay chips and Taco Bell, Pizza Hut, and KFC (Kentucky Fried Chicken) restaurants. But as a former Pepsi CEO was fond of stating, "We're proud of the U.S. business. But 95 percent of the world doesn't live here."[10] And Pepsi seemed unable to hold its own against Coke in this world market.

COKE TRAVAILS IN EUROPE, 1999

The Trials of Douglas Ivester

In early 1998, Douglas Ivester took over as chairman and chief executive of Coca-Cola. Things seemed to go downhill from then on, but it was not entirely his fault. The first quarter of 1999 witnessed a sharp slowdown in Coca-Cola's North American business, at least partly due to price increases designed to overcome weakness resulting from overseas economic woes. While most analysts thought the sticker shock of higher prices would be temporary, some thought the company needed to be more innovative, needed to do more than offer supersize drinks.[11] Other problems emanated from a racial discrimination lawsuit, as well as from Mr. Ivester's brassy

---

[10] Ibid.

[11] Nikhil Deogun, "Coke's Slower Sales Are Blamed on Price Increases," *Wall Street Journal,* 31 March 1999, pp. A3, A4.

attempts to make acquisitions such as Orangina and Cadbury Schweppes, angering overseas regulators and perhaps motivating them to make life difficult for Coke.

Such concerns paled before what was to come.

Contamination Scares

On June 8, a few dozen Belgian schoolchildren began throwing up after drinking Cokes. This was to result in one of the greatest crises in Coca-Cola's 113-year history. An early warning had seemingly been ignored when in mid-May the owner of a pub near Antwerp complained of four people becoming sick from drinking bad-smelling Coke. The company claimed to have investigated but found no problems.

The contamination news could not have hit at a worse time. Belgium was still reeling from a dioxin-contaminated food scare in Belgian poultry and other foods, and European agencies were coming under fire for a breakdown in their watchdog responsibilities. Officials were inclined to be overzealous in their dealings with this big U.S. firm.

The problems worsened. Coca-Cola officials were meeting with Belgium's health minister, seeking to placate him, telling him that their analyses "show that it is about a deviation in taste and color" that might cause headaches and other symptoms, but "does not threaten the health of your child." In the middle of this meeting, news came that another fifteen students at another school had gotten sick.[12]

It was thought that the contamination came from bottling plants in Antwerp, Ghent, and from the Dunkirk plant that produced cans for the Belgium market. European newspapers were speculating that Coke cans were contaminated with rat poison.

Soon hundreds of people in France were sick and blaming their illnesses on Coke, and France banned products from the Dunkirk plant. These two countries rebuffed Coca-Cola's urgent efforts to lift the ban, and scolded the company for not supplying enough information about the cause of the problem. The setback left Coke out of the market in parts of Europe because the company had badly underestimated how much explanation governments would demand before letting it back in business.

Not until June 17 did Belgium and France lift restrictions, and then only on some products; the bans were continued on Coca-Cola's Coke, Sprite, and Fanta. Then the Netherlands, Luxembourg, and Switzerland also imposed selective bans until health risks could be evaluated. Some 14 million cases of Coke products eventually were recalled in the five countries, and estimates were that Coke was losing $3.4 million per day in revenues. Case volume for the European division was expected to fall 6 to 7 percent from the year earlier.[13] The peak soft-drink summer season had arrived, and the timing of the scare could not have been worse.

The European Union requested further study as the health scare spread. At the same time, Coca-Cola and its local distributors launched an advertising campaign

---

[12] "Anatomy of a Recall: How Coke's Controls Fizzled Out in Europe," *Wall Street Journal*, 29 June 1999, p. A6.

[13] Will Edwards, "Coke Chairman Tries to Assure Europeans," *Cleveland Plain Dealer*, 19 June 1999, pp. 1-C, 3-C; and Nikhil Deogun, "Coke Estimates European Volume Plunged 6 to 7 in 2nd Quarter," *Wall Street Journal*, 1 July 1999, p. A4.

defending the quality of their products. The company blamed defective carbon dioxide (used for fizz) for problems at Antwerp. It also said the outside of cans made in Dunkirk were contaminated with a wood preservative during shipping. One company-commissioned study suggested that health problems were in the victim's heads. Meanwhile, the Ivory Coast seized 50,000 cans of Coke imported from Europe as a precautionary measure, though there was no evidence that anyone in the Ivory Coast had become ill by drinking imported Coke.

Problems continued to spread. All glass bottles of Bonaqua, a bottled-water brand of Coca-Cola, were recalled in Poland because about 1,500 bottles were found to contain mold. This recall in Poland soon spread to glass bottles of Coke. Company officials believed the mold was caused by inadequate washing of returnable bottles. Barely a week later, the company recalled 180,000 plastic bottles of Bonaqua after discovering nonhazardous bacteria. Coca-Cola also had to recall some soft drinks in Portugal after small bits of charcoal from a filtration system were found in some cans.

Coca-Cola Finally Acts Aggressively

In the initial contamination episodes, Coca-Cola was accused of dragging its feet. Part of the problem in ameliorating the situation was the absence of an explanation by any top Coca-Cola officials. Ivester was criticized for this delay when he finally made an appearance in Brussels on June 18, ten days after the initial scare. He visited Brussels again four days later, meeting with the prime minister. Strenuous efforts to improve the company's image and public relations then began.

Ivester, in a major advertising campaign, apologized to Belgian consumers and explained "how the company allowed two breakdowns to occur." The ads showed his photograph along with these opening remarks: "My apologies to the consumers of Belgium; I should have spoken with you earlier." Ivester further promised to buy every Belgian household a Coke. A special consumer hotline was established, and fifty officials, including several top executives, were temporarily shifted from the Atlanta headquarters to Brussels.

Five thousand delivery people then fanned out across the country, offering a free 1.5-liter bottle of Coke's main brands to 4.37 million households. Around Belgium, Coke trucks and displays proclaimed, "Your Coca-Cola is coming back." In newspaper ads, the company explained its problems, noting that it was destroying old products and using fresh ingredients for new drinks. A similar marketing strategy was planned for Poland, where 2 million free beverages were distributed to consumers.

Pepsi's Competitive Maneuvers near the Millennium

Pepsi's Role in Coke's European Problems

Some thought that Coca-Cola's problems should have been Pepsi's gain. Yet, Pepsi did nothing to capitalize on the situation, did not gloat, and did not increase advertising for its brand. Worldwide, Pepsi experienced some temporary gains in sales, most surprisingly in countries far removed from the scare—such as China. A Pepsi bottler in

Eastern Europe probably expressed the prevailing company attitude when he observed that people were buying bottled water and juices instead of soda pop: "That's why we don't wish this stuff on anyone," he said, referring to the health scare.[14]

But Pepsi was not idle in Europe.

Pepsi's Antitrust Initiations against Coca-Cola

In late July 1999, European Union officials raided offices of Coca-Cola and its bottlers in four countries in Europe—Germany, Austria, Denmark, and Britain—on suspicions that the company used a dominant market position to shut out competitors. Coming at a time when Coca-Cola was still trying to recover from the contamination problems, this was a cruel blow. All the more so since such alleged noncompetitive activities affected its plans to acquire some additional businesses in Europe.

The raids were expected to lead to a full-blown antitrust action against Coke. The major suspicion was that Coke was illegally using rebates to enhance its market share. The several types of rebates under investigation were rebates on sales that boosted Coke's market share at the expense of rivals, as well as rebates given to distributors who agreed either to sell the full range of Coke products or to stop buying from competitors.

Coca-Cola's huge market share in most countries of Europe fed the concern. See Table 3.3 for Coke's market shares of the total soft-drink market in selected European countries.

While the huge market share of Coke was being scrutinized by European antitrust officials, the investigation was sparked by a complaint—filed by Pepsi—that Coke was illegally trying to force competitors out of the market.

TABLE 3.3. Coca-Cola's Market Share of Soft-Drink Market in Selected European Countries, 1998

France	59%
Spain	58
Germany	55
Central Europe	47
Italy	45
Nordic and Northern Eurasia	41
Great Britain	35

Source: Company published reports.

Commentary: The dominance of Coke in almost all countries of Europe, not surprisingly, makes it vulnerable to antitrust scrutiny.

---

[14] Nikhil Deogun and James R. Hagerty, "Coke Scandal Could Boost Rivals, But Also Could Hurt Soft Drinks," *Wall Street Journal*, 23 June 1999, p. A4.

Pepsi also filed a complaint with Italian regulators, who were quicker to act. A preliminary report found that Coca-Cola and its bottlers had violated antitrust laws by abusing a dominant market position through practices such as discounts, bonuses, and exclusive deals with wholesalers and retailers. The Italian regulators also said there was evidence that Coke had a "strategic plan" to remove Pepsi from the Italian market, one of the biggest in Europe, by paying wholesalers to remove Pepsi fountain equipment and replace it with Coke. At about this time, Australian and Chilean officials also began conducting informal inquiries in their markets.

Coca-Cola officials responded to the Italian report as follows: "we believe this is a baseless allegation by Pepsi and we believe that Pepsi's poor performance in Italy is due to their lack of commitment and investment there. As a result, they are attempting to compete with us in the courtroom instead of the marketplace."[15]

ANALYSIS

What Went Wrong with the New Coke Decision?

The most convenient scapegoat was the marketing research that preceded the decision. Yet Coca-Cola spent about $4 million and devoted two years to the marketing research. During that time, the company contacted about 200,000 consumers. The error in judgment was surely not from want of trying. But when we dig deeper into the research, some flaws become apparent.

Flawed Marketing Research

The major design of the marketing research involved taste tests by representative consumers. After all, the decision point was whether to go with a different-flavored Coke, so what could be more logical than to conduct taste tests to determine acceptability of the new flavor, not only versus the old Coke but also versus Pepsi? The results were strongly positive for the new formula, even among Pepsi drinkers. This was a clear "go" signal.

With benefit of hindsight, however, some deficiencies in the research design merited concern. Research participants were not told that by picking one cola, they would lose the other. This proved to be a significant distortion: Any addition to the product line would naturally be far more acceptable than completely eliminating the traditional product would be.

While three to four new tastes were tested with almost 200,000 people, only 30,000 to 40,000 of these testers tried the specific formula for the new Coke. Research was geared more to the idea of a new, sweeter cola than that used in the final formula. In general, a sweeter flavor tends to be preferred in blind taste tests. This is particularly true with youths, the largest drinkers of sugared colas and the very group drinking more Pepsi in recent years. Interestingly, preference for sweeter-tasting products tends to diminish with use.[16]

---

[15] Betsy McKay, "Coke, Bottlers Violated Antitrust Laws in Italy, a Preliminary Report States," *Wall Street Journal,* 13 August 1999, p. A4.

[16] "New Cola Wins Round 1, But Can It Go the Distance?" *Business Week,* 24 June 1985, p. 48.

Consumers were asked whether they favored change as a concept, and whether they would likely drink more, less, or the same amount of Coke if there were a change. But such questions could hardly prove the depth of feelings and emotional ties to the product.

Symbolic Value

The symbolic value of Coke was the sleeper. Perhaps this should have been foreseen. Perhaps the marketing research should have considered this possibility and designed the research to map it and determine the strength and durability of these values— that is, would they have a major effect on any substitution of a new flavor?

Admittedly, when we get into symbolic value and emotional involvement, any researcher is dealing with vague attitudes. But various attitudinal measures have been developed that can measure the strength or degree of emotional involvement.

Herd Instinct

Here we see a natural human phenomenon: the herd instinct, the tendency of people to follow an idea, a slogan, a concept, to "jump on the bandwagon." At first, acceptance of new Coke appeared to be reasonably satisfactory. But as more and more outcries were raised—fanned by the media—about the betrayal of the old tradition (somehow this became identified with motherhood, apple pie, and the flag), public attitudes shifted strongly against the perceived unworthy substitute. The bandwagon syndrome was fully activated. It is doubtful that by July 1985 Coca-Cola could have done anything to reverse the unfavorable tide. To wait for it to die down was fraught with danger—for who would be brave enough to predict the durability and possible heights of such a protest movement?

Could, or should, such a tide have been predicted? Perhaps not, at least regarding the full strength of the movement. Coca-Cola expected some protests. But perhaps it should have been more cautious, by considering a worst-case scenario in addition to what seemed the more probable, and by being better prepared to react to such a contingency.

Pepsi, and Later Coca-Cola's, International Problems

Pepsi's Defeats in South America

With hindsight we can identify many of the mistakes Pepsi made. It tried to expand too quickly in Argentina and Brazil, imprudently putting all its chips on a distributor with a checkered past. Instead of building up relationships more slowly and carefully, it did not monitor foreign operations closely enough or soon enough to prevent rash expansion of facilities and burdensome debt accumulations by affiliates. It did not listen closely enough to old distributors and their changing wants, and so lost Venezuela to Coca-Cola. Pepsi apparently did not learn from its mistakes: For example, three times before, it had tried to enter Brazil and failed. Why the failures? Why was it not more careful to prevent failure the next time?

Finally, we can speculate that maybe Pepsi was not so bad, but rather that its major competitor was so good. Coca-Cola had slowly built up close relationships with foreign bottlers over decades. It was aggressive in defending its turf. Perhaps not the least of its strengths, at least in the lucrative Latin American markets, was a CEO who was also a Latino, who could speak Spanish and share the concerns and build on the egos of its local bottlers. In selling, this is known as a dyadic relationship, and it is discussed further in the Information Box: The Dyadic Relationship. After all, why can't a CEO do a selling job on a distributor and capitalize on a dyadic relationship?

Coca-Cola's Problems in Europe

Could Coca-Cola have handled the Belgian crisis better? With hindsight we see a flawed initial reaction. Still, the first incident of twenty-four schoolchildren getting ill and throwing up after drinking Coke hardly seemed a major crisis at the time. But crises often start slowly with only minor indications, and then mushroom to even catastrophic proportions. Eventually, hundreds of people reported real or imagined illnesses from drinking the various Coca-Cola products.

The mistakes of Coca-Cola in handling the situation were (1) not taking the initial episodes seriously enough; (2) not realizing the intense involvement and skepticism of governmental officials, who demanded complete explanations of the cause(s) and were reluctant to lift bans; and (3) not involving Coke Chairman Douglas Ivester and other high-level executives soon enough. Allowing ten days to go by before his personal intervention was a long time for Ivester to let problems fester. Added to that, the quality-control lapses should not have been allowed to occur in the first place.

Eventually, Ivester and Coke acted aggressively in restoring Coca-Cola, but lost revenues could not be fully recovered.

Of interest in the environment of cola wars was Pepsi's restraint in not trying to take advantage of Coke's problems. This was not altruism but fear that the whole soft-drink

---

INFORMATION BOX

THE DYADIC RELATIONSHIP

Sellers are now recognizing the importance of the buyer-seller interaction, *a dyadic relationship*. A transaction, negotiation, or relationship can often be helped by certain characteristics of the buyer and seller in the particular encounter. Research suggests that salespeople tend to be more successful if they have characteristics similar to those of their customers in age, size, and other demographic, social, and ethnic variables.

Of course, in the selling situation this suggests that selecting and hiring sales applicants most likely to be successful might require careful study of the characteristics of the firm's customers. Turning to the Pepsi/Coke confrontation in Brazil and Venezuela, the same concepts should apply and give a decided advantage to Coca-Cola and Roberto Goizueta in influencing government officials and local distributors. After all, in interacting with customers and affiliates, even a CEO needs to be persuasive in presenting ideas as well as handling problems and objections.

Can you think of any situations where the dyadic theory may not work?

industry would face decreased demand, so Pepsi did not want to aggravate the situation. Anyway, Pepsi saved its competitive thrusts for antitrust challenges.

With its great size and market-dominating visibility in country after country, Coca-Cola was vulnerable to regulatory scrutiny and antitrust allegations, especially when stimulated by its No. 1 competitor, PepsiCo. Does this mean that it is dangerous for a firm to become too big? In certain environments, such as that facing a foreign firm in some European countries, this may well be the case. The firm then needs to tread carefully, tone down inclinations toward arrogance, and be subtle and patient in seeking acquisitions on foreign turf.

UPDATE—2003

By 2003 both Pepsi and Coca-Cola were facing an aggressive new rival. Cott Corp., the world's biggest maker of private-label soft drinks, had been moribund with production and delivery problems and no new products when Frank Weise, former chief financial officer of Campbell Soup Co., took over in June 1998. He kicked its production and delivery problems into efficiency and began introducing new, copycat products in flashy packages at competitive prices. A shrewd acquisition of a flavor laboratory from British drink-maker Cadbury Schweppes PLC in 2001 for $94 million gave Cott the means to create new products quickly.

Now Cott is quietly building market share in the U.S. carbonated soft-drink market, increasing market share from 3.1 percent in 1999 to 3.8 percent through 2001, for an increase of 22.5 percent. During that same period, Coke fell from 44.1 percent to 43.7 percent; Pepsi barely inched up to 31.6 percent from 31.4 percent. In a competitive marketplace where small gains or losses in market share are causes for celebration or worry, Cott's 22.5 percent gain was momentous. Does this portend worse things to come for Pepsi and Coke?

Source: Elena Cherney, "After Flat Sales, Cott Challenges Pepsi, Coca-Cola," *Wall Street Journal,* 8 January 2003, pp. B1, B4.

WHAT CAN BE LEARNED?

Public Taste Is Inconstant

Taste tests are commonly used in marketing research, but I have always been skeptical of their validity. Take beer, for example. I know of few people—despite their strenuous claims—who can in blind taste tests unerringly identify which is which among three or four disguised brands of beer. We know that people tend to favor the sweeter products in taste tests. But does this mean that a sweeter flavor will always win out in the marketplace? Hardly; something else is operating with consumer preference other than the fleeting essence of a taste—unless the flavor difference is extreme.

Brand image usually is a more powerful sales stimulant. Advertisers consistently have been more successful in cultivating a desirable image or personality for their brands or the types of people who use them, than by making such vague statements as "better tasting."

Don't Tamper with Tradition

Not many firms have a hundred-year-old tradition to be concerned with—or even twenty-five years, or ten years. Most products have much shorter life cycles. No other product has been so widely used and so deeply entrenched in societal values and culture as Coke.

The psychological components of the great Coke protest make interesting speculation. Perhaps in an era of rapid change, many people wish to hang onto the one symbol of security or constancy in their lives—even if it's only the traditional Coke flavor. Perhaps many people found this protest to be an interesting way to escape the humdrum, by making waves in a rather harmless way, in the process seeing if a big corporation might be forced to cry "uncle."

One is left to wonder how many consumers would even have been aware of any change in flavor had the new formula been quietly introduced without fanfare. But, of course, the advertising siren song of "New" would have been muted.

So, do we dare tamper with tradition? In Coke's case the answer is probably not, unless very quietly; but then Coke is unique.

Don't Try to Fix Something that Isn't Broken

Conventional wisdom may advocate that changes are best made in response to problems, that when things are going smoothly the success pattern or strategy should not be tampered with. Perhaps. But perhaps not.

Actually, things were not going all that well for Coke by early 1985. Market share had steadily been lost to Pepsi for some years. So it was certainly worth considering a change, and the obvious one was a different flavor. I do not subscribe to the philosophy of "don't rock the boat." But Coke had another option.

Don't Burn Your Bridges

Coke could have introduced the New Coke, but kept the old one. Goizueta was concerned about dealer resentment at having to stock an additional product in the same limited space. Furthermore, he feared that Pepsi might emerge as the No. 1 soft drink due to the two competing Cokes. This rationale is flawed, as events soon proved.

Consider the Power of the Media

Press and broadcast media are powerful influencers of public opinion. With new Coke, the media exacerbated the herd instinct by publicizing the protests. News seems to be spiciest when someone or something can be criticized or found wanting. We saw this fanning of protests in Coke's contamination problems in Europe, to the extent that some people came up with psychosomatic illnesses after drinking Coca-Cola products. The power of the media should not only be recognized, but be a factor in making decisions that may affect an organization's public image.

International Growth Requires Tight Controls

In Pepsi's problems with Baesa, we saw the risks of placing too much trust in a distributor. One could question the selection of Charles Beach to spearhead the

Pepsi invasion of Coke strongholds in South America. Prudence would dictate close monitoring of plans and performance, with major changes—in expansion planning, marketing strategy, financial commitments—approved by corporate headquarters. In international dealings, the tendency is rather to loosen controls due to the distances, different customs, and bureaucratic procedures as well as unfamiliar cultures. We will see an extreme example of this in the Maytag case.

The Human Factor May Be More Important in International Dealings

Rapport with associates and customers may be even more important internationally than domestically. The distances involved usually necessitate more decentralization and therefore more autonomy. If confidence and trust in foreign associates are misplaced, serious problems can result. Customers and affiliates may need a closer relationship with corporate management if they are not to be wooed away. Furthermore, in some countries the political climate is such that the major people in power must be catered to by the large firm wanting to do business in that country.

Sound Crisis Management Requires Prompt Participation by Top Management

The chief executive is both an expediter and a public relations figure in crises, particularly in foreign environments. Ivester's delay in rushing to Belgium may have held up resolution of the crisis for several weeks, and it cost Coca-Cola millions in lost revenues. No other person is as well suited as the CEO to handle serious crises. Some sensitive foreign officials see an affront to their country without top management involvement and are likely to express their displeasure in regulatory delays, calls for more investigations, and bad publicity toward a foreign firm. In the case of Coca-Cola, even though Ivester eventually made a conciliatory appearance, by that time some countries were receptive to antitrust allegations made by Pepsi against Coca-Cola.

CONSIDER

After reading the preceding material, can you think of other learning insights?

QUESTIONS

1. In the new Coke fiasco, how could Coca-Cola's marketing research have been improved? Be as specific as you can.

2. When a firm faces a negative press—as Coca-Cola did with the New Coke, and almost fifteen years later in Europe—what recourse does a firm have? Support your conclusions.

3. "If it's not broken, don't fix it." Evaluate this statement.

4. Do you think Coca-Cola engineered the whole scenario with the new Coke, including fanning initial protests, in order to get a bonanza of free publicity? Defend your position.

5. Critique Pepsi's handling of Baesa. Could it have prevented the South American disaster? If so, how?

6. With hindsight, how might Enrico, CEO of PepsiCo, have kept Cisneros, his principal bottler in Venezuela, in the fold instead of defecting to Coke?

7. How could Coca-Cola have lessened the chances of antitrust and regulatory scrutiny in Europe?

8. Do you think Pepsi can ever make big inroads in Coke's market share in Europe? Why or why not?

9. A big stockholder complains, "All this fuss over a few kids getting sick to their stomach. The media have blown this all out of proportion." Discuss.

HANDS-ON EXERCISES

1. Assume that you are Robert Goizueta, and you are facing increased pressure in early July 1985 to abandon the New Coke and bring back the old formula. However, your latest marketing research suggests that only a small group of agitators are making all the fuss. Evaluate your options and support your recommendations to the board.

2. As a market analyst for PepsiCo, you have been asked to present recommendations to Roger Enrico, CEO, and the executive board, for the invasion of Brazil's soft-drink market. The major bottler, Baesa, is already in place and waiting for Pepsi's final plans and objectives. You are to design a planning blueprint for the invasion, complete with an estimated timetable.

3. You are a staff assistant to Ivester. It is 1998, and he has just assumed the top executive job with Coca-Cola. One of his first major decisions concerns raising soft-drink prices 5 percent to improve operating margins and make up for diminished revenues in a depressed European market. He wants you to provide pro and con information on this important decision.

TEAM-DEBATE EXERCISES

1. "There is no way Pepsi can ever win the war with Coca-Cola. We are best off to try to hang onto what we have with soft drinks, and devote our efforts to diversify outside the soft-drink industry." Debate this issue: Should Pepsi essentially leave the battlefield to Coke and diversify, or should it continue to focus on the soft-drink core and try to win the cola war?

2. Debate Ivester's plan to distribute millions of free bottles of Coke products to people in Belgium and Poland. In particular, debate the costs versus benefits of this marketing strategy. Are the benefits likely to be worth the substantial cost?

INVITATION TO RESEARCH

What is the newest development in the Cola wars? Has Coke lost market share in Europe? Has Pepsi been able to make any inroads in Latin America? How do the two firms stack up in profitability? Have there been any innovations in this arena?

CHAPTER FOUR

Airliner Wars: Boeing vs. Airbus

The commercial jet business had long been subject to booms and busts: major demand for new aircraft and then years of little demand. By the second half of the 1990s, demand burgeoned as never before. Boeing, the world's leading producer of commercial airplanes, seemed in the catbird seat amid the worldwide surge of orders. This was an unexpected windfall, spurred by markets greatly expanding in Asia and Latin America at the same time that domestic demand, helped by deregulation and prosperity, boomed. In the midst of these good times, Boeing in 1997 incurred its first loss in fifty years.

During this same period, Airbus (Airbus Industrie), a European aerospace consortium, an underdog, began climbing toward its long-stated goal of winning 50 percent of the over-100-seat airplane market. The battle was all-out, no holds barred, and Boeing was blinking.

BOEING

Background of the Company

Boeing's is a fabled past. The company was a major factor in the World War II war effort, and in the late 1950s led the way in producing innovative, state-of-the-art commercial aircraft. It introduced the 707, the world's first commercially viable jetliner. In the late 1960s it almost bankrupted itself to build a jetliner twice the size of any other then in service, while the critics predicted it could never fly profitably. But the 747 dramatically lowered costs and airfares and brought passenger comfort previously undreamed of in flying. In the mid-1990s, Boeing introduced the high-technology 777, the first commercial aircraft designed entirely with the use of computers.

In efforts to reduce the feast-or-famine cycles of the commercial aircraft business, Boeing acquired Rockwell International's defense business in 1996. In 1997 Boeing purchased McDonnell Douglas for $16.3 billion.

In 1997 Boeing's commercial aircraft segment contributed 57 percent of total revenues. This segment ranged from 125-passenger 737s to giant 500-seat 747s. In 1997,

Boeing delivered 374 aircraft, up from 269 in 1996. The potential seemed enormous: Over the next twenty years, air passenger traffic worldwide was projected to rise 4.9 percent a year, and airlines were predicted to order 16,160 aircraft to expand their fleets and replace aging planes.[1] As the industry leader, Boeing had 60 percent of this market. At the end of 1997, its order backlog was $94 billion.

Defense and space operations comprised 41 percent of 1997 revenues. This included airborne warning and control systems (AWACS), helicopters, B-2 bomber subcontract work, and the F-22 fighter, among other products and systems.

Problems with the Commercial Aircraft Business Segment

Production Problems

Boeing proved to be poorly positioned to meet the surge in aircraft orders. Part of this resulted from drastic layoffs it had made of experienced workers during the industry's last slump, in the early 1990s. Though Boeing hired 32,000 new workers over 18 months starting in 1995, the experience gap upped the risk of costly mistakes. Boeing had also cut back its suppliers in strenuous efforts to slash parts inventories and increase cost efficiency.

But Boeing had other problems. Its production systems were a mess. It had somehow evolved some four hundred separate computer systems, and these were not linked. Its design system was labor intensive, paper dependent, and very expensive as it tried to cater to customer choices. A $1 billion program had been launched in 1996 to modernize and computerize the production process. But this was too late: The onslaught of orders had already started. (It is something of an anomaly for a firm with the sophistication to design the 777 entirely by computers to be so antiquated in its use of computers otherwise.)

Demands for increased production were further aggravated by unreasonable production goals and too many plane models. Problems first hit with the 747 Jumbo, and then with a new version of the top-selling 737, the so-called next-generation 737NG. Before long, every program was affected—also the 757, 767, and 777. While Boeing released over 320 planes to customers in 1997 for a 50 percent increase over 1996, this was far short of the planned completion rate. For example, by early 1998 a dozen 737NGs had been delivered to airlines, but this was less than one-third of the forty aircraft Boeing was supposed to have delivered by then. Yet, the company maintained through September 1997 that everything was going well, that there was only a month's delay in the delivery of some planes.

Soon it became apparent that problems were much greater. In October, the 747 and 737 assembly lines were shut down for nearly a month to allow workers to catch up and ease part shortages. The *Wall Street Journal* reported horror stories of parts being rushed in by taxicab, of executives spending weekends trying to chase down needed parts, of parts needed for new planes being shipped out to replace defective

---

[1] Boeing 1997 Annual Report.

parts on an in-service plane. Overtime pay brought some assembly-line workers incomes over $100,000, while rookie workers muddled by on the line.[2]

Despite its huge order backlog, Boeing took a loss for 1997, the first in over fifty years. See Table 4.1 for the trend in revenues and net income from 1988 to 1998.

The loss mostly resulted from two massive write-downs. One, for $1.4 billion, arose from the McDonnell Douglas acquisition and, in particular, from its ailing commercial aircraft operation at Long Beach, California. The bigger write-off, $1.6 billion, reflected production problems, particularly on the new 737NG. Severe price competition with Airbus resulted in not enough profits on existing business to bring the company into the black. Production delays continued, with more write-downs on the horizon.

As Boeing moved into 1998, analysts wondered how much longer it would take to clear up the production snafus.

This would be longer than anyone had been led to believe. Unexpectedly, a new problem arose for Boeing. Disastrous economic conditions in Asia now brought major order cancellations.

TABLE 4.1. Boeing's Trend of Revenues and Income, 1988–1998

	(million $)	
	Revenue	Net Income
1988	16,962	614
1989	20,276	675
1990	27,595	1,385
1991	29,314	1,567
1992	30,184	1,554
1993	25,438	1,244
1994	21,924	856
1995	19,515	393
1996	22,681	1,095
1997	45,800	–177
1998	56,100	1,100

Commentary: Note the severity of the decline in revenues and profits during the industry downturn in 1993, 1994, and 1995. It is little wonder that Boeing was so ill-prepared for the deluge of orders starting in 1995. Then, in an unbelievable anomaly, the tremendous increase in revenues in 1997 to the highest ever—partly reflecting the acquisitions—was accompanied by a huge loss.

Source: Boeing Annual Reports.

---

[2] Frederic M. Biddle and John Helyar, "Behind Boeing's Woes: Clunky Assembly Line, Price War with Airbus," *Wall Street Journal*, 24 April 1998, p. A16.

Customer Relations

Not surprisingly, Boeing's production problems resulting in delayed shipments had a serious impact on customer relations. For example, Southwest Airlines had to temporarily cancel adding service to another city because the ordered planes were not ready. Boeing paid Southwest millions of dollars of compensation for the delayed deliveries. Continental also had to wait for five overdue 737s.

Other customers switched to Boeing's only major competitor—Airbus Industrie, of Toulouse, France.

AIRBUS INDUSTRIE

Airbus had to salivate at Boeing's troubles. It was a distant second in market share to the 60 percent of Boeing. Now this was changing, and Airbus could see achieving a sustainable 50 percent market share. See the Information Box: Importance of Market Share for a discussion of market share.

Background of Airbus

Airbus was founded in 1970 as a consortium that came to include four countries: British Aerospace, DaimlerChrysler Aerospace (Germany), France's Aerospatiale,

---

INFORMATION BOX

IMPORTANCE OF MARKET SHARE

The desire to surpass a competitor is a common human tendency, whether in sports or business. A measurement of performance relative to competitors encourages this desire and can be highly motivating for management and employees alike. Furthermore, market-share performance is a key indicator not only in ascertaining how well a firm is doing and in spotting emerging problems but also sometimes in allaying blame. As an example of the latter, declining sales over the preceding year, along with a constant and improving market share, can suggest that the firm is doing a good job, even though certain factors adversely affected the whole industry.

Market share is usually measured by (1) share of overall sales, and/or (2) share relative to certain competitors, usually the top one or several in the industry. Of particular importance is trend data: Are things getting better or worse? If worse, why is this, and what needs to be done to improve the situation?

Since Boeing and Airbus were the only real competitors in this major industry, relative market shares became critical. The perceived importance of gaining, or not losing, market share led to severe price competition that cut into the profits of both firms, as will be discussed later.

How would you respond to the objection that market-share data is not all that useful, since "it doesn't tell us what the problem really is"?

Can emphasizing market share be counterproductive? If so, why?

and Spain's Casa. Each of the partners supplied components such as wings and fuse-lages; the partners also underwrote the consortium's capital expenses (sometimes with government loans) and were prepared to cover its operating losses.

The organizational structure seemed seriously flawed. It was politicized, with the partners voting on major issues in proportion to their country's ownership stakes. From this fragmented leadership, public squabbles frequently arose, some very seri-ous. For example, plans to produce a new 107-seat A318 were held up by the French, who thought they were not getting their fair share of the production. Finances were also tangled—components supplied by the various countries were charged to Airbus at suspiciously high prices.

The result was that in 1998, Boeing made $1.1 billion on sales of $56.1 billion, while Airbus was losing $204 million on sales of $13.3 billion. Boeing accused Airbus of selling below cost in order to steal business from Boeing, and Airbus blamed Boeing for the low bids.

The competition between the two companies became increasingly bitter after 1996. In that year, Boeing and several Airbus partners discussed the joint develop-ment of a superjumbo. The talks ended when they could not agree on a single design. But Airbus suspected Boeing was not sincerely interested in this collaboration, that its main purpose in the talks was to stall Airbus's plans.

Airbus went ahead with its plans, while Boeing pooh-poohed the idea of such a huge plane.

Airbus Chairman Noel Forgeard

A slight Frenchman with a cheery disposition, Noel Forgeard, 52, joined the consor-tium in 1998 from Matra, a French aerospace manufacturer. He came with several major goals: to centralize decision-making, to impose sensible bookkeeping, and to make Airbus consistently profitable. The task was not easy. For example, plans to build the world's largest airplane, code-named A3XX, were even threatened by dis-agreements over where it would be assembled. Both France and Germany thought it should be produced in their country. Forgeard stated, "The need for a single corpo-rate entity is well recognized. Everybody here is focused on it."[3] Still, while the need for reorganizing into something like a modern corporation was evident to most exec-utives, the major partners were divided over how to proceed.

The World's Largest Plane

The A3XX was designed as a double-decker plane that on overseas routes could carry 555 passengers comfortably—137 more than a Boeing 747-400 (it could even carry 750 people on routes around Asia, where people did not care as much about seating comfort). It was expected to fly by 2004, with prices starting somewhat over $200 mil-lion. Development costs could reach $15 billion, so essentially the A3XX was a bet-the-company project with an uncertain outlook, much as was Boeing's 747 thirty years before. To pay for these costs, Airbus expected to get 40 percent from suppliers such

---

[3] Alex Taylor II, "Blue Skies for Airbus," *Fortune,* 2 August 1999, p. 103.

as Sweden's Saab, 30 percent from government loans arranged by its partners, and the rest from its own resources.

The huge financing needed for this venture could hardly be obtained without a corporate reorganization, one that would provide a mechanism for handling internal disputes among the various partner countries, not the least of which was where the plane would be assembled. So, Forgeard had necessity on his side for reorganizing. But the A3XX faced other issues and concerns.

Should a Plane Like the A3XX Even Be Built?

Boeing's publicly expressed opinion was that such a plane would never be profitable. "Let them launch it," said one Boeing official, with a hint of malice.[4] Boeing took the position that consumers want frequent, nonstop flights, such as Southwest Airlines had brought to prominence with its saturation of city-pair routes with frequent flights. An ultra-large aircraft would mean far less frequency.[5]

Airbus, meantime, surveyed big airlines and discerned enough interest in a superjumbo to proceed. It also consulted with more than 60 airports around the world to determine whether such a big plane would be able to take off and land easily. Weight is critical to these maneuvers, and Airbus pledged that the A3XX would be able to use the same runways as the 747 because of a new lightweight material. Instead of regular aluminum, the planes would use a product called Glare, made of aluminum alloy and glass-fiber tape.

Airbus promised ambitious plans for passenger comfort in this behemoth. It built a full-size 237-foot mockup of the interior to show prospective customers, and enlisted 1,200 frequent flyers to critique the cabin mockup. To reduce claustrophobia, the designers added a wide staircase between upper and lower decks. Early plans also included exercise rooms and sleeping quarters fitted with bunk beds.

Airbus claimed that the 555-seat A3XX would be 15 percent cheaper to operate per seat-mile than Boeing's 747. Boeing maintained this was wildly optimistic. United Airlines Frederick Brace, vice president of finance, also expressed doubts: "The risk for Airbus is whether there's a market for A3XX. The risk for an airline is: Can we fill it up? We have to be prudent in how we purchase it."[6]

Competitive Position of Airbus

Airbus was well positioned to supply planes to airlines whose needs Boeing couldn't meet near term. Some thought it was even producing better planes than Boeing.

United Airlines chose Airbus's A320 twinjets over Boeing's 737s, saying passengers preferred the Airbus product. Several South American carriers also chose A320s over the 737, placing a $4 billion order with Airbus. For 1997, Airbus hacked out a 45 percent market share, the first time Boeing's 60 percent market share had eroded.

---

[4] Steve Wilhelm, "Plane Speaking," *Puget Sound Business Journal*, 18 June 1999, p. 112.

[5] Ibid.

[6] Taylor, "Blue Skies for Airbus," p. 108.

The situation worsened drastically for Boeing in 1998. US Air, which had previously ordered 400 Airbus jets, announced in July that it would buy 30 more. But the biggest defection came in August, when British Airlines announced plans to buy 59 Airbus jetliners and take options for 200 more. This broke its long record as a Boeing-loyal customer. The order, worth as much as $11 billion, would be the biggest victory of Airbus over Boeing.[7]

Beyond the production delays of Boeing, Airbus had other competitive strengths. While it had less total production capability than Boeing (235 planes vs. Boeing's 550), the Airbus production line was efficient and the company had done better in trimming its costs. This meant it could go head to head with Boeing on price. And price seemed to be the name of the game in the late 1990s. This contrasted with earlier days when Boeing rose to world leadership with performance, delivery, and technology more important than cost. "They [the customers] do not care what it costs us to make the planes," Boeing Chairman and Chief Executive Philip Condit admitted. With airline design stabilized, he saw the airlines buying planes today as chiefly interested in how much carrying capacity they could buy for a buck.[8]

Increasingly, passengers were grousing about the cramped interiors of planes designed for coast-to-coast trips, and the dearth of lavatories to accommodate 126 to 189 passengers on long flights. Passenger rage appeared to be cropping up more and more. *Forbes* magazine editorialized that "the first carrier that makes an all-out effort to treat passengers as people rather than oversized sardines will be an immense money-maker."[9]

Boeing's new 737-700s and 737-800s were notorious for giving customer comfort low priority. Airbus differentiated itself from Boeing by designing its A320 150-seat workhorse with a fuselage 7.5 inches wider than Boeing's, thus adding an inch to every seat in a typical six-across configuration.

In the first four months of 1999, Airbus won an amazing 78 percent of orders. US Airways Chairman Stephen Wolf, whose airline had ordered 430 Airbus planes since 1996, said, "Airbus aircraft offer greater flexibility for wider seats, more overhead bin space, and more aisle space—all important in a consumer-conscious business."[10]

A Donnybrook

An interesting marketing brawl occurred in mid-1999 that was indicative of the intensity of this airliner war. Boeing won a $1.9 billion order for ten of its 777 jetliners from Singapore Airlines. This in itself would not have raised eyebrows, but there was more to it. As a condition, Boeing agreed to purchase for resale seventeen competing Airbus A340-300 jets from Singapore Airlines, which would allow the airline to phase out these Airbus planes.

---

[7] "British to Order Airbus Airliners," *Cleveland Plain Dealer,* 25 August 1998, p. 6-C.

[8] Howard Banks, "Slow Learner," *Forbes,* 4 May 1998, p. 54.

[9] "Plane Discomfort," *Forbes,* 6 September 1999, p. 32.

[10] Taylor, "Blue Skies for Airbus," p. 104.

Airbus officials claimed that Boeing had agreed to unprofitable terms out of desperation to close a 777 sale agreement and that this signaled a new price war involving trade-ins to provide a discount rather than direct price-cutting. Boeing crowed that the carrier's decision to eliminate the competing version of the A340 from its fleet was a victory for Boeing.[11]

A month later, still stung by the marketing move of Boeing, and in an effort to thwart it, Airbus announced that it would not provide its standard support services for the jets it sold to Singapore Airlines if Boeing buys and resells them. Such a countermove could prove costly to Boeing. On the other hand, Boeing was likely to offer the jets first to airlines with fleets of the same planes, several of which had already expressed interest. Refusing to provide support service would put Airbus in the position of denying support for a small number of planes within the fleet of a major customer. Move and countermove, this.[12]

WHO CAN WE BLAME FOR BOEING'S TROUBLES?

Was It CEO Philip Condit?

Philip Condit became the Boeing chief executive in 1996, just in time for the emerging problems. He had hardly assumed office before becoming deeply involved in the defense industry's merger mania, first buying Rockwell's aerospace operation and then McDonnell Douglas. Condit later admitted that he probably spent too much time on these acquisitions and not enough time on watching the commercial part of the operation.[13]

Condit's credentials were good. His association with Boeing began in 1965 when he joined the firm as an aerodynamics engineer. The same year, he obtained a design patent for a flexible wing called the sailwing. Moving through the company's engineering and managerial ranks, he was named CEO in 1996 and chairman in 1997. Along the way, he earned a master's degree in management from the Massachusetts Institute of Technology in 1975, and in 1997 a doctorate in engineering from Science University of Tokyo, where he was the first Westerner to earn such a degree.

Was Condit's pursuit of the Rockwell and McDonnell Douglas mergers a major blunder? While analysts did not agree on this, prevailing opinion was more positive than negative, mostly because these businesses could smooth the cyclical nature of the commercial sector.

Interestingly, in the face of severe adversity, no heads rolled, as they might have in other firms. See the Issue Box: Management Climate during Adversity.

---

[11] Jeff Cole, "Airbus Industrie Charges Boeing Is Inciting Price War in Asian Deal," *Wall Street Journal,* 21 June 1999, p. A4.

[12] Daniel Michaels, "Airbus Won't Provide Support Service for Jets It Sold to Singapore Air If Boeing Resells Them," *Wall Street Journal,* 28 July 1999, p. A17.

[13] Howard Banks, "Slow Learner," *Forbes,* 4 May 1998, p. 56.

ISSUE BOX

MANAGEMENT CLIMATE DURING ADVERSITY: WHAT IS BEST FOR MAXIMUM EFFECTIVENESS

Management shake-ups during adversity can range from practically none to widespread head-rolling. In the first scenario, a cooperative board is usually necessary, and it helps if the top executive(s) controls a lot of stock. But the company's problems will probably continue. In the second scenario, at the extreme, wielding a mean ax with excessive worker and management layoffs can wreak havoc on a company's morale and longer-term prospects.

In general, neither extreme—complacency or upheaval—is good. A sick company usually needs drastic changes, but not necessarily widespread bloodletting that leaves the entire organization cringing and sending out resumes. But we need to further define *sick*. At what point is a company so bad off it needs a drastic overhaul? Was Boeing such a sick company? Would a drastic overhaul have quickly changed things? Certainly Boeing management had made some miscalculations, mostly in the area of too much optimism and too much complacency, but these were finally recognized.

Major competitor Airbus was finally aggressively attacking, and that certainly had something to do with Boeing's problems. Executive changes and resignations might not have helped.

How do you personally feel about the continuity of management at Boeing during these difficult times? Should some heads have rolled? What criteria would you use in your judgment of whether to roll heads or not?

Were the Problems Mostly Due to Internal Factors?

The airlines' unexpected buying binge, which was brought about by the worldwide prosperity fueling air travel, maybe should have been anticipated. However, even the most prescient decision maker probably would have missed the full extent of this boom. For example, orders jumped from 124 in 1994 to 754 in 1996. With hindsight we know that Boeing made a grievous management mistake in trying to bite off too much, by promising expanded production and deliveries that were wholly unrealistic. We know what triggered such extravagant promises: trying to keep ahead of archrival Airbus.

Huge layoffs in the early 1990s contributed to the problems of gearing up for new business. An early retirement plan had been taken up by 9,000 of 13,000 eligible people. This was twice as many as Boeing expected, and it removed a core of production-line workers and managers who had kept a dilapidated system working. New people could not be trained or assimilated quickly enough to match those lost.

Boeing had begun switching to the Japanese practice of lean inventory management that delivers parts and tools to workers precisely as needed, so that production costs could be reduced. Partly due to this change, and to the early 1990s economic downturn, Boeing's supplier base changed significantly. Some suppliers quit the aviation business; others had suffered so badly in the slump that their credit was affected and they were unable to boost capacity for the suddenly increased business. The result was serious parts shortages.

Complicating production problems was Boeing's long-standing practice of customizing. Because it permitted customers to choose from a host of options, Boeing was fine-tuning not only for every airline, but for every order. For example, it offered the 747's customers 38 different pilot clipboards and 109 shades of the color white.[14] Such tailoring added significantly to costs and production time. This perhaps was acceptable when these costs could be easily passed on to customers in a more leisurely production cycle, but it was far from maximizing efficiency. With deregulation, fare wars made extreme customizing archaic. Boeing apparently got the message with the wide-bodied 777, designed entirely by computers. Here, choices of parts were narrowed to standard options, such as carmakers offer in their transmissions, engines, and comfort packages.

Cut-rate pricing between Boeing and Airbus epitomized the situation by the mid-1990s. Then, costs became critical if a firm was to be profitable. In that climate, Boeing was so obsessed with maintaining its 60 percent market share that it fought for each order with whatever price it took. Commercial airline production had somehow become a commodity business, with neither Boeing nor Airbus having products all that unique to sell. Innovation seemed disregarded, and price was the only factor in getting an order. So, every order became a battleground, and prices might be slashed 20 percent off list in order to grab all the business possible.[15] And Boeing did not have the low-cost advantage over Airbus.

Such price competition worked to the advantage of the airlines, and they grew skillful at gaining big discounts from Boeing and Airbus by holding out huge contracts and negotiating hard.

The cumbersome production systems of Boeing—cost inefficient—became a burden in this cost-conscious environment. While some of the problems could be attributed to computer technology not well applied to the assembly process, others involved organizational myopia regarding even such simple things as a streamlined organization and common parts. For example, before recent changes the Boeing commercial group had five wing-design groups, one for each aircraft program. It now has one. Another example cited in *Forbes* tells of different tools needed in the various plane models to open their wing access hatches.[16] Why not use the same tool?

There is a paradox in Boeing's dilemma. Its 777 was the epitome of high technology and computer design, as well as efficient production planning. Yet, much of the other production was mired in a morass with supplies, parts management, and production inefficiency.

Harry Stonecipher, former CEO of McDonnell Douglas before the acquisition and then president and chief operating officer of Boeing, cited arrogance as the mind-set behind Boeing's problems. He saw this as coming from a belief that the company could do no wrong, that all its problems came from outside, and that business as usual would solve them.[17]

---

[14] John Greenwald, "Is Boeing Out of Its Spin?" *Time*, 13 July 1998, p. 68.

[15] Biddle and Helyar, "Behind Boeing's Woes," A1, A16.

[16] Banks, "Slow Learner," 60.

[17] Bill Sweetman, "Stonecipher's Boeing Shakeup," *Interavia Business & Technology*, September 1998, p. 15.

The Role of External Factors

Adding to the production and cost-containment difficulties of Boeing were increased regulatory demands. These came not only from the U.S. Federal Aviation Administration but also from the European Joint Airworthiness Authority (a loose grouping of regulators from more than twenty European countries). The first major consequence of this increased regulatory climate concerned the new 730NG. Boeing apparently thought it could use the same over-the-wings emergency exits as it had on the older 737. But the European regulators wanted a redesign. They were concerned that the older type of emergency exits would not permit passengers in the larger version of the plane to evacuate quickly enough. So Boeing had to design two new over-the-wing exits on each side. This was no simple modification since it involved rebuilding the most crucial aspect of the plane. The costly refitting accounted for a major part of the $1.6 billion write-down Boeing took in 1997.

Europe's Airbus Industrie had made no secret of its desire to achieve parity with Boeing and have 50 percent of the international market for commercial jets. This mind-set led to the severe price competition of the latter 1990s as Boeing stubbornly tried to maintain its 60 percent market share even at the expense of profits. While its total production capacity was somewhat below that of Boeing, Airbus had already overhauled its manufacturing process and was better positioned to compete on price. Airbus's competitive advantage seemed stronger with single-aisle planes, those in the 120- to 200-seat category, mostly 737s of Boeing and A320s of Airbus. But this accounted for 43 percent of the $40 billion expected to be spent on airliners in 1998.[18]

The future was something else. Airbus placed high stakes on a superjumbo successor to the 747, with seating capacity well beyond that of the 747. Such a huge plane would operate from hub airports such as New York City's JFK. Meantime, Boeing staked its future on its own 767s and 777s, which could connect smaller cities around the world without the need for passenger concentration at a few hubs.

Have you ever heard of a firm complaining of too much business? Probably not, but then we're confronted with Boeing's immersion in red ink, caused by trying to cope with too many orders. However, Boeing's feast of too much business abruptly ended. Financial problems in Asia brought cancellations and postponements of orders and deliveries.

In October 1998, Boeing disclosed that thirty-six completed aircraft were sitting in company storage areas in the desert, largely because of canceled orders. By December 1998, Boeing warned that its operations could be hurt by the Asian situation for as long as five years, and it announced that an additional 20,000 jobs would be eliminated and production cut 25 percent.[19] Of course, it didn't help that Airbus was capitalizing on Boeing's production difficulties by wresting orders from the stable of long-term Boeing customers, nor that Airbus planned a 30 percent production increase for 1999.

---

[18] Banks, "Slow Learner," 60.

[19] Frederick M. Biddle and Andy Pasztor, "Boeing May Be Hurt Up to 5 Years by Asia," *Wall Street Journal*, 3 December 1998, p. A3.

Later Developments

By 2001 the competition between Airbus and Boeing continued unabated. Airbus had gone ahead with its superjumbo A-380, the world's largest passenger jet, with delivery to start in 2006 for a list price of $239 million. In its standard configuration, it would carry 555 passengers between airport hubs. With delivery still five years away, Airbus already had orders for 72 of the jumbos, and expected to reach the 100 milestone early in 2002. It would break even with 250 of the wide bodies.

In March 2001, Boeing scrapped plans for an updated, but still smaller, 747-X project. Instead, it announced plans for a revolutionary delta-winged "Sonic Cruiser," carrying 150 to 250 passengers higher and faster than conventional planes. The savings in time would amount to 50 minutes from New York City to London, and almost two hours between Singapore and London. Further time savings would come from the plane flying to point-to-point destinations, bypassing layovers at such congested hubs as London and Hong Kong. Delivery was expected in 2007 or 2008.

Both companies had undergone major organizational changes. As of January 1, 2001, Airbus was no longer a four-nation consortium, but now an integrated company with centralized purchasing and management systems. Operations were streamlined toward bottom-line responsibilities.

Boeing had previously diversified itself away from so much dependence on commercial aircraft through its acquisitions of Rockwell's aerospace and defense business, McDonnell Douglas, Hughes Space & Communications, and several smaller companies. Boeing expected that within five years more than half its revenues would come from new business lines, including financing aircraft sales, providing high-speed Internet access, and managing air-traffic problems.[20]

Everything changed with 9/11.

UPDATE—LATE 2002

The airline industry's woes that began with 9/11 intensified in 2002. By late that year two major carriers, US Air and United, were in bankruptcy. But other airlines, with the exception of a few discount carriers, notably Southwest and JetBlue, were experiencing horrific losses. Airlines were placing no new orders and even reneging on accepting delivery of previously ordered planes. Boeing's jet production fell to half of what it had been a year earlier, and forecasts for 2003 and 2004 were little better.

In this environment, the competition between Airbus and Boeing for winning the few customers still buying became even fiercer and was influenced almost entirely by price. The biggest prize was capturing the 120-plane order from British budget carrier, easyJet, and this customer milked its power position to the utmost, repeatedly sending Boeing and Airbus back to improve their offers.

---

[20] Compiled from such sources as David J. Lynch, "Airbus Comes of Age with A-380," *USA Today,* 21 June 2001, pp. 1B, 2B; J. Lynn Lunsford, Daniel Michaels, and Andy Pasztor, "At Paris Air Show, Boeing-Airbus Duel Has New Twist," *Wall Street Journal,* 15 June 2001, p. B4.

During the aviation slump in the early 1990s, Boeing had beefed up its order backlog by selling at steep discounts—only to find itself in a serious bind in 1997 when it could not keep up with the built-up demand, and production costs skyrocketed. Now, Boeing refused to follow Airbus into unprofitable terrain, and Airbus got the order. Though Airbus claimed it was not selling its planes at a loss, many people in the industry thought otherwise.

In late December 2002, Boeing announced it was shelving the ambitious development program for its high-speed Sonic Cruiser. In talks with potential customers to gauge interest in such a plane in this post-9/11 environment, few expressed any interest; most wanted a replacement plane that would be cheaper to operate than existing ones. So Boeing began changing its focus to developing a new 250-seat plane that would be 20 percent cheaper to operate than existing jetliners. At last report, Airbus was still garnering orders for its planned 555-passenger A380.

Be a Devil's Advocate (one who argues an opposing position to assure that all aspects of a course of action are considered): Amass all the arguments and rationale you can for Boeing to continue with the high-speed Sonic Cruiser.

Sources: J. Lynn Lunsford, "Boeing to Drop Sonic Cruiser, Build Plane Cheaper to Operate," *Wall Street Journal*, 19 December 2002, p. B4; Daniel Michaels and J. Lynn Lunsford, "Airbus Is Awarded easyJet Order for 120 New Planes over Boeing," *Wall Street Journal*, 15 October 2002, pp. A3 and A6; and Scott McCartney and J. Lynn Lunsford, "Skies Darken for Boeing, AMR and UAL as Aviation Woes Grow," *Wall Street Journal*, 17 October 2002, pp. A1 and A9.

WHAT CAN BE LEARNED?

Beware the "King-of-the-Hill" Three-Cs Mind-Set

Firms that have been well entrenched in their industry and that have dominated for years tend to fall into a particular mind-set that leaves them vulnerable to aggressive and innovative competitors.

The "three Cs" are detrimental to a front-runner's continued success:

- Complacency
- Conservatism
- Conceit

Complacency is smugness—a complacent firm is self-satisfied, content with the status quo, no longer hungry and eager for innovative growth. *Conservatism,* when excessive, characterizes a management that is wedded to the past, to the traditional, to the way things have always been done. Conservative managers see no need to change because they believe nothing is different today (e.g., "Our 747 jumbo jet is the largest that can be profitably used"). Finally, *conceit* further reinforces the myopia of the mind-set: conceit regarding current and potential competitors. The beliefs that "we are the best" and "no one else can touch us" can easily permeate an organization that has dominated its industry for years. Usually the three Cs insidiously move in at the highest levels and readily filter down to the rest of the organization.

Stonecipher, former CEO of McDonnell Douglas and then president of Boeing, admitted to company self-confidence bordering on arrogance. The current problems of Boeing should have destroyed any vestiges of the three Cs mind-set. But the company's former king-of-the hill position may be lost.

Growth Must Be Manageable

Boeing certainly demonstrated the fallacy of attempting growth beyond immediate capabilities in a growth-at-any-cost mind-set. The rationale for embracing great growth is that firms "need to run with the ball" if they ever get that rare opportunity to suddenly double or triple sales. But there are times when a slower, more controlled growth is prudent.

Risks lie on both sides as businesses reach for these opportunities. When a market begins to boom and a firm is unable to keep up with demand without greatly increasing capacity and resources, it faces a dilemma: (1) Stay conservative in fear that the opportunity will be short-lived, but thereby abdicate some of the growing market to competitors; or (2) Expand vigorously to take full advantage of the opportunity, but risk being overextended and vulnerable should the potential suddenly fade. Regardless of the commitment to a vision of great growth, a firm must develop an organization and systems and controls to handle it, or find itself in the same morass as Boeing, with quality control problems, inability to meet production targets, alienated customers, and costs far out of line. And, not the least, having its stock price savaged by Wall Street investors while its market share tumbles. Growth must not be beyond a firm's ability to manage it.

Perils of Downsizing

Boeing presents a sobering example of the risks of downsizing in this era when downsizing is so much in fashion. With incredibly bad timing, Boeing encouraged many of its most experienced and skilled workers and supervisors to take early retirement, just a few years before the boom began. Boeing found out the hard way that it could replace bodies, but not the skills needed to produce the highly complex planes under severe deadlines for output. The company would have been better off to have maintained a core of experienced workers during the downturn, rather than lose them forever. It would have been better to have suffered with higher labor costs during the lean times, disregarding management's typical attitude of paring costs to the bone during such times. Yet, when we look at Table 4.1 and see the severe decreases of revenues and income in 1993, 1994, and lasting well into 1995, we can appreciate the dilemma of Boeing's management.

Problems of Competing Mostly on Price

Price competition almost invariably leads to price-cutting and even price wars to win market share. In such an environment, the lowest-cost, most efficient producer wins.

More often, all firms in an industry have rather similar cost structures, and severe price competition hurts the profits of all competitors without bringing much additional business. Any initial pricing advantage is quickly matched by competitors unwilling to lose market share. In this situation, competing on non-price bases has much to recommend it. Non-price competition emphasizes uniqueness, perhaps in some aspects of product features and quality, perhaps through service and quicker deliveries or maybe better quality control. A firm's reputation, if good, is a powerful non-price advantage.

Usually new and rapidly growing industries face price competition as marginal firms are weeded out and more economies of operation are developed. The more mature an industry, the greater likelihood of non-price competition since cutthroat pricing causes too much hardship to all competitors.

Certainly the commercial aircraft industry was mature, and much has been made of airlines being chiefly interested in how much passenger-carrying capacity they can buy for the same buck, and of their pitting Airbus and Boeing against each other in bidding wars.[21] Non-price competition badly needed to be reinstated in this industry. At that point, Airbus appeared to be doing a better job of finding uniqueness, with its passenger-friendly planes and its charting new horizons with the superjumbo.

The Synergy of Mergers and Acquisitions Is Suspect

The concept of synergy says that a new whole is better than the sum of its parts. In other words, a well-planned merger or acquisition should result in a better enterprise than the two separate entities. Theoretically, this would seem possible since operations can be streamlined for more efficiency and since greater management and staff competence can be brought to bear as more financial and other resources are tapped; or in Boeing's case, since the peaks and valleys of commercial demand could be countered by defense and space business.

Unfortunately, such synergy often is absent, at least in the short and intermediate term. More often such concentrations incur severe digestive problems—problems with people, systems, and procedures—that take time to resolve. Furthermore, greater size does not always beget economies of scale. The opposite may in fact occur: an unwieldy organization, slow to act and vulnerable to more aggressive, innovative, and agile smaller competitors. The siren call of synergy is often an illusion.

The acquisitions of McDonnell Douglas and Rockwell may work out well for Boeing. But their assimilation came at a most troubling time for Boeing. The Long

---

[21] For example, see Banks, "Slow Learner," 54.

Beach plant of McDonnell Douglas alone led to a massive $1.4 billion write-off, and contributed significantly to the losses of 1997. Less easily calculated, but certainly a factor, was the management time involved in coping with these new entities.

CONSIDER

After reading the preceding material, can you think of additional learning insights?

QUESTIONS

1. Do you think Boeing should have anticipated the impact of Asian economic difficulties long before it did?

2. If it had more quickly anticipated the drying up of the Asian market for planes, could Boeing have prevented most of the problems now confronting it? Discuss.

3. Do you think top management at Boeing should have been fired after the disastrous miscalculations in the late 1990s? Why or why not?

4. A major stockholder grumbles, "Management worries too much about Airbus, and to hell with the stockholders." Evaluate this statement. Do you think it is valid?

5. What do you see for Boeing three to five years down the road? For Airbus?

6. Do you think it likely that Boeing will have to contend with new competitors over the next ten years? Why or why not?

7. Discuss synergy in mergers. Why does synergy so often seem to be lacking, despite expectations?

8. You are a skilled machinist for Boeing and have always been quite proud of participating in the building of giant planes. You have just received notice of another lengthy layoff, the second in five years. Discuss your likely attitudes and actions.

9. How wise do you think it was for Airbus to "bet the company" on the super-jumbo A-380, the world's largest jet?

10. Do you think Airbus's more passenger-friendly planes give it a significant competitive advantage? Why or why not? Discuss as many aspects of this issue as you can.

HANDS-ON EXERCISES

Before

1. You are a management consultant advising top management at Boeing. It is 1993 and the airline industry is in a slump, but early indications are that things will improve greatly in a few years. What would you advise that might have prevented the problems Boeing faced a few years later? Be as specific

as you can, and support your recommendations as to practicality and probable effectiveness.

After

2. It is late 1998, and Boeing has had to announce drastic cutbacks with little improvement likely before five years. Boeing's stock has collapsed, and Airbus is charging ahead. What do you recommend now? (You may need to make some assumptions; if so, state them clearly and keep them reasonable.)

TEAM DEBATE EXERCISE

1. A business columnist writes: Boeing could "have told customers 'no thanks' to more orders than its factories could handle. … It "could have done itself a huge favor by simply building fewer planes and charging more for them."[22] Debate the merits of this suggestion.

2. Debate the controversy of Airbus Chairman Forgeard's decision to go for broke with the A3XX superjumbo. Is the risk/reward probability worth such a mighty commitment? Debate as many pros and cons as you can, and consider how much each should be weighted or given priority consideration.

INVITATION TO RESEARCH

What is the situation with Boeing today? Has it recovered its profitability? How is the competitive position with Airbus?

What is the situation with the A-380 of Airbus? Is it still an ongoing project with delivery scheduled for 2006?

How has 9/11 affected the fortunes of the two companies? Has it changed the competitive picture?

---

[22] Holman W. Jenkins Jr., "Boeing's Trouble: Not Enough Monopolistic Arrogance," *Wall Street Journal,* 16 December 1998, p. A23.

CHAPTER FIVE

Sneaker Wars:
Reebok vs. Nike

*B*y the late 1970s and early 1980s, Nike had wrested first place in the athletic shoe industry from Adidas—the firm that had been supreme since the 1936 Olympics when Jesse Owens, wearing Adidas shoes, won his medals in front of Hitler, the German nation, and the world.

In the early 1980s, Reebok emerged as Nike's major competitor, showing a tremendous growth and becoming No. 1 in this industry by 1987. But Nike fought back, and three years later had regained the top-dog position. By the latter 1990s and into the new millennium, Nike had decisively pulled away in revenues and profitability. How did Reebok fight its way to the top in the first place? Why did it permit Nike to dislodge it so soon? Or did Nike use some inspired marketing strategy to do so?

REEBOK

History

The ancestor to Reebok goes back to the 1890s when Joseph William Foster made himself the first known running shoes with spikes. By 1895, he was hand-making shoes for top runners. Soon, the fledgling company, J. W. Foster & Sons, was furnishing shoes for distinguished athletes around the world.

In 1958 two of the founder's grandsons started a companion company, which they named—fittingly they thought—after an African gazelle: Reebok. This company eventually absorbed J. W. Foster & Sons.

In 1979 Paul Fireman, a partner in an outdoor sporting goods distributorship, saw Reebok shoes at an international trade show. He negotiated for the North American distribution license and introduced three running shoes in the United States that year. It was the height of the running boom. These Reeboks were the most expensive running shoes on the market at the time, retailing for $60. But no matter; demand burgeoned, outpacing the plant's capacity, and production facilities were established in Korea.

In 1981, sales were $1.5 million. But a breakthrough came the next year. Reebok introduced the first athletic shoe designed especially for women. It was a shoe for aerobic dance exercise, and was called the Freestyle. Whether accidentally or with brilliant foresight, Reebok anticipated three major trends that were to transform the athletic footwear industry: (1) the aerobic exercise movement, (2) the great embracing by women of sports and exercise, and (3) the transference of athletic footwear to street and casual wear.

Sales exploded from $13 million in 1983 to $307 million in 1985. Almost unbelievably, sales tripled in 1986 to $919 million, and by 1991 they reached $2.7 billion.

A company publication in 1993 said:

> For more than a decade, the semi-official corporate motto has called for the company, its products and its people to always strive to "make a difference"; and one of the company's business objectives is to become "the best, most innovative and exciting sporting goods company in the world."[1]

Shifting Competitive Picture for Reebok

In 1987, Reebok's share of the U.S. athletic footwear market surpassed archrival Nike's as it racked up sales of $1.4 billion against Nike's plateauing sales of $900 million. Somehow, Reebok's sales growth then slowed, and in 1990 Nike overtook it, with $2.25 billion in sales to Reebok's $2.16 billion. The margin widened as Reebok began to lose ground, not sporadically but steadily. Its meteoric sales increases of a few years before were no more, and stock market valuations and investor enthusiasm reflected this decline in fortunes.

Part of the shift in competitive position could be attributed to Nike's savvy advertising and to its two well-paid athlete endorsers—Michael Jordan and Pete Sampras. But perhaps Reebok could blame itself more for the change in its fortunes. Certainly as the 1990s moved toward mid-decade, the flaws of Reebok were becoming more obvious and self-destructing.

Paul Fireman had purchased Reebok in 1984 and led it to more than a tenfold increase in sales in only five years. But with such growth, directors felt they needed an executive with experience running a big operation. Fireman, who owned 20 percent of the company's stock, didn't object. He maintained that he was glad to give up day-to-day responsibilities. While retaining the titles of chairman and CEO, he turned his attentions to private pursuits, including building a golf course on Cape Cod.

The new management was to prove inept. Amid unimproving performance, Reebok went through three different top executives in the next five years—the last being John Duerden, formerly with Xerox. Nothing seemed to stem the tide; Reebok continued losing ground against Nike. Finally, in August 1992, Fireman again took active charge, and he wasted little time bringing in a new management team. At the same time, he introduced aggressive plans for the company to regain its competitive position.

---

[1] *Reebok International, Ltd. Corporate Background,* January 1993, pp. 13–14.

Aggressive Thrusts of Reebok

Fireman first attacked Nike in the basketball arena. Nike's share of basketball shoes was almost 50 percent, against Reebok's 15 percent. But at about this time, Michael Jordan retired from basketball to try baseball. "Nike's success has become their albatross," Fireman exalted. "Jordan is no longer on the radar screen."[2] He signed up Shaquille O'Neal, "the next enduring superstar," and planned to destroy the market dominance of Nike.

The pressure was stepped up on Nike at the NBA All-Star Game in February 1994, when Reebok launched a national ad campaign for its Instapump. This was a sneaker that had no laces, but instead was inflated with CO_2 to fit the foot. It was pricey, retailing for $130, but seemed on the cutting edge. Fireman expected this innovation to account for 10 percent of all Reebok's sales in three years.

Reebok also attacked another Nike stronghold—the $250 million market for cleated shoes, of which Nike had 80 percent. In January 1993 Reebok introduced a new line of cleated shoes aimed at high-school athletes. Fireman predicted that these sales should triple by 1994 to $45 million. In 1994 he also aimed an offensive into the outdoor hiking and mountaineering market, with twelve new shoes that he predicted would produce $100 million in new sales.

During the years Fireman was not at the helm, Reebok had tried a number of advertising slogans, such as "UBU" and "Physics behind Physique." None of them were notably effective compared to the Nike "Just Do It" theme. Fireman now approved a new unifying theme for all ads, "Planet Reebok."

Fireman also did an about-face with his endorsement promotions. Despite Nike's heavy use of endorsements in its advertising, Reebok always had been reluctant to do much, thinking the huge sums celebrity athletes demanded were unreasonable. Suddenly Fireman signed O'Neal in 1992 for $3 million, and then went on to sign endorsement deals with some four hundred football, baseball, and soccer stars. The brand logo was also changed to an inverted "V" with a slash through it that he hoped consumers would identify with high performance. "We'll be the market leader by the end of 1995," Fireman predicted.[3]

Consequences

Unfortunately, Fireman's aggressive efforts to rejuvenate the company and win back market leadership from Nike continued to sputter. Some flaws were coming to light. For example, with Shaquille O'Neal, the Shaq Attaq shoe seemed a sure thing for teens. But it bombed. The problems: The shoes were white with light blue trim, and they cost $130. But now black shoes were the hot look, and how many teens could afford $130? In the first six months of 1993, sales of Reebok basketball shoes fell 20 percent, despite the Shaq's influence.

---

[2] Geoffrey Smith, "Can Reebok Regain Its Balance?" *Business Week,* 20 December 1993, p. 109.

[3] Ibid., p. 108.

By 1995, operating costs were surging, totaling 32.7 percent of sales compared with 24.4 percent in 1991. They also exceeded the industry average of 27 percent. Reebok admitted that the increased costs were partly due to its aggressive pursuit of endorsement contracts with athletes as well as to sporting-event sponsorships. For example, the company had signed up 3,000 athletes to wear Reebok shoes and apparel at the 1996 Olympics in Atlanta, up from 400 four years before. It had also bought endorsements from the San Francisco 49ers and other NFL teams, as well as basketball star Rebecca Lobo, to wear its products.

Some of the prior endorsements had not worked out well: Tennis pro Michael Chang had a $15 million endorsement contract; but Sampras and Agassi, both Nike endorsers, had eclipsed Chang. And Shaquille O'Neal became unhappy with his $3 million Reebok contract and began looking around for bigger money.

Reebok's costs also were increased by investments aimed at fixing distribution snags and opening a new facility in Memphis.

Other Reebok problems stemmed from management turmoil, including the departures and resignations of top executives. Some shareholders questioned whether Fireman was too difficult a boss: "How do you attract first-rate talent when there's been a history of turnover at the top?"[4]

Adding to Reebok's difficulties were price-fixing charges brought by the Federal Trade Commission. The government contended that Reebok had told retailers their supplies would be cut off if they discounted Reebok shoes too much. In May 1995, Reebok agreed to pay $9.5 million to settle the price-fixing charges, saying that while no evidence of wrongdoing was established, still it settled to avoid costly litigation.

But the major Reebok problem was in its relations with the major retailer player in the athletic footwear industry—Foot Locker.

The Struggle to Win Foot Locker

By 1995, Woolworth's Foot Locker, a chain of some 2,800 stores, had become the biggest seller of athletic footwear. It and related Woolworth units accounted for $1.5 billion of the $6.5 billion U.S. sales, this being some 23 percent. Nike had a winning relationship with this behemoth customer. In 1993, Nike's sales in Foot Lockers were $300 million; Reebok was slightly behind, with $228 million. Two years later, Nike's Foot Locker sales had risen to $750 million, while Reebok's dropped to $122 million.[5] The decline of Reebok's fortunes with Foot Locker can be attributed to poor handling by top management of this important relationship. Fireman seemed to resent the demands of Foot Locker almost from the beginning. For example, in the 1980s when Reebok's aerobics shoes were facing robust demand, Foot Locker wanted exclusivity, that is, special lines only for itself. The retailer saw exclusive lines as one of its major weapons against discounters, and was getting such protection from other manufacturers—but not from Reebok, which persisted in selling its shoes to anybody, including discounters near Foot Locker stores.

[4] Joseph Pereira, "In Reebok–Nike War, Big Woolworth Chain Is a Major Battlefield," *Wall Street Journal*, 22 September 1995, p. A6.

[5] Ibid., p. A1.

In contrast, Nike had been working with Foot Locker for some years, and by 1995 had a dozen items sold only by the chain, including Flights 65 and 67, high-priced basketball shoes. While Fireman began belatedly trying to fix the relationship, little had apparently been accomplished by the end of 1995.[6] Adding to Reebok's troubles in cracking this major chain, Foot Locker's customers were mainly teens and Generation-X customers willing to pay $80 to $90 for shoes. But Reebok had given up that high-end niche with most of its products. Reebok's primary customer base had become older people and preteens unwilling or unable to pay the high prices. Aggravating the poor relationship with Foot Locker was Reebok's carelessness in providing samples on time to Foot Locker buyers. Because of the chain's size, buying decisions had to be made early in the season. Late-arriving samples, or no samples, virtually guaranteed that such new items would not be purchased in any appreciable quantity. See the Information Box: Importance of Major Account Management for a discussion of the importance of major customers.

NIKE

History

Phil Knight was a miler of modest accomplishments. His best time was a 4:13, hardly in the same class as the below-4:00 world-class runners. But he had trained under the

---

INFORMATION BOX

IMPORTANCE OF MAJOR ACCOUNT MANAGEMENT

Recognizing the importance of major customers has come belatedly to some sellers, probably none more belatedly than Reebok. These very large customers often represent a major part of a firm's total sales volume, and satisfying them in an increasingly competitive environment requires special treatment. Major account management should be geared to developing long-term relationships. Service becomes increasingly important in cementing such relations. To this end, understanding and catering to customer needs and wants is a must. If this means giving such important customers exclusivity, and making them the absolute first to see new goods and samples, this ought to be done unhesitatingly.

Such account management has resulted in changes in many organizations. Separate sales forces are often developed, such as "account managers" who devote all their time to one or a few major customers while the rest of the sales force calls on smaller customers in the normal fashion. For a customer the size of Foot Locker, senior executives, even firm presidents, need to become part of this relationship.

Given that you think the demands of a major retailer are completely unreasonable, what would you do if you were Mr. Fireman: give in completely, hold to your principles, negotiate, or what?

---

[6] Ibid., p. A6.

renowned coach Bill Bowerman at the University of Oregon in the late 1950s. Bowerman had put Eugene, Oregon, on the map when year after year he turned out world-record-setting long-distance runners. Bowerman was constantly experimenting with shoes: He had a theory that an ounce off a running shoe might make enough difference to win a race.

In the process of completing his MBA at Stanford University, Phil wrote a research paper based on the theory that the Japanese could do for athletic shoes what they were doing for cameras. After receiving his degree in 1960, Knight went to Japan to seek an American distributorship from the Onitsuka Company for Tiger shoes. Returning home, he took samples of the shoes to Bowerman.

In 1964 Knight and Bowerman went into business. They each put up $500 and formed the Blue Ribbon Shoe Company, sole distributor in the United States for Tiger running shoes. They put the inventory in Knight's father-in-law's basement, and they sold $8,000 worth of these imported shoes that first year. Knight worked by days as a Coopers & Lybrand accountant, while at night and on weekends he peddled these shoes mostly to high-school athletic teams.

Knight and Bowerman finally developed their own shoe in 1972 and decided to manufacture it themselves. They contracted the work out to Asian factories where labor was cheap. They named the shoe Nike after the Greek goddess of victory. At that time they also developed the "swoosh" logo, a highly distinctive emblem that was subsequently placed on every Nike product. The Nike shoe's first appearance in competition came during the 1972 Olympic trials in Eugene, Oregon. Marathon runners who had been persuaded to wear the new shoes placed fourth through seventh in the trials, whereas Adidas wearers finished first, second, and third.

On a Sunday morning in 1975, Bowerman began tinkering with a waffle iron and some urethane rubber. He fashioned a new type of sole, a "waffle" sole whose tiny rubber studs made it springier than those of other shoes currently on the market. This product improvement—seemingly so simple—gave Knight and Bowerman an initial impetus, helping to bring Nike's 1976 sales to $14 million, up from $8.3 million the year before and only $2 million in 1972.

Now Nike was off and running. It was to stay in the forefront of the industry with its careful research and development of new models. By the end of the decade Nike was employing almost one hundred people in the research and development section of the company. Over 140 different shoe models were offered, many of these the most innovative and technologically advanced on the market. Such diversity came from models designed for different foot types, body weights, sexes, running speeds, training schedules, and skill levels. By 1981, Nike led all athletic shoe makers with approximately 50 percent of the total market. Adidas, the decades-long market leader, had seen its market share fall well below that of Nike.

In 1980 Nike went public and Knight became an instant multimillionaire, reaching the coveted Forbes Richest Four Hundred Americans with a net worth estimated at just under $300 million.[7] Bowerman, who at age seventy had sold most of his stock earlier and owned only 2 percent of the company, was worth a mere $9.5 million.

---

[7] "The Richest People in America—The Forbes Four Hundred," *Forbes*, Fall 1983, p. 104.

In the January 4, 1982, edition of *Forbes,* Nike was rated number one in profitability over the previous five years, ahead of all other firms in all other industries.[8]

But by the late 1980s, Reebok had emerged as Nike's greatest competitor and was threatening its dynasty. A good part of the reason for this was Nike's underestimation of an opportunity. Consequently, it was late into the fast-growing market for shoes worn in the aerobics classes that were sweeping the country, fueled by bestselling books by Jane Fonda and others. Reebok was there with the first athletic shoe designed especially for women: a shoe for aerobic dance exercise.

Figure 5.1 shows the sales growth of Reebok and Nike from their beginnings to 1995. Of particular note is the great growth of Reebok in the mid-80s; in only a few years it surpassed Nike, which had plateaued as it missed the new fitness opportunity. Then, as can graphically be seen, Reebok began slowing down—a slowdown it was unable to turn around through the mid-1990s, while Nike again surged. Table 5.1 shows the net income comparisons. Both firms had somewhat erratic incomes, but the early income growth promise of Reebok relative to Nike, as with sales, could not be sustained. This is confirmed with later revenue and income figures from 1995 to 1998, shown in Table 5.2.

Nike's Rejuvenation

The recharge of Nike, after letting its guard down to the wildly charging Reebok, has to be a significant success story. Usually when a front-runner loses momentum, the trend is difficult to reverse. But Phil Knight and Nike were not to be denied.

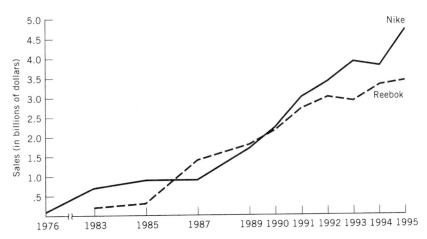

Figure 5.1. Sneaker Wars: Sales, Nike and Reebok 1976–1995 (billions of dollars).

Source: Company annual reports.

Commentary: Here we can graphically see the charge of Reebok in the later 1980s that for a few years surpassed Nike, but then faltered by 1990 as Nike surged ever farther ahead.

[8] "Annual Report on American Industry," *Forbes,* 4 January 1982, p. 246.

TABLE 5.1.   Sneaker Wars: Net Income
Comparisons, Nike and Reebok
1985–1994 (billions of dollars)

	Nike	Reebok
1985	$10.3	$39.0
1986	59.2	132.1
1987	35.9	165.2
1988	101.7	137.0
1989	167.0	175.0
1990	243.0	176.6
1991	287.0	234.7
1992	329.2	114.8
1993	365.0	223.4
1994	298.8	254.5

Source: Company annual reports.

Commentary: Note how much more profitable Reebok
was than Nike in the late 1980s. In one year, 1987, it
was almost five times more profitable. But then in 1990
the tide swung strongly in Nike's favor. Note also that
Nike's profitability was far steadier than Reebok's during
this period.

TABLE 5.2.   Nike versus Reebok Comparative Operating
Statistics, 1995–1998

	Nike	Reebok	Nike % of Total
Revenues (million $):			
1995	$4,761	$3,481	57.8%
1996	6,471	3,478	65.0
1997	9,187	3,644	71.6
1998	9,553	3,225	74.8
Net Income (million $):			
1995	400	165	70.8
1996	553	139	79.9
1997	796	135	85.5
1998	400	24	82.2

Source: Calculated from company reports.

Commentary: In this comparative analysis, the further widening of the gap
between Nike and Reebok is clearly evident. In revenues, Nike's market share
against Reebok has grown from 57.8 percent to 74.8 percent in these four
years—a truly awesome increase in market dominance. In net income, Nike's
comparative performance is even more impressive, despite the poor 1998 profit
performance partly due to poor economic conditions in the Asian markets.
Nike's profits were down, but not nearly as much as Reebok's.

Still, in 1993, Nike did not look very much a winner, even though it had wrested market dominance from Reebok. From the high 80s in February of that year, share prices had plummeted to the mid-50s. The reason? Nike's sales were up only 15 percent and earnings just 11 percent, nothing outstanding for a once-hot stock. So Wall Street began questioning: How many pairs of sneakers does the world need? (Critics had once assailed McDonald's under the same rationale: How many hamburgers can the world eat?) Knight's response was that the Nike mystique could sell other kinds of goods: outdoor footwear, from sandals to hiking boots; apparel lines, such as uniforms, for top-ranked college football and basketball teams—from pants and jerseys to warm-up jackets and practice gear; even golf clothing and equipment. And these same products would be eagerly sought by the general public.

The greatest boost to the Nike image in the years around the millennium was Tiger Woods. Phil Knight had given him a $40 million contract in 1996 just after Woods won his third straight U.S. Amateur Golf Championship and was about to turn pro. The next year Woods won the prestigious Masters Golf Tournament by the biggest margin ever achieved, in the most-watched golf finale in the history of television. In the golf tournaments, while wearing the conspicuous swoosh, Tiger focused attention on Nike as not even Michael Jordan had been able to do.

Could it be that an athletic shoe company could still face a growth industry? Apparently so, through wise diversifications within the larger athletic goods industry. See the Issue Box: How Should We Define Our Business? for a discussion of how a business should define itself.

In his quest to remain the dominant player, Knight recalled what he learned from his old coach and Nike cofounder, Bill Bowerman: "Play by the rules, but be ferocious."[9]

ISSUE BOX

HOW SHOULD WE DEFINE OUR BUSINESS?

Nike has developed its business horizons through the following sequence:

running shoes ⇒ athletic shoes ⇒ athletic clothing ⇒ athletic goods

In so doing, it has greatly expanded its growth potential. This idea of expanding perception of one's business was first put down on paper by Theodore Levitt in a seminal article, "Marketing Myopia," in the *Harvard Business Review* in July–August 1960. Levitt suggested that it was shortsighted for railroads to consider themselves only in the railroad business, and not in the much larger transportation business. Similarly, petroleum companies should consider themselves in the energy business, and plan their strategies accordingly.

Can such expansion of a firm's business definition go too far? Even in Levitt's day, could a railroad really have the expertise to run an airline? Looking to Nike today, and its expanding views of tapping into the athletic goods market, do you think golf clubs and bags are a viable expansion opportunity? Football equipment? Fishing tackle?

[9] Fleming Meeks, "Be Ferocious," *Forbes,* 2 August 1993, p. 41.

But Knight and Nike were not ferocious to their customers. They pampered them, as we have seen in the relations with Foot Locker. And by the end of 1995, Nike's sales lead over Reebok was 38 percent. By 1999 it was 213 percent.

Handling Adversity

In the summer of 1996, Nike, as well as many other U.S. manufacturers, came under fire for farming production out to so-called sweatshops in poor countries of the world in order to reduce manufacturing costs. Nike became the major target for critics of these "abuses."

Then came another blow to Nike's image in April 1997. Thirty-nine members of the Heaven's Gate cult committed suicide, all wearing Nikes with the swoosh logo readily visible. The "Just Do It" slogan of Nike was trumpeted as being entirely apt, and some even spoofed that Nike's slogan should be changed to "Just Did It."

Environmental factors, by no means unique to Nike, also tormented the firm. Demand in Asia was drastically reduced due to deep recession there. Another troubling portent was the public's growing disenchantment with athletes. Fan interest seemed to be dropping, perhaps reflecting a growing tide of resentment at overpriced athletes proving to be selfish, arrogant, and decadent—the very role models that Nike, Reebok, and other firms spent millions to enlist.

Knight had to wonder at another disturbing possibility: Had Nike grown too big? Was its swoosh logo too pervasive, to the point that it turned some people off? Was even the tag line, "Just Do It," becoming counterproductive?

Concerned about such questions, Nike began reassessing. A new advertising campaign had the softer tag line, "I can." Nike began toning down its use of the swoosh, removing it from corporate letterheads and most advertising and replacing it with a lowercase "nike."

Later Developments

At the beginning of the new millennium, Nike's dominant position continued to strengthen. Changing fashion trends, new products, cost cutting, and an Asian revival aided Nike. The company found that with the public's growing disenchantment with many athlete endorsers, it could shave its marketing budget by $100 million. Furthermore, prospects for 2000 were optimistic. Sales of athletic gear peak in Olympic years, and expectations were reasonable that the summer games in Sydney, Australia, would stimulate a big buying spree in merchandise—where Nike had a 35 percent share.[10]

Reebok turned out to benefit most by the Olympics; its shoes were seen on 2,500 pairs of feet. It had also scored a coup in sponsoring the CBS hit, *Survivor.* But after years of missteps the Reebok market share was just 12 percent, although Paul Fireman was predicting that figure would rise to 25 percent within the next six years. The company was pursuing a smarter distribution strategy with less emphasis on discount chains and more on courting mall retailers, such as Foot Locker, for whom

[10] Leigh Gallagher, "Rebound," *Forbes,* 3 May 1999, p. 60.

Fireman was now giving some exclusive rights. Reebok also was trying to win back teenage boys—who were spurning its conservative, even frumpy, shoes—by introducing new colorful designs endorsed by professional basketball player Allen Iverson, the latest endorser.

Nike continued to push its apparel lines, which in 2001 accounted for about a third of the total $9 billion in sales, giving particular attention to women's wear. It opened NikeTown stores where shoppers could see the full range of products, displayed in a hands-on environment. But it was also trying to boost its exposure in department stores, which were notorious for driving hard bargains.

See Table 5.3 for the most recent operating results of Nike and Reebok as we research this market in late 2002. You can see from these statistics that Nike's dominance was increasing. Despite Reebok's improved showing in 2000 and 2001, it still lagged far behind.

ANALYSIS

The case shows the whipsawing of the two major competitors in what was once merely the athletic shoe industry, an industry now expanded far beyond its original focus. In its youth, Nike had outgunned the old entrenched Adidas, only to find Reebok surpassing it in the mid-1980s as it failed to respond soon enough to a new opportunity. Somehow Nike came back stronger than ever. The explanation lies in the mistakes of Reebok as well as the luck and aggressiveness of Nike after its brief hiccup.

The most controllable factor in the divergent success patterns of these competitors had to be customer relations. Nike cultivated its customers, especially the larger dealers such as Foot Locker, while Reebok was surprisingly nonchalant, and even arrogant, in such relationships. A maker of even high-demand goods is myopic in being

TABLE 5.3. **Nike versus Reebok Comparative Operating Statistics, 1999–2001**

	Nike	Reebok	Nike % of Total
Revenues (million $):			
1999	$8,995	$2,872	75.8%
2000	9,449	2,865	76.7
2001	9,893	2,993	76.8
Net Income (million $):			
1999	579	11	98.1
2000	590	81	87.9
2001	663	103	86.6

Source: Calculated from company reports.

Commentary: In this latest comparative analysis, Nike dominance has grown well beyond that during 1995–1998 (see Table 5.2). In revenues, Nike's market share against Reebok averaged 76.4 percent in those three years, while Nike has over 90 percent of the combined profitability of the two firms.

arbitrary and dictatorial toward dealers. This relationship should be viewed as symbiotic, with both parties benefiting from it, though the temptation is to capitalize on the perceived king-of-the-hill position. But the caprice of fashions and fads can quickly destroy this smugness, leaving the previous year's winner at the gate the next year, as was the case with the Shaq Attaq shoes and the expensive endorsements of Shaquille.

In other aspects of its comeback, Nike may have lucked out. It chose for its endorsing athletes ones who grew to become the dominant figures in their sport, ones lionized by fans. The advertising theme of Nike caught on: "Just Do It" had great appeal to youth. But such home runs in advertising can never be guaranteed.

The success and visibility of Nike and its products brought with it critical public scrutiny. Was Nike—and other U.S. manufacturers as well—guilty of violations of accepted moral and ethical standards in farming out production to foreign subcontractors in Third World countries using child labor at low wages? Critics condemned this as exploitation to maximize profits. But others pointed out that while long hours in a smelly shoe or garment factory may be less than idyllic, it was superior to subsistence farming or laboring in even harsher workplaces.

Could Reebok rejuvenate itself as Nike had? That seems less likely today, with Nike's revenues four times greater than Reebok's and its net income six times greater. Still, it could close the gap with a striking new product innovation—or if Nike becomes complacent. Remember the three Cs of the last chapter as Boeing opened the gates for Airbus. And, dare we forget, Nike vanquished the dominant Adidas in its early days.

WHAT CAN BE LEARNED?

No One Is Immune from Mistakes; Success Does Not Guarantee Continued Success

Some executives delude themselves into thinking success begets continued success. It is not so! No firm, market leader or otherwise, can afford to rest on its laurels, to disregard a changing environment and aggressive but smaller competitors. Adidas had as commanding a lead in its industry as IBM once had in computers. But it was overtaken and surpassed by Nike, a rank newcomer, and a domestic firm with few resources in an era when foreign brands (of beer, watches, cars) had a mystique and attraction for affluent Americans that few domestic brands could achieve. But Adidas let down its guard at a critical point. Similarly, but to a lesser degree, Nike then lagged against Reebok as it underestimated or was unaware of the growing interest among women in aerobic dancing and other physical activities.

Don't Underestimate the Importance of Catering to Major Customers

A firm should seek to satisfy all its customers; but for the larger ones, the major accounts, the need to satisfy their needs and wants is absolutely vital. In few cases is the stark contrast between effective and ineffective dealings with larger customers more obvious than between Nike and Reebok in their relations with the huge Foot Locker retail chain. Even though a manufacturer may resent the demands made by a powerful retailer, the alternatives are either to meet these demands or to lose part or all of the business to someone else. However, a better course of action is to work closely with the large customer in a spirit of cooperation and mutual interest, not in an adversarial power struggle.

Consider the Power of Public Image

Granted that technological differences in running shoes have narrowed so that any tangible advantage of a brand is practically imperceptible, what makes Nike stand out? Isn't it the image and the Nike swoosh that identifies the brand? See the Information Box: The Nike "Swoosh" Logo for a discussion of the swoosh.

Items like running shoes, athletic equipment, and apparel have high visibility. For many youth, the sight of famous and admired athletes actively using the brand is an irresistible lure, feeding the desire to emulate them even if only through wearing the same brand ... and maybe dreaming a little. The popularity of a brand becomes a further attraction: being cool, belonging to the in-group.

Is Nike's success in building its image transferable to other firms whose products cannot be identified with use by the famous? Do such firms have any possibilities for developing image-enhancing qualities for their brands? They certainly do.

Consider the long-advertised lonesome Maytag repairman. Maytag has been highly successful in building a reputation, an image, for dependability and assured quality. In so doing it has been able to sustain a higher price advantage over its competitors. A carefully nurtured image of good quality, dependability, reliable service, and being in the forefront of technology or fashion can bring a firm great success in its particular industry.

Is There a Point of Diminishing Returns with Celebrity Endorsements?

One would think so, and public attitudes today seem to bear this out. Athlete celebrities demand big bucks. Are their endorsements worth the price? Perhaps only in moderation, and only with the best of the best. But one cannot always predict with

INFORMATION BOX

THE NIKE "SWOOSH" LOGO

The Nike "swoosh" is one of the world's best-recognized logos. In the very early days of Nike, a local design student at Portland State University was paid $35 for creating it. The curvy, speedy-looking blur turned out to be highly distinctive and has from then on been placed on all Nike products. Phil Knight even has the swoosh logo tattooed on his left calf. Because it has become so familiar, Nike no longer adds the name Nike to the logo. (Tiger Woods wears a cap and other clothing with the swoosh well visible.)

The power of such a well-known logo makes Nike's sponsorship of famous athletes unusually effective as they wear shoes and apparel displaying it in their sports exploits.

In your judgment, do you think Nike could have achieved its present success without this unique but simple logo? What do you think of the Reebok logo?

certainty the future exploits of any athlete, even someone as talented as Michael Jordan or Tiger Woods. Yet, contracts are binding. While some would criticize Nike for too much emphasis on celebrity advertising, the right role models can play dividends. But the overkill of Reebok in seeking celebrity endorsements led to burgeoning costs and a mediocre payoff in sales. The message seems clear: Overuse of celebrity endorsements can be a financial drain. Added to this is the always-present risk that the athlete celebrity in contact sports may have a career-ending injury, or be guilty of some nefarious activity that destroys his or her image.

Is a Great Executive the Key?

Were the rejuvenation of Nike and the decline of Reebok due mostly to the talents of Phil Knight versus Paul Fireman? Does the success of an enterprise depend almost entirely on the ability of its leader? Such questions have long baffled experts.

Several aspects of this issue are worth noting. The incompetent is usually clearly evident and identifiable. The great business leader may also be, but perhaps he or she simply lucked out. In most situations, competing executives are reasonably similar in competence. They have vision, the support of their organizations, and reasonable judgment and prudence. What then makes the difference? A good assessment of opportunities, an advertising slogan that really hits, a hunch of competitor vulnerability? Yes. But how much is due just to a fortuitous call, a gamble that paid off?

We know that Phil Knight had a history of great successes. After all, he beat Adidas, and he brought Nike from nowhere to become the premier athletic footwear firm. Add to this his handling of a great challenge by moving Nike, for a second time, into the heady air of market leader. Was his ability as a top executive so much greater than that of Fireman? Would his absence have destroyed the promise of Nike?

Perhaps the basic question is: Can one person make a difference? Does that person have to be infallible? But Phil Knight was not infallible. He had a major perceptual lapse in the mid-1980s. But Fireman's lapses were more serious.

In the final analysis, Knight made a great difference for Nike. Certainly we can identify other leaders who made great differences: Sam Walton of Wal-Mart, Herb Kelleher of Southwest Airlines, Lee Iacocca of Chrysler, Ray Kroc of McDonald's come readily to mind. Sometimes, one person can make a major difference; but they can still make bad decisions, misjudgments. Perhaps their success was in having a higher percentage of good decisions and, yes, having a little luck on their side.

CONSIDER

After reading the preceding material, can you think of additional learning insights?

QUESTIONS

1. "The success of Nike was strictly fortuitous and had little to do with great decision making." Evaluate this statement.

2. In recent years Nike has moved strongly to develop markets for running shoes in the Far East, particularly in China. Discuss how Nike might go about stimulating such underdeveloped markets.

3. How could anyone criticize Fireman for signing up Shaquille O'Neal to a lucrative endorsement contract? Discuss.

4. Do you think the swoosh logo has become too widespread, to the point that it is turning off many people?

5. Given that all decision makers will sometimes make bad calls, how might the batting average of correct decision be improved? Can it really be improved?

6. Do you think the athletic goods industry has limited potential? Or is it still a growth industry? Your opinions, and rationale, please.

7. Is there a danger in catering too much to major customers? Discuss.

8. What do you think of the inverted V slash logo of Reebok? How would you evaluate it against Nike's swoosh?

HANDS-ON EXERCISES
Before

1. It is 1985. Your production of shoes can hardly meet the burgeoning demand. The future seems unlimited. Design a program for Reebok to build stronger relations with its major customers, including Foot Locker.

After

1. It is 1995. Nike has again achieved market dominance, and its position seems unassailable. Some shareholders are calling for your resignation, Mr. Fireman. Design a strategy for again bringing Reebok to victory in this war against Nike. Be as specific as you can, and defend your recommendations.

2. *Be a Devil's Advocate* (one who argues an opposing viewpoint to test the decision). Array all the rationale you can for *not* deemphasizing the swoosh. Be persuasive.

TEAM DEBATE EXERCISE

Debate the issue of endorsements for athletes. How much is too much? Where do we draw the line? Should we go only for the few famous? Or should we gamble on lesser-knowns eventually making it big and offer them long-term contracts? Argue the two sides of the issue: aggressive and conservative.

INVITATION TO RESEARCH

How has the battle gone between Reebok and Nike? Has Reebok been able to gain any ground? How are the two firms doing in overseas markets? What is your prognosis for their future competitive positions? Are any "sleeper" competitors emerging, such as a newly energized Adidas?

PART
TWO

GREAT COMEBACKS

CHAPTER SIX

Continental Airlines— From the Ashes

*M*assive marketing and management blunders almost destroyed Continental Airlines. In a remarkable turnaround by new management, in only a few years Continental became a star of the airline industry. The changemaker, CEO Gordon Bethune, wrote a best-selling book on how he turned around the moribund company, titled *From Worst to First*. In this chapter we will look at the scenario leading to the difficulties of Continental, and then examine the ingredients of the·great comeback.

THE FRANK LORENZO ERA

Lorenzo was a consummate manipulator, parlaying borrowed funds and little of his own money to build an airline empire. By the end of 1986, he controlled the largest airline network in the non-Communist world: Only Aeroflot, the Soviet airline, was larger. Lorenzo's network was a leveraged amalgam of Continental, People Express, Frontier, and Eastern, with $8.6 billion in sales—all this from a small investment in Texas International Airlines in 1971. In the process of building his network, Lorenzo defeated unions and shrewdly used the bankruptcy courts to further his ends. When he eventually departed, his empire was swimming in red ink, had a terrible reputation, and was burdened with colossal debt and aging planes.

The Start

After getting an MBA from Harvard, Lorenzo's first job was as a financial analyst at Trans World Airlines. In 1966, he and Robert Carney, a buddy from Harvard, formed an airline consulting firm, and in 1969 the two put together $35,000 to form an investment firm, Jet Capital. Through a public stock offering they raised an additional $1.15 million. In 1971 Jet Capital was called in to fix ailing Texas International and wound up buying it for $1.5 million, and Lorenzo became CEO. He restructured the debt as well as the airline's routes, found funds to upgrade the almost obsolete planes, and brought Texas International to profitability.

In 1978, acquisition-minded Lorenzo lost out to Pan Am in a bidding war for National Airlines, but he made $40 million on the National stock he had acquired. In 1980 he created nonunion New York Air and formed Texas Air as a holding company. In 1982 Texas Air bought Continental for $154 million.

Lorenzo's Treatment of Continental

In 1983 Lorenzo took Continental into bankruptcy court, filing for Chapter 11. This permitted the corporation to continue operating but spared its obligation to meet heavy interest payments and certain other contracts while it reorganized as a more viable enterprise. The process nullified the previous union contracts, and this prompted a walkout by many union workers.

Lorenzo earned the lasting enmity of organized labor and the reputation of union-buster as he replaced strikers with nonunion workers at much lower wages. (A few years later, he reinforced this reputation when he used the same tactics with Eastern Airlines.)

In a 1986 acquisition achievement that was to backfire a few years later, Lorenzo struck deals for a weak Eastern Airlines and a failing People Express/Frontier Airlines. That same year Continental emerged out of bankruptcy. Now Continental, with its nonunion workforce making it a low-cost operator, was Lorenzo's shining jewel. The low bid accepted for Eastern reinforced Lorenzo's reputation as a visionary builder.

What kind of executive was Lorenzo? Although he was variously described as a master financier and visionary, his handling of day-to-day problems bordered on the inept.[1] One former executive was quoted as saying, "If he agreed with one thing at 12:15, it would be different by the afternoon.[2] Inconsistent planning and poor execution characterized his lack of good operational strength. Furthermore, his domineering and erratic style alienated talented executives. From 1983 to 1993, nine presidents left Continental.

But Lorenzo's treatment of his unions brought the most controversy. He became the central figure of confrontational labor-management relations to a degree perhaps unmatched by any other person in recent years. Although he won the battle with Continental's unions and later with Eastern's, he was burdened with costly strikes and the residue of ill feeling that impeded any profitable recovery during his time at the helm.

The Demise of Eastern Airlines

In an environment of heavy losses and its own militant unions, Eastern in 1986 accepted the low offer of Lorenzo. With tough contract demands and the stockpiling

---

[1] For examples, see Todd Vogel, Gail DeGeorge, Pete Engardio, and Aaron Bernstein, "Texas Air Empire in Jeopardy," *Business Week*, 27 March 1989, p. 30.

[2] Mark Ivey and Gail DeGeorge, "Lorenzo May Land a Little Short of the Runway," *Business Week*, 5 February 1990, p. 48.

of $1 billion in cash as strike insurance, Lorenzo seemed eager to precipitate a strike that he might crush. He instituted a program of severe downsizing, and in 1989, after 15 months of fruitless talks, some 8,500 machinists and 3,800 pilots went on strike. Lorenzo countered the strike at Eastern by filing for Chapter 11 bankruptcy, and replaced many of the striking pilots and machinists within months.

At first Eastern appeared to be successfully weathering the strike, while Continental benefited with increased business. But soon revenue dropped drastically with Eastern planes flying less than half full amid rising fuel costs. Fares were slashed in order to regain business, and a liquidity crisis loomed. Then, on January 16, 1990, an Eastern jet sheared the top off a private plane in Atlanta. Even though the accident was attributed to air controller error, Eastern's name received the publicity.

Eastern creditors now despaired of Lorenzo's ability to pay them back in full and they pushed for a merger with Continental, which would expose Continental to the bankruptcy process. On December 3, 1990, Continental again tumbled into bankruptcy, burdened with overwhelming debt. In January 1991, Eastern finally went out of business.

CONTINENTAL'S EMERGENCE FROM BANKRUPTCY, AGAIN

Lorenzo was gone. The legacy of Eastern remained, however. Creditors claimed more than $400 million in asset transfers between Eastern and Continental, and Eastern still had $680 million in unfunded pension liabilities. The board brought in Robert Ferguson, veteran of Braniff and Eastern bankruptcies, to make changes. On April 16, 1993, the court approved a reorganization plan for Continental to emerge from bankruptcy, the first airline to have survived two bankruptcies. However, creditors got only pennies on the dollar.[3]

Still, despite its long history of travail and a terrible profit picture, Continental in 1992 was the nation's fifth-largest airline, behind American, United, Delta, and Northwest, and it served 193 airports. Table 6.1 shows the revenues and net profits (or losses) of Continental and its major competitors from 1987 through 1991.

The Legacy of Lorenzo

Continental was savaged in its long tenure as a pawn in Lorenzo's dynasty-building efforts. He had saddled it with huge debts, brought it into bankruptcy twice, and left it with aging equipment. Perhaps a greater detriment was a ravished corporate culture. The Information Box: Importance of Corporate Culture discusses corporate culture and its relationship to public image or reputation.

---

[3] Bridget O'Brian, "Judge Backs Continental Airlines Plan to Regroup, Emerge from Chapter 11," *Wall Street Journal*, 19 April 1993, p. A4.

TABLE 6.1. Performance Statistics, Major Airlines, 1987–1991

	1987	1988	1989	1990	1991	Percent 5-Year Gain
Revenues: (millions $)						
American	6,368	7,548	8,670	9,203	9,309	46.0
Delta	5,638	6,684	7,780	7,697	8,268	46.6
United	6,500	7,006	7,463	7,946	7,850	20.8
Northwest	3,328	3,395	3,944	4,298	4,330	30.1
Continental	3,404	3,682	3,896	4,036	4,031	18.4
Income (millions $)						
American	225	450	412	(40)	(253)	
Delta	201	286	467	(119)	(216)	
United	22	426	246	73	(175)	
Continental	(304)	(310)	(56)	(1,218)	(1,550)	

Source: Company annual reports.

Commentary: Note the operating performance of Continental relative to its major competitors during this period. It ranks last in sales gain. It far and away has the worst profit performance, having massive losses during each of the years in contrast to its competitors, who, while incurring some losses, had neither the constancy nor the magnitude of losses of Continental. And the relative losses of Continental are even worse than they at first appear: Continental is the smallest of these major airlines.

INFORMATION BOX

IMPORTANCE OF CORPORATE CULTURE

A corporate or organizational culture can be defined as the system of shared beliefs and values that develops within an organization and guides the behavior of its members.[4] Such a culture can be a powerful influence on performance and customer satisfaction:

> If employees know what their company stands for, if they know what standards they are to uphold, then they are much more likely to make decisions that will support those standards. They are also more likely to feel as if they are an important part of the organization. They are motivated because life in the company has meaning for them.[5]

Lorenzo had destroyed the former organizational climate as he beat down the unions. Replacement employees had little reason to develop a positive culture or esprit de corps given the many top management changes, the low pay relative to other airline employees, and the continuous possibility of corporate bankruptcy. They had little to be proud of, and this impacted on the service and consequent reputation among the traveling public.

But this was to change abruptly under new management.

Can a corporate climate be too upbeat? Discuss.

[4] Edgar H. Schein, "Organizational Culture," *American Psychologist*, vol. 45 (1990), pp. 109–119.
[5] Terrence E. Deal and Alan A. Kennedy, *Corporate Cultures: The Rites and Rituals of Corporate Life* (Reading, MA: Addison-Wesley, 1982) p. 22.

A devastated reputation proved to be a major impediment. The reputation of a surly labor force had repercussions far beyond the organization itself. For years Continental had a problem wooing the better-paying business travelers. Being on expense accounts, they wanted quality service rather than cut-rate prices. A reputation for good service is not easily or quickly achieved, especially when the opposite reputation is well entrenched.

On another dimension, Continental's reputation also hindered competitive parity. Surviving two bankruptcies does not engender confidence among investors, creditors, or travel agents.

A Sick Airline Industry

Domestic airlines lost a staggering $8 billion in the years 1990 through 1992. Fare wars and excess planes proved to be albatrosses. Even when planes were filled, discount prices often did not cover overhead.

A lengthy recession drove both firms and individuals to fly more sparingly. Business firms found teleconferencing a viable substitute for business travel, and consumers, facing less discretionary income as well as the threat of eventual layoffs or forced retirements, were hardly optimistic. The airlines suffered.

Part of the blame for the red ink lay directly with the airlines—they were expansion-reckless—yet they did not deserve total blame. In the late 1980s, passenger traffic climbed 10 percent per year, and in response the airlines ordered hundreds of jetliners.[6] The recession arrived just as new planes were being delivered. The airlines greatly increased their debt in these expansion efforts: the big three, for example—American, United, and Delta—doubled their leverage in the four years after 1989, with debt at 80 percent of capitalization by 1993.[7]

In such a climate, emphasis was on cost-cutting. But how much can be cut without jeopardizing service and even safety? Some airlines found that hubs, heralded as the great strategy of the 1980s, were not as cost-effective as expected. With hub cities, passengers were gathered from outlying "spokes" and then flown to final destinations. Maintaining too many hubs, however, brought costly overheads. While the concept was good, some retrenchment seemed necessary to be cost effective.

Airlines such as Continental with heavy debt and limited liquidity had two major concerns: first, how fast the country could emerge from recession; second, the risk of fuel price escalation in the coming years. Despite Continental's low operating costs, external conditions impossible to predict or control could affect viability.

THE GREAT COMEBACK UNDER GORDON BETHUNE

In February 1994, Gordon Bethune left Boeing and took the job of president and chief operating officer of Continental. He faced a daunting challenge. While it was

---

[6] Andrea Rothman, "Airlines: Still No Wind at Their Backs," *Business Week*, 11 January 1993, p. 96.
[7] Ibid.

the fifth-largest airline, Continental was by far the worst among the nation's 10 biggest, according to these quality indicators of the Department of Transportation:

- In on-time percentage (the percentage of flights that land within 15 minutes of their scheduled arrival)
- In number of mishandled-baggage reports filed per 1,000 passengers
- In number of complaints per 100,000 passengers
- In involuntarily denied boarding (i.e., passengers with tickets who are not allowed to board because of overbooking or other problems)[8]

In late October he became chief executive officer. Now he sat in the pilot's seat.

He made dramatic changes. In 1995, through a "renewed focus on flight schedules and incentive pay," he greatly improved on-time performance, along with lost-baggage claims and customer complaints. Now instead of being dead last in these quality indicators of the Department of Transportation, Continental by 1996 was third best or better in all four categories.

Customers began returning, especially the higher-fare business travelers, climbing from 32.2 percent in 1994 to 42.8 percent of all customers by 1996. In May 1996, based on customer surveys Continental was awarded the J.D. Power Award as the best airline for customer satisfaction on flights of 500 miles or more. It also received the award in 1997, the first airline to win two years in a row. Other honors followed. In January 1997, it was named "Airline of the Year" by *Air Transport World,* the leading industry monthly. In January 1997, *Business Week* named Bethune one of its top managers of 1996.

Bethune had transformed the workforce into a happy one, as measured by these statistics:

- Wages up an average of 25 percent
- Sick leave down more than 29 percent
- Personnel turnover down 45 percent
- Workers compensation down 51 percent
- On-the-job injuries down 54 percent[9]

Perhaps nothing illustrates the improvement in employee morale as much as this: In 1995, not long after he became top executive, employees were so happy with their new boss's performance that they chipped in to buy him a $22,000 Harley-Davidson.[10]

Naturally such improvement in employee relations and customer service had major impact on revenues and profitability. See Table 6.2 for the trend since 1992.

---

[8] Gordon Bethune, *From Worst to First* (New York: Wiley, 1998) p. 4.

[9] Ibid., pp. 7–8.

[10] Ibid., frontpiece.

TABLE 6.2. Continental Sales and Profits, before and after Bethune, 1992–1997

	Before Bethune			After Bethune		
	1992	1993	1994	1995	1996	1997
Revenues (millions $)	5,494	3,907	5,670	5,825	6,360	7,213
Net income (millions $)	–110	–39	–612	224	325	389
Earnings per share $		–1.17	–11.88	3.60	4.25	5.03

Source: Company annual reports.

Commentary: While the revenue statistics do not show a striking improvement, the net income certainly does. Most important to investors, the earnings per share show a major improvement.

These statistics suggest the fallacy of a low price strategy at the expense of profitability in the 1992–1994 era. At the same time, we have to realize that the early 1990s were recession years, particularly for the airline industry.

Gordon Bethune

Bethune's father was a crop duster, and as a teenager Gordon helped him one summer and learned first hand the challenges of responsibility: in this case, preparing a crude landing strip for nightime landings, with any negligence disastrous. He joined the navy at 17, before finishing high school. He graduated second in his class at the Naval Technical School to become an aviation electronics technician, and over 19 years worked his way up to lieutenant. After leaving the navy he joined Braniff, then Western, and later Piedmont Airlines as senior vice president of operations. He finally left Piedmont for Boeing as VP/general manager of customer service. There he became licensed as a 757 and 767 pilot: "An amazing thing happened. All the Boeing pilots suddenly thought I was a great guy," he writes. "I hope I hadn't given them any reason to think otherwise of me before that, but this really got their attention."[11]

How Did He Do It?

Introducing the Human Element

Bethune stressed the human element in guiding the comeback of a lethargic, even bitter, organization. Even by simple things: "On October 24, 1994, I did a very significant thing in the executive suite of Continental Airlines.... I opened the doors.... [Before] The doors to the executive suite were locked, and you needed an ID to get through. Security cameras added to the feeling of relaxed charm.... So the day I began running the company, I opened the doors. I wasn't afraid of my employees, and I wanted everybody to know it."[12]

Still, he had to entice employees to the twentieth floor of headquarters, and he did this with open houses, supplying food and drink, and personal tours and chat sessions. "I'd take a group of employees into my office, open up the closet, and say, 'You see?

[11] Ibid., p. 268.
[12] Ibid., p. 14.

Frank's not here.' Frank Lorenzo had left Continental years before; the legacy of cost cutting and infighting of that era was finally gone, and I wanted them to know it."[13]

Of course, the improved employee relations needed tangible elements to cement and sustain it, and to improve the morale. Bethune worked hard to instill a spirit of teamwork. He did this by giving on-time bonuses to all employees, not just pilots. He burned the employee procedure manual that bound them to rigid policies instead of being able to use their best judgments. He even gave the planes a new paint job to provide tangible evidence of a disavowal of the old and an embracing of new policies and practices. This new image impressed both employees and customers.

Better communications was also a key element in improving employee relationships and the spirit of teamwork. Information was shared with employees through newsletters, updates on bulletin boards, e-mail, voice-mail, and electronic signs over worldwide workplaces. To Bethune it was a cardinal sin for any organization if employees first heard of something affecting them through the newspaper or other media.

Marketing Strategy for Winning Back Customers

Now Continental had to win back customers. Instead of the company's old focus on cost savings, efforts were directed to putting out a better product through better service. This meant emphasis on on-time flights, better baggage handling, and the like. By giving employees bonuses for meeting these standards, the incentive was created.

Bethune sought to do a better job of designing routes with good demand, to "fly places people wanted to go." This meant, for example, cutting back on six flights a day between Greensboro, North Carolina and Greenville, South Carolina. It meant not trying to compete with Southwest's Friends Fly Free Fares, which "essentially allowed passengers to fly anywhere within the state of Florida for $24.50.[14] The frequent flyer program was reinstated. Going a step further, the company apologized to travel agents, business partners, and customers and showed them how it planned to do better and earn their business back.

Continental queried travel agents about their biggest clients, the major firms that did the most traveling, asking how could it better serve their customers. As a result, more first-class seats were added, particular destinations were given more attention, discounts for certain volumes were instituted. Travel agents themselves were made members of the team and given special incentives beyond normal airline commissions. The result was to greatly improve the public image or reputation of Continental. See the Information Box for a discussion of the importance of public image.

This still left financial considerations. Bethune was aggressive in renegotiating loans and poor airplane lease agreements, and in getting supplier financial cooperation. Controls were set up to monitor cash flow and stop waste. Tables 6.3 and 6.4 show the results of Bethune's efforts from the dark days of 1992–94, and how the competitive position of Continental changed. Remember, Bethune joined the firm in February 1994 and did not become the top executive until late October of that year.

---

[13] Ibid., p. 32.

[14] Ibid., pp. 51–52.

INFORMATION BOX

IMPORTANCE OF PUBLIC IMAGE

The public image of an organization is its reputation, how it and its output (products, services, or both) are viewed by its various publics: customers, suppliers, employees, stockholders, creditors, the communities in which it dwells, and the various governments, both local and federal. And to these groups must be added the press, which is influenced by the subject's reputation and cannot always be relied upon to deliver objective and unbiased reporting.

In some situations it is impossible to satisfy all the diverse publics: For example, a new, highly automated plant may meet the approval of creditors and investors, but it will undoubtedly find resistance from employees who see jobs threatened. On the other hand, high-quality products and service standards should bring almost complete approval and pride of association—given that operating costs are competitive—while shoddy products, poor service, and false claims would be widely decried.

A firm's public image, if it is good, should be cherished and protected. It is a valuable asset built up from a satisfying relationship with the various publics. If a firm has developed a quality image, this image is not easily countered or imitated by competitors. Such an image may enable a firm to charge higher prices, to woo the best distributors and dealers (or travel agents), to attract the best employees, and to expect the most favorable creditor relationships and the lowest borrowing costs. It should enable a firm's stock to command a higher price-to-earnings ratio than other firms in the same industry that lack such a good image. Herein lies a great competitive advantage.

A bad image, on the other hand, hurts a firm with its various publics. All can turn critical and even litigious. At best, present and potential customers may simply seek alternative sources for goods and services and switch to competitors.

What do you think is the effectiveness of advertising in enhancing the public image?

WHAT CAN BE LEARNED?

It Is Possible to Quickly Turn Around an Organization

This idea flies in the face of conventional wisdom. How can a firm's bad reputation with employees, customers, creditors, stockholders, and suppliers be overcome without years of trying to prove that it has changed for the better? This conventional wisdom is usually correct: A great comeback does not often occur easily or quickly. But it sometimes does, with a streetwise leader, and perhaps a bit of luck. Gordon Bethune is proof that negative attitudes can be turned around quickly.

This possibility of a quick turnaround should be inspiring to other organizations mired in adversity.

Still, reputation should be carefully guarded. In most cases, a poor image is difficult to overcome, with trust built up only over time. The prudent firm is careful to safeguard its reputation.

TABLE 6.3. Competitive Position of Continental before and after Bethune, 1992–1997

	Before Bethune			After Bethune		
	1992	1993	1994	1995	1996	1997
Revenues (millions $):						
AMR (American)	14,396	15,701	16,137	16,910	17,753	18,570
UAL (United)	12,890	14,511	13,950	14,943	16,362	17,378
Delta	10,837	11,997	12,359	12,194	12,455	13,590
Northwest	NA	8,649	9,143	9,085	9,881	10,226
Continental	5,494	3,907	5,670	5,825	6,360	7,213
Continental's Market Share (Percent of total shares of Big Five Airlines):		7.1%	9.9%	9.9%	10.1%	10.8%

Source: Company annual reports.

NA = information not available.

Commentary: Most significant is the gradual increase in market share of Continental over its four major rivals. This is an improving competitive position.

TABLE 6.4. Profitability Comparison of Big Five Airlines, 1992–1997

	Before Bethune			After Bethune		
	1992	1993	1994	1995	1996	1997
Net Income (millions $):						
AMR	−474	−96	228	196	1,105	985
UAL	−416	−31	77	378	600	958
Delta	−505	−414	−408	294	156	854
Northwest	NA	−114	296	342	536	606
Continental	−110	−39	−696	224	325	389

Source: Company annual reports. NA = information not available.

Commentary: Of interest is how the good and bad times for the airlines seem to move in lockstep. Still, the smallest of the Big Five, Continental, incurred the biggest loss of any airline in 1994. Under Bethune, it has seen a steady increase in profitability, but so have the other airlines, although AMR and Delta have been more erratic.

Give Employees a Sense of Pride and a Caring Management

Bethune proved a master at changing employees' attitudes and their sense of pride. Few top executives ever faced such a negative workforce, reflecting the Lorenzo years. But Bethune changed all this, and in such a short time. His open-door policy and open houses to encourage employees to interact with him and other top executives was such a simple gesture, but so effective, as was his opening wide the channels of communication about company plans. The incentive plans for improving performance, and the encouragement of employee initiatives by abolishing the rigidity of formal policies, were further positives. He engendered an atmosphere of teamwork and a personal image of an appreciative CEO. It is remarkable how quickly such simple actions could turn around the attitudes of a workforce from adversarial with morale in the pits to pride and an eagerness to build an airline.

Contradictory and Inconsistent Strategies Are Vulnerable

Lorenzo was often described as mercurial and subject to knee-jerk planning and poor execution.[15] Clearly focused objectives and strategies mark effective firms. They bring stability to an organization and give customers, employees, and investors confidence in undeviating commitments. Admittedly, some objectives and strategies may have to be modified occasionally to meet changing environmental and competitive conditions, but the spirit of the organization should be resolute, provided it is a positive influence and not a negative one.

Try to Avoid an Adversarial Approach to Employee Relations

Lorenzo used a confrontational and adversarial approach to his organization and the unions. He was seemingly successful in destroying the unions and hiring nonunion replacements at lower pay scales. This resulted in Continental becoming the lowest-cost operator of the major carriers, but there were negatives: service problems, questionable morale, diminished reputation, and devastated profitability.

Bethune used the opposite tack. It is hard to argue against nurturing and supporting an existing organization, avoiding the adversarial mindset of "them or us" if at all possible. Admittedly this may sometimes be difficult—sometimes impossible, at least in the short-run—but it is worth trying. It should result in better morale, motivation, and commitment to the company's best interest.[16]

The Dangers of Competing Mostly on Low Price

Bethune inherited one of the lowest-cost air carriers, and it was doing badly. He says, "you can make an airline so cheap nobody wants to fly it," [just as] "you can make a pizza so cheap nobody wants to eat it." "Trust me on this—we did it. ... In fact, it was making us lousy, and people didn't want to buy what we offered."[17]

We might add here that competing strictly on a price basis usually leaves any firm vulnerable. Low prices can easily be matched or countered by competitors if such low prices are attracting enough customers. On the other hand, competition based on such nonprice factors as better service, quality of product, and a good public image or reputation, are not so easily matched, and can be more attractive to many customers.

In Chapter 20, with Southwest Airlines, we find a firm competing ever so successfully with a low-price strategy. But Southwest has operational efficiency unmatched in the industry.

---

[15] For example, Ivey and DeGeorge, p. 48.

[16] See Chapter 20 for Southwest Airlines' approach to organizational relations.

[17] Bethune, p. 50.

CONSIDER

Can you add any other learning insights?

QUESTIONS

1. Could Lorenzo's confrontation with the unions of Continental have been more constructively handled? How?

2. Do you see any limitations to Bethune's employee relations, especially in the areas of discipline and acceptance of authority?

3. Compare Bethune's handling of employees with that of Kelleher of Southwest Airlines in Chapter 20. Are there commonalities? contrasts?

4. Compare Bethune's management style with that of Lorenzo. What conclusions can you draw?

5. Bethune gave great credit to his open-door policy when he became CEO. Do you think this was a major factor in the turnaround? How about changing the paint of the planes?

6. How do you motivate employees to give a high priority to customer service?

7. Evaluate the causes and the consequences of frequent top executive changes such as Continental experienced in the days of Lorenzo.

8. How can replacement workers—in this case pilots and skilled maintenance people hired at substantially lower salaries than their unionized peers at other airlines—be sufficiently motivated to provide top-notch service and a constructive esprit de corps?

HANDS-ON EXERCISES

1. It is 1994 and Bethune has just taken over. As his staff adviser, he has asked you to prepare a report on improving customer service as quickly as possible. He has also asked you to design a program to inform both business and nonbusiness potential customers of this new commitment. Be as specific as possible in your recommendations.

2. You are the leader of the machinists' union at Eastern. It is 1986 and Lorenzo has just acquired your airline. You know full well how he broke the union at Continental, and rumors are flying that he has similar plans for Eastern. Describe your tactics under two scenarios:

   (a) You decide to take a conciliatory stance.

   (b) You plan to fight him every step of the way.

   How successful do you think you will be in saving your union?

TEAM DEBATE EXERCISE

Bethune was quoted as saying, "You can make an airline so cheap nobody wants to fly it." Debate this issue, and the related issue of how an airline can make itself sufficiently unique that it can command higher prices than competitors.

INVITATION TO RESEARCH

What is the situation with Continental today? Is Bethune still CEO? Whatever happened to Lorenzo?

CHAPTER SEVEN

IBM—A Fading
Giant Rejuvenates

*I*BM exhibited similar roller-coaster fortunes as did Continental Air, with the major difference that it was so much bigger and had so many years of industry domination. The common notion is that the bigger the firm, the more difficult it is to turn it around, just as the grand ship needs far more room to maneuver to avoid catastrophe than a smaller vessel.

THE REALITY AND THE FLAWED ILLUSION

On January 19, 1993, International Business Machines Corporation reported a record $5.46 billion loss for the fourth quarter of 1992, and a deficit for the entire year of $4.97 billion, the biggest annual loss in American corporate history. (General Motors recorded a 1991 loss of $4.45 billion, after huge charges for cutbacks and plant closings. And Ford Motor Company reported a net loss of more than $6 billion for 1992, but that was a non-cash charge to account for the future costs for retiree benefits.) The cost in human lives, as far as employment was concerned, was also consequential, as some 42,900 had been laid off during 1992, with an additional 25,000 planned to go in 1993. In its fifth restructuring, seemingly endless rounds of job cuts and firings had eliminated 100,000 jobs since 1985. Not surprisingly, IBM's share price, which was above $100 in the summer of 1992, closed at an 11-year low of $48.375. Yet IBM had long been the ultimate blue-chip company, reigning supreme in the computer industry. How could its problems have surfaced so suddenly and so violently?

THE ROAD TO INDUSTRY DOMINANCE

"They hired my father to make a go of this company in 1914, the year I was born," said Thomas J. Watson Jr. "To some degree I've been a part of IBM ever since."[1] Watson took over his father's medium-sized company in 1956 and built it into a

---

[1] Michael W. Miller, "IBM's Watson Offers Personal View of the Company's Recent Difficulties," *Wall Street Journal*, 21 December 1992, p. A3.

technological giant. Retired for almost 19 years by 1992, he now was witnessing the company in the throes of its greatest adversity.

IBM had become the largest computer maker in the world. With its ever-growing revenues since 1946 it had become the bluest of blue-chip companies. It had 350,000 employees worldwide and was one of the largest U.S.-based employers. Its 1991 revenues had approached $67 billion, and while profits had dropped some from the peak of $6.5 billion in 1984, its common stock still commanded a price-earnings ratio of over 100, making it a darling of investors. In 1989, it ranked first among all U.S. firms in market value (the total capitalization of common stock, based on the stock price and the number of shares outstanding), fourth in total sales, and fourth in net profits.[2]

During the days of Watson, IBM was known for its centralized decision making. Decisions affecting product lines were made at the highest levels of management. Even IBM's culture was centralized and standardized, with strict behavioral and dress codes. For example, a blue suit, white shirt, and dark tie was the public uniform, and IBM became widely known as "Big Blue."

One of IBM's greatest assets was its research labs, by far the largest and costliest of their kind in the world, with staffs that included three Nobel Prize winners. IBM treated its research and development function with tender, loving care, regularly budgeting 10 percent of sales for this forward-looking activity: For example, in 1991, the R&D budget was $6.6 billion.

The past success of IBM and the future expectations for the company with a seeming stranglehold over the technology of the future made it esteemed by consultants, analysts, and market researchers. Management theorists, all the way from Peter Drucker to Tom Peters (of *In Search of Excellence* fame), lined up to analyze what made IBM so good. And the business press regularly produced articles of praise and awe of IBM.

Alas, the adulation was to change abruptly by 1992. Somehow, insidiously, IBM had gotten fat and complacent over the years. IBM's problems, however, went deeper, as we will explore in the next section.

CHANGING FORTUNES

Perhaps the causes of the great IBM debacle of 1992 started in the early 1980s with a questionable management decision. Perhaps the problems were more deep-rooted than any single decision; perhaps they were more a consequence of the bureaucracy that often typifies behemoth organizations (Sears and General Motors faced somewhat similar worsening problems): growing layers of policies and entrenched interests.

In the early 1980s, two little firms, Intel and Microsoft, were upstarts, just emerging in the industry dominated by IBM. Their success by the 1990s can be largely attributed to their nurturing by IBM. Each got a major break when it was "anointed" as a key supplier for IBM's new personal computer (PC). Intel was signed

---

[2] "Ranking the Forbes 500s," *Forbes*, 30 April 1990, p. 306.

on to make the chips and Microsoft the software. The aggressive youngsters proceeded to set standards for successive PC generations, and in the process wrested from IBM control over the PC's future. And the PC was to become the product of the future, shouldering aside the giant mainframe that was IBM's strength.

As IBM began losing ground in one market after another, Intel and Microsoft were gaining dominance. Ten years before, in 1982, the market value of stock of Intel and Microsoft combined amounted to about a tenth of IBM's. By October 1992, their combined stock value surpassed IBM's; by the end of the year, they topped IBM's market value by almost 50 percent. See Table 7.1 for comparative operating statistics of IBM, Intel, and Microsoft. Table 7.2 shows the market valuation of IBM, Intel, and Microsoft from 1989 to 1992, the years before and during the collapse of investor esteem.

Defensive Reactions of IBM

As the problems of IBM became more visible to the entire investment community, chairman John Akers sought to institute reforms to turn the behemoth around. His problem—and need—was to uproot a corporate structure and culture that had developed when IBM had no serious competition.

A cumbersome bureaucracy stymied the company from being innovative in a fast-moving industry. Major commitments still went to high-margin mainframes, but these were no longer necessary in many situations given the computing power of

TABLE 7.1. Growth of IBM and the Upstarts, Microsoft and Intel, 1983–1992 ($ million)

	1983	1985	1987	1989	1991	1992
IBM:						
Revenues	$40,180	$50,056	$54,217	$62,710	$64,792	$67,045
Net income	5,485	6,555	5,258	3,758	(2,827)	(2,784)
% of Revenue	13.6%	13.1%	9.7%	6.0%	—	—
Microsoft:						
Revenues	$50	$140	$346	$804	$1,843	$2,759
Net Income	6	24	72	171	463	708
% of Revenue	12.0%	17.1%	20.8%	21.3%	25.1%	25.7%
Intel:						
Revenues	$1,122	$1,365	$1,907	$3,127	$4,779	$5,192
Net Income	116	2	176	391	819	827
% of Revenue	10.3%	0.1%	9.2%	12.5%	17.1%	15.9%

Source: Company annual statements; 1992 figures are estimates from *Forbes,* "Annual Report of American Industry," 4 January 1993, pp. 115–116.

Commentary: Note the great growth of the "upstarts" in recent years, both in revenues and in profits, compared with IBM. Also note the great performance of Microsoft and Intel in profit as a percent of revenues.

TABLE 7.2. Market Value and Rank among All U.S.
Companies of IBM and the Upstarts, Microsoft and Intel,
1989 and 1992

	Rank		*Market Value ($mil)*	
	1989	1992	1989	1992
IBM	1	13	$60,345	$30,715
Microsoft	92	25	6,018	23,608
Intel	65	22	7,842	24,735

Source: Forbes Annual Directory Issue, "The Forbes Market Value 500," 13
April 1990, pp. 258–259, and 26 April 1993, p. 242. The market value is the per-
share price multiplied by the number of shares outstanding for all classes of
common stock.

Commentary: The market valuation reflects the stature of the firms in the eyes of
investors. Obviously, IBM has lost badly during this period, while Microsoft and
Intel have more than tripled their market valuation, almost approaching that of
IBM. Yet, IBM's sales were $65.5 billion in 1992, against sales of Microsoft of
$3.3 and Intel of $5.8.

desktop PCs. IBM had problems getting to market quickly with the technological
innovations that were revolutionizing the industry. In 1991, Akers warned an unbe-
lieving group of IBM managers of the coming difficulties. "The business is in crisis."[3]

He attempted to push power downward, to decentralize some of the decision-
making that for decades had resided at the top. His more radical proposal was to
break up IBM, to divide it into 13 divisions and to give each more autonomy. He
sought to expand the services business and make the company more responsive to
customer needs. Perhaps most important, he saw a crucial need to pare costs by cutting the fat from the organization.

The need for cost-cutting was evident to all but the entrenched bureaucracy.
IBM's total costs grew 12 percent a year in the mid-1980s, while revenues were not
keeping up with this growth.[4] Part of the plan for reducing costs involved cutting
employees, which violated a cherished tradition dating back to Thomas Watson's
father and the beginning of IBM: a promise never to lay off IBM workers for economic reasons.[5] (Most of the downsizing was indeed accomplished by voluntary
retirements and attractive severance packages, but eventually outright layoffs
became necessary.)

The changes decreed by Akers would leave the unified sales division untouched,
but each of the new product group divisions would act as a separate operating unit, with
financial reports broken down accordingly. Particularly troubling to Akers was the
recent performance of the personal computer (PC) business. At a time when demand,
as well as competition, was burgeoning for PCs, this division was languishing. Early in

[3] David Kirkpatrick, "Breaking up IBM," *Fortune*, 27 July 1992, p. 44.

[4] Ibid., p. 53.

[5] Miller, p. A4.

1992 Akers tapped James Cannavino to head the $11 billion Personal Systems Division, which also included workstations and software.

IBM PC

PCs had been the rising star of the company, despite the fact that mainframes still accounted for about $20 billion in revenues. But in 1990, market share dropped drastically as new competitors offered PCs at much lower prices than IBM; many experts even claimed that these clones were at least equal to IBM's PCs in quality. Throughout 1992, IBM had been losing market share in an industry price war. Even after it attempted to counter Compaq's price cuts in June, IBM's prices still remained as much as one-third higher than its competitors' prices. Even worse, IBM had announced new fall models, and this development curbed sales of current models. At the upper end of the PC market, firms such as Sun Microsystems and Hewlett-Packard were bringing out more powerful workstations that tied PCs together with mini- and mainframe computers. James Cannavino faced a major challenge in reviving the PC.

Cannavino planned to streamline operations by slicing off a new unit to focus exclusively on developing and manufacturing PC hardware. By so doing, he would cut PCs loose from the rest of Personal Systems and the workstations and software. This, he believed, would create a streamlined organization that could cut prices often, roll out new products several times a year, sell through any kind of store, and provide customers with whatever software they wanted, even if it was not IBM's.[6] Such autonomy was deemed necessary in order to respond quickly to competitors and opportunities, without having to deal with the IBM bureaucracy.

THE CRISIS

On January 25, 1993, John Akers announced that he was stepping down as IBM's chairman and chief executive. He had lost the confidence of the board of directors. Until mid-January, Akers seemed determined to see IBM through its crisis, at least until he would reach IBM's customary retirement age of 60, which would be December 1994. But the horrendous $4.97 billion loss in 1992 changed that, and investor and public pressure mounted for a top management change. The fourth quarter of 1992 was particularly shocking, brought on by weak European sales and a steep decline in sales of minicomputers and mainframes. Now IBM's stock sank to a 17-year low, below 46.

Other aspects of the operation also accentuated IBM's fall from grace: most notably, the jewel of its operation, its mainframe processors and storage systems.

For 25 years IBM had dominated the $50 billion worldwide mainframe industry. In 1992, overall sales of such equipment grew at only 2 percent, but IBM experienced a 10 to 15 percent drop in revenue. At the same time, its major mainframe rivals, Amdahl Corp. and Unisys Corp., had respective sales gains of 48 percent and 10 percent.[7]

---

[6] "Stand Back, Big Blue—And Wish Me Luck," *Business Week*, 17 August 1992, p. 99.

[7] John Verity, "Guess What: IBM Is Losing Out in Mainframes, Too," *Business Week*, 8 February 1993, p. 106.

IBM was clearly lagging in developing new computers that could out-perform the old ones, such as IBM's old System/390. Competitors' models exceeded IBM's old computers not only in absolute power but in prices, selling at prices a tenth or less of IBM's price per unit of computing. For example, with IBM's mainframe computers, customers paid approximately $100,000 for each MIPS, or the capacity to execute 1 million instructions per second, this being the rough gauge of computing power. Hewlett-Packard offered similar capability at a cost of only $12,000 per MIPS, and AT&T's NCR unit could sell a machine for $12.5 million that outperformed IBM's $20 million ES/9000 processor complex.[8]

In a series of full-page advertisements appearing in such business publications as the *Wall Street Journal,* IBM defended the mainframe and attacked the focus on MIPS:

> One issue surrounding mainframes is their cost. It's often compared using dollars per MIPS with the cost of microprocessor systems, and on that basis mainframes lose. But...dollars per MIPS alone is a superficial measurement. The real issue is function. Today's appetite for information demands serious network and systems management, around-the-clock availability, efficient mass storage and genuine data security. MIPS alone provides none of these, but IBM mainframes have them built in, and more fully developed than anything available on microprocessors.[9]

On March 24, 1993, 51-year-old Louis V. Gerstner Jr. was named the new chief executive of IBM. The two-month search for a replacement for Akers had captivated the media, with speculation ranging widely. The choice of an outsider caught many by surprise: Gerstner was chairman and CEO of RJR Nabisco, a food and tobacco giant, but Nabisco was a far cry from a computer company. And IBM had always prided itself on promoting from within, with most IBM executives—for example, John Akers—being lifelong IBM employees. Not all analysts supported the selection of Gerstner. While most did not criticize the board for going outside IBM to find a replacement for Akers, some questioned going outside the computer industry or other high-tech industries. Geoff Lewis, senior editor of *Business Week,* fully supported the choice. He had suggested the desirability of bringing in some outside managers to Akers in 1988:

> Akers seemed shocked—maybe even offended—by my question. After a moment, he answered: "IBM has the best recruitment system anywhere and spends more than anybody on training. Sometimes it might help to seek outsiders with unusual skills, but the company already had the best people in the world.[10]

See the Issue Box: Should We Promote from Within? for a discussion of promotion from within.

---

[8] Ibid.

[9] Taken from advertisement, *Wall Street Journal,* 5 March 1993, p. B8.

[10] Geoff Lewis, "One Fresh Face at IBM May Not Be Enough," *Business Week,* 12 April 1993, p. 33.

ISSUE BOX

SHOULD WE PROMOTE FROM WITHIN?

A heavy commitment to promoting from within, as had long characterized IBM, is sometimes derisively called "inbreeding." The traditional argument against this stand maintains that an organization with such a policy is not alert to needed changes, that it is enamored with the status quo, "the way we have always done it." Proponents of promotion from within talk about the motivation and great loyalty it engenders, with every employee knowing that he or she has a chance of becoming a high-level executive.

However, the opposite course of action—that is, heavy commitment to placing outsiders in important executive positions—plays havoc with morale of trainees and lower-level executives and destroys the sense of continuity and loyalty. A middle ground seems preferable: filling many executive positions from within, promoting this idea to encourage both the achievement of current executives and the recruiting of trainees, and at the same time bringing the strengths and experiences of outsiders into the organization.

Do you think there are particular circumstances in which one extreme or the other regarding promotion policy might be best? Discuss.

Later in this chapter we will describe and make commentary on the great comeback engineered by Gerstner. But for now, let us examine the factors leading to the decline in IBM's fortunes.

ANALYSIS

In examining the major contributors to IBM's fall from grace, we will analyze the predisposing or underlying factors, resultants, and controversies.

Predisposing Factors

Cumbersome Organization

As IBM grew with its success, it became more and more bureaucratic. One author described it as big and bloated. Another called it "inward-looking culture that kept them from waking up on time."[11] Regardless of phraseology, by the late 1980s IBM could not bring new machines quickly into the market, nor was it able to make the fast pricing and other strategic decisions of its smaller competitors. Too many layers of management, too many vested interests, a tradition-ridden mentality, and a gradually emerging contentment with the status quo shackled it in an industry that some thought to be mature, but which in reality had important sectors still gripped by burgeoning change. As a huge ship

---

[11] Jennifer Reese, "The Big and the Bloated: It's Tough Being No. 1," *Fortune*, 27 July 1992, p. 49.

requires a considerable time and distance to turn or to stop, so the giant IBM found itself at a competitive disadvantage to smaller, hungrier, more aggressive, and above all, more nimble firms. Impeding all efforts to effect major changes was the typical burden facing all large and mature organizations: resistance to change. The Information Box: Resistance to Change discusses this phenomenon.

Overly Centralized Management Structure

Often related to a cumbersome bureaucratic organization is rigid centralization of authority and decision making. Certain negative consequences may result when all major decisions have to be made at corporate headquarters rather than down the line. Decision making is necessarily slowed, since executives feel they must investigate fully all aspects, and not being personally involved with the recommendation, they may be not only skeptical but critical of new projects and initiatives. More than this, the enthusiasm and creativity of lower-level executives may be curbed by the typical conservatism of a higher-management team divorced from the intimacy of the problem or the opportunity. The motivation and morale needed for a climate of

INFORMATION BOX

RESISTANCE TO CHANGE

People, as well as organizations, have a natural reluctance to embrace change. Change is disruptive. It can destroy accepted ways of doing things and familiar authority-responsibility relationships. It makes people uneasy because their routines will likely be disrupted; their interpersonal relationships with subordinates, co-workers, and superiors may well be modified. Positions that were deemed important before the change may be downgraded. And persons who view themselves as highly competent in a particular job may be forced to assume unfamiliar duties.

Resistance to change can be combatted by good communication with participants about forthcoming changes. Without such communication, rumors and fears can assume monumental proportions. Acceptance of change can be facilitated if managers involve employees as fully as possible in planning the changes, solicit and welcome their participation, and assure them that positions will not be impaired, only different. Gradual rather than abrupt changes also make a transition smoother, as participants can be initially exposed to the changes without drastic upheavals.

In the final analysis, however, needed changes should not be delayed or canceled because of their possible negative repercussions on the organization. If change is necessary, it should be initiated. Individuals and organizations can adapt to change—although it may take some time.

The worst change an employee may face is layoff. And when no one knows when the next layoff will occur or who will be affected, morale and productivity may both be devastated. Discuss how managers might best handle the necessity of upcoming layoffs.

innovation and creativity is stifled under the twin bureaucratic attitudes, "Don't take a chance" and "Don't rock the boat."

The Three Cs Mindset of Vulnerability

Firms that have been well entrenched in their industry and that have dominated it for years tend to fall into a particular mindset that leaves them vulnerable to aggressive and innovative competitors. (We first encountered this syndrome in Chapter 4 with Boeing, but it bears repeating.)

The "three Cs" that are detrimental to a frontrunner's continued success are:

Complacency

Conservatism

Conceit

Complacency is smugness—a complacent firm is self-satisfied, content with the status quo, no longer hungry and eager for growth. *Conservatism,* when excessive, characterizes a management that is wedded to the past, to the traditional, to the way things have always been done. Conservative managers see no need to change because they believe nothing is different today (e.g., "Mainframe computers are the models of the industry and will always be"). Finally, *conceit* further reinforces the myopia of the mindset: conceit regarding present and potential competitors. The beliefs that "we are the best" and "no one else can touch us" can easily permeate an organization that has enjoyed success for years.

The three Cs mindset leaves no incentive to undertake aggressive and innovative actions, and contributes to growing disinterest in such important facets of the business as customer relations, service, and even quality control. Furthermore, it inhibits interest in developing innovative new products that may cannibalize—that is, take business away from—existing products or disrupt entrenched interests. (We will discuss cannibalization in more detail shortly.)

Resultants

Overdependence on High-Margin Mainframes

The mainframe computers had long been the greatest source of market power and profits for IBM. But the conservative and tradition-minded IBM bureaucracy could not accept the reality that computer power was becoming a desktop commodity. Although a market still existed for the massive mainframes, it was limited and had little growth potential; the future belonged to desktop computers and work stations. And here IBM in a lapse of monumental proportions relinquished its dominance. First there were the minicomputers, and these opened up a whole new industry, one with scores of hungry competitors. But the cycle of industry creation and decline started anew by the early 1980s as personal computers began to replace minicomputers in defining new markets and fostering new competitors. While the mainframe was not replaced, its markets became more limited, and cannibalization became the fear. See the Information Box: Cannibalization.

INFORMATION BOX

CANNIBALIZATION

Cannibalization occurs when a company's new product takes some business away from an existing product. The new product's success consequently does not contribute its full measure to company revenues since some sales will be switched from older products. The amount of cannibalization can range from virtually none to almost total. In this latter case, then, the new product simply replaces the older product, with no real sales gain achieved. If the new product is less profitable than the older one, the impact and the fear of cannibalization becomes all the greater.

For IBM, the PCs and the other equipment smaller than mainframes would not come close to replacing the bigger units. Still, some cannibalizing was likely. And the profits on the lower-price computers were many times less than those of mainframes.

The argument can justifiably be made that if a company does not bring out new products then competitors will, and that it is better to compete with one's own products. Still the threat of cannibalization can cause a hesitation, a blink, in a full-scale effort to rush to market an internally competing product. This reluctance and hesitation needs to be guarded against, lest the firm find itself no longer in the vanguard of innovation.

Assume the role of a vocal and critical stockholder at the annual meeting. What arguments would you introduce for a crash program to rush the PC to market, despite possible cannibalization? What contrary arguments would you expect, and how would you counter them?

Neglect of Software and Service

At a time when software and service had become ever more important, IBM still had a fixation on hardware. In 1992, services made up only 9 percent of IBM's revenue. Criticisms flowed:

Technology is becoming a commodity, and the difference between winning and losing comes in how you deliver that technology. Service will be the differentiator.
As a customer, I want a supplier who's going to make all my stuff work together.
The job is to understand the customer's needs in detail.[12]

In the process of losing touch with customers, the sales force had become reluctant to sell low-margin open systems if it could push proprietary mainframes or minicomputers.

Bloated Costs

As indications of the fat that had insidiously grown in the organization, some 42,900 jobs were cut in 1992, thankfully all through early-retirement programs. An

[12] Kirkpatrick, pp. 49, 52.

additional 25,000 people were expected to be laid off in 1993, some without the benefit of early-retirement packages. Health benefits for employees were also scaled down. Manufacturing capacity was reduced 25 percent, and two of three mainframe development labs were closed. But perhaps the greatest bloat was R&D.

Diminishing Payoff of Massive R&D Expenditures

As noted earlier, IBM spent heavily on research and development, often as much as 10 percent of sales (see Table 7.3). Its research labs were by far the largest and costliest of their kind in the world.

And IBM labs were capable of inventing amazing things. For example, they developed the world's smallest transistor, 1/75,000th the width of a human hair.

Somehow, with all these R&D resources and expenditures, IBM lagged in transferring its innovation to the marketplace. The organization lacked the ability to quickly translate laboratory prototypes into commercial triumphs. Commercial R&D is wasted without this.

Controversies

Questionable Decisions

No executive has a perfect batting average of good decisions. Indeed, most executives do well to bat more than 500, that is, to have more good decisions than bad decisions. But, alas, decisions are all relative. Much depends on the importance, the consequences, of these decisions.

IBM made a decision of monumental long-term consequences in the early 1980s. At that time, IBM designated two upstart West Coast companies to be the key suppliers for its new personal computer. Thus, it gave away its chances to control the personal computer industry. Over the next ten years, each of these two firms would develop a near-monopoly—Intel in microprocessors and Microsoft in operating-systems software—by setting standards for successive PC generations. Instead of keeping such developments proprietary (that is, within its own organization) IBM, in an urge to save developmental time, gave these two small firms a golden opportunity,

TABLE 7.3. IBM Research and Development Expenditures as a Percent of Revenues, 1987–1991

	1987	1988	1989	1990	1991
Revenues ($ million)	$54,217	$59,681	$62,710	$64,792	$67,045
Research, development, and engineering costs	5,434	5,925	6,827	6,554	6,644
Percent of revenues	10.0%	9.9%	10.9%	10.1%	9.9%

Source: Company annual reports.

Commentary: Where has been the significant contribution from about 10 percent of sales budgeted for R&D?

which both grasped to the fullest. By 1992, Intel and Microsoft had emerged as the computer industry's most dominant firms.

The decision still is controversial. But it saved IBM badly needed time in bringing its PC to market, and as computer technology becomes ever more complex, not even an IBM can be expected to have the ability and resources to go it alone. Linking up with competitors offers better products and services and a faster flow of technology today, and seems the wave of the future.

Former IBM CEO, Thomas Watson Jr., has criticized his successors Frank Cary and John Opel for phasing out rentals and selling the massive mainframe computer outright. Originally, purchasers could only lease the machines, thus giving IBM a dependable cushion of cash each year ("my golden goose," Mr. Watson called it.)[13] Doing away with renting left IBM, and John Akers, a newly volatile business, just as the industry position began worsening. Akers, newly installed as CEO, was thus left with a hostile environment without the cushion or support of steady revenues coming from such rentals, according to Watson's argument. But the counterposition holds that selling brought needed cash quickly into company coffers. Furthermore, it is unlikely, given the more competitive climate that was emerging in the 1980s, that big customers would continue to tolerate the leasing arrangement when they could buy their machines, if not from IBM, then from another supplier whose machines were just as good or better.

Breaking Up IBM

The general consensus of management experts favored the reforms of Akers to break up Big Blue into 13 divisions and give them increasing autonomy—even to the point that shares of some of these new Baby Blues might be distributed to stockholders. The idea is not unlike that of Japan's *keiretsu*, in which alliances of companies with common objectives but with substantial independence seek and develop business individually.

The assumption in favor of such breaking up is that the sum of the parts is greater than the whole, that the autonomy and motivation will bring more total revenues and profits. But these hypothesized benefits are not assured. At issue is whether the good of the whole would be better served by suboptimizing some business units—that is, by reducing the profit maximizing of some units in order to have the highest degree of coordination and cooperation. Giving disparate units of an organization goals of individual profit maximization lays the seeds for intense intramural competition, with cannibalization and infighting likely. Is the whole better served by a less intensely competitive internal environment?

THE COMEBACK UNDER GERSTNER

Louis Gerstner took command in March 1993. The company, as we have seen, was reeling. In a reversal of major proportions, he brought IBM back to record profitability. Table 7.4 shows the statistics of a sensational turnaround. In 1994, the

---

[13] Miller, p. A4.

TABLE 7.4.   IBM's Resurgence under Gerstner, 1993–1995

	1993	1994	1995
	(millions of dollars)		
Revenue	$62,716	$64,052	$71,940
Net Earnings (loss)	(8,101)	3,021	4,178
Net Earnings (loss) per Share of Common Stock	(14.22)	5.02	7.23
Working Capital	6,052	12,112	9,043
Total Debt	27,342	22,118	21,629
Number of Employees	256,207	219,839	225,347

Source: Company annual reports.

Commentary: In virtually all measures of performance, IBM has made a significant turnaround from 1993 to 1995. Note in particular the decrease in debt and the great profit turnaround.

company earned $3 billion, its first profitable year since 1990. Perhaps of greater significance, compared with the previous year this represented a profit swing of $11 billion. And revenues grew for the first time since 1990. Equally important, 1994 finished with financial strength: IBM had more than $10 billion in cash and basic debt was reduced by $3.3 billion.

The winning ways continued. In 1995, record revenues topped $70 billion for the first time. The rate of growth—12 percent over the previous year—was the best in more than a decade. And earnings doubled, excluding a onetime charge related to the acquisition of Lotus Development Corp. Not surprising, the stock market value of IBM improved nearly $27 billion from the summer of 1993 through year-end 1995, and continued to improve significantly in 1996.

By all such performance statistics, Gerstner had done an outstanding job of turning the giant around. At first there had been doubters. For the most part, their skepticism was rooted in the notion that Gerstner was not aggressive enough, that he did not tamper mightily with the organizational structure of IBM. For example, a 1994 *Fortune* article questioned, "Is He Too Cautious to Save IBM?" The article went on to say, "After running IBM for more than a year and a half, CEO Lou Gerstner has revealed himself to be something other than the revolutionary whom the directors of this battered and demoralized enterprise once seemed to want … he seems to be attempting a conventional turnaround: deep-cleaning and redecorating the house rather than gutting and renovating it."[14]

Before Gerstner took over, IBM was moving toward a breakup into 13 independent units: one for mainframes, one for PCs, one for disk drives, and so on. But he saw IBM's competitive advantage to be offering customers a complete package, a one-stop shopping to all those seeking help in solving technological problems: a unified IBM—somehow, an IBM with a single, efficient team.

---

[14] Allison Rogers, "Is He Too Cautious to save IBM?" *Fortune*, 3 October 1994, p. 78.

The Quiet Revolution

The critics inclined toward revolutionary measures had to be disappointed. "Transforming IBM is not something we can do in one or two years," Gerstner had stated. "The better we are at fixing some of the short-term things, the more time we have to deal with the long-term issues."[15] His efforts were contrasted with those of Albert Dunlap, who overhauled Scott Paper at about the same time. Dunlap replaced 9 of the 11 top executives in the first few days and laid off one-third of the total workforce. Gerstner brought in only eight top executives from outside IBM to sit on the 37-person Worldwide Management Council.

A nontechnical man, Gerstner's strengths were in selling: cookies and cigarettes at RJR, travel services during an 11-year career at American Express Company. Weeks after taking over, he talked to IBM's top 100 customers at a retreat in Chantilly, Virginia. He asked them what IBM was doing right and wrong. They were surprised and delighted: This was the first time the chairman of the 72-year-old company had ever polled its customers. The input was revealing:

> The customers told him IBM was difficult to work with and unresponsive to customers' needs. For example, customers who needed IBM's famed mainframe computers were being told that the machines were dinosaurs and that the company would have to consider getting out of the business.[16]

Gerstner told these customers that IBM was in mainframes to stay, and would aggressively cut prices and focus on helping them set up, manage, and link the systems. And IBM's hardware sales turned around also, rising from $30.6 billion in 1993 to $35.6 billion in 1995.

Perhaps the most obvious change Gerstner instituted was the elimination of a dress code that once kept IBM salespeople in blue suits and white shirts.

By the spring of 1997, *Fortune* highlighted Gerstner on its cover with the feature article, "The Holy Terror Who's Saving IBM."[17] Total company sales for 1996 were $75.947 billion, up 5.6 percent from the previous year, and net profits gained 30 percent over 1995, to $5.429 billion.

The growth continued. Revenues in 1997 were $78.508 billion and net income $6.093 billion. The first three quarters of 1998 showed surprisingly robust sales growth, with practically all the portfolios of businesses contributing to the sparkling performance. For example, third-quarter earnings were up 10 percent, on an unexpectedly healthy sales growth of 8 percent. For the year, IBM shares were one of the leading gainers among the companies that make up the Dow Jones Industrial Average.[18]

Gerstner's turnaround was no fluke.

---

[15] Ibid., p. 78.

[16] "IBM Focuses on Sales," *Cleveland Plain Dealer*, 10 September 1996, p. 6-C.

[17] Betsy Morris, "He's Saving Big Blue," *Fortune*, 14 April 1997, pp. 68–81.

[18] *1998 Annual Report;* and Raju Narisetti, "IBM Profit Rose 10% in 3rd Period, Topping Estimates, Amid Robust Sales," *The Wall Street Journal*, 21 October 1998, p. A3.

UPDATE—LATE 2002

Louis Gerstner, age sixty, stepped down from chairman of IBM at the end of 2002 to become chairman of the Carlyle Group investment firm. He succeeded former U.S. Defense Secretary Frank Carlucci, seventy-two years old, who had been chairman for a decade. Carlyle oversees $13.5 billion in investments for institutions and wealthy clients, and has long been politically connected with such notables as former President Bush, ex-Secretary of State James Baker, and former British Prime Minister John Major. Carlyle isn't the first private-equity firm to recruit a high-ranking corporate executive. In October 2001, former General Electric Co. Chairman John F. Welch joined Clayton, Dubilier & Rice as a senior adviser.

The founding partner of Carlyle, Daniel D'Anielio, said Mr. Gerstner could help Carlyle unify its culture and strategy: "That's exactly what [Mr. Gerstner] did at IBM and it's directly applicable" here.

Managerial skills are often transferable.

Source: Kara Scannell and William M. Bulkeley, "IBM's Gerstner to Join Carlyle as Chairman," *Wall Street Journal,* 22 November 2002, p. AS.

WHAT CAN BE LEARNED

Beware of the Cannibalization Phobia

We have just set the parameters of the issue of cannibalization, that is, how far a firm should go in developing products and encouraging intramural competition that will take away sales from other products and other units of the business. The issue is particularly troubling when the part of the business that is likely to suffer is the most profitable in the company. Yet cannibalization should not even be an issue. At stake is the forward-leaning of the company, its embracing of innovation and improved technology, as well as its competitive stance. Unless a firm has an assured monopoly position, it can expect competitors to introduce advances in technology and/or new efficiencies of productivity and customer service.

In general we can conclude that no firm should rest on its laurels, that it must introduce improvements and change as soon as possible, hopefully ahead of competition—all this without regard to any possible impairment of sales and profits of existing products and units.

Need to Be "Lean and Mean" (Sometimes Called "Acting Small")

The marketplace is uncertain. This is especially true in high-tech industries. In such environments a larger firm needs to keep the responsiveness and flexibility of smaller firms. It must avoid layers of management, of delimiting policies, and a tradition-bound mindset. Otherwise our big firm is like the behemoth vessel, unable to stop or change course without losing precious time and distance. But how can a big firm keep the maneuverability and innovative-mindedness of a smaller firm? How can it remain lean and mean with increasing size?

We can identify certain conditions or factors of lean-and-mean firms:

1. They have simple organizations. Typically, they are decentralized, with decision-making moved lower in the organization. This discourages the buildup of cumbersome bureaucracy and staff, which tends to add both increasing overhead expenses and the red tape that stultifies fast reaction time.

   With a simple organization comes a relatively flat one, with fewer levels of management than comparable firms. This also has certain desirable consequences. Overhead is greatly reduced because there are fewer executives with their expensive staffs. But communication is also improved, since higher executives are more accessible and directions and feedback are less distorted because of more direct communications channels. Even morale is improved because of the better communication and the accessibility of leaders of the organization.

2. Receptivity and encouragement of new ideas. A major factor in the inertia of large firms are the vested interests who see their power threatened by new ideas and innovative directions. Consequently, real creativity is stymied by not being appreciated; often it is even discouraged.

   A firm that wishes to be lean and mean must seek new ideas. This implies rewards and recognition for creativity but, even more, acting upon worthwhile ideas. Few things are more thwarting to creativity in an organization than pigeon-holing the good ideas of eager employees.

3. Participation in planning should be moved as low in the organization as possible. Important employees and lower-level managers should be involved in decisions concerning their responsibilities, with their ideas receiving reasonable weight in final decisions. Performance goals—and rewards—should be moved as low in the organization as possible. Such an organizational climate encourages innovation, improves motivation and morale, and can lead to the fast-reaction time that so often characterizes small organizations and so seldom the large.

4. A final factor that characterizes some highly successful proactive larger organizations is minimum frills, even austerity at the corporate level. Two of our most successful firms today, Wal-Mart and Southwest Airlines, evince this philosophy to the furthest degree. A no-frills management orientation is the greatest corporate model for curbing frivolous costs throughout an organization.

Beware the "King-of-the-Hill" Three Cs Mindset

As a firm gains dominance and maturity, a natural mindset evolution can occur, and must be guarded against. Conservatism, complacency, and conceit insidiously move in. Usually this happens at the highest levels, and readily filters down to the rest of the organization. As discussed earlier, this mindset leaves a firm highly vulnerable to competitors who are smaller and hungrier. And so the king of the hill is toppled.

While top management usually initiates such a mindset, top management can also lead in inhibiting it. The lean-and-mean organization is anathema to the three Cs mindset. If we can curb bureaucratic buildup, then the seeds are thwarted.

Perhaps most important in preventing this mindset is encouragement of innovative thinking throughout the organization, as well as bringing in fresh blood from outside the organization to fill some positions. A strict adherence to promotion from within is inhibiting.

The Power of Greater Commitment to Customers

One of the bigger contributions Gerstner may have made to the turnaround of IBM was his customer focus: putting the needs of customers first and relying on his in-house experts for the technology; asking, not merely talking—finding out what customers wanted, and seeing what could be done to best meet these needs as quickly as possible; at the same time, toning down the arrogance of an "elite" staff of sales representatives. Perhaps the style change from blue suits and white shirts was the visible sign of a change in culture and attitudes.

Many firms profess a great commitment to customers and service. So common are such statements that one wonders how much is mere lip service. It is so easy to say this, and then not really to follow up. In so doing, the opportunity to develop a trusting relationship is lost.

We Can Overcome Adversity!

We saw this with Continental Airlines and now with IBM. Such examples should be motivating and inspiring for all organizations and the executives trying to turn them around. Firms and their managers should be capable of learning from mistakes. As such, mistakes should be valuable learning experiences, leading the way to better performance and decisions in the future.

CONSIDER

What additional learning insights do you see emerging from the IBM case?

QUESTIONS

1. Assess the pro and con arguments for the 1982 decision to delegate to Microsoft and Intel a foothold in software and operating systems. (Keep your perspective to that of the early 1980s; don't be biased with the benefit of hindsight.)

2. Do you see any way that IBM could have maintained its nimbleness and technological edge as it grew to a $60 billion company? Reflect on this, and be as creative as you can.

3. "Tradition has no place in corporate thinking today." Discuss this statement.

4. Can you defend the position that the problems besetting IBM were not its fault—that they were beyond its control?

5. Would you say that the major problems confronting IBM were marketing rather than organizational? Why or why not?

6. Which of the three Cs do you think was most to blame for IBM's problems? Why do you conclude this?

HANDS-ON EXERCISES

1. *Be a Devil's Advocate* (one who argues a contrary position to test the decision). It is early 1993, and Louis Gerstner, an outsider and not even a computer man, being chief executive of Nabisco, a food and tobacco firm, is on the verge of being selected for chief executive of IBM. You have been asked to argue against this decision. Array all the negative arguments you can for this appointment, and be as persuasive as possible. (You must not be swayed by what actually happened; place yourself in 1993.)

2. As the new CEO brought in to turn around IBM in 1993, how would you propose to do so? (State any assumptions you find necessary, but keep them reasonable. And don't be influenced by what actually happened. Perhaps better actions could have been taken.) Be as specific as you can, and discuss the constraints likely to face your turnaround program.

3. You are a marketing consultant reporting to the CEO in the late 1980s. IBM is still racking up revenue and profit gains, but you detect serious emerging weaknesses. What would you advise management at this time? (Make any assumptions you feel necessary, but state them clearly.) Persuasively explain your rationale.

TEAM DEBATE EXERCISE

At issue: Whether to break up the company into ten to fifteen semiautonomous units, or to keep basically the same organization. Debate the opposing views as persuasively as possible.

INVITATION TO RESEARCH

What is the current situation of IBM? Have any new problems arisen for IBM?

CHAPTER EIGHT

Harley-Davidson: At Last

*I*n the early 1960s, a staid and unexciting market was shaken up, was rocked to its core, by the most unlikely invader. This intruder was a smallish Japanese firm that had risen out of the ashes of World War II and was now trying to encroach on the territory of a major U.S. firm—a company that had in the space of sixty years destroyed all of its U.S. competitors, and now had a solid 70 percent of the motorcycle market.

Yet, almost inconceivably, in half a decade this market share was to fall to 5 percent, and the total market was to expand many times over what it had been for decades. A foreign invader had furnished a textbook example of the awesome effectiveness of carefully crafted marketing efforts. In the process, this confrontation between Honda and Harley-Davidson was a harbinger of the Japanese invasion of the auto industry.

Eventually, by the late 1980s, Harley was to make a comeback. But only after more than two decades of travail and mediocrity.

THE INVASION

Sales of motorcycles in the United States were around 50,000 per year during the 1950s, with Harley-Davidson, Britain's Norton and Triumph, and Germany's BMW accounting for most of the market. By the turn of the decade, Honda began to penetrate the U.S. market. In 1960 less than 400,000 motorcycles were registered in the United States. While this was an increase of almost 200,000 from the end of World War II fifteen years before, it was far below the increase in other motor vehicles. But by 1964, only four years later, the number had risen to 960,000; two years later it was 1.4 million; and by 1971 it was almost 4 million.

In expanding the demand for motorcycles, Honda instituted a distinctly different strategy. The major elements of this strategy were lightweight cycles and an advertising approach directed toward a new customer. Few firms have ever experienced such a shattering of market share as did Harley-Davidson in the 1960s. (Although its market share declined drastically, its total sales remained nearly constant, indicating that it was getting none of the new customers for motorcycles.)

Reaction of Harley-Davidson to the Honda Threat

Faced with an invasion of its staid and static U.S. market, how did Harley react to the intruder? It did not react—at least not until far too late. Harley-Davidson considered itself the market leader in full-size motorcycles. While the company might shudder at the image tied in with its product's usage by the leather-jacket types, it took solace in knowing that almost every U.S. police department used its machines. Perhaps this is what led Harley to stand aside and complacently watch Honda make deep inroads into the American motorcycle market. The management saw no threat in Honda's thrust into the market with lightweight machines. The Harley attitude was exemplified in this statement by William H. Davidson, president of the company and son of the founder:

> Basically, we don't believe in the lightweight market. We believe that motorcycles are sport vehicles, not transportation vehicles. Even if a man says he bought a motorcycle for transportation, it's generally for leisure-time use. The lightweight motorcycle is only supplemental. Back around World War I, a number of companies came out with lightweight bikes. We came out with one ourselves. They never got anywhere. We've seen what happens to these small sizes.[1]

Eventually Harley recognized that the Honda phenomenon was not an aberration, and that there was a new factor in the market. The company attempted to fight back by offering an Italian-made lightweight in the mid-1960s. But it was far too late; Honda was firmly entrenched. The Italian bikes were regarded in the industry to be of lower quality than the Japanese. Honda—and toward the end of the 1960s, other Japanese manufacturers—continued to dominate what had become a much larger market than anyone ever dreamed.

AFTERMATH OF THE HONDA INVASION: 1965–1981

In 1965, Harley-Davidson made its first public stock offering. Soon after, it faced a struggle for control. The contest was primarily between Bangor Punta, an Asian company, and AMF, an American company with strong interests in recreational equipment including bowling. In a bidding war, Harley-Davidson's stockholders chose AMF over Bangor Punta, even though the bid was $1 less than Bangor's offer of $23 a share. Stockholders were leery of Bangor's reputation of taking over a company, squeezing it dry, and then scrapping it for the remaining assets. AMF's plans for expansion of Harley-Davidson seemed more compatible.

But the marriage was troubled: Harley-Davidson's old equipment was not capable of the expansion envisioned by AMF. At the very time that Japanese manufacturers—Honda and others—were flooding the market with high-quality motorcycles, Harley was falling down on quality. One company official noted, "Quality was going down just as fast as production was going up."[2] Indicative of the depths of the problem at a

---

[1] Tom Rowan, "Harley Sets New Drive to Boost Market Share," *Advertising Age*, 29 January 1973, pp. 34–35.

[2] Peter C. Reid, *Well Made in America—Lessons from Harley-Davidson on Being the Best* (New York: McGraw-Hill, 1990), 10.

demoralized Harley-Davidson, quality-control inspections failed 50–60 percent of the motorcycles produced. In comparison, only 5 percent of Japanese motorcycles failed their quality-control checks.

AMF put up with an average $4.8 million operating loss for eleven years. Finally, the firm called it quits and put the division up for sale in 1981. Vaughan Beals, vice president of motorcycle sales, still had faith in the company: He led a team that used $81.5 million in financing from Citicorp to complete a leveraged buyout. All ties with AMF were severed.

VAUGHAN BEALS

Vaughan Beals was a middle-aged Ivy Leaguer, a far cry from what might be thought of as a heavyweight motorcycle aficionado. He had graduated from MIT's Aeronautical Engineering School and was considered a production specialist.[3] But Beals was far more than that. He was truly committed to motorcycles, personally as well as professionally. Deeply concerned with AMF's declining attention to quality, he achieved the buyout from AMF.

The prognosis for the company was bleak. Its market share, which had dominated the industry before the Honda invasion, was now 3 percent. In 1983 Harley-Davidson would celebrate its eightieth birthday; some doubted it would still be around by then. Tariff protection seemed Harley's only hope, and massive lobbying paid off. In 1983, Congress passed a huge tariff increase on Japanese motorcycles. Instead of a 4 percent tariff, Japanese motorcycles would be subject to a 45 percent tariff for the coming five years.

The tariff gave the company new hope, and Harley slowly began to rebuild market share. Key to this recovery was restoring confidence in the quality of its products. And Beals took a leading role. He drove Harley-Davidsons to rallies, where he met Harley owners. There he learned of their concerns and their complaints, and he promised changes. At these rallies a core of loyal Harley-Davidson users, called HOGs (for Harley Owners Group), were to be trailblazers for the successful growth to come.

Beals had company on his odyssey—Willie G. Davidson, grandson of the company's founder, and the vice president of design. Willie was an interesting contrast to the more urbane Beals. His was the image of a middle-age hippie. He wore a Viking helmet over his long, unkempt hair while a straggly beard hid some of his wind-burned face. An aged leather jacket completed the picture. Beals and Davidson fit in nicely at the HOG rallies.

THE STRUGGLE BACK

In December 1986, Harley-Davidson asked Congress to remove the tariff barriers, more than a year earlier than originally planned. The company's confidence had been restored, and it believed it could begin competing with the Japanese head to head.[4]

---

[3] Rod Willis, "Harley-Davidson Comes Roaring Back," *Management Review*, March 1986, pp. 20–27.

[4] "Harley Back in High Gear," *Forbes*, 20 April 1987, p. 8.

Production Improvements

Shortly after the buyout, Beals and other managers visited Japanese plants both in Japan and in Honda's assembly plant at Marysville, Ohio. They were impressed that they were being beaten not by "robotics, or culture, or morning calisthenics and company songs, [but by] professional managers who understood their business and paid attention to detail."[5] As a result, Japanese operating costs were as much as 30 percent lower than Harley's.

Beals and his managers tried to implement some of the Japanese management techniques. Each plant was divided into profit centers, with managers assigned total responsibility within their particular area. Just-in-time (JIT) inventory and a materials-as-needed (MAN) system sought to control and minimize all inventories both inside and outside the plants. Quality circles (QCs) were formed to increase employee involvement in quality goals and to improve communication between management and workers. See the Information Box: Quality Circles for further discussion. Another new program called statistical operator control (SOC) gave employees the responsibility for checking the quality of their own work and making proper correcting adjustments. Efforts were made to improve labor relations by more sensitivity to employees and their problems as well as better employee assistance and benefits. Certain product improvements were also introduced, notably, a new engine and mountings on rubber to reduce vibration. A well-accepted equipment innovation was to build stereo systems and intercoms into the motorcycle helmets.

The production changes between 1981 and 1988 resulted in:

- Inventory reduced by 67 percent
- Productivity up by 50 percent
- Scrap and rework down two-thirds
- Defects per unit down 70 percent[6]

In the 1970s, the joke among industry experts was, "If you're buying a Harley, you'd better buy two—one for spare parts."[7] This situation had obviously changed by the 1980s, but the change still had to be communicated to consumers, and believed.

Marketing Moves

Despite its bad times and its poor quality, Harley had an almost unparalleled cadre of loyal customers. Company research maintained that 92 percent of its customers remained with Harley.[8] Despite such hard-core loyalists, the company had always had a serious public image problem. It was linked to an image of the pot-smoking, beer-drinking, woman-chasing, tattoo-covered, leather-clad biker: "When your company's logo is the number one requested in tattoo parlors, it's time to get a

[5] Dexter Hutchins, "Having a Hard Time with Just-in-Time," *Fortune*, 19 June 1986, p. 65.

[6] Ibid., p. 66.

[7] Ibid.

[8] Mark Marvel, "The Gentrified HOG," *Esquire*, July 1989, p. 25.

INFORMATION BOX

QUALITY CIRCLES

Quality circles were adopted by Japan in an effort to rid its industries of poor quality control and cheapness after World War II. Quality circles are worker-management committees that meet regularly, usually weekly, to talk about production problems, plan ways to improve productivity and quality, and resolve job-related gripes on both sides. They have been described as "the single most significant explanation for the truly outstanding quality of goods and services produced in Japan."[9] For example, Mazda had 2,147 quality circles with more than 16,000 employees involved.[10] They usually consisted of seven to eight volunteer members who met on their own time to discuss and solve the issues they were concerned with. In addition to making major contributions to increased productivity and quality, the Mazda quality circles gave employees an opportunity to participate and gain a sense of accomplishment.

The idea—like so many ideas adopted by the Japanese—did not originate with them: It came from two American personnel consultants. The Japanese refined the idea and ran with it. In the 1980s, American industry rediscovered quality circles. Some firms found them a desirable way not only to promote teamwork and good feelings but also to avoid at least some of the adversarial relations stemming from collective bargaining and union grievances that must be negotiated.

Despite sterling claims for quality circles, they have not always worked out well. Some workers claim they smack of "tokenism," and are more a facade than anything practical. Questions are also raised about the lasting benefits of such circles, once the novelty has worn off. Others doubt that the time invested in quality circles by management and workers is that productive. And few U.S. workers accept the idea of participating in quality circles on their own time.

How would you feel about devoting an hour or more to quality circle meetings every week or so, on your own time? If your answer is, "No way," do you think this is a fair attitude on your part? Why or why not?

[9] "A Partnership to Build the New Workplace," *Business Week,* 30 June 1980, p. 101.
[10] As described in a Mazda ad in *Forbes,* 24 May 1982, p. 5.

licensing program that will return your reputation to the ranks of baseball, hot dogs, and apple pie." [11]

Part of Harley's problem had been with bootleggers ruining the name by placing it on unlicensed goods of poor quality. Now the company began to use warrants and federal marshals to crack down on unauthorized uses of its logo at motorcycle conventions. And it began licensing its name and logo on a wide variety of products, from leather jackets to cologne to jewelry—even to pajamas, sheets, and towels. Suddenly retailers realized that these licensed goods were popular, and were even being bought

[11] "Thunder Road," *Forbes,* 18 July 1983, p. 32.

by a new customer segment, undreamed of until now: bankers, doctors, lawyers, and entertainers. This new breed of customers soon expanded their horizons to include the Harley-Davidson bikes themselves. They joined the HOGs, only now they became known as rubbies—the rich urban bikers. And high prices for bikes did not bother them in the least.

Beals was quick to capitalize on this new market with an expanded product line of expensive heavyweights. In 1989 the largest motorcycle was introduced, the Fat Boy, with 80 cubic inches of V-twin engine and capable of a top speed of 150 mph. By 1991, Harley had twenty models, ranging in price from $4,500 to $15,000.

The rubbies brought Harley back to a leading position in the industry by 1989, with almost 60 percent of the super heavyweight motorcycle market; by the first quarter of 1993, this had become 63 percent (see Figure 8.1). The importance of this customer to Harley could be seen in the demographic statistics supplied by the *Wall Street Journal* in 1990:

> One in three of today's Harley-Davidson buyers are professionals or managers. About 60 percent have attended college, up from only 45 percent in 1984. Their median age is 35, and their median household income has risen sharply to $45,000 from $36,000 five years earlier.[12]

In 1989 Beals stepped down as CEO, turning the company over to Richard Teerlink, who was chief operating officer of Harley-Davidson's Motorcycle Division. Beals, however, retained his position as chairman of the board. The legacy of Beals in Harley's renaissance was particularly notable for his role in bringing it out of the internal production orientation that had long characterized the firm. See the Information Box: Internal vs. External (Marketing) Orientation for a further discussion of the topic.

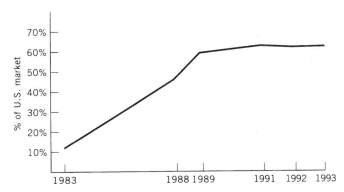

Figure 8.1. Harley-Davidson's share of the U.S. heavyweight motorcycle market, selected years, 1983–1993.

Source: Company annual reports.

[12] Robert L. Rose, "Vrooming Back," *Wall Street Journal,* 31 August 1990, p. 1.

INFORMATION BOX

INTERNAL VS. EXTERNAL (MARKETING) ORIENTATION

Managers sometimes focus primarily on internal factors, such as technology and cost cutting. They consequently believe the key to attracting customers lies in improving production and distribution efficiency and lowering costs if possible. Henry Ford pioneered this philosophy in the early 1900s with his Model T. Harley stuck for decades with this orientation in the absence of competition. The internal orientation is most appropriate in three situations (with the third often being a dubious risk):

- When demand for a product exceeds supply, such as in new technologies and in developing countries.
- When the product cost is high and the market can be expanded only if costs can be brought down.
- Where there is a present lack of significant competition, and no competitive threat is expected either because of severe entry requirements in the industry or because the market is limited.

Obviously, Harley-Davidson in the 1960s had made a major miscalculation with the third situation, assuming that the motorcycle market would be forever limited.

An external, or marketing, orientation recognizes the fallacy of the assumption that products will forever sell themselves "if we maintain our production and technological superiority." Looking outside the firm to the market environment results in giving major priority to determining customers' needs and wants, assessing how these may be changing as evidenced by shifts in buying patterns, and adapting products and services accordingly. The external focus also permits more responsiveness to other external forces, such as major competitive thrusts, changing laws and regulations, economic conditions, and the like. With such an external orientation, attention will more likely be directed to locating new opportunities brought about by changing conditions, rather than focusing on internal production and technology. Such an orientation is more geared to meeting and even anticipating change.

Do all firms need a marketing orientation? Can you think of any that probably do not and will not?

SUCCESS

By 1993 Harley-Davidson had a new problem, one born of success: It could not even come close to meeting demand. Customers faced empty showrooms, except perhaps for rusty trade-ins or antiques. Waiting time for a new bike could be six months or longer, unless the customer was willing to pay a 10 percent or higher premium to some gray marketer advertising in biker magazines.

Some of the six hundred independent U.S. dealers worried that these empty showrooms and long waiting lists would induce their customers to turn to foreign imports, much as they had several decades before. But other dealers recognized that somehow Beals and company had engendered a brand loyalty unique in this industry, and perhaps in all industries. Assuaging the lack of big bike business, dealers were finding other sources of revenues. Harley's branded line of merchandise, available only at Harley dealers and promoted through glossy catalogs, had really taken off. Harley black leather jackets were bought eagerly at $500; fringed leather bras went for $65; even shot glasses brought $12—all it seemed to take was the Harley name and logo. So substantial was this ancillary business that in 1992, non-cycle business generated $155.7 million in sales, up from $130.3 million in 1991.

Production

In one sense, Harley's production situation was enviable—it had far more demand than production capability. More than this, it had such a loyal body of customers that delays in product gratification were not likely to turn many away to competitors. The problem, of course, was that full potential was not being realized.

Richard Teerlink, the successor to Beals, expressed the corporate philosophy to expanding quantity to meet the demand: "Quantity isn't the issue, quality is the issue. We learned in the early 1980s you do not solve problems by throwing money at them."[13]

The company increased output slowly. In early 1992 it was making 280 bikes a day; by 1993, production had risen to 345 a day. With increased capital spending, goals were to produce 420 bikes a day, but not until 1996.

Export Potential

Some contrary concerns with the conservative expansion plans of Teerlink surfaced regarding international operations. The European export market beckoned. Harleys had become very popular in Europe. But the company had promised its domestic dealers that exports would not go beyond 30 percent of total production until the North American market was fully satisfied. Suddenly the European big-bike market grew by an astounding 33 percent between 1990 and 1992. Yet, because of its production constraints, Harley could maintain only a 9 to 10 percent share of this market. In other words, it was giving away business to foreign competitors.

To enhance its presence in Europe, Harley opened a branch office of its HOG club in Frankfurt, Germany, for its European fans.

Specifics of the Resurgence of Harley-Davidson

Table 8.1 shows the trend in revenues and net income of Harley from 1982 through 1994. The growth in sales and profits did not go unnoticed by the investment community. In 1990, Harley-Davidson stock sold for $7; in January of 1993, it hit $39. Its market share of heavyweight motorcycles (751 cubic centimeters displacement and larger) had soared from 12.5 percent in 1983 to 63 percent by 1993. Let the Japanese have the lightweight bike market—Harley would dominate the heavyweights.

Harley acquired Holiday Rambler in 1986. As a wholly owned subsidiary, this manufacturer of recreational and commercial vehicles was judged by Harley management

---

[13] Gary Slutsker, "Hog Wild," *Forbes*, 24 May 1993, p. 46.

TABLE 8.1. Harley-Davidson's Growth
in Revenue and Income 1982–1994
(Millions of dollars)

Year	Revenue	Net Income
1982	$ 210	def. $25.1
1983	254	1.0
1984	294	2.9
1985	287	2.6
1986	295	4.3
1987	685	17.7
1988	757	27.2
1989	791	32.6
1990	865	38.3
1991	940	37.0
1992	1,100	54.0
1993	1,210	68.0
1994	1,537	83.0

Source: Company annual reports.

Commentary: The steady climb in sales and profits, except for a pause in 1985, is noteworthy. The total gain in revenues over these years was 631.9%, while income rose more than eighty-fold since 1983.

not only as compatible with the existing motorcycle business but also as moderating some of the seasonality of the motorcycle business. The diversification proved rather mediocre. In 1992, it accounted for 26 percent of total corporate sales, but only 2 percent of profits.[14]

Big motorcycles, made in America by the only U.S. manufacturer, continued to be the rage. Harley's ninetieth anniversary was celebrated in Milwaukee on June 12, 1993. As many as 100,000 people, including 18,000 HOGS, were there to celebrate. Hotel rooms were sold out for a sixty-mile radius. Harley-Davidson was up and doing real well.

More Recent Developments

The 1990s continued to be kind to Harley. Demand grew, and the mystique was as strong as ever. The company significantly increased its motorcycle production capacity by opening a new engine plant in Milwaukee in 1997 and a new assembly plant in Kansas City in 1998. It expected that demand in the United States would still exceed the supply of Harley bikes.

[14] Company annual reports.

The following numbers show how motorcycle shipments (domestic and export) increased from 1993 to 1997 (in thousands of units):

	U.S.	Exports
1997	96.2	36.1
1993	57.2	24.5

Despite continuous increases in production, U.S. consumers still had to wait to purchase a new Harley-Davidson bike, but the wait only added to the mystique.

The following chart shows the growth in revenues and income from 1993 to 1997:

	Revenues ($M)	Net Income ($M)
1997	$1,763	$174.0
1993	$1,217	$ 18.4

As an indication of the popularity of the Harley-Davidson logo, Wolverine World Wide, originally maker of Hush Puppies shoes but now the largest manufacturer of footwear in the United States, entered into a licensing agreement with Harley to use its "sexy" name for a line of boots and fashion shoes to come out in late 1998.[15]

In its January 7, 2002 issue, *Forbes* declared Harley to be its "Company of the Year," a truly prestigious honor. In supporting its decision, *Forbes* noted that:

> In a disastrous year for hundreds of companies, Harley's estimated 2001 sales grew 15 percent to $3.3 billion and earnings grew 26 percent to $435 million. Its shares were up 40 percent in 2001, while the S&P stock averages dropped 15 percent. Since Harley went public in 1986, its shares have risen an incredible 15,000 percent. Since 1986, GE, generally considered the paragon of American business, had risen only 1,050 percent.

Jeffrey Bleustein, a twenty-six-year company veteran and the current Harley CEO, was diversifying into small, cheaper bikes to attract younger riders as well as women. These groups had shunned the big, lumbering machines and together represented only 9 percent of Harley riders. The cult image was stronger than ever. Half of the company's eight thousand employees rode Harleys, and many of them appeared at rallies around the country for pleasure and to promote the company. There were now 640,000 owners, the parts-and-accessories catalog numbered 720 pages, and the Harley-Davidson name was on everything from blue jeans to pickup trucks. Harley would celebrate its hundredth birthday in 2002, and some 250,000 riders were expected at the rally in Milwaukee.[16]

ANALYSIS

One of the first moves Vaughan Beals made after the 1981 leveraged buyout was to improve production efficiency and quality control. This became the foundation for

---

[15] Carleen Hawn, "What's in a Name? Whatever You Make It," *Forbes*, 27 July 1998, p. 88.

[16] Jonathan Fahey, "Love into Money," *Forbes*, 7 January 2002, pp. 60–65.

the strategic regeneration moves to come. In this quest, he borrowed heavily from the Japanese, in particular by cultivating employee involvement.

The cultivation of a new customer segment for the big bikes had to be a major factor in the company's resurgence. To some, discovering that more affluent consumers embraced the big, flashy Harley motorcycles was a surprise of no small moment. After all, how could you have two more incompatible groups than the stereotypical black-jacketed cyclists and the rubbies? Perhaps part of the change was due to high-profile people such as Beals and some of his executives frequently participating at motorcycle rallies and charity rides. Technological and comfort improvements in motorcycles and their equipment added to the new attractiveness. Dealers were also coaxed to make their stores more inviting.

Along with this, expanding the product mix not only made such Harley-branded merchandise a windfall for company and dealers alike but also piqued the interest of upscale customers in motorcycles themselves. The company was commendably aggressive in running with the growing popularity of the ancillary merchandise, making it into a well over $100 million revenue booster.

Some questions remained. How durable was this popularity, both of the big bikes and the complementary merchandise, with the affluent customer segment? Would it prove to be only a passing fad? If so, then Harley needed to seek diversifications as quickly as possible, even though the Holiday Rambler Corporation had brought no notable success by 1992. Diversifications often bring disappointed earnings compared with a firm's core business.

Another question concerned Harley's slowness in expanding production capability. Faced with a burgeoning demand, was it better to go slowly, to be extremely protective of quality, and to refrain from heavy debt commitments? This had been Harley's most recent strategy, but it raised the risk of permitting competitors to gain market share in the United States and especially in Europe. The Issue Box: Should We Be Aggressive or Conservative in Our Planning? discusses the issues in more depth.

WHAT CAN BE LEARNED?

Again, a Firm Can Come Back from Adversity

The resurrection of Harley-Davidson almost from the point of extinction proves that adversity can be overcome. It need not be fatal or forever. This should be encouraging to all firms facing difficulties—and to their investors.

Noteworthy, however, in comparing Harley with the previous cases of Continental Airlines and IBM, is the great difference in time these two firms took to turn around. Continental under Bethune achieved spectacular results in only months; IBM became profitable in the year that Gerstner took over. It took Harley decades before Vaughan Beals came on the scene as change maker.

What does a turnaround require? Above all, it takes a leader who has the vision and confidence that things can be changed for the better. The change may not necessitate anything particularly innovative. It may involve only a rededication to basics, such as better quality control or an improved commitment to customer

---

ISSUE BOX

SHOULD WE BE AGGRESSIVE OR CONSERVATIVE IN OUR PLANNING?

The sales forecast—the estimate of sales for the periods ahead—serves a crucial role because it is the starting point for all detailed planning and budgeting. A volatile situation presents some high-risk alternatives: Should we be optimistic or conservative?

On one hand, with conservative planning in a growing market, a firm risks underestimating demand and being unable to expand its resources sufficiently to handle the potential. It may lack the manufacturing capability and sales staff to handle growth potential, and it may have to abdicate a good share of the growing business to competitors who are willing and able to expand their capability to meet the demands of the market.

On the other hand, a firm facing burgeoning demand should consider whether the growth is likely to be a short-term fad or a more permanent situation. A firm can easily become overextended in the buoyancy of booming business, only to see the collapse of such business jeopardizing its viability.

Harley's conservative decision was undoubtedly influenced by concerns about expanding beyond the limits of good quality control. The decision was probably also influenced by management's belief that Harley-Davidson had a loyal body of customers who would not switch despite the wait.

Do you think Harley-Davidson made the right decision to expand conservatively? Why or why not? Defend your position.

---

service brought about by a new positive attitude of employees. But such a return to basics requires that a demoralized or apathetic organization be rejuvenated and remotivated. This calls for leadership of a high order. If the core business has still been maintained, it at least provides a base to work from.

Preserve the Core Business at all Costs

Every viable firm has a basic core or distinctive position—sometimes called an ecological niche—in its business environment. This unique position may be due to its particular location, or to a certain product. It may come from somewhat different operating methods or from the customers served. Here, a firm is better than its competitors. This strong point is the core of a company's survival. Though it may diversify and expand far beyond this area, the firm should not abandon its main bastion of strength.

Harley almost did this. Its core—and indeed, only—business was its heavyweight bikes sold to a limited and loyal, though not at the time particularly savory, customer segment. Harley almost lost this core business by abandoning reasonable quality control to the point that its motorcycles became the butt of jokes. To his credit, upon assuming leadership Beals acted quickly to correct the production and employee motivation problems. By preserving the core, Beals could pursue other avenues of expansion.

Consider the Power of a Mystique

We first discussed this point in Chapter 2 in describing how Gateway Computer hoped to gain devoted followers as it thought Apple had. But it is worth repeating here, even though few products are able to gain a mystique or cult following. Coors beer did for a few years in the 1960s and early 1970s, when it became the brew of celebrities and the emblem of the purity and freshness of the West. In the cigarette industry, Marlboro rose to become the top seller from a somewhat similar advertising and image thrust—the Marlboro man. The Ford Mustang had a mystique at one time. Somehow the big bikes of Harley-Davidson developed a more enduring mystique by appealing to two disparate customer segments: the HOGS and the rubbies. Different they might be, but both were loyal to their Harleys. The mystique was so strong, it led to "logo magic": Simply put the Harley-Davidson name and logo on all kinds of merchandise, and watch the sales take off.

How does a firm develop (or acquire) a mystique? We can give no simple answer, no guarantee. Certainly a product has to be unique, but though most firms strive for this differentiation, few achieve a mystique. Image-building advertising, focusing on the target buyer, may help. Perhaps even better is image-building advertising that highlights the people customers might wish to emulate. But the black leather-jacketed, possibly bearded, cyclist?

Perhaps in the final analysis, acquiring a mystique is more accidental and fortuitous than something that can be deliberately orchestrated. Two lessons, however, can be learned about mystiques: First, they do not last forever (even though Harley's seems to). Second, firms should run with them as long as possible and try to expand the reach of the name or logo to other goods, even unrelated ones, through licensing.

CONSIDER

What additional learning insights can you see coming from this Harley-Davidson resurgence?

QUESTIONS

1. Do you think the rejuvenation strategy developed by Beals for Harley-Davidson was the best policy? Discuss and evaluate other strategies that he might have pursued.

2. How durable do you think the rubbies' infatuation with the heavyweight Harleys will be? What leads you to this conclusion?

3. A Harley-Davidson stockholder criticizes present management: "It is a mistake of the greatest magnitude that we abdicate a decent share of the European motorcycle market to foreign competitors, simply because we do not gear up our production to meet the demand." Discuss.

4. Given the resurgence of Harley-Davidson in the 1990s, would you invest money now in the company? Discuss, considering as many factors bearing on this decision as you can.

5. "Harley-Davidson's resurgence is only the purest luck. Who could have predicted, or influenced, the new popularity of big bikes with the affluent?" Discuss.

6. "The tariff increase on Japanese motorcycles in 1983 gave Harley-Davidson badly needed breathing room. In the final analysis, politics is more important than management in competing with foreign firms." What are your thoughts?

HANDS-ON EXERCISES

1. *Be a Devil's Advocate* (one who opposes a position to establish its merits and validity). Your mutual fund has a major investment in Harley-Davidson, and you are concerned because Vaughn Beals attends motorcycle rallies to hobnob with black-jacketed motorcycle gangs. Beals maintains that it's the way to cultivate a loyal core of customers. Argue against this practice.

2. As a vice president at Harley-Davidson in the 1990s, you believe the recovery efforts should have gone well beyond the heavyweight bikes into lightweights. What arguments would you present for this change in strategy, and what specific recommendations would you make for such a new course of action? What contrary arguments would you expect? How would you counter them?

3. As a staff assistant to Vaughan Beals when he first took over, you have been charged to design a strategy to bring a mystique to the Harley-Davidson name. How would you propose to do this? Be as specific as you can, and defend your reasoning.

TEAM DEBATE EXERCISE

A major schism has developed in the executive ranks of Harley-Davidson. Many executives believe a monumental mistake is being made not to gear up production to meet the burgeoning worldwide demand for Harleys. Others see the present go-slow approach to increasing production as more prudent. Persuasively support your position and attack the other side.

INVITATION TO RESEARCH

What is the situation with Harley-Davidson today? Has the cult following remained as strong as ever? How are the new lightweight bikes faring? Are many women being attracted to Harleys? Have any new competitors emerged?

PART THREE

MANAGING CHANGE
AND CRISES

CHAPTER NINE

Scott Paper, Sunbeam, and Al Dunlap

Al Dunlap was hired in July 1996 by two large Sunbeam investors to turn Sunbeam around. He had gained a reputation as a turnaround artist extraordinaire, most recently from his efforts at Scott Paper. His philosophy was to cut to the bone, and the press frequently called him "Chainsaw Al." But he met his comeuppance with Sunbeam. In the process, his philosophy came under bitter attack, as did his character. But was his strategy for managing crises all that bad?

ALBERT J. DUNLAP

Dunlap wrote an autobiography, *Mean Business; How I Save Bad Companies and Make Good Companies,* describing his business philosophy and how it had evolved. The book became a best seller. Dunlap grew up in the slums of Hoboken, New Jersey, the son of a shipyard worker, and was imbued with the desire to make something of himself. He played football in high school and graduated from West Point. A former army paratrooper, he was known as a quick hitter, a ruthless cost cutter, a tough boss. But he got results, at least in the short term.

In 1983 Dunlap became chief executive of Lily Tulip Co., a maker of disposable cups that was heavily in debt after a buyout. He quickly exhibited the management philosophy that was to make him famous. He slashed costs by decimating the headquarters staff, closing plants, and selling the corporate jet. When he left in the mid-1980s, the company was healthy. In the latter 1980s, Dunlap became the No. 1 operations man for Sir James Goldsmith, a notorious raider of corporations. Dunlap was involved in restructuring Goldsmith's acquisitions of Crown Zellerbach and International Diamond. In 1991, he worked on a heavily debt-laden Australian conglomerate, Consolidated Press Holdings. Two years later, after his "chainsaw approach," Consolidated Press was one hundred divisions lighter and virtually free of debt.

By then Dunlap was a wealthy man, having made close to $100 million on his various restructurings. Still, at fifty-six, he was hardly ready to retire. When the board of

Scott Paper heard that he was available, they wooed him, even purchasing his $3.2 million house in Florida from him.

SCOTT PAPER—A SICK COMPANY— AND DUNLAP'S RESULTS

An aged Scott Paper was reeling in the early 1990s. Per-share earnings had dropped 61 percent since 1989 on flat sales growth. In 1993, the company had a $277 million loss.

Part of the problem stemmed from Scott's commercial paper division, S. D. Warren. In 1990, the company spent to increase capacity at Warren. Unfortunately, the timing could not have been worse. One of the worst industry slumps since the Great Depression was just beginning. Three subsequent "restructurings" had little positive effect.

Table 9.1 shows the decline in sales from 1990 through 1993. Table 9.2 shows the net income and loss during these four years. Of even more concern was Scott's performance relative to the major competitors Procter & Gamble and Kimberly-Clark during these four years. Table 9.3 shows the comparisons of profits as a percentage of sales, with Scott again showing up most poorly. Undoubtedly this was a company needing fixing.

TABLE 9.1. Sales of Scott, 1990–1993 (billions)

1990	$3.9
1991	3.8
1992	3.9
1993	3.6
Total change, 1990–1993	(7.7%)

Source: Company annual reports.

Commentary: The company's deteriorating sales come at a time of great economic growth and advancing revenues for most firms.

TABLE 9.2. Net Income of Scott and Percent of Sales, 1990–1993

	(millions)	% of sales
1990	$148	3.8%
1991	(70)	(1.8)
1992	167	4.3
1993	(277)	(7.7)

Source: Company annual reports.

Commentary: The company's erratic profit picture, culminating in the serious loss of 1993, deserved deep concern, which it received.

TABLE 9.3. Profit as a Percentage of Sales: Scott, Kimberly-Clark, and Procter & Gamble, 1990–1993

	1990	1991	1992	1993
Scott	3.8%	(1.8%)	4.3%	(7.7%)
P&G	6.6	6.6	6.4	(2.1)°
Kimberly-Clark	6.8	7.5	1.9	7.3

Source: Company annual reports.

° Extraordinary charges reflecting accounting changes.

Commentary: Scott again shows up badly against its major competitors, both in the low percentage of earnings to sales and their severe fluctuations into earnings losses.

In characteristic fashion, Dunlap acted quickly once he took over as chief executive officer on April 19, 1994. That same day, to show his confidence and commitment, he invested $2 million of his own money in Scott. A few months later, after the stock had appreciated 30 percent, he invested another $2 million.

After only a few hours on the job, Dunlap offered three of his former associates top positions in the company. On the second day, he disbanded the powerful management committee. On the third day, he fired nine of the eleven highest-ranking executives. To complete his blitzkrieg, on the fourth day Dunlap destroyed four bookshelves crammed with strategic plans prepared by previous administrations.

Can such drastic and abrupt changes be overdone? Should change be introduced more slowly and with more reflection? See the Issue Box: How Soon to Introduce Drastic Changes? for a discussion of these questions.

At the annual meeting in June 1994, barely two months after assuming command, Dunlap announced four major goals for the first year. First, he vowed to divest the company of nonstrategic assets, most notably S. D. Warren, the printing and publishing papers subsidiary that had received major expansion funding only a few years before. Second, he would develop a core team of accomplished senior managers. Third, Scott was to be brought to "fighting trim" through a one-time-only global restructuring. Last, Dunlap promised to develop new strategies for marketing Scott products around the world.

In one of the largest relative restructurings in corporate America, more than 11,000 positions out of a total of 25,900 worldwide were eliminated. This included 71 percent of the headquarters staff, 50 percent of the salaried employees, and 20 percent of the production workers. Such draconian measures certainly cut costs. But were they overdone? Might such cuts potentially have detrimental long-term consequences? Please see the Issue Box: How Deep to Cut? for a discussion of these topics.

In addition to cutting staff, Dunlap sought to reduce other costs, including outsourcing some operations and services. If these could be provided cheaper by other firms, then they should be farmed out. Dunlap announced that with the restructuring completed by year-end, pretax savings of $340 million were expected.[1]

[1] The New Scott 1994 Annual Report, p. 5.

ISSUE BOX

HOW SOON TO INTRODUCE DRASTIC CHANGES?

Some new administrators believe in instituting major changes as quickly as possible. They reason that an organization is expecting this and is better prepared to make the adjustments needed than it ever will be again. Such managers are often referred to as gunslingers—those who "shoot from the hip." Other managers believe in moving more slowly, gathering more information, and taking action only when all the pros and cons can be weighed. But sometimes such delays can lull an organization into a sense of false calm, and make for even more trauma when the changes eventually come.

Relevant to the issue of moving swiftly or slowly is the health of the entity. If a firm is sick, in drastic need of help, we would expect a new manager to move more quickly and decisively. A firm doing well, although perhaps not as well as desired, reasonably should not require such drastic and abrupt disruption.

It has always baffled me how a fast-acting executive can acquire sufficient information to make the crucial decisions of who to fire and who to retain, what operations need to be pruned and which supported, all within a few days. Of course, operating statistics can be studied before formally taking charge, but the causes of the problems or successes—the whys—can hardly be understood so soon.

Boards, investors, and creditors want a fast turnaround. Waiting months before taking action to fix a sick company is not acceptable. However, not all companies are easily fixable. For example, Borden, a food and chemical conglomerate, has gone through five restructurings in six years, with little improvement. But maybe Borden needed an Albert Dunlap, a person with a clear vision and willingness to clean house. And, yes, a supportive board.

Do you think Dunlap acted too hastily in his initial sweeping changes? Playing the devil's advocate (one who takes an opposing view for the sake of debate), support a position that he did indeed act far too hastily.

By late fall of 1994, Dunlap's plans to divest the company of nonstrategic assets bore fruit. S. D. Warren was sold for $1.6 billion to an international investment group. Other asset sales generated more than $2 billion. Dunlap was able to lower debt by $1.5 billion and repurchase $300 million of Scott stock. This led to the credit rating being upgraded.

The results of Dunlap's efforts were impressive indeed. Second-quarter earnings rose 71 percent; third-quarter earnings increased 73 percent, the best quarterly performance for Scott in four years. Fourth-quarter earnings were 159 percent higher than in 1993, establishing an all-time record. For the whole year, net income increased 82 percent over the previous year, and the stock price performance since Dunlap took over stood at the top 1 percent of major companies traded on the New York Stock Exchange.[2]

[2] Ibid., p. 6.

ISSUE BOX

HOW DEEP TO CUT?

Bloated bureaucratic organizations are the epitome of inefficiency and waste, whether in business corporations or in governmental bodies, including school systems. Administrative overhead might even exceed actual operating costs. But corrections can be overdone—they can go too far. In Scott's case, was the axing of 11,000 of 25,900 employees overdone?

Although we are not privy to the needed cost/productivity records, we can raise some concerns. Did the massive layoffs go well beyond fat and bloat into bone and muscle? If so, future operations might be jeopardized. Other concerns ought to be: Does an organization owe anything to its loyal and senior employees, or should they simply be considered pawns in the pursuit of maximizing profits? Where do we draw the line between efficiency and responsibility to faithful employees? And even to the community itself?

You may want to consider some of these questions and issues. They are current in today's downsizing mindset.

Still, the cost slashing was not helping market share. In the fiscal year ended April 2, 1995, Scott's bath-tissue sales in key U.S. markets slipped 1 percent, and paper towel sales fell 5.2 percent.[3]

On July 17, 1995, Dunlap's efforts to make Scott an attractive acquisition candidate were capped by Kimberly-Clark's $7.38 billion offer for the firm. In the process, Dunlap himself would be suitably rewarded, leaving far richer than after any of his seven previous restructuring efforts. But Dunlap insisted, "I am still the best bargain in corporate America."[4]

THE SUNBEAM CHALLENGE

Sunbeam was a maker of blenders, electric blankets, and gas grills. These old-line products had shown little growth, and revenues and profits languished. After the well-publicized turnaround success of Dunlap at Scott, it was no surprise when he was courted for the top job at Sunbeam, and he entered the fray with gusto.

The day Dunlap was hired, Sunbeam stock rose 50 percent, "on faith." It eventually rose 300 percent. With his customary modus operandi, he terminated half of Sunbeam's 12,000 employees and cut back its product offerings. Gone were such items as furniture and bed linens, and efforts were concentrated on things like grills, humidifiers, and kitchen appliances. In 1996 Dunlap took massive write-offs amounting to $338 million, of which almost $100 million was inventory.

In 1997, it looked like Dunlap was accomplishing another of his patented "miracles." Sales were up 22 percent to $1.168 billion, while income had risen from a loss

[3] Joseph Weber and Paula Dwyer, "Scott Rolls Out a Risky Strategy," *Business Week*, 22 May 1995, p. 45.

[4] Joann S. Lublin and Steven Lipin, "Scott Paper's 'Rambo in Pin Stripes' Is on the Prowl for Another Company to Fix," *Wall Street Journal*, 18 July 1995, p. B1.

of $196 million the previous year to a gain of $123 million in 1997. For stockholders this translated into earnings per share of $1.41 from a $2.37 loss in 1996. Table 9.4 shows the trend in revenues and income of Sunbeam through 1997.

In October 1997, after barely a year on the job, Dunlap announced that the turnaround was complete; he was seeking a buyer for Sunbeam. Stockholders had much to be pleased about. From a low of $12 a share in 1996, the price had risen to $50. Unfortunately, there was a serious downside to this, as Dunlap was soon to find: The high price for Sunbeam stock took it out of the range for any potential buyer; $50 gave a market capitalization of $4.6 billion, or four times revenues, a multiple reserved for only a few of the premier companies. So, for the time being, the stockholders were stuck with Dunlap.

Since he was not successful in selling the company, Dunlap went on a buying spree. He began talking about his "vision," in such words as, "We have moved from constraining categories to expanding categories. Small kitchen appliances become kitchen appliances. We'll move from grills to outdoor cooking. Health care moves from just a few products to a broad range of products."[5]

So, Dunlap bought Coleman Company, Signature Brands and its Mr. Coffee, and First Alert for an aggregate of approximately $2.4 billion in cash and stock. Part of this was financed with $750 million of convertible debentures, as well as $60 million of accounts receivable that were sold to raise cash. Critics maintained he had paid too much for these, especially the $2.2 billion for money-losing Coleman. The effect of these acquisitions on Sunbeam's balance sheet was sobering if any stockholders had looked closely.

When Dunlap took over Sunbeam, though it was performing poorly, it had only $200 million in debt. By 1998, Sunbeam was over $2 billion in debt, and its net worth had dropped from $500 million to a negative $600 million.[6]

TABLE 9.4.   **Trend of Sunbeam Revenues and Income, 1991–1997**

	1991	1992	1993	1994 (millions $)	1995	1996	1997
Revenues	886	967	1,066	1,198	1,203	964	1,168
Net Income	47.4	65.6	88.8	107	50.5	−196	123

Sources: Company annual reports.

Commentary: Dunlap came on the scene in July 1996, the year that Sunbeam incurred $196 million in losses. The $123 million profit for 1997 showed a remarkable and awesome recovery, and would seemingly make Dunlap a hero with his slash-and-burn strategy. Unfortunately, a reaudit did not confirm these figures. The inaccurate figures were blamed on questionable accounting, including prebooking sales and incorrectly assigning costs to the restructuring. The auditors said the company overstated its loss for 1996 and overstated profits for 1997. The revised figures showed a loss of $6.4 million for 1997, instead of the $123 million profit. (*Sources:* Martha Brannigan, "Sunbeam Audit to Repudiate '97 Turnaround," *Wall Street Journal,* 20 October 1998, p. A3; and "Audit Shows Sunbeam's Turnaround Really a Bust," *Cleveland Plain Dealer,* 21 October 1998, pp. 1-C, 2-C.)

[5] As quoted in Holman W. Jenkins Jr., "Untalented Al? The Sorrows of a One-Trick Pony," *Wall Street Journal,* 24 June 1998, p. A19.

[6] Matthew Schifrin, "The Unkindest Cuts," *Forbes,* 4 May 1998, p. 45.

THE DEBACLE OF 1998, AND THE DEMISE OF DUNLAP

The first quarter of 1998 showed a complete reversal of fortunes. Revenues were down and a first-quarter loss was posted of $44.6 million—all this far below expectations. Sunbeam's stock price plunged 50 percent, from $53 to $25. By midsummer it was to reach a low of $4.62.

Dunlap conceded that he and top executives had concentrated their attention too much on "sealing" the acquisitions of Coleman and the two smaller companies, allowing underlings to offer "stupid, low-margin deals" on outdoor cooking grills. He pointed to glitches with new products, a costly recall, and even El Niño. "People don't think about buying outdoor grills during a storm," he said. "Faced with sluggish sales, a marketing executive offered excessive discounts," he further said. More job cuts were promised, through eliminating one-third of the jobs at the newly acquired companies.[7]

On Monday, June 15, 1998, after deliberating over the weekend, Sunbeam's board abruptly fired Al Dunlap, having "lost confidence in his ability to carry out the long-term growth potential of the company."[8] Then a legal fight ensued as to what kind of severance package, if any, Dunlap deserved because of his firing. A severance package for Mr. Dunlap would be "obscene—an obscenity on top of an obscenity, capitalism gone crazy," said Michael Cavanaugh, union leader.[9] Other comments were reported in the media; a sampling is in the Information Box: The Popularity of "Chainsaw" Al Dunlap.

Allegations of Fraud

At the end of a three-month audit after Dunlap's departure, auditors discovered accounting irregularities that struck down the amazingly high reported profits for 1997, the first full year of Dunlap's leadership. Rather than a turnaround, the good results came from improper accounting moves that adversely affected 1996 and 1998 results. The restated numbers showed that Sunbeam actually had a small operating loss in 1997, while 1996 showed a modest profit.

On May 15, 2001, the Securities and Exchange Commission (SEC) formally charged that Dunlap and some of his executives broke security laws to make Sunbeam look healthier and more attractive for a buyer. This was done by fraudulently shifting revenue to inflate losses under the old management and boosting income to create the false impression of the rapid turnaround in financial performance for 1997. Furthermore, revenue was increased in 1997 at the expense of future results by inducing retail customers to sell merchandise more quickly than normal, a practice known as *channel stuffing*. By the next year, the company was getting desperate to hide its mounting financial problems and misrepresented its performance and prospects in quarterly reports, bond offerings material, press releases, and statements to stock analysts. Dunlap denied any

---

[7] James R. Hagerty and Martha Brannigan, "Sunbeam Plans to Cut 5,100 Jobs as CEO Promises Rebound from Dismal Quarter," *Wall Street Journal*, 12 May 1998, pp. A3, A4.

[8] Martha Brannigan and James Hagerty, "Sunbeam, Its Prospects Looking Ever Worse, Fires CEO Dunlap," *Wall Street Journal*, 15 June 1998, pp. A1, A14.

[9] Martha Brannigan and Joann S. Lublin, "Dunlap Faces a Fight Over His Severance Pay," *Wall Street Journal*, 16 June 1998, p. B3.

INFORMATION BOX

THE POPULARITY OF "CHAINSAW" AL DUNLAP

Not surprisingly, the slashing policy of Dunlap did not bring him a lot of friends, even though he may have been admired in some circles. Here are some comments reported in the press immediately after his firing:

"He finally got what he's been doing to a lot of people. It was a taste of his own medicine." (Union representative)

"I'm happy the son of a bitch is fired." (Former supervisor)

"Somebody at that company finally got some sense." (Small-town mayor)

"I couldn't think of a better person to deserve it. It tickled me to death. We may need to have a rejoicing ceremony." (Small-town mayor)

"I guess the house of cards came tumbling down ... when you reduce your workforce by 50 percent, you lose your ability to manage." (Former plant manager)

Is there a lesson to be learned from such comments as these? Perhaps it is that the human element in organizations and communities needs to be considered.

Taking a devil's advocate position (one who takes an opposing viewpoint for the sake of argument and full discussion), defend the philosophy of Dunlap.

Sources: Thomas W. Gerdel, "Workers at Glenwillow Plant Cheer Firing of 'Chainsaw' Al," *Cleveland Plain Dealer,* 16 June 1998, p. 2-C; "No Tears for a Chainsaw," *Wall Street Journal,* 16 June 1998, p. B1.

---

involvement or knowledge of such matters and said that any accounting changes by the auditors were "judgment calls" on matters subject to interpretation.[10]

The company was forced to restate financial results for eighteen months, and it filed for bankruptcy protection in February 2001.

In early September 2002, Dunlap agreed to settle the SEC suit by paying $500,000 and agreeing never to be an officer or director of another public company. He neither admitted nor denied the SEC's claim that he masterminded the accounting fraud. A month earlier, Dunlap also paid $15 million in a settlement of a class-action suit filed by shareholders for their losses due to Sunbeam's fraudulent business practices.[11] All thoughts of a severance package for Dunlap after his firing were long forgotten.

The SEC also came to believe there was funny accounting at Scott Paper when Dunlap was running it. But this suspicion came at the height of the Enron furor, and the SEC had bigger game to pursue.[12]

[10] Martha Brannigan, "Sunbeam Slashes Its 1997 Earnings in Restatement," *Wall Street Journal,* 21 October 1998, p. B23.

[11] Jill Barton, "Sunbeam's 'Chain Saw Al' to Pay $500,000 Judgment," Associated Press as reported in *Cleveland Plain Dealer,* 5 September 2002, p. C1.

[12] Floyd Norris, "Fraud Surrounded 'Chainsaw Al', Yet Little Was Done," *New York Times,* as reported in *Cleveland Plain Dealer,* 8 September 2002, p. G3.

ANALYSIS

Was Dunlap's Management Style of "Slash and Burn" Appropriate?

We see conflicting evidence in the Scott and Sunbeam cases. Without doubt, Dunlap achieved his goal to make Scott an attractive acquisition candidate and thus reward shareholders and himself (although suspicions later arose that the sterling results may have been tainted). That he did this so quickly seemed at the time a strong endorsement of his strategy for turning around sick companies—simply decimate the organization, sell off all ancillary units, cut costs to the bone, and virtually force the company into increased profitability.

The flaw with this reasoning is that it tends to boost short-term performance at the expense of the longer term. Morale and dedication of surviving employees are devastated. Vision and innovative thinking may be impaired since the depleted organization lacks time and commitment to deal effectively with more than day-to-day basic operations.

Dunlap's strategy backfired with Sunbeam. When he couldn't sell the company after manipulating the performance statistics for 1997, he was left with a longer-term management challenge that he was by no means equal to. It is ironic that the reputation for turning around sick companies acted against him with Sunbeam. Investors were so confident of his ability to quickly turn around the company that they bid the price up so high no other firm would buy it. And they were stuck with Dunlap.

Did the Adversity Require Such Drastic Changes?

Sales of both Scott and Sunbeam were flat, with profit performance deteriorating. Stock prices were falling counter to a bull market, and investors were disillusioned. Did such situations call for draconian measures?

Neither company was in danger of going belly-up. True, they both were off the growth path, but their brands continued to be well regarded by consumers. On the other hand, many firms become too bureaucratic, burdened with high overhead and chained to established policies and procedures. Such organizations desperately need paring down, eliminating bloated staff and executive levels, and—not the least— curbing the red tape that destroys flexibility and creativity.

The best answer lies in moderation, cutting the deadwood but not bone and muscle. The worst scenario is to cut with little investigation and reflection. This cost-cutting climate may degenerate to the extent that worthy operations and individuals are cut regardless of their merit and future promise. We would expect better long-term performance in an organization that is not decimated with shattered morale.

Dunlap quickly sold off the S. D. Warren unit of Scott, and this added $1.6 billion to Scott coffers. Previous Scott management had invested heavily in what seemed a reasonable diversification into commercial paper, only to encounter an unexpected industry downturn. How could this have been predicted? Was Warren worth keeping? Research and investigation might have found that it was.

Creeping Bureaucracy

Bureaucratic excesses often come about after years of reasonable success and viability. The Information Box: The Bureaucratic Organization describes this type of organization.

INFORMATION BOX

THE BUREAUCRATIC ORGANIZATION

The bureaucratic organization is a natural consequence of size and age. Its characteristics include the following:

- A clear-cut division of labor
- A strict hierarchy of authority
- Staffing by technical competence
- Formal rules and procedures
- Impersonal approaches to decision making

Although a well-structured organization would appear to be best in many circumstances, it tends to be too rigid. It relies heavily on rules and procedures and as a result is often slow to adapt to change. Red tape usually predominates, as do many layers of hierarchy, an abundance of staff, and overspecialization. Consequently, creativity and initiative are stifled, and communication between upper management and lower operations is cumbersome and often distorted. Perhaps even more serious, a bureaucratic organization, with its entrenched administrators and staff positions, has a built-in high overhead that makes it difficult to compete against leaner competitors.

A bureaucratic organization does not have to be inevitable as a firm attains large size and dominance. As shown in Table 9.5, a firm can still mold itself as an adaptive organization. But the temptation is otherwise.

TABLE 9.5. Contrasts of Bureaucratic and Adaptive Organizations

Organizational Aspects	Bureaucratic	Adaptive
Hierarchy of authority	Centralized	Decentralized
Rules and procedures	Many	Few
Division of labor	Precise	Open
Spans of control	Narrow	Wide
Coordination	Formal/impersonal	Informal/personal

Can you identify the type of person who tends to work best in a bureaucracy? The one who performs worst in this setup?

Source: This section is adapted from John R. Schermerhorn, Jr., *Management*, 6th ed. (New York: Wiley, 1999), pp. 75, 223.

Bureaucracy seemed to have been rampant at pre-Dunlap Scott. After all, Dunlap eliminated 71 percent of the headquarters staff and four bookshelves crammed with strategic plans of previous administrations. Too many administrators and staff bring higher overhead costs than leaner competitors, thus placing the firm at a competitive disadvantage. Some pruning needed to be done.

Was the same thing true with Sunbeam? Perhaps not to the same extent, although without more specific information we cannot know for sure. We can suspect, however, that Dunlap, caught up in his success at Scott, simply transferred his strategy to Sunbeam with no consideration of their differences. We might call this slashing by formula, and it suggests a rigid mind-set devoid of flexibility or compassion.

Paying Too Much for Acquisitions

With Sunbeam, Dunlap made three questionable acquisitions, and burdened the firm with several billions of dollars of debt. In particular, the $2.2 billion paid for money-losing Coleman seemed another of Dunlap's shoot-from-the-hip decisions. Such questionable research in acquisitions decisions followed the pattern of his personnel-slashing decisions and the quick sale of S. D. Warren. Furthermore, the reckless accumulation of debt for these acquisitions almost suggests a masochistic mind-set. Or did Dunlap think that if the share price now dropped drastically, the firm would become attractive for an acquisition?

Detection of Fraud Destroys
Any Perception of Management Competence

Dunlap apparently had a long history of manipulating records to make himself look better, as we will further see in the next section. While this fraud pales in comparison with the massive misdeeds of Enron, Tyco, WorldCom, and others—simply because Dunlap's were much smaller firms—it can no more be condoned than their fraudulent practices. Dunlap could yet face jail time, should the SEC decide to turn its attention to less publicized cases.

LATER DEVELOPMENTS

Dunlap's exploits brought turmoil to the executive-search industry. It seems major search firms checking his employment history prior to being hired by Sunbeam failed to uncover that he had been fired from two previous positions. He was terminated at Max Phillips & Sons in 1973 after only seven weeks. Three years later in 1976, he had been fired as president of Nitec Paper Corp. under circumstances of alleged fraud involving misstated profits, a situation not unlike his departure from Sunbeam.

While these episodes took place twenty years before the recruiting for Scott Paper and Sunbeam, and were apparently overlooked because of his supposedly strong track record in recent years, significant and pertinent omissions in Dunlap's job history were not caught by search firms supposedly conducting thorough background checks. Along the way, Dunlap erased both jobs from his employment history, and no one who checked his background discovered the omissions.[13]

[13] Joann S. Lublin, "Search Firms Have Red Faces in Dunlap Flop," *Wall Street Journal,* 17 July 2001, pp. B1, B4; Floyd Norris, "Uncovering Lost Years of Sunbeam's Fired Chief," *New York Times,* reported in *Cleveland Plain Dealer,* 17 July 2001, pp. C1, C4.

WHAT CAN BE LEARNED?

How to Jump-start a Languid Organization

Can we find any keys to stimulating an organization not performing up to potential? Or maybe even to inspire it to perform beyond its potential? The challenge is similar to that of motivating a discouraged and downtrodden athletic team to rise up and have faith in itself and recommit itself to quality of performance.

In both athletics and business, the common notion is that personnel changes have to be made. Dunlap introduced the idea of severe downsizing. But this is controversial, and in view of Dunlap's problems with Sunbeam, now almost discredited. So how much should be cut, how quickly should changes be made and how sweeping should they be, and what kind of information is most vital in making such decisions? Furthermore, there is the question of morale and its importance in any restoration.

We find more art than science in this mighty challenge of restoration. In particular, the right blend or degree of change is crucial. Let us look at some considerations:

- *How much do we trim?* In most revival situations, some pruning of personnel and operations is necessary. But how much is too much, and how much is not enough? Is an ax always required for a successful turnaround? One would hope not. Certainly those personnel who are not willing to accept change may have to be let go. And weak persons and operations that show little probability of improvement need to be pruned, just as the athlete who can't seem to perform up to expectations may have to be let go. Still, it is often better to wait for sufficient information as to the "why" of poor performance, before assigning blame for the consequences.

- *How long do we wait?* Mistakes can be made both in taking action before all the facts are known, and in waiting too long. If the change maker procrastinates for weeks, an organization that at first was psychologically geared to major change might find it more traumatic and disruptive.

- *What should be the role of strategic planning?* Major actions should hardly be taken without *some* research and planning, but strategic plans too often delay change implementation. They tend to be the products of a fumbling bureaucracy and of some abdication of responsibility. (Despite the popularity of strategic planning, it often is a vehicle for procrastination and blame-dilution; e.g., "I simply followed the strategy recommendations of the consultants.") Dunlap had an aversion to strategic planning; he saw it as indicative of a top-heavy bureaucratic organization. Perhaps he was right on this, when carried to an extreme. But going into an organization and heedlessly slashing positions without considering the individuals involved and their potential promise is akin to shooting from the hip, with little regard for careful aiming. Then there is the matter of morale.

- *Morale considerations.* Major restructuring usually is demoralizing to the organizations involved. The usual result is massive layoffs and forced retirements, complete reassignment of people, traumatic personnel and policy changes, and destruction of accustomed lines of communication and authority. This is hardly conducive to preserving stability and morale and any faint spark of teamwork. (You may want to review the Continental Airlines case to see how Gordon Bethune achieved an amazing revitalization of employee morale.)

Moderation Is Usually Best

Much can be said for moderation, for choosing the middle position, for example, between heavy cost cutting and light cost cutting. Of course, the condition of the firm is a major consideration; one on the verge of bankruptcy, unable to meet its bills, needs drastic measures promptly. But the problems of both Scott and Sunbeam were by no means so serious. More moderate action could have been taken.

It is better to view the restoration challenge as a *time for building rather than tearing down.* This focuses attention more on the longer view than on short-term results that may come back to haunt the firm as well as the change maker, someone like Dunlap.

Periodic Housecleaning Produces Competitive Health

To minimize the buildup of deadwood, periodically all aspects of an organization ought to be objectively appraised. Weak products and operations should be pruned, unless solid justification exists for keeping them. Such justification might include good growth prospects or complementing other products and operations or even providing a desired customer service. In particular, staff and headquarters personnel and functions should be scrutinized, perhaps every five years, with the objective of weeding out the redundant and superfluous. Most important, these "axing" evaluations should be done objectively, with decisive actions taken where needed. While some layoffs may result, they might not be necessary if suitable transfers are possible.

CONSIDER

Can you add any other learning insights?

QUESTIONS

1. "Periodic evaluations of personnel and departments aimed at pruning cause far too much harm to the organization. Such 'axing' evaluations should themselves be pruned." Argue this position as persuasively as you can.

2. Now marshal the most persuasive arguments for such "axing" evaluations.

3. Describe a person's various stages of morale and dedication to the company as it goes through a restructuring, with massive layoffs expected and realized, but with the person finding himself or herself one of the survivors. How, in your opinion, would this affect productivity and loyalty?

4. Is it likely that any decades-old organization will be bloated with excessive bureaucracy and overhead? Why or why not?

5. What decision guides should be used to determine which divisions and subsidiaries are to be divested or sold?

6. What arguments would you make in a time of restructuring for keeping your particular business unit? Which are likely to be most persuasive to an administration committed to a program of heavy pruning?

HANDS-ON EXERCISES

1. You are one of the nine high-ranking executives fired by Dunlap his third day on the job. Describe your feelings and your action plan at this point. (If you want to make some assumptions, state them specifically.)

2. You are one of the two high-level executives kept by Dunlap as he sweeps into office. Describe your feelings and your likely performance on the job.

3. You are one of the three outsiders brought into Scott vice-presidential jobs by Dunlap. You have worked for him before and must have impressed him. Describe your feelings and your likely performance on the job. What specific problems, if any, do you foresee?

TEAM DEBATE EXERCISE

It is early 1996. The board of Sunbeam is considering bringing in a turnaround team. One is the team of Dunlap, which argues for major and rapid change. Another team under consideration is Clarence Ripley's, who advocates more modest immediate changes. Array your arguments and present your positions as persuasively as possible. Attack the recommendations of the other side as aggressively as possible—we are talking about millions of dollars in fees and compensation at stake for the winning team.

INVITATION TO RESEARCH

What is Dunlap up to after being fired by the Sunbeam board in mid-1998? Has he gracefully retired, or is he running scared pending legal charges? Is he still fighting for severance pay? Who replaced Dunlap, and how well is he doing? Are his policies much different from Dunlap's?

CHAPTER TEN

The Great Firestone/Ford Explorer Tire Disaster

$\mathbf{A}$ product defect that leads to customer injuries and deaths through manufacturer carelessness constitutes the most serious crisis that any firm should face. In addition to destroying brand reputation, ethical and social responsibility abuses are involved, and then legal and regulatory consequences. Managing such a crisis becomes far worse, however, when the manufacturer knew about the problems and concealed them, or denied them.

This case is unique in that two manufacturers were culpable, but each blamed the other. As a result, Firestone and Ford were savaged by the press, public opinion, the government, and a host of salivating lawyers. Massive tire recalls destroyed the bottom line and even endangered the viability of Bridgestone/Firestone, while sales of the Ford Explorer, the world's best-selling sport-utility vehicle (SUV), plummeted 22 percent in April 2001 from the year before, while domestic sales of SUVs overall climbed 9 percent.

A HORROR SCENARIO

Firestone tires mounted on Ford Explorers were linked to more than 200 deaths from rollovers in the United States, as well as more than 60 in Venezuela and a reported 14 in Saudi Arabia and neighboring countries. A widely publicized lawsuit took place in Texas in the summer of 2001. It had been expected that the jury would determine who was most to blame for the deaths and injuries from Explorers outfitted with Firestone tires.

Ford settled its portion of the suit for $6 million, one month before the trial began. While Firestone now became the sole defendant, jurors were also asked to assess Ford's responsibility for the accident.

The lawsuit was brought by the family of Marisa Rodriguez, a mother of three who was left brain-damaged and paralyzed after the steel belt and tread of a Firestone tire tore apart during a trip to Mexico in March 2000. As a result, the Explorer rolled over three times, crushing the roof above Mrs. Rodriguez in the rear seat; her husband

139

Joel, who was asleep in the front passenger seat, was also injured. The live pictures of Mrs. Rodriguez in a wheelchair received wide TV coverage.

After the federal court jury in the Texas border town of McAllen had been dead-locked for four days, a settlement was reached with Bridgestone/Firestone for $7.85 million. (The plaintiffs originally had asked for $1 billion.)

The out-of-court settlements with both Ford and Firestone did not resolve the issue of who was most to blame for this and the hundreds of other injuries and deaths. But a lawyer for the Rodriguez family predicted that sooner or later a verdict would emerge: "There's going to be trials and there's going to be verdicts. We've got Marisa Rodriguezes all over the country."[1]

ANATOMY OF THE PROBLEM

The Ford/Firestone Relationship

Ford and Firestone had a long, intimate history. In 1895, Harvey Firestone sold tires to Henry Ford for his first automobile. In 1906, the Firestone Tire & Rubber Company won its first contract for Ford Motor Company's mass-produced vehicles, a commitment that continued through the decades.

Henry Ford and Harvey Firestone became business confederates and best friends who went on annual summer camping trips, riding around in Model T's along with Thomas Edison and naturalist John Burroughs. Further cementing the relationship, in 1947 Firestone's granddaughter, Martha, married Ford's grandson, William Clay Ford, in a dazzling ceremony in Akron, Ohio, that attracted a *Who's Who* of dignitaries and celebrities. Their son, William Clay Ford Jr., was to become Ford's chairman.

In 1988, Tokyo-based Bridgestone Corporation bought Firestone, twenty years after the Japanese company sold its first tires in the United States under the Bridgestone name. In 1990, Ford introduced the Explorer SUV to replace the Bronco II in the 1991 model year. It became the nation's top-selling SUV, and the Explorer generated huge profits for more than a decade. Bridgestone/Firestone was the sole supplier of the Explorer's tires.

The Relationship Worsens

The first intimation of trouble came in 1999 when, after fourteen fatalities occurred, Ford began replacing tires of Explorers in Saudi Arabia and nearby countries. The tire failures were blamed on hot weather and underinflated tires. At the time, over-seas fatalities did not have to be reported to U.S. regulators, so the accidents received scant attention in the media.

The media caught the scent in early 2000 when television reports in Houston revealed instances of tread separation on Firestone's ATX tires, and the National Highway Traffic Safety Administration (NHTSA) started an investigation. By May,

---

[1] "Firestone Agrees to Pay $7.5 Million in Tire Suit," *Cleveland Plain Dealer,* 25 August 2001, pp. A1, A13; also, Milo Geyelin and Timothy Aeppel, "For Firestone, Tire Trial Is Mixed Victory," *Wall Street Journal,* 27 August 2001, pp. A3, A4.

four U.S. fatalities had been reported, and NHTSA expanded the investigation to 47 million ATX, ATXII, and Wilderness tires.

In August 2000, as mounting deaths led to increasing pressure from consumers and multiple lawsuits, Firestone voluntarily recalled 14.4 million 15-inch radial tires because of tread separation. The plant in Decatur, Illinois, was implicated in most of these accidents. Ford and Firestone agreed to replace the tires, but estimated that 6.5 million were still on the road. Consumer groups sought a still wider recall, charging that Explorers with other Firestone tire models were also prone to separation leading to rollovers.

In December 2000, Firestone issued a report blaming Ford for the problems, claiming that the Explorer's design caused rollovers with any tread separations. On April 20, 2001, Ford gave NHTSA a report blaming Firestone for flawed manufacturing.

In May 2001, Ford announced that it was replacing all remaining 13 million Firestone Wilderness AT tires on its vehicles, saying the move was necessary because Ford had no confidence in the tires' safety. "We feel it's our responsibility to act immediately," Ford CEO Jacques Nasser said. Ford said the move would cost the automaker $2.1 billion, although it hoped to get this money back from Firestone.

Firestone Chairman and CEO John Lampe defended his tires, saying, "no one cares more about the safety of the people who travel on our tires than we do. When we have a problem, we admit it and we fix it."[2]

The Last Days

It is lamentable when a long-lasting, close relationship is severed. But on May 21, 2001, Lampe abruptly ended the 95-year association, accusing Ford of refusing to acknowledge safety problems with its vehicles, thus putting all the blame on Firestone.

The crisis had been brewing for months. Many Firestone executives did not trust Ford and even exchanging documents was done with rancor, with major disagreements in interpreting the data. Firestone argued that tread-separation claims occurred ten times more frequently on Ford Explorers than on Ranger pickups with the same tires, thus supporting their contention that the Explorer was mostly at fault. Ford rejected Firestone's charges about the Explorer, saying that for 10 years the model "has ranked at or near the top in terms of safety among the 12 SUVs in its class." It stated that 2.9 million Goodyear tires mounted on more than 500,000 Explorers had "performed with industry-leading safety."[3]

The climax came in a May 21 meeting attended by Lampe and a contingent of Ford officials, during which both sides maintained that the other was to blame. Discussions broke down regarding any working together to examine Explorer's role in the accidents. At that point, Lampe ended their relationship. Each party then was left to defend itself before Congress, the court of public opinion, and ultimately a siege of lawsuits. See the Information Box: How Emotion Influences Company Reputation for a discussion of how emotion drives consumers in their perception, good and bad, of companies.

---

[2] Ed Garsten, Associated Press, as reported in "Ford Tire Tab $2.1 Billion," *Cleveland Plain Dealer,* 23 May 2001, pp. 1-C, 4-C.

[3] Timothy Aeppel, Joseph B. White, and Stephen Power, "Firestone Quits as Tire Supplier to Ford," *Wall Street Journal,* 22 May 2001, pp. A3, A12.

INFORMATION BOX

HOW EMOTION INFLUENCES COMPANY REPUTATION

The second annual corporate-reputation survey conducted by the Harris market-research firm and the Reputation Institute, involving 26,011 respondents, found that Emotional Appeal—trust, admiration and respect, and generally good feelings toward—was the driving force in how people rated companies. The survey found that advertising did not necessarily change opinions. For example, despite a $100 million advertising campaign about what a good citizen Philip Morris Company was in feeding the hungry and helping victims of domestic violence, the company still received low marks on trust, respect, and admiration. But the most recent poll showed that Philip Morris no longer had the worst reputation in America. This distinction went to Bridgestone/Firestone, with Ford receiving the lowest reputation rating among auto companies.

Once lost, a company's reputation or public image is usually difficult to regain. For example, Exxon Mobil's reputation for environmental responsibility was still given low grades more than a decade after the destructive Alaskan oil spill involving the tanker *Exxon Valdez*.

Do you think Firestone's quest to improve its reputation would face the same problems as those occurring from the *Exxon Valdez?* Why or why not?

Source: Ronald Alsop, "Survey: Emotion Drives Public Perception of Companies," *Wall Street Journal*, 11 February 2001, p. 5-H.

Advantage to Competitors

Major competitors Goodyear and Michelin, as well as smaller competitors and private-label tire makers, predictably raised tire prices 3 to 5 percent. Goodyear then tried to increase production robustly to replace the millions of Firestone tires recalled or soon to be, but it was trying to avoid overtime pay to bolster profits. In a written statement, Goodyear said, "We are working very closely with Ford to jointly develop an aggressive plan to address consumers' needs as quickly as possible."[4]

The decrease in auto sales in the slowing economy that began in 2000 had led Goodyear to production cutbacks, including cutting 7,200 workers worldwide as it posted an 83 percent decline in profits in 2000. Now it was challenged to gear up to handle the windfall of the ending of the Ford/Firestone relationship.

WHEREIN LIES THE BLAME?

In years to come, courts and lawyers will sort out the culpability controversy. The outcome is in doubt, and the finger of blame points to a number of sources, though the weighting is uncertain. While Ford and Firestone should share major responsibility, NHTSA and the motoring public were hardly blameless.

[4] Thomas W. Gerdel, "Goodyear, Michelin Raising Consumer Tire Prices," *Cleveland Plain Dealer*, 23 May 2001, pp. 1-C, 4-C.

Ford

The question whether the design of Ford's Explorer made it more prone to rollover than other SUVs will be decided in the courtroom. One thing seems clear: Ford recommended a low inflation level for its Firestone-equipped tires, and this would subject them to more flex in the sidewall and greater heat buildup. With high-speed driving in hot weather, such a high-profile vehicle would be more prone to roll over with any tire trouble, especially with inexperienced drivers. For example, Ford's recommended tire pressure was 26 pounds, which would bring the car's center of gravity lower to the ground. This would seem good, but only at first look. Required by the government, the Uniform Tire Quality Grade (UTQG) provides comparative manufacturer information. Tires are subjected to a series of government-mandated tests that measure performance in treadwear, traction, and temperature resistance. All testing is done by the tire manufacturer. Ford was alone among SUV makers in equipping the Explorer with grade C tires rather than the more heat-resistant B tires that were the near universal standard on most sport utility vehicles. To make the C grade, tires had to withstand only 2 hours at 50 miles per hour (mph) when properly inflated and loaded, plus another 90 minutes at speeds up to 85 mph. This standard dated back to 1968, when sustained highway speeds were much lower than today. Now, people drive hour after hour at speeds well above 70 mph.

The C-rated Firestones were used on millions of Ford pickup trucks without problems. However, in contrast with SUVs, most pickup trucks are not taken on long-haul, high-speed road trips filled with family and luggage.

Ford CEO Jacques Nasser justified replacing 13 million tires by claiming the Firestones were failing at a rate higher than Goodyears mounted on 2 million Explorers in the mid-1990s. But the Goodyears carried the B rating. The dangerous effect of heat buildup was shown by most Explorers' accidents taking place in hot Southern states and other hot-climate countries with high speed limits.

Ford engineers should have been aware of these dangers—if not immediately, certainly after a few years—and adapted the Explorer to customers who drive fast, pay little attention to tire maintenance, and are prone to panic with a blowout and flip the car. Unfortunately, the American legal environment, the tort system, makes the manufacturer vulnerable to lawsuits and massive damage claims should it acknowledge in retrospect that it had made a bad mistake in its tire selection and pressure recommendation. So the temptation was to blame the tire maker, and spend millions turning it into a media monster.

Bridgestone/Firestone

Firestone tires were far from blameless. Early on, investigations of deadly vehicle accidents linked the causes to tire failure, notably due to shoddy manufacturing practices at the Firestone plant in Decatur, Illinois; the 6.5 million tire recall by Firestone was of the 15-inch radial ATX and ATX11 tires and Wilderness AT tires made at that plant. In June 27, 2001, the company announced the plant would be closed. But Firestone's poorly controlled manufacturing process proved not to be limited to this single operation. See the Information Box: A Whistle-Blower "Hero" about the whistle-blower who exposed another plant's careless disregard of safe tire production.

INFORMATION BOX

A WHISTLE-BLOWER "HERO"

Alan Hogan was honored in June 2001 by the Civil Justice Foundation for exposing how employees at a Bridgestone/Firestone plant in North Carolina routinely made defective tires. This consumer advocacy group, founded by the Association of Trial Lawyers of America, bestowed similar "community champion" awards on tobacco whistle-blower Jeffrey Wigand and on Erin Brockovich, who exposed hazardous waste dangers and was the subject of a popular movie.

With his insider's knowledge of shoddy tire-building practices, Hogan was widely credited with bringing about the first recall. He testified at a wrongful death lawsuit in 1999 that he witnessed the crafting of countless bad tires built with dried-out rubber and wood bits, cigarette butts, screws, and other foreign materials mixed in. Hogan, who had quit the company and opened an auto-body shop in his hometown, became a pariah among many people for his revelations about the community's major employer, and company attorneys looked into his work and family life for anything they could use to discredit him. They tried to portray him as a disgruntled former employee. An anonymous fax accused him of spreading "vicious, malicious allegations" about the company. Employees were warned not to do business with car dealerships that dealt with his body shop.

But Hogan persevered, and eventually won recognition and accolades. "I'm surprised it took this long," he said. "Maybe now people will see this is the way it's been since 1994, 1995, when they started covering this up." His whistle-blowing credentials were then in high demand as an expert witness in other lawsuits.

Do you see any reasons why Hogan may not have been completely objective in his whistle-blowing efforts?

Source: Dan Chapman, Cox News, as reported in "Firestone Ex-Worker Called Hero in Recall," *Cleveland Plain Dealer*, 29 May 2001, p. 1-C.

Still, there were contrary indications that the fault was not all Bridgestone/Firestone's, that Ford shared the blame. General Motors had detected no problems with the Firestones it used as standard equipment in fourteen of its models. In fact, in July 2001 GM named Firestone as its supplier of the year for the sixth consecutive time. Honda of America was also loyal to Firestones, which it used on best-selling Civics and Odysseys.[5]

On September 14, 2001, months after all Firestones had been recalled from Ford Explorers, an apparently skilled driver—a deputy bailiff driving home from court—was killed when he lost control of his Explorer and it flipped over a guardrail, slid down an embankment, and rolled over several times.[6]

---

[5] Garsten, "Ford Tire Tab," pp. 1-C, 4-C; and Alison Grant, "Bridgestone/Firestone Faces Struggle to Survive," *Cleveland Plain Dealer*, 5 August 2001, pp. H1, H5.

[6] "SUV Flips, Killing Deputy Bailiff, 24," *Cleveland Plain Dealer*, 15 September 2001, p. B5.

Government

Public Citizen and other consumer groups were critical of the government, maintaining that it was too slow in completing its initial Firestone investigation and had dragged its feet in any investigation of the Explorer. A Public Citizen study saw the use of the specific Firestone tires as coming from cost- and weight-saving miscalculations and gambles by Ford, "making what was already a bad problem into a lethal one." Not just the companies were at fault, but federal regulators were lax in not toughening standards on SUVs to prevent roofs from collapsing in rollover crashes. "The human damage caused is barbaric and unnecessary," the study concluded.[7]

The Driver

There is no doubt that drivers contributed to accidents. They did so by neglecting tire pressure so that it was often below even the low recommendations of Ford, by heavily loading vehicles, and by driving too fast over long periods so that heat could build up to danger levels. Added to this, the lack of driving expertise to handle emergency blowouts was often the fatal blow. Yet, could a carmaker, tire maker, or government really expect the average consumer to act with strict prudence? Precautions, be they car standards or tire standards, needed to be imposed with worst scenarios in mind as to consumer behavior.

CONSEQUENCES

Each company maneuvered to cast blame primarily on the other. Ford announced in May 2001 it would triple the size of the Firestone recall—a $2.8 billion prospect, a cost Ford wanted to shift to the tire maker. Firestone, at that point, severed its long relationship with Ford by refusing to supply the company with more tires. CEO Lampe maintained Ford was trying to divert scrutiny of the rollover-prone Explorer by casting doubt on the safety of Firestone tires.

Both parties suffered in this name-calling and buck-passing. By fall 2001, sales of Explorers were off sharply, as consumers wondered whether the hundreds of Explorer crashes were due to the SUV's design, or Firestone tires, or both. Ford lost market share to Toyota and other foreign rivals in the SUV market. In July 2001, it reported its first loss from operations since 1992. It also faced two hundred product liability lawsuits involving Explorer rollovers. Still, Ford was big enough to absorb problems with one of its models.

Smaller Bridgestone/Firestone faced a more dangerous situation. In 2000 its earnings dropped 80 percent, reflecting the costs of recalling millions of tires as well as a special charge to cover legal expenses. The Firestone unit, which accounted for 40 percent of the parent company's revenue, posted a net loss of $510 million after it took a $750 million charge for legal expenses. Sales were forecast to plunge 20 percent in 2001, and costs of lawsuits could eventually reach billions of dollars, to the point where some analysts doubted that Firestone as a brand could survive.[8]

---

[7] Alison Grant, "Government, Goodyear Still Navigating a Bumpy Road," *Cleveland Plain Dealer,* 5 August 2001, p. H5.

[8] Akiko Kashiwagi, "Recalls Cost Bridgestone Dearly; Firestone's Parent's Profit Drops 80%," *Washington Post,* 23 February 2001, p. E-3.

Options Firestone Faced

The esteemed Firestone brand, launched more than a century ago, had been the exclusive tire supplier to the Indy 500. Now its future was in doubt, despite decades of brand loyalty. The brand faced three options.

Option 1

Some thought the company should try to deemphasize Firestone and push business to the Bridgestone label. This would likely result in some loss of market segmentation and the flexibility of having distinct low-end, mid-level, and premium tires. Others thought such a halfhearted approach would simply prolong the agony of hanging onto a besmirched brand.

Option 2

Obliterate the Firestone name, it being irretrievable. "Firestone should just give up," said one public relations analyst. "They've damaged themselves so severely." A University of Michigan Business School professor called the brand dead: "Can you imagine any jury claiming that somebody who's suspected of building bad tires is innocent?"[9]

Option 3

Try to salvage the brand. Some questioned the wisdom of abandoning the century-old Firestone name, with its rich tradition and millions of cumulative advertising dollars. They thought that with money, time, and creative advertising, Bridgestone/Firestone should be able to restore its image. But to do so, Roger Blackwell of Ohio State University thought the company needed to make an admission of regret: "The lawyers will tell them not to admit blame.... But they need to do what Johnson & Johnson did when someone was killed by their product [cyanide-tainted Tylenol]. A credible spokesman got on TV and had tears in his eyes when he spoke." An independent tire dealer who lost $100,000 in sales in 2000, but was confident of a rebound, supported this option: "The American public is quick to forget," he said.[10]

POSTMORTEM

Buyers of Ford Explorers with Firestone tires for years faced far higher risks of deaths and injuries, both in the United States and abroad, than they would have from other models. The *New York Times* reported that the tire defects, and their contribution to accidents, were known in 1996.[11] Not until August 1999 did Ford begin replacing tires on Explorers in Saudi Arabia, calling the step a "customer notification enhancement program." Fourteen fatalities had already been reported. Not until March 2000, after television reports of problems, did federal regulators and the two manufacturers take all this seriously.

---

[9] Grant, "Struggle to Survive," p. H5.

[10] Ibid.

[11] Keith Bradsher, "SUV Tire Defects Were Known in '96 But Not Reported; 190 Died in Next 4 years," *New York Times*, 24 June 2001, p. 1N.

Ford, in its concern with the bottom line, stubbornly refused to admit that anything was wrong with its SUV; meanwhile Firestone couldn't seem to clean up its act in the Decatur, Illinois, plant—and even in some other plants, where carelessness and lack of customer concern prevailed. Minor ethical abuses became major when lives were lost, but the foot-dragging continued until lawyers came on the scene. Then these two companies tried to cover their mistakes with finger-pointing, while a vulnerable public continued to be in jeopardy. Throughout this whole time, saving lives did not apparently have a very high priority. Eventually the consequences came back to haunt the companies, with hundreds of lawsuits, millions of tire recalls, and denigration of their public images.

How could this have been permitted to happen? After all, those in top management were not deliberately vicious men. They were well intentioned, albeit badly misguided. Perhaps their worst sin was first to ignore, and then refuse to admit and try to cover up the increasingly apparent serious risk factors.

Part of the problem was the stubborn mind-set of top executives that nothing was wrong: A few accidents reflected driver carelessness, not a defective product. Neither company would assume the worst scenario: that this was a dangerous product used on a dangerous product that was killing people, and neither Ford nor Firestone could escape blame.

Forty years ago a somewhat similar situation occurred with the GM Corvair, a rear-engine car that exhibited instability under extreme cornering conditions, causing it to flip over. Ralph Nader gained his reputation as a consumer advocate in his condemnation of this "unsafe" car with a best-selling book, *Unsafe at Any Speed.* But GM executives refused to admit there was any problem—until eventually the evidence was overwhelming, lawsuits flourished, and the federal government stepped in with the National Traffic and Motor Vehicle Safety Act of 1966. Among other things, this act required manufacturers to notify customers of any defects or flaws later discovered in their vehicles.

GM executives, like those of Ford and Firestone forty years later, were honorable men. Yet, something seems to happen to the conscience and the moral sensitivity of top executives. They commission actions in their corporate personas that they would hardly dream of doing in their private lives. John DeLorean, former GM executive, was one of the first to note this dichotomy:

> These were not immoral men who were bringing out this car [the Corvair]. These were warm, breathing men with families and children who as private individuals would never have approved [this project] for a minute if they were told, "You are going to kill and injure people with this car." But these same men, in a business atmosphere, where everything is reduced to terms of costs, corporate goals, and production deadlines, were able to approve a product most of them wouldn't have considered approving as individuals.[12]

We have to raise the question: Why this lockstep obsession with sales and profits at all costs? See the Information Box: The "Groupthink" Influence on Unethical Behavior for a discussion of this issue.

[12] J. Patrick Wright, *On a Clear Day You Can See General Motors* (Grosse Point, Mich.: Wright Enterprises, 1979), 5–6.

INFORMATION BOX

THE "GROUPTHINK" INFLUENCE ON UNETHICAL BEHAVIOR

The callousness about "killer" cars would, as John DeLorean theorized, probably never have prevailed if an individual was making the decision outside the corporate environment. But bring in *groupthink*, which is decision by committee, and add to this a high degree of organizational loyalty (versus loyalty to the public interest), and such callousness can manifest itself. Why can the moral standards of groupthink be so much lower than individual moral standards?

Perhaps the answer lies in the "pack mentality" that characterizes certain committees or groups highly committed to organizational goals. All else then becomes subordinated to these goals, being a single-minded perspective. Within any committee, individual responsibility for decision is diluted since this is a committee decision. Furthermore, without the contrary arguments of a strong devil's advocate a follow-the-leader syndrome can take place, with no one willing to oppose the majority views.

But there is more to it than that. Chester Barnard, a business executive, scholar, and philosopher, noted the paradox: People have a number of private moral codes that affect behavior in different situations, and these codes are not always compatible. Codes for private life, regarding family and religion, may be far different from codes for business life. Throughout the history of business, it has not been unusual to find that the scrupulous and God-fearing churchgoer is far different when he or she conducts business during the week: A far lower ethical standard prevails during the week than on the Sabbath. Nor has it been unusual to find that a person can be a paragon of love, understanding, and empathy with his or her family but be totally lacking in such qualities with employees or customers.[13] We might add that even tyrants guilty of the most extreme atrocities, such as Adolf Hitler and Saddam Hussein, have been known to exude great tenderness and consideration for their intimates.

What does it take for a person to resist and not accept the majority viewpoint? What do you think would be the characteristics of such a person? Do you see yourself as such a rebel?

---

[13] Chester I. Barnard, *The Functions of the Executive* (Cambridge, Mass.: Harvard University Press, 1938), 263.

UPDATE—2002

On October 30, 2001, Ford Motor Company announced that Jacques Nasser would be replaced as CEO by William Clay Ford Jr., 44—the first Ford family member to be in charge since 1979. Ford is the son of William Clay Ford Sr., who is the grandson of founder Henry Ford and brother of Henry Ford II. Nasser had been under pressure for months for Ford's loss of market share and tumbling profitability and the adverse publicity of the Explorer.

In December 2001, the newly designed 2002 Ford Explorer received a top score in a crash test from the Insurance Institute for Highway Safety. Changes in the 2002 Explorer to improve passenger protection were part of the automaker's "commitment to continuous improvements," a Ford spokesperson said.[14]

Firestone also bounced back, despite dire predictions of the brand's demise as U.S. operations suffered a $1.7 billion loss in 2001 on top of a $510 million loss in 2000.

Some called this "the most unlikely brand resurrection in marketing history." Much of the credit for the survival was credited to Firestone CEO John Lampe, who crisscrossed the country giving pep talks to hundreds of Firestone's 10,000 dealers. These dealers became fiercely loyal at a time when 75 percent of tire buyers were influenced by dealers' recommendations, according to industry estimates. Several splashy new tires were brought out, including the Firehawk Indy 500, which became a hit with racing fans. "We are selling as many Firestone tires as we've ever sold," one large dealer noted.

With communication improving between the two companies, Lampe could see signs that the rift with Ford was ending, and William Clay Ford even mentioned his great-grandfather Harvey Firestone in a Ford commercial. "It was a very honest thing to do. He didn't have to do that," Lampe observed.[15]

WHAT CAN BE LEARNED?

A Firm Today Must Zealously Guard against Product Liability Suits

Any responsible executive needs to recognize that product liability suits, in today's litigious environment, can even bankrupt a firm. The business arena has become riskier, more fraught with peril for the unwary or the naively unconcerned. Consequently, any firm needs careful and objective testing of any product that can affect customer health and safety. Sometimes such testing may require that production be delayed, even if competition gains some advantage from this delay. The risks of putting an unsafe product on the market outweigh competitive concerns.

Suspicions and Complaints about Product Safety Must Be Thoroughly Investigated

We should learn from this case that immediate and thorough investigation of any suspicions or complaints must be undertaken, regardless not only of the confidence management may have in the product but also of the glowing recommendations of persons whose objectivity could be suspect. To procrastinate or ignore complaints poses what should be unacceptable risks.

Sometimes the root of the problem is not obvious, or is more complex than first thought. In this Ford/Firestone case, objective research should have focused on both the Explorer and the Firestone tires, and how the situation could be remedied to minimize rollovers and save lives.

[14] Christopher Jensen, *Cleveland Plain Dealer,* 12 December 2001, pp. C1, C4.

[15] Todd Zaun, "Defying Expectations, Bridgestone Embarks on a Turnaround, *Wall Street Journal,* 12 March 2002, p. A21; and Jonathan Fahey, "Flats Fixed," *Forbes,* 27 May 2002, pp. 40–41.

The Health and Safety of Customers
Is Entirely Compatible with the Well-being of the Firm

It is a lose-lose situation if this is ignored: The customer is jeopardized, but eventually the firm is, too, as lawsuits grow and damages increase. Why, then, the corporate mind-set of "us versus them"? There should be no conflicting goals. Both win when customer welfare is maximized.

In the Worst Scenario, Go for a Conciliatory Salvage Strategy

Ford and Firestone faced a crossroads by late 1999 and early 2000. Reports of fatalities linked to Ford Explorers and Firestone tires were trickling in, the first occurring in the hot climate of Saudi Arabia, and these were in a matter of months to become a flood. How should a company react?

A salvage strategy can be attempted by toughing it out, trying to combat the bad press, denying culpability, blaming someone else, and resorting to the strongest possible legal defense. This essentially is what Ford opted to do, since it blamed Firestone for everything and spent millions in advertising to promote this contention.

Firestone was more vulnerable since its shredded tires could hardly be denied. It was forced to recall millions of tires, although it stoutly maintained that the cause of the shredding was underinflation and the wrong quality of tire, as well as the Explorer itself. At stake were company reputations, economic positions, viability for Firestone, and, most importantly, the lives of hundreds of users.

Conciliation usually is the better salvage strategy. This involves recognition and full admission of the problem and removal of the risk, even if this involved a full-market withdrawal until the source of the problem could be identified and correction made. Expensive, yes, but far less risky for the viability of the company and certainly for the health of those customers involved.

Neither strategy is without substantial costs. But the first course of action puts major cost consequences in the future, where they may turn out to be vastly greater as legal expenses and damage awards skyrocket. The second course of action poses an immediate impact on profitability, and will not avoid legal expenses, but may save the company and its reputation and return it to profitability in the near future.

Where Blame Is Most Likely Shared, the Solution of the Problem
Lies not in Confrontation but in Cooperation

This is the most grievous component of the violations of the public trust by Ford and Firestone: denial and confrontation, rather than both parties working together to solve the problem of product safety.

CONSIDER

Can you think of additional learning insights?

QUESTIONS

1. Can a firm guarantee complete product safety? Discuss.

2. Based on the information we discussed in this chapter, which company do you think is most to blame for the deaths and injuries? What led you to your conclusion?

3. "If an Explorer driver never checks the tire pressure and drives well above the speed limit, he has no one to blame but himself in an accident—not the vehicle and not the tires." Discuss.

4. Do you think the government should be blamed in the Explorer deaths and injuries? Why or why not?

5. Would you give credence to the "community champion" awards bestowed by the Civil Justice Foundation and given to Alan Hogan in June 2001 for exposing careless tire production? Why or why not?

6. "Admittedly the groupthink mind-set may be responsible for a few unethical and bad decisions, but isn't this mind-set more likely to consider the consequences to the company of delivering unsafe products and to support aggressive corrective action?" Evaluate this.

7. Have you had any experience with a Ford Explorer? If so, what is your perception of its performance and safety?

8. Have you had any experience with Firestone tires? What is your perception of their performance and safety?

HANDS-ON EXERCISES

1. Place yourself in the position of John Lampe, CEO of Firestone, as the crisis worsens and accusations mount. Discuss how you would try to change the climate with Jacques Nasser of Ford from confrontational to cooperative. Be as specific as you can. Do you think you would be successful?

2. Firestone is on its knees after massive tire recalls and monstrous damage suits. You are a consultant brought in to help the firm recover. Be as specific as you can in recommendations, and in the priority of things to do. Make any assumptions you need to, but keep them reasonable. Defend your recommendations. (Do not be swayed by what actually happened. Maybe things could have been done better.)

3. You are a trusted aide of Nasser. Support his confrontational stance with Firestone before the Ford board of directors.

4. *Be a Devil's Advocate.* In a staff meeting the topic comes up that your SUVs have been involved in a number of deaths. The group passes this off as due to reckless drivers. Argue persuasively a contrary position.

TEAM DEBATE EXERCISE

Debate the issue of dropping or keeping the Firestone name. Defend your position and attack the other side.

INVITATION TO RESEARCH

Can you find statistics about how other competing tire companies, particularly Goodyear and Michelin, fared during and after the Firestone recall?

Are Ford and Firestone friends again?

Is the Ford Explorer still the top SUV?

CHAPTER ELEVEN

Perrier—Overresponding to a Crisis

On a Friday in early February 1990, the first news reached Perrier executive suites that traces of benzene had been found in its bottled water. Ronald Davis, president of the Perrier Group of America, ordered a sweeping recall of all bottles in North America. Just a few days later, Source Perrier S.A., the French parent, expanded the recall to the rest of the world while the company sought to identify the source of the problem and correct it.

Although at first view such a reaction to an unexpected crisis seems zealous and the ultimate in customer concern and social responsibility, a deeper study reveals marketing mistakes of major proportions.

BEFORE

In late 1989, Ronald Davis, 43-year-old president of Perrier's U.S. operations, had reason to be pleased. During his 10-year tenure, Perrier's U.S. sales had risen from $40 million to more than $800 million at retail, which was a significant 25 percent of the company's worldwide sales. He was also proud of his firm being depicted in a May 1989 issue of *Fortune* as one of six companies that compete best. *Fortune* captions: "These are companies you don't want to come up against in your worst nightmare. In the businesses they're in, they amass crushing market share."[1]

A company report in 1987 described the French source, a spring in Vergeze, as follows:

> One of Perrier's identifying qualities is its low mineral (particularly sodium) content. This is because the water spends only a short time filtering through minerals. While flowing underground, the water meets gas flowing vertically through porous volcanic rocks. This is how Perrier gets its fizz ... the company assured us that production has never been limited by the source output. The company sells approximately one billion bottles of which 600 million are exported.[2]

---

[1] Bill Saporito, "Companies That Compete Best," *Fortune,* 22 May 1989, pp. 36ff.

[2] B. Facon, *Source Perrier—Company Report,* 13 November 1987, p. 4.

Davis recognized that he was in two businesses, albeit both involved bottled water: (1) sparkling water, in the famous green bottle, which he had been successful in positioning as an adult soft drink with a French mystique, an alternative to soft drinks or alcohol; and (2) still water, a tap-water replacement, with the product delivered to homes and offices and dispensed through watercoolers. This latter business he saw as more resembling package delivery such as UPS and Federal Express, and less akin to pushing soft drinks. Accordingly, he emphasized quality of professional service for his route drivers. While best known for the green-bottled Perrier, a mainstay of most restaurants and bars, the company owned nine other brands of bottled water, including Poland Spring, Great Bear, Calistoga, and Ozarka.

At a price of 300 to 1,200 times that of tap water, bottled water was the fastest growing segment of the U.S. beverage industry (see Table 11.1). Perrier controlled 24 percent of the total U.S. bottled-water business. Of the imported bottled water sector, the green bottle dominated with almost 50 percent of the market, although this market share had fallen when more competitors attempted to push into the rapidly growing market. In the 1980s more than 20 firms had taken a run at the green bottle, but without notable success; these included such behemoths as Coca-Cola, PepsiCo, and Anheuser-Busch. Now Davis was more concerned with expanding the category and was trying to shift the brand's image from chic to healthy, so as to make the brand more acceptable to the "masses."

THE CRISIS

The North American Recall

Davis, as he prepared his five-year plan in early 1990, wrote that competing in the 1990s would require not strategic planning, but "flexibility planning."[3] In retrospect, he seemed to be prophetic.

TABLE 11.1. **Average Annual Growth of Beverage Sales, 1985–1989**

Beverage Type	Percent of Growth
Bottled water	+11.1
Soft drinks	+3.2
Milk	+1.5
Tea	+1.2
Beer	+0.4
Coffee	−0.4
Wine	−2.0
Distilled spirits	−2.6

Source: Beverage Marketing Corporation, as reported in *Fortune,* 23 April 1990, p. 277.

[3] Patricia Sellers, "Perrier Plots Its Comeback," *Fortune,* 23 April 1990, p. 277.

As he was fine-tuning his plan, the first news trickled in that a lab in North Carolina had discovered traces of benzene, a carcinogen, in some of the bottles. That same day, February 9, he ordered Perrier removed from distribution in North America.

Source Perrier officials were soon to inform reporters that the company believed the contamination occurred because an employee had mistakenly used cleaning fluid containing benzene to clean the production-line machinery that fills bottles for North America. Frederik Zimmer, managing director of Source Perrier, said that the machinery in question had been cleaned and repaired over the weekend. But in another news conference, Davis announced that he expected Perrier to be off the market for 2 to 3 months.

Such a long absence was seen by some marketing observers as potentially devastating to Perrier, despite it being the front-runner of the industry. Al Ries, chairman of a consulting firm and well-known business writer, was quoted in the *Wall Street Journal* article as saying: "If I were Perrier, I would make a desperate effort to reduce that time as much as possible, even if I had to fly it in on 747s from France."[4]

Without doubt, competitors were salivating at a chance to pick up market share of the $2.2 billion annual U.S. sales. Major competitors included Evian and Saratoga, both owned by BSN of France, and San Peligrino, an Italian import. In 1989 PepsiCo had begun test marketing $H_2OH!$, and in January 1990, Adolph Coors Company introduced Coors Rocky Mountain Sparkling Water. The Perrier absence was expected to accelerate their market entry.

Despite competitive glee at the misfortune of Perrier, some in the industry were concerned. They feared that consumers would forsake bottle water altogether, with its purity now being questioned. Would the public be as willing to pay a substantial premium for any bottled brand? See the Information Box: Is Quality Best Judged by Price? for a discussion of the relationship between *price and quality*.

Worldwide Recall

A few days later, the other shoe fell. After reports of benzene being found in Perrier bottles in Holland and Denmark, Source Perrier expanded its North American recall to the rest of the world on February 14 and acknowledged that all production lines for its sparkling water had been contaminated in recent months by tiny amounts of benzene.

At a news conference in Paris, company officials acknowledged for the first time that benzene occurs naturally in Perrier water and that the current problem came about because workers failed to replace filters designed to remove it. This was a critical reversal of previous statements that the water was tainted only because an employee mistakenly used cleaning fluid containing benzene to clean machinery. Zimmer even went further, revealing that Perrier water naturally contains several gases, including benzene, that have to be filtered out.

The company insisted that its famous spring was unpolluted. But now questions were being raised about this and other contradictory statements made about

---

[4] Alix M. Freedman and Thomas R. King, "Perrier's Strategy in the Wake of Recall," *Wall Street Journal*, 12 February 1990, p. B1.

INFORMATION BOX

IS QUALITY BEST JUDGED BY PRICE?

We as consumers have difficulty in judging the quality of competing products. With their complex characteristics and hidden ingredients, we cannot rely on our own expertise to determine the best. So what sources of information can we use? We can rely on our past experiences with the brand; we can be swayed by our friends and neighbors, we might be influenced by advertising and salespeople (but more and more we become skeptical of their claims); we can study *Consumer Reports* and other consumer information publications. But all of these sources are flawed in that the experience and information usually is dated, and is a limited sample—usually of one—so that we can seriously question how representative the experience is.

Most people judge quality by price: the higher the price, the better the quality. But such a price/quality perception sets us up. While it may be valid, it also may not be. With the publicity about the impurity of Perrier, we are brought to the realization that paying many times the price of tap water gives us no assurance of better quality, as measured by purity.

Is a price/quality misperception limited mostly to bottled water, do you think? How about liquor? Designer clothes? Perfume?

the problem. For example, how widespread was the contamination? Was benzene a naturally occurring phenomenon, or does it represent man-made pollution? Suspicions were tending toward the man-made origin. While benzene occurs naturally in certain foods, it is more commonly found as a petroleum-based distillate used in many manufacturing processes.

Particularly surprising was the rather nonchalant attitude of Perrier executives. Zimmer, the president, even suggested that "all this publicity helps build the brand's renown."[5]

Ronald Davis was quick to point out that the company did not have to recall its entire 70-million-bottle U.S. inventory. After all, health officials both in the U.S. and France had noted that the benzene levels found in Perrier did not pose any significant health risk. The major risk really was to the image of Perrier: it had gone to great lengths to establish its water as naturally pure. And while not particularly dangerous, it was certainly not naturally pure—as all the world was finding out from the publicity about it. Add to this the undermining of the major attraction of bottled water that it was safer than ordinary tap water, and the recall and subsequent publicity assumed more ominous proportions.

[5] Alix M. Freedman and Thomas R. King, "Perrier Expands North American Recall to Rest of Globe," *Wall Street Journal,* 15 February 1990, p. B1.

THE COMEBACK

It took until mid-July before Perrier was again widely available in the United States; this was 5 months after the recall rather than the expected 3 months. Still, Davis was confident that Perrier's sales would return to 85 percent of normal by the end of 1991. Actually, he was more worried about short supply than demand. He was not sure the one spring in Vergeze, France, would be able to replace the world's supply before the beginning of 1991.

Davis's confidence in the durability of the demand stemmed from his clout with retailers, where the brand does a majority of its business. He believed the brand's good reputation, coupled with the other brands marketed by Perrier that had replaced some of the supermarket space relinquished by Perrier, would bring quick renewal. To help this, he wrote letters to 550 CEOs of retail firms, pledging heavy promotional spending. The marketing budget was increased from $6 million to $25 million for 1990, with $16 million going into advertising and the rest into promotions and special events. A highly visible discount strategy was instituted, which included a buy-two, get-one-free offer. Supermarket prices had dropped, with bottles now going for $0.89 to $0.99, down from $1.09 to $1.19. To win back restaurant business, a new 52-member sales force supplemented distributor efforts. However, a setback of sorts was the Food and Drug Administration order to drop the words "naturally sparkling" from Perrier labels.

Still, a recent consumer survey indicated that 84 percent of Perrier's U.S. drinkers intended to buy the product again.[6] Davis could also take heart from the less-than-aggressive actions of his competitors during the hiatus. None appeared to have strongly reacted, although most improved their sales considerably. The smaller competitors proved to be short of marketing money and bottling capacity and apparently were fearful that a beleaguered Perrier would negatively affect the overall market. Big competitors, such as PepsiCo and Coors, who were introducing other bottled waters, somehow also appeared reluctant to move in aggressively.

CONSEQUENCES

By the end of 1990, however, it was clear that Perrier was not regaining market position as quickly and completely as Davis had hoped. Now more aggressive competitors were emerging. Some, such as Saratoga, La Croix, and Quibell, had experienced major windfalls in the wake of the recall. Evian, in particular, a nonsparkling water produced by the French firm BSN S.A., was the biggest winner. Through aggressive marketing and advertising it had replaced Perrier by the end of 1990 as the top-selling imported bottled water.

Perrier's sales had reached only 60 percent of prerecall levels, and its share of the imported bottled-water market had sunk to 20.7 percent from the 44.8 percent of one year earlier. While the Perrier Group of America expected to report a sales gain

---

[6] Sellers, p. 278.

for 1990 of 3.7 percent, this was largely because of the strong performance of such domestic brands as Calistoga and Poland Spring.

Particularly worrisome for Davis was the slow return of Perrier to bars and restaurants, which had formerly accounted for about 35 percent of its sales. A sampling of comments of restaurant managers, as reported in such prestigious papers as the *Wall Street Journal* and *Washington Post,* were far from encouraging. For example:

> The manager of the notable Four Seasons restaurant in New York City said his patrons had begun to shift to San Pellegrino: "I think Perrier is finished," he said. "We can write it off."[7]

> The general manager of Spago Restaurant in Los Angeles said: "Now consumers have decided that other brands are better or at least as good, so Perrier no longer holds the monopoly on water." And Spago no longer carries Perrier.[8]

> Le Pavillon restaurant in Washington, D.C., switched to Quibell during the recall, and has not gone back to Perrier. "Customers still ask for Perrier, but it's a generic term like Kleenex, and customers aren't unhappy to get a substitute."[9]

Evian

David Daniel, 34, was Evian's U.S. CEO since June 1988. He joined the company in 1987 as the first director of marketing at a time when the American subsidiary was a two-person operation. By 1990 there were 100 employees.

Daniel came from PepsiCo, and his background was marketing. He saw Evian's sphere to be portable water that is good for you, a position well situated to capitalize on the health movement. He was particularly interested in broadening the distribution of Evian, and he sought out soft-drink and beer distributors, showing them that their basic industries were only growing at 1 to 3 percent a year, while bottled water was growing at over 10 percent per year. In 1989, Evian sales doubled to $65 million, with $100 million in sight for 1990. The attractiveness of such growth to these distributors was of no small moment.

Daniel made Evian the most expensive water on the market. He saw the price as helping Evian occupy a certain slot in the consumer's mind—remember the price/quality perception discussed earlier. For example, at a fancy grocery in New York's West Village, a 1-liter bottle of Evian sold for $2.50; the city charges a fraction of a penny for a gallon of tap water[10]—a lot of perceived quality in that. This type of pricing along with the packaging that made Evian portable—plastic nonbreakable bottles and reusable caps—were seen as keys in the selling of bottled water.

Then, late in 1990, Evian benefited greatly from the Persian Gulf War, with free publicity from several newspapers and from all three national TV networks: GIs were shown gulping water from Evian bottles.

---

[7] Freedman and King, "Perrier's Strategy," p. B3.

[8] Alix M. Freedman, "Perrier Finds Mystique Hard to Restore," *Wall Street Journal,* 1 December 1990, p. B1.

[9] Lori Silver, "Perrier Crowd Not Taking the Waters," *Washington Post,* 4 July 1990, p. 1.

[10] Seth Lubove, "Perched Between Perrier and Tap," *Forbes,* 14 May 1990, p. 120.

ANALYSIS

Was the massive recall overkill, or was it a prudent necessity? Did it show a concerned corporate citizen, or rather a panicked executive? Were consumers impressed with the responsibleness of the company, or were they more focused on its carelessness? These questions are all directed at the basic impact of the recall and the subsequent actions and admissions: Was it to have favorable, neutral, or unfavorable public reactions?

Perrier did *not* have to recall its product. It was a North Carolina county laboratory that first noticed the excessive amounts of benzene in Perrier and reported its findings to the state authorities. The state agriculture and health departments did not believe that a recall was necessary, but they did insist on issuing a health advisory, warning that Perrier should not be consumed until further tests could be made. It was the state's plan to issue the health advisory that was reported to Davis on the afternoon of the critical day, February 9. He announced the recall later that same day.

ISSUE BOX

ARE BOTTLED WATER CLAIMS BUNK?[11]

The bottled water industry came under serious attack in April 1991. As if the Perrier massive recall was not enough, now a congressional panel with wide media coverage accused the Food and Drug Administration of "inexcusably negligent and complacent oversight of the bottled-water industry." Despite its high price, the panel said, bottled water may be less safe than tap water. The panel noted that although consumers pay 300 to 1,200 times more for bottled water than for tap water, 25 percent of all bottled water comes from public drinking water sources. For example:

> Lithia Springs Water Company touts its "world's finest" bottled mineral water as "naturally pure" and recommends its special Love Water as an "invigorator" before bedtime. Yet, it was found to be tainted with bacteria.
>
> Artisia Waters, Inc., promotes its "100% pure sparkling Texas Natural Water." But it comes from the same underground source that San Antonio uses for its municipal water supply.

Furthermore, the FDA released a list of 22 bottled-water recalls because of contaminants such as kerosene and mold. For the most part, these went unnoticed by consumers, being overshadowed by the Perrier recall.

At issue: Are we being hoodwinked? Debate two positions: (1) the bottled-water industry really is a throwback to the snake-oil charlatans of the last century; and (2) a few unscrupulous or careless bottlers are denigrating the image of the entire industry, an industry that is primarily focused on health and purity.

---

[11] Examples are taken from Bruce Ingersoll, "FDA Finds Bunk in Bottled-Water Claims," *Wall Street Journal,* 10 April 1991, p. B1.

We are left to wonder: Perhaps a full and complete recall was not needed. Perhaps things could have been worked out entirely satisfactorily with less drastic measures. Given that a recall meant a 3- to 5-month absence from the marketplace, should it not have been the action of last resort?

But let us consider Davis's thought process on that ill-fated afternoon in February. He did not know the source of the problem; he certainly had no reason to suspect that it emanated from the spring in southern France or that it was a worldwide problem. He probably considered it of less magnitude. Perhaps he thought of the total North American recall as a gesture showing the concerned thinking of the management of this product that had developed such a reputation of health and purity and, yes, status. Only with the experience after the fact do we know the error of this decision: that it was to result in a 5-month absence from the hotly competitive market; that it was to result in revelations of far more serious implications than a simple employee error or even a natural occurrence largely beyond the company's control.

So, perhaps Davis's drastic decision was fully justified and prudent. But it turned out to be confounded by circumstances he did not envision.

A lengthy complete absence from the marketplace is a catastrophe of rather monumental proportions—all the more so for a product that is habitually and frequently consumed, in Perrier's case, sometimes several times daily. Such an absence forces even the most loyal customers to establish new patterns of behavior, in this case switching brands. Once behavior becomes habituated, at least for some people, a change back becomes less likely. This is especially true if the competitive offerings are reasonably similar and acceptable. Anything that Perrier could have done to lessen the time away from the market would have been desirable—regardless of expense.

Perhaps the biggest problem for Perrier concerned the false impressions, and even outright deception, that the company had conveyed regarding the purity of its product. Now, in the wake of this total recall and the accompanying publicity, all was laid bare. Company officials in France had to own up that the contamination had occurred "in recent months," and not suddenly and unexpectedly on February 9.

But more than this, under intense pressure from the media to explain what caused the problem, Source Perrier ultimately conceded that its water does not bubble up pure, already carbonated and ready to drink, from its renowned spring in southern France. Instead, contrary to the image that it had spent tens of millions of dollars to promote, the company extracts the water and carbon dioxide gas separately, and must pipe the gas through charcoal filters before combining it mechanically with the water to give the fizz. Without the filters, Perrier water would contain benzene and, even worse, would taste like rotten eggs.

Finally, the public relations efforts were flawed. Source Perrier officials issued a confusing series of public statements and clarifications. Early on, the company tried to maintain the mystique of Perrier by concealing information about the cause of the contamination and by blaming it on a mistake by cleaning personnel in using an oily rag, which could have contained some benzene, to wipe equipment used for bottles to be shipped to the United States. But the spokespeople knew the problem was more fundamental than that.

An aura of nonchalance was conveyed by corporate executives and reported in the press. This was hardly in keeping with a serious problem having to do with the possible safety of customers. Furthermore, Source Perrier relied mainly on media reports to convey information to consumers. Misinformation and rumors are more likely with this approach to public relations than in a more proactive strategy of direct company advertisement and statements.

The reputation of Perrier was on the ropes. And top management seemed unconcerned about the probability of severe public image damage. The Information Box: Ignoring Possible Negative Image Consequences discusses the topic of ignoring possible image damage.

UPDATE—2001

Despite occasional publicity about the rip-off accomplished by the bottled-water industry—charging exorbitant prices for water little better than tap water—public demand has continued to grow. In 2001 soft-drink sales were flat; but bottled-water sales were up 11.5 percent, continuing the double-digit rate of the preceding decade. Bottled water was a $5.2 billion industry in 2001, in line to surpass coffee and tea and become second only to soft drinks in liquid consumption sales. More than nine hundred brands of bottled water were on the market. With the marketing clout of major firms, Pepsi's Aquafina and Coke's Dasani were becoming U.S. market leaders. This boom reflected a remarkable turnabout from 1980, when sales of Perrier fizzy water were limited mostly to upscale restaurants.

INFORMATION BOX

IGNORING POSSIBLE NEGATIVE IMAGE CONSEQUENCES

We can identify several factors that induce a firm to ignore public image considerations until sometimes too late. First, a firm's public image often makes a nonspecific impact on company performance. The cause-and-effect relationship of a deteriorating image is virtually impossible to assess, at least until and unless image problems worsen. Image consequences may be downplayed because management is unable to single out the specific profit impact.

Second, an organization's image is not easily and definitively measured. Although some tools are available for tracking public opinion, they tend to be imprecise and of uncertain validity. Consequently, image studies are often spurned or given short shrift relative to more quantitative measures of performance.

Third, it is difficult to determine the effectiveness of image-building efforts. While firms may spend thousands, and even millions, of dollars for institutional and image-building advertising, measures of the effectiveness of such expenditures are inexact and also of questionable validity. For example, a survey may be taken of attitudes of a group of people before and after the image-building campaign is run. Presumably if a few more people profess to be favorably disposed toward the company after the campaign than before, this is an indication of its success. But an executive can question how much this really translates into sales and profits.

Given the near impossibility of measuring the effectiveness of image-enhancing promotion, how do you account for the prevalence of institutional advertising, even among firms that have no image problems?

Critical studies still found the product no cleaner or safer than big-city tap water; a third of the bottles sampled were contaminated by synthetic chemicals, bacteria, and arsenic. Out of the average $1.50 spent for a bottle of water, 90 percent went for bottling, packaging, marketing, retailing, and other expenses. The industry in defense claimed that the federal Centers for Disease Control had never found a U.S. outbreak of disease or illness linked to bottled water.

Source: Lance Gay, "Bottlers Tap Profits from Designer Water," Scripps Howard reported in *Cleveland Plain Dealer,* 11 September 2001, pp. Al, A8.

WHAT CAN BE LEARNED?

Exiting a Market for Several Months or More Poses Critical Risks, Particularly for a Habitually Consumed Product

To allow new habits to be established and new loyalties to be created not only among consumers but also dealers may be impossible to fully recover from. This is especially true if competing products are comparable, and if competitors are aggressive in seizing the proffered opportunity. Since a front-runner is a target anyway, abandoning the battlefield simply invites competitive takeover.

Deception Discovered and Grudgingly Admitted Destroys a Mystique

No mystique is forever. Consumer preferences change, competitors become more skilled at countering, or perhaps a firm becomes complacent in its quality control or innovative technology. These conditions act to nibble away at a mystique and eventually destroy it. As in the case of Perrier, where long-believed images of a product, its healthfulness and purity, are suddenly revealed to be false—that the advertising was less than candid and was even deceptive—then any mystique comes tumbling down and is unlikely to ever be regained. This scenario can only be avoided if the publicity about the deception or misdeed is not widespread. But, with a popular product such as Perrier, publicity reaches beyond business journals to the popular press. Such is the fate of large, well-known firms.

A Price/Quality Misperception Strongly Exists

Without doubt, most consumers judge quality by price: the higher the price, the higher the quality. Is a $2.50 liter of Evian better quality than a gallon of tap water costing a fraction of a cent? Perhaps. But is it a hundred times better? And yet many people embrace the misconception that price is the key indicator of quality, and are consequently taken advantage of every day.

An Industry Catering to Health Is Particularly Vulnerable to a Few Unscrupulous Operators

We, the general public, are particularly vulnerable to claims for better health, beauty, and youthfulness. It is human nature to reach out, hopefully, for the false promises that can be made about such important personal concerns. We become gullible in our desire to find ways to change our condition. And so we have become victims of quacks and snake-oil charmers through the ages. Governmental agencies try to exercise strong monitoring in these areas, but budgets are limited, and all claims cannot be investigated. As recent congressional scrutiny has revealed, the bottled-water industry had long been overlooked by governmental watchdogs. Now this is changing, thanks at least partly to the Perrier recall.

Should an Organization Have a Crisis-Management Team?

Perrier did a poor job in its crisis management. Would a more formal organizational unit devoted to this have handled things better, instead of leaving it to top executives unskilled in handling catastrophes? The issue can hardly be answered simply and all-inclusively. Crises occur rarely; and a serious crisis may never happen to a particular organization. A crisis team then would have to be composed of executives and staff who have other primary responsibilities. And their decisions and actions under fire may be no better than a less formal arrangement. For severe crises—and Perrier's was certainly that—top executives who bear the ultimate responsibility therefore have to be the final decision makers. Some will be cooler under fire than others, but this usually cannot be fully ascertained until the crisis occurs. More desirable for most organizations would seem to be contingency plans, with plans formulated for various occurrences, including the worst scenarios. With such action plans drawn up under more normal conditions, better judgments are likely to result.

CONSIDER

Can you think of other learning insights from this case?

QUESTIONS

1. How could the public relations efforts of Perrier have been better handled?
2. Discuss the desirability of Perrier's price-cutting during its comeback.
3. Whom do you see as the primary customers for Perrier? For Evian? For other bottled waters? Are these segments likely to be enduring in their commitment to bottled water?
4. Why do you think the big firms, such as Coca-Cola, PepsiCo, and Coors, have been so slow and unaggressive in entering the bottled-water market?
5. Are we being hoodwinked by bottled-water claims and images?
6. "The success of bottled water in the United States, unlike the situation in many countries of the world where bottled water is often essential for good health, attests to the power of advertising." Evaluate this statement.
7. Is the consumer appeal of bottled water largely attributable to an image developed of sophistication and status?

HANDS-ON EXERCISES

1. Put yourself in the position of Ronald Davis on the afternoon of February 9, 1990. The first report of benzene found by a Carolina lab has just come in. What would you do? Be as specific as you can, and describe the logic behind your decisions.

2. How would you attempt to build up or resurrect the mystique of Perrier after the recall?

TEAM DEBATE EXERCISE

Debate the issue of extreme measures (a massive recall) undertaken in a product safety situation versus more moderate reactions (a modest recall). Consider as many aspects of this issue as you can, and make educated judgments of various probable consumer and governmental reactions.

INVITATION TO RESEARCH

What is the popularity of bottled water today? Has it increased or lessened since the events described? Has Perrier regained market position? Where are the biggest markets for bottled water?

CHAPTER TWELVE

United Way—A Not-for-Profit Tries to Cope with Image Destruction

*T*he United Way, the preeminent charitable organization in the United States, celebrated its 100-year anniversary in 1987. It had evolved from local community chests, and its strategy for fund raising had proven highly effective: funding local charities through payroll deductions. The good it did seemed unassailable.

Abruptly in 1992, the image that United Way had created was jolted by revelations from investigative reporters of free spending and other questionable deeds of its greatest builder and president, William Aramony. A major point of public concern was Aramony's salary and uncontrolled perks in a lifestyle that seemed inappropriate for the head of a charitable organization that depended mostly on contributions from working people.

We are left to question the callousness and lack of concern with the public image of such a major charitable and not-for-profit entity. After all, unlike business firms that offer products or services to potential customers, charitable organizations depend on contributions that people give freely out of a desire to help society, with no tangible personal benefits. An image of high integrity and honest dealings without any semblance of corruption or privilege would seem essential for such organizations.

THE STATURE AND ACCOMPLISHMENTS OF THE UNITED WAY

For its 100-year anniversary, then President Ronald Reagan summed up what the United Way stood for (see the following page).

Organizing the United Way as the umbrella charity to fund other local charities through payroll deductions established a most effective means of fund-raising. As a not-for-profit marketer, the United Way became the recipient of 90 percent of all charitable donations. Employers sometimes used extreme pressure to achieve 100 percent participation of employees, which qualified companies for organizational

December 10, 1986

United Way Centennial, 1887–1987
By The President Of The United States Of America
A Proclamation

Since earliest times, we Americans have joined together to help each other and to strengthen our communities. Our deep-roots spirit of caring, of neighbor helping neighbor, has become an American trademark—and an American way of life. Over the years, our generous and inventive people have created an ingenious network of voluntary organizations to help give help where help is needed.

United Way gives that help very well indeed, and truly exemplifies our spirit of voluntarism. United Way has been a helping force in America right from the first community-wide fund-raising campaign in Denver, Colorado, in 1887. Today, more than 2,200 local United Ways across the land raise funds for more than 37,000 voluntary groups that assist millions of people.

The United Way of caring allows volunteers from all walks of life to effectively meet critical needs and solve community problems. At the centennial of the founding of this indispensable voluntary group, it is most fitting that we Americans recognize and commend all the good United Way has done and continues to do.

The congress, by Public Law 99–612, has expressed gratitude to United Way, congratulated it, and applauded and encouraged its fine work and its goals.

NOW, THEREFORE, I, RONALD REAGAN, President of the United States of America, by virtue of the authority vested in me by the Constitution and laws of the United States, do hereby proclaim heartfelt thanks to a century of Americans who have shaped and supported United Way, and encourage the continuation of its efforts.

IN WITNESS WHEREOF, I have hereunto set my hand this tenth day of December, in the year of our Lord nineteen hundred and eighty-six, and of the independence of the United States of America the two hundred and eleventh.

Ronald Reagan

bonuses. Business organizations achieved further cooperation by involving their executives as leaders of annual campaigns, amid widespread publicity. It would consequently cause such an executive acute loss of face if his or her own organization did not go "over the top" in meeting campaign goals. A local United Way executive admitted that "if participation is 100 percent, it means someone has been coerced."[1]

---

[1] Susan Garland, "Keeping a Sharper Eye on Those Who Pass the Hat," *Business Week,* 16 March 1992, p. 39.

For many years, except for some tight-lipped gripes of corporate employees, the organization moved smoothly along, generally increasing local contributions every year, although the needs for charitable contributions invariably increased all the more.

The national organization, United Way of America (UWA), is a separate corporation and has no direct control over the approximately 2,200 local United Ways. But most of the locals voluntarily contributed 1 cent on the dollar of all funds they collected. In return, the national organization provided training and promoted local United Way agencies through advertising and other marketing efforts.

Much of the success of the United Way movement in becoming the largest and most respected charity in the United States was due to the 22 years of William Aramony's leadership of the national organization. When he first took over, the United Ways were not operating under a common name. He built a nationwide network of agencies, all operating under the same name and all using the same logo of outstretched hands, which became nationally recognized as the symbol of charitable giving. Unfortunately, in 1992 an exposé of Aramony's lavish lifestyle, as well as other questionable dealings, led to his downfall and burdened local United Ways with serious difficulties in fund-raising.

WILLIAM ARAMONY

During Aramony's tenure, United Way contributions increased from $787 million in 1970 to $3 billion in 1990. He increased his headquarters' budget from less than $3 million to $29 million in 1991. Of this, $24 million came from the local United Ways, with the rest coming from corporate grants, investment income, and consulting.[2] He built up the headquarters' staff to 275 employees. Figure 12.1 shows the organizational chart as of 1987.

Aramony moved comfortably among the most influential people in our society. He attracted a prestigious board of governors, many of these top executives from America's largest corporations, with only 3 of the 37 from not-for-profit organizations. The board was chaired by John Akers, chairman and CEO of IBM. Other board members included Edward A. Brennan, CEO of Sears; James D. Robinson III, CEO of American Express; and Paul J. Tagliabue, commissioner of the National Football League. The presence on the board of such top executives brought prestige to United Way and spurred contributions from some of the largest and most visible organizations in the United States.

Aramony was the highest paid executive in the charity field. In 1992 his compensation package was $463,000—nearly double that of the next highest paid executive in the industry, Dudley H. Hafner of the American Heart Association.[3] The board fully supported Aramony, regularly giving him 6 percent annual raises.[4]

---

[2] Charles E. Shepard, "Perks, Privileges and Power in a Nonprofit World," *Washington Post,* 16 February 1992, p. A38.

[3] Shepard, p. A38; and Charles E. Shepard, "United Way of America President Is Urged to Resign," *Washington Post,* 27 February 1992, p. A1.

[4] Joseph Finder, "Charity Case," *New Republic,* 4 May 1992, p. 11.

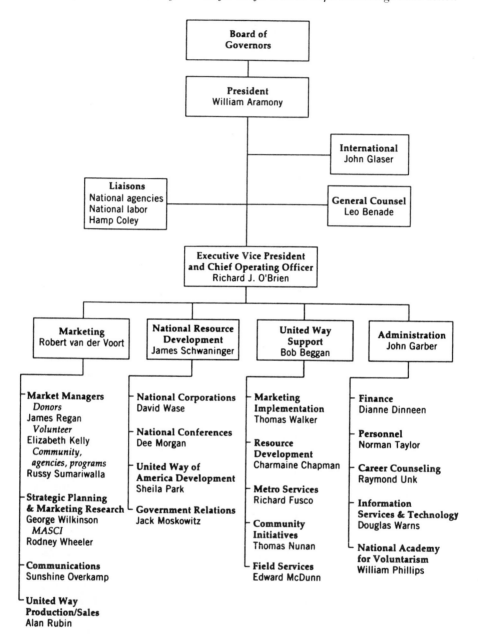

Figure 12.1. Organizational chart, United Way of America, 1987.

Source: E.L. Brilliant, "Appendix B," *United Way: Dilemmas of Organized Charity* (New York: Columbia University Press, 1990) p. 272.

Investigative Disclosures

The *Washington Post* began investigating Aramony's tenure as president of United Way of America in 1991, raising questions about his high salary, travel habits, possible cronyism, and dubious relations with five spinoff companies. In February 1992 it released the following information of Aramony's expense charges:[5]

- Aramony had charged $92,265 in limousine expenses to the charity during the previous five years.
- He had charged $40,762 on airfare for the supersonic Concorde.
- He had charged more than $72,000 on international airfare, which included first class flights for himself, his wife, and others.
- He had charged thousands more for personal trips, gifts, and luxuries.
- He had made 29 trips to Las Vegas between 1988 and 1991.
- He had expensed 49 journeys to Gainesville, Florida, the home of his daughter and a woman with whom he had had a relationship.
- He had allegedly approved a $2 million loan to a firm run by his chief financial officer.
- He had approved the diversion of donors' money to questionable spin-off organizations run by long-time aides and had provided benefits to family members as well.
- He had passed tens of thousands of dollars in consulting contracts from the UWA to friends and associates.

United Way of America's corporate policy prohibited the hiring of family members within the actual organization, but Aramony skirted the direct violation by hiring friends and relatives as consultants within the spin-off companies. The United Way paid hundreds of thousands of dollars in consulting fees, for example, to two aides in vaguely documented and even undocumented business transactions.

The use of spin-off companies provided flexible maneuvering. One of the spin-off companies Aramony created to provide travel and bulk purchasing for United Way chapters purchased a $430,000 condominium in Manhattan and a $125,000 apartment in Coral Gables, Florida, for use by Aramony. Another of the spin-off companies hired Aramony's son, Robert Aramony, as its president. Loans and money transfers between the spin-off companies and the national organization raised questions. No records showed that the board members had been given the opportunity to approve such loans and transfers.[6]

---

[5] Shepard, "Perks, Privileges and Power"; Shepard, "Urged to Resign"; Kathleen Teltsch, "United Way Awaits Inquiry on its President's Practices," *New York Times*, 24 February 1992, p. A12 (L); Charles E. Shepard, "United Way Report Criticizes Ex-Leader's Lavish Lifestyle," *Washington Post*, 4 April 1992, p. A1.

[6] Shepard, "Perks, Privileges and Power," A38.

CONSEQUENCES

When the information about Aramony's salary and expenses became public, reaction was severe. Stanley C. Gault, CEO of Goodyear Tire & Rubber Co., asked, "Where was the board? The outside auditors?"[7] Robert O. Bothwell, executive director of the National Committee for Responsive Philanthropy, said, "I think it is obscene that he is making that kind of salary and asking people who are making $10,000 a year to give 5 percent of their income."[8] At this point, let us examine the issue of executive compensation: Are many executives overpaid? See the Issue Box: Executive Compensation: Is it Too Much?

ISSUE BOX

EXECUTIVE COMPENSATION: IS IT TOO MUCH?

A controversy is mounting over multimillion-dollar annual compensations of corporate executives. For example, in 1992 the average annual pay of CEOs was $3,842,247; the 20 highest paid ranged from over $11 million to a mind-boggling $127 million (for Thomas F. Frist, Jr., of Hospital Corporation of America).[9]

Activist shareholders, including some large mutual and pension funds, began protesting pay practices, especially for top executives of those firms that were not even doing well. New disclosure rules imposed in 1993 by the Securities & Exchange Commission (SEC) spotlighted questionable executive-pay practices. In the past, complacent boards, themselves well paid and often closely aligned with the top executives of the organizations, condoned liberal compensations. Now this may be changing. Still, the major argument supporting high executive compensations is that compared to some entertainers' and athletes', their salaries are modest. And are their responsibilities not far greater than those of any entertainer or athlete?

In light of the for-profit executive compensations, Aramony's salary was modest. And results were on his side: He made $369,000 in basic salary while raising $3 billion; Lee Iacocca, on the other hand, made $3 million while Chrysler lost $795 million. Where is the justice?

Undoubtedly as head of a large for-profit corporation Aramony could have earned several zeros more in compensation and perks, with no raised eyebrows. But is the situation different for a not-for-profit organization? Especially when revenues are derived from donations of millions of people of modest means? This is a real controversy. On one side, shouldn't a charity be willing to pay for the professional competence to run the organization as effectively as possible? But how do revelations of high compensation affect the public image and fund-raising marketing of such not-for-profit organizations?

What is your position regarding Aramony's compensation and perks, relative to the many times greater compensations of for-profit executives?

---

[9] John A. Byrne, "Executive Pay: The Party Ain't Over Yet," *Business Week*, 26 April 1993, pp. 56–64.

---

[7] Susan Garland, p. 39.

[8] Felicity Barringer, "United Way Head Is Forced Out In a Furor Over His Lavish Style," *New York Times*, 28 February 1992, p. A1.

As a major consequence of the scandal, some United Way locals withheld their funds, at least pending a thorough investigation of the allegations. John Akers, chairman of the board, noted that by March 7, 1992, dues payments were running 20 percent behind those of the previous year, and he admitted, "I don't think this process that the United Way of America is going through, or Mr. Aramony is going through, is a process that's bestowing a lot of honor."[10]

In addition to the decrease in dues payments, UWA was in danger of having its not-for-profit status revoked by the Internal Revenue Service due to the relationship of loans made to the spin-off companies. For example, it loaned $2 million to a spin-off corporation of which UWA's chief financial officer was a director—a violation of not-for-profit corporate law. UWA also guaranteed a bank loan taken out by one of the spin-offs, another violation of not-for-profit corporate law.[11]

The adverse publicity benefitted competing charities, such as Earth Share, an environmental group. United Way, at one time the only major organization to receive contributions through payroll deductions, now found itself losing market share to other charities able to garner contributions in the same manner. All the building that William Aramony had done for the United Way as the primary player in the American charitable industry was now in danger of disintegration owing to his uncontrolled excesses.

On February 28, amid mounting pressure from local chapters threatening to withhold their annual dues, Aramony resigned. In August 1992 the United Way board of directors hired Elaine Chao, director of the Peace Corps, to replace Aramony.

ELAINE CHAO

Chao's story is one of great achievement for one only 39 years old. She is the oldest of six daughters in a family that came to California from Taiwan when Elaine was 8 years old. She did not know a word of English. Through hard work, the family prospered. "Despite the difficulties … we had tremendous optimism in the basic goodness of this country, that people are decent here, that we would be given a fair opportunity to demonstrate our abilities," she told an interviewer.[12] Chao's parents instilled in their six daughters the conviction that they could do anything they set their minds to, and the daughters all went to prestigious universities.

Elaine Chao earned an economics degree from Mount Holyoke in 1975, then went on for a Harvard MBA. She was a White House fellow, an international banker, chair of the Federal Maritime Commission, deputy secretary of the U.S. Transportation Department, and director of the Peace Corps before accepting the presidency of the United Way of America.

Chao's salary was $195,000, less than one-half that of Aramony. She cut budgets and staffs: no transatlantic flights on the Concorde, no limousine service, no plush condominiums. She expanded the board of governors to include more local representatives, and she established committees on ethics and finance. Still, she had no illusions

[10] Felicity Barringer, "United Way Head Tries to Restore Trust," *New York Times*, 7 March 1992, p. 8L.

[11] Shepard, "Perks, Privileges and Power," p. A38; Charles E. Shepard, "United Way Chief Says He Will Retire," *Washington Post*, 28 February 1992, p. A1.

[12] "United Way Chief Dedicated," *Cleveland Plain Dealer*, 28 March 1993, p. 24-A.f.

about her job: "Trust and confidence once damaged will take a great deal of effort and time to heal."[13] The Information Box: Public Image for Not-for-Profit Organizations discusses the particular importance of the public image for not-for-profit agencies.

A Local United Way's Concerns

In April 1993, for the second time in a year, United Way of Greater Lorain County (Ohio) withdrew from the United Way of America. The board of the local chapter was still concerned about the financial stability and accountability of the national agency.

INFORMATION BOX

PUBLIC IMAGE FOR NOT-FOR-PROFIT ORGANIZATIONS

Product-oriented firms ought to be concerned and protective of their public image; even more so not-for-profit organizations such as schools, police departments, hospitals, politicians, and, most of all, charitable organizations, should be concerned. Let us consider here the importance of public image for representative not-for-profits.

Large city police departments often have a poor image among important segments of the population. The need to improve this image is hardly less important than for a manufacturer faced with a deteriorating brand image. A police department can develop a "marketing" campaign to win friends; examples of possible activities aimed at creating a better image are promoting tours and open houses of police stations, crime laboratories, police lineups, and cells; speaking at schools; and sponsoring recreation projects, such as a day at the ballpark for youngsters.

Public school systems, faced with taxpayers' revolts against mounting costs and image damage owing to teacher strikes, need conscious effort to improve their image in order to obtain more public support and funds.

Many nonbusiness organizations and institutions, such as hospitals, governmental bodies, even labor unions, have grown self-serving, dominated by a bureaucratic mentality so that perfunctory and callous treatment is the rule and the image is in the pits. Improvement of the image can come only through a greater emphasis on satisfying the public's needs.

Not-for-profits are particularly vulnerable to public image problems because they may depend solely on voluntary support. The need to be untainted by any scandal becomes crucial. In particular, great care should be exerted that contributions are being spent wisely and equitably, that overhead costs are kept reasonable, and that no opportunities exist for fraud and other misdeeds. The threat of investigative reporting must be feared and guarded against.

How can a not-for-profit organization be absolutely assured that moneys are not being misspent and that there are no ripoffs?

---

[13] Ibid.

In particular, it was concerned about the retirement settlement for Aramony. A significant "golden parachute" retirement package was being negotiated by the national board and Aramony; it was in the neighborhood of $4 million. Learning of this triggered the decision to again withdraw from UWA.

There were other reasons as well for this decision. The national agency was falling far short of its projected budget, as only 890 of the 1,400 affiliates that had paid membership dues two years before were still paying. Roy Church, president of the Lorain Agency, explained their decision: "Since February ... it has become clear that United Way of America's financial stability and ability to assist locals has been put in question. The benefit of being a United Way of America member isn't there at this time for Lorain's United Way."[14]

Elaine Chao's task of resurrecting United Way of America would not be easy.

Chao's Remedial Efforts

As it turned out, Elaine Chao did a fine job. She was hired to restore public faith and confidence in the United Way. And this she did. She oversaw formation of new oversight committees and established policies that would ensure "that United Way of America will be accountable and responsive to local United Ways."[15] The board of governors was expanded from 30 to 45 members and included more local representatives.

On May 20, 1996, she announced her resignation effective September 1. "My job is complete," she said.[16] Her plans were to lecture, join a Washington think tank, volunteer for Bob Dole's presidential campaign and work for the re-election of her husband, Sen. Mitch McConnell (R., Ky.).

Still, had United Way recovered completely from the scandal? The enduring aftereffects say not completely. For the nation's leading chapter, Cleveland, donations have slipped considerably from the 1989–90 campaign that raised $52 million. Total contributions in 1995 were only $40 million, and more than $1 million below the goal set at the beginning of the campaign.[17]

The stigma of an abuse to the public image can be enduring. This may especially be true of public service organizations that derive their revenues from voluntary contributions.

See the Information Box: Another Controversy: Girl Scouts and Their Cookies for a discussion of a related example of nonprofit callousness to its parties.

---

[14] Karen Henderson, "Lorain Agency Cuts Ties with National United Way," *Cleveland Plain Dealer*, 16 April 1993, p. 7C.

[15] Matthew Tungate, "United Way Chief Hails Local Efforts," *Cleveland Plain Dealer*, 25 May 1996, p. 2-B.

[16] "Head of United Way to Leave Her Post Saying Job Is Done," *Wall Street Journal*, 20 May 1996, p. B8.

[17] Michael K. McIntyre, "United Way Changing Fund Drive Strategies," *Cleveland Plain Dealer*, 1 September 1996, p. 4-B.

INFORMATION BOX

**ANOTHER CONTROVERSY:
GIRL SCOUTS AND THEIR COOKIES**

The main funding source for the nation's 2.6 million Girl Scouts is the annual cookie sale, estimated to generate $400 million in revenue. The practice goes back some 70 years, although in the 1920s the girls sold homemade cookies. Now each regional council negotiates with one or two bakeries that produce the cookies; sets the price per box, which ranges from $2 to $3; and divides the proceeds as it sees fit. Typically, the Girl Scout troops get 10 to 15 percent, the council takes more than 50 percent, and the rest goes to the manufacturer.[18]

Criticisms have emerged and received public attention regarding the dictatorial handling of these funds by the councils. There are 332 regional councils in the United States, each having an office and a paid staff overseen by a volunteer board. Some councils have dozens of employees, with most serving mainly as policy enforcers and supervisors. At the troop level, volunteer leaders, often women with daughters in the troop, guide their units in the true tradition of scouting, giving their time tirelessly. For the cookie drives, the girls are an unpaid sales force—child labor, as critics assail—that supports a huge bureaucratic structure. Little of the cookie revenue comes back to the local troops.

The bureaucracy does not tolerate dissent well. The *Wall Street Journal* cites the case of a West Haven, Connecticut, troop leader, Beth Denton, who protested both the way the Connecticut Trails council apportioned revenue and the $1.6 million in salaries and benefits paid to 42 council employees. After she complained to the state attorney general, the council dismissed her as leader.[19]

Admittedly, the individual salaries in the bureaucracy were not high by corporate standards or even by not-for-profit standards. Council administrators' salaries ranged up to about $90,000. Perhaps more disturbing was that volunteer leaders saw no annual financial statements of their councils' expenditures and activities.[20]

Evaluate the council's position that annual financial records of their council's activities should be entirely confidential and limited to full-time staff.

---

[18] Ellen Graham, "Sprawling Bureaucracy Eats Up Most Profits of Girl Scout Cookies," *Wall Street Journal*, 13 May 1992, p. A1.

[19] Graham, p. A4.

[20] Ibid.

ANALYSIS

The lack of accountability to the donating public was a major contributor to UWA's problems. Such a loosely run operation, with no one to approve or halt administrators' actions, encouraged questionable practices. It also opened the way for great shock and criticism, come the revelation. The fact that voluntary donations were the principal source of revenues made the lack of accountability all the more crucial. The situation was similar for the Girl Scouts. In a for-profit organization, lack of account-ability primarily affects stockholders; for a major charitable organization, it affects mil-lions of contributors, who see their money and commitment being squandered.

Where full disclosure and a system of checks and balances is lacking, two conse-quences tend to prevail, neither one desirable nor totally acceptable. The worst case scenario is outright "white-collar theft," when the unscrupulous see it as an opportu-nity for personal gain. The absence of sufficient controls and accountability can make even normally honest persons succumb to temptation. Second, insufficient controls tend to promote a mindset of arrogance and allow people to play fast and loose with the system. Aramony seemed to fall into this mindset, with his spending extravagances, cronyism, and other conflict-of-interest activities. (At least some of the Girl Scout Councils, too, perceived themselves as aloof from the dedicated volunteer troop lead-ers, tolerating no criticism or questioning, dictating and enforcing all policies without consultation or participation, and allowing no scrutiny of their own operation.)

The UWA theoretically had an overseer: the board, similar to the board of direc-tors of business corporations. But when such boards act as rubber stamps, where they are solidly in the camp of the chief executives, they are not really exercising control. This appeared to be the case with United Way of America during the "reign" of Aramony; similarly with the regional councils of the Girl Scouts, many of the volun-teer boards appear to have exercised little or no oversight.

Certainly such a situation of a board's failure to fulfill its responsibility is not unique to not-for-profits. Corporate boards have often been notorious for pro-moting the interests of the incumbent executives. Although this situation is chang-ing today, it still prevails. See the Issue Box: What Should Be the Role of the Board of Directors? for a discussion.

UPDATE

William Aramony was convicted of defrauding the United Way out of $1 million. He was sentenced to seven years in prison for using the charity's money to finance a lavish lifestyle.

Despite this, a federal judge ruled in late 1998 that the charity must pay its former president more than $2 million in retirement benefits. "A felon, no matter how despised, does not lose his right to enforce a contract," U.S. District Judge Shira Scheindlin in New York ruled.[22]

WHAT CAN BE LEARNED?

Beware the Arrogant Mindset

A leader's mindset that he or she is so superior to subordinates—and even to con-cerned outsiders—that other opinions are unacceptable is a formula for disaster, both

---

[22] Reported in *Cleveland Plain Dealer,* 25 October 1998, p. 24–A.

ISSUE BOX

WHAT SHOULD BE THE
ROLE OF THE BOARD OF DIRECTORS?

In the past, most boards of directors have tended to be rubber stamps, closely allied with top executives and even composed mostly of corporate officials. In some organizations today this is changing, mostly in response to criticism of board tendencies always to support the status quo and to perpetuate the "establishment."

More and more, opinion is shifting to the idea that boards must assume a more activist role:

> The board can no longer play a passive role in corporate governance. Today, more than ever, the board must assume ... a role that is protective of shareholder rights, sensitive to communities in which the company operates, responsive to the needs of company vendors and customers, and fair to its employees.[21]

Incentives for more active boards have been the increasing risks of liability for board decisions, as well as liability insurance costs. Although the board of directors has long been seen as responsible for establishing corporate objectives, developing broad policies, and selecting top executives, this is no longer viewed as sufficient. Boards must also review management's performance to ensure that the company is well run and that stockholders' interests are furthered. And, today, they must ensure that society's best interests are not disregarded. All of this translates into an active concern for the organization's public image or reputation.

But the issue remains: To whom should the board owe its greatest allegiance—the entrenched bureaucracy or the external publics? Without having board members representative of the many special interests affected by the organization, board members may be inclined to support the interests of the establishment.

Do you think a more representative and active board will prevent a similar scenario for United Way in the future? Why or why not?

---

[21] Lester B. Korn and Richard M. Ferry, *Board of Directors Thirteenth Annual Study* (New York: Korn/Ferry International, February 1986), pp. 1–2.

---

for an organization and for a society. It promotes dictatorship, intolerance of contrary opinions, and an attitude that "we need answer to no one." The consequences are such as we have seen with William Aramony: moving over the edge of what is deemed by most as acceptable and ethical conduct, assuming the role of the final judge who brooks no questions or criticisms. The absence of real or imagined controls or reviews seems to bring out the worst in humans. We seem to need periodic scrutiny to avoid the trap of arrogant decision making devoid of responsiveness to other concerns. The Girl Scout bureaucracy's dealings with its volunteers corroborates the inclination toward arrogance and dictatorship in the absence of objective oversight.

Checks and Balances Are Even More Important in Not-for-profit and Governmental Bodies than in Corporate Entities

For-profit organizations have "bottom-line" performance (i.e., profit and loss statistics) as the ultimate control and standard. Not-for-profit and governmental organizations do not have this control, so they have no ultimate measure of their effectiveness.

Consequently, not-for-profit organizations should be subject to the utmost scrutiny of objective outsiders. Otherwise, abuses seem to be encouraged and perpetuated. Often these not-for-profit organizations are sheltered from competition, which protects them from demands for greater efficiency. Thus, without objective scrutiny, not-for-profits have a tendency to get out of hand, to be run as little dynasties unencumbered by the constraints that face most businesses. Fortunately, investigative reports and increased litigation by allegedly abused parties today act as needed controls for such organizations. In view of the revelations of investigative reporters, we are left to wonder how many other abusive and reprehensible activities have not yet been detected.

Marketing of Not-for-profits Depends on Trust and Is Particularly Vulnerable to Bad Press

Not-for-profits depend on donations for the bulk of their revenues. They depend on people to give without receiving anything tangible in return (unlike most businesses). And the givers must have trust in the particular organization, trust that the contributions will be well spent, that beneficiaries will receive the maximum benefit, that administrative costs will be held low. Consequently, when publicity surfaces that causes such trust to be questioned, the impact can be devastating. Contributions can quickly dry up or be shunted to other charities.

With governmental bodies, of course, their perpetuation is hardly at stake with bad publicity. However, administrators can be recalled, impeached, or not reelected.

CONSIDER

Can you add to these learning insights?

QUESTIONS

1. How do you feel, as a potential or actual giver to United Way campaigns, about Aramony's "high living"? Would these allegations affect your gift giving? Why or why not?

2. What prescriptions do you have for thwarting arrogance in not-for-profit and/or governmental organizations? Be as specific as you can, and support your recommendations.

3. How do you personally feel about the coercion that some organizations exert for their employees to contribute substantially to the United Way? What implications, if any, emerge from your attitudes about this?

4. Given the information supplied about the dictatorial relationships between Girl Scout councils and the local volunteers—and recognizing that such anecdotal information may not be truly representative—what do you see as the pros and cons of Girl Scout cookie drives? On balance, is this marketing fund-raising effort still desirable, or might other alternatives be better?

5. "Since there is no bottom-line evaluation for performance, not-for-profits have no incentives to control costs and prudently evaluate expenditures." Discuss.

6. How would you feel, as a large contributor to a charity, if you learned that it spent $10 million for advertising? Discuss your rationale for this attitude.

7. Do you think the UWA's action after Aramony left was the best way to salvage the public image? Why or why not? What else might have been done?

HANDS-ON EXERCISES

1. You are an advisor to Elaine Chao, who has taken over the scandal-ridden United Way. What advice do you give her for as quickly as possible restoring the confidence of the American public in the integrity and worthiness of this preeminent national charity organization?

2. You are a member of the board of governors of United Way. Allegations have surfaced about the lavish lifestyle of the highly regarded Aramony. Most of the board members, being corporate executives, see nothing at all wrong with his perks and privileges. You, however, feel otherwise. How do you convince the other board members of the error of condoning Aramony's activities? Be as persuasive as you can in supporting your position.

3. You are the parent of a Girl Scout, who has assiduously worked to sell hundreds of boxes of cookies. You now realize that her efforts and that of thousands of other girls are primarily supporting a bloated central and regional bureaucracy, and not the local troops. You feel strongly that this situation is an unacceptable use of child labor. Describe your proposed efforts to institute change.

TEAM DEBATE EXERCISE

Debate this issue: No not-for-profit organization can ever attain the efficiency of a business firm that always has the bottom line to be concerned about.

INVITATION TO RESEARCH

What is the situation with the United Way today? Are local agencies contributing to the national? Have donations matched or exceeded previous levels? Has Elaine Chao restored public confidence? What is Elaine Chao doing now?

MARKETING
MANAGEMENT
MISTAKES

CHAPTER THIRTEEN

Maytag—Bungling a Promotion in England

*T*he atmosphere at the annual meeting in the little Iowa town of Newton had turned contentious. As Leonard Hadley faced increasingly angry questions from disgruntled shareholders the thought crossed his mind: "I don't deserve this!" After all, he had only been CEO of Maytag Corporation for a few months, and this was his first chairing of an annual meeting. But the earnings of the company had been declining every year since 1988, and in 1992, Maytag had had a $315.4 million loss. No wonder the stockholders in the packed Newton High School auditorium were bitter and critical of their management. But there was more. Just the month before, the company had the public embarrassment and costly atonement resulting from a monumental blunder in the promotional planning of its United Kingdom subsidiary.

Hadley doggedly saw the meeting to its close, and limply concluded: "Hopefully, both sales and earnings will improve this year."[1]

THE FIASCO

In August 1992, Hoover Limited, Maytag's British subsidiary, launched this travel promotion: Anyone in the United Kingdom buying more than 100 U.K. pounds worth of Hoover products (about $150 in American dollars) before the end of January 1993 would get two free round-trip tickets to selected European destinations. For 250 U.K. pounds worth of Hoover products, they would get two free round-trip tickets to New York or Orlando.

A buying frenzy resulted. Consumers had quickly figured out that the value of the tickets easily exceeded the cost of the appliances necessary to be eligible for them. By the tens of thousands, Britishers rushed out to buy just enough Hoover products to qualify. Appliance stores were emptied of vacuum cleaners. The Hoover factory in Cambuslang, Scotland, that had been making vacuum cleaners only three days a week was suddenly placed on a 24-hour, seven days a week production

---

[1] Richard Gibson, "Maytag's CEO Goes Through Wringer at Annual Meeting," *Wall Street Journal*, 28 April 1993, p. A5.

schedule—an overtime bonanza for the workers. What a resounding success for a promotion! Hoover managers, however, were unhappy.

Hoover had never ever expected more than 50,000 people to respond. And of those responding, it expected far less would go through all the steps necessary to qualify for the free trip and really take it. But more than 200,000 not only responded but qualified for the free tickets. The company was overwhelmed. The volume of paperwork created such a bottleneck that by the middle of April only 6,000 people had flown. Thousands of others either never got their tickets, were not able to get the dates requested, or waited for months without hearing the results of their applications. Hoover established a special hot line to process customer complaints, and these were coming in at 2,000 calls a day. But the complaints quickly spread, and the ensuing publicity brought charges of fraud and demands for restitution. This raises the issue of loss leaders—how much should we use loss leaders as a promotional device?—discussed in the Issue Box.

Maytag dispatched a task force to try to resolve the situation without jeopardizing customer relations any further. But it acknowledged that it's "not 100% clear" that all eligible buyers will receive their free flights.[2] The ill-fated promotion

---

ISSUE BOX

SHOULD WE USE LOSS LEADERS?

Leader pricing is a type of promotion with certain items advertised at a very low price—sometimes even below cost, in which case they are known as loss leaders—in order to attract more customers. The rationale for this is that such customers are likely to purchase other regular price items as well with the result that total sales and profits will be increased. If customers do not purchase enough other goods at regular prices to more than cover the losses incurred from the attractively priced bargains, then the loss leader promotion is ill advised. Some critics maintain that the whole idea of using loss leaders is absurd: the firm is just "buying sales" with no regard for profits.

While U.K. Hoover did not think of their promotion as a loss leader, in reality it was: they stood to lose money on every sale if the promotional offer was taken advantage of. Unfortunately for its effectiveness as a loss leader, the likelihood of customers purchasing other Hoover products at regular prices was remote, and the level of acceptance was not capped, so that losses were permitted to multiply. The conclusion has to be that this was an ill-conceived idea from the beginning. It violated these two conditions of loss leaders: they should stimulate sales of other products, and their losses should be limited.

Do you think loss leaders really are desirable under certain circumstances? Why or why not?

---

[2] James P. Miller, "Maytag U.K. Unit Find a Promotion Is Too Successful," *Wall Street Journal*, 31 March 1993, p. A9.

was a staggering blow to Maytag financially. It took a $30 million charge in the first quarter of 1993 to cover unexpected additional costs linked to the promotion. Final costs were expected to exceed $50 million, which would be 10 percent of UK Hoover's total revenues. This for a subsidiary acquired only four years before that had yet to produce a profit.

Adding to the costs were problems with the two travel agencies involved. The agencies were to obtain low-cost space available tickets, and would earn commissions selling "packages," including hotels, rental cars, and insurance. If consumers bought a package, Hoover would get a cut. However, despite the overwhelming demand for tickets, most consumers declined to purchase the package, thus greatly reducing support money for the promotional venture. So, Hoover greatly underestimated the likely response, and overestimated the amount it would earn from commission payments.

If these cost overruns added greatly to Maytag and Hoover's customer relations and public image, the expenditures would have seemed more palatable. But with all the problems, the best that could be expected would be to lessen the worst of the agitation and charges of deception. And this was proving to be impossible. The media, of course, salivated at the problems and were quick to sensationalize them:

> One disgruntled customer, who took aggressive action on his own, received the widest press coverage, and even became a folk hero. Dave Dixon, claiming he was cheated out of a free vacation by Hoover, seized one of the company's repair vans in retaliation. Police were sympathetic: They took him home, and did not charge him, claiming it was a civil matter.[3]

Heads rolled also. Initially, Maytag fired three UK Hoover executives involved, including the president of Hoover Europe. Mr. Hadley, at the annual meeting, also indicated that others might lose their jobs before the cleanup was complete. He likened the promotion to "a bad accident... and you can't determine what was in the driver's mind."[4]

The issue receiving somewhat less publicity was why corporate headquarters allowed executives of a subsidiary such wide latitude that they could saddle parent Maytag with tens of millions in unexpected costs. Did not top corporate executives have to approve ambitious plans? A company spokesman said that operating divisions were "primarily responsible" for planning promotional expenses. While the parent may review such outlays, "if they're within parameters, it goes through."[5] This raises the issue, discussed in the Issue Box, of how loose a rein foreign subsidiaries should be allowed.

[3] "Unhappy Brit Holds Hoover Van Hostage," *Cleveland Plain Dealer,* 1 June 1993, p. D1; and Simon Reeve and John Harlow, "Hoover Is Sued Over Flights Deal," *London Sunday Times,* 6 June 1993.

[4] Gibson, p. A5.

[5] Miller, p. A9.

ISSUE BOX

HOW LOOSE A REIN FOR A FOREIGN SUBSIDIARY?

In a decentralized organization, top management delegates considerable decision-making authority to subordinates. Such decentralization—often called a "loose rein"—tends to be more marked with foreign subsidiaries, such as UK Hoover. Corporate management in the United States understandably feels less familiar with the foreign environment and is more willing to let the native executives operate with less constraints than it might with a domestic subsidiary. In the Maytag/Hoover situation, decision-making authority by British executives was evidently extensive, and corporate Maytag exercised little operational control, being content to judge performance by ultimate results achieved. Major deviations from expected performance goals, or widespread traumatic events—all of which happened to UK Hoover—finally gained corporate management attention.

Major advantages of extensive decentralization or a loose rein are: first, top management effectiveness can be improved since time and attention is freed for presumably more important matters; second, subordinates are permitted more self-management, which should improve their competence and motivation; and third, in foreign environments, native managers presumably better understand their unique problems and opportunities than corporate management, located thousands of miles away, possibly can. But the drawbacks are as we have seen: parameters within which subordinate managers operate can be so wide that serious miscalculations may not be stopped in time. Since top management is ultimately responsible for all performance, including actions of subordinates, it faces greater risks with extensive decentralization and giving a free rein.

"Since the manager is ultimately accountable for whatever is delegated to subordinates, then a free rein reflects great confidence in subordinates." Discuss.

BACKGROUND ON MAYTAG

Maytag is a century-old company. The original business, formed in 1893, manufactured feeder attachments for threshing machines. In 1907, the company moved to Newton, Iowa, a small town thirty miles east of Des Moines, the capital. Manufacturing emphasis turned to home-laundry equipment, and wringer-type washers.

A natural expansion of this emphasis occurred with the commercial laundromat business in the 1930s, when coin meters were attached to Maytag washers. Rapid growth of these coin-operated laundries took place in the U.S. during the late 1950s and early 1960s. The 1970s hurt laundromats with increased competition and soaring energy costs. In 1975, Maytag introduced new energy-efficient machines, and "Home Style" stores that rejuvenated the business.

The Lonely Maytag Repairman

For years Maytag reveled in a marketing coup, with its washers and dryers enjoying a top-quality image, thanks to decades-long ads in which a repairman laments his loneliness because of Maytag's trouble-free products. (The actor who portrayed this repairman died in early 1997.) The result of this dependability and quality image was that Maytag could command a price premium: "Their machines cost the same to make, break down as much as ours—but they get $100 more because of the reputation," grumbled a competitor.[6]

During the 1970s and into the 1980s, Maytag continued to capture 15 percent of the washing machine market, and enjoyed profit margins about twice that of competitors. Table 13.1 shows operating results for the period 1974–1981. Whirlpool was the largest factor in the laundry equipment market, with a 45 percent share, but this was largely because of sales to Sears under the Sears' brand.

Acquisitions

For many years, until his retirement on December 31, 1992, Daniel J. Krumm had influenced Maytag's destinies. He had been CEO for eighteen years and chairman since 1986, and his tenure with the company encompassed 40 years. In that time, the home-appliance business encountered some drastic changes. The most ominous occurred in the late 1980s with the merger mania, in which the threat of takeovers by hostile raiders often motivated heretofore conservative executives to greatly increase corporate indebtedness, thereby decreasing the attractiveness of their firms. Daniel Krumm was one of these running-scared executives, as rumors persisted that the company was a takeover candidate.

Largely as a defensive move, Krumm pushed through a deal for a $1 billion buyout of Chicago Pacific Corporation (CPC), a maker of vacuum cleaners and

TABLE 13.1. Maytag Operating Results, 1974–1981 (in millions)

	Net Sales	Net Income	Percent of Sales
1974	$229	$21.1	9.2%
1975	238	25.9	10.9
1976	275	33.1	12.0
1977	299	34.5	11.5
1978	325	36.7	11.3
1979	369	45.3	12.3
1980	346	35.6	10.2
1981	409	37.4	9.1
Average net income percent of sales: 10.8%			

Source: Company operating statistics.

Commentary: These years show a steady, though not spectacular growth in revenues, and a generally rising net income, except for 1980. Of particular interest is the high net income percentage of sales, with this averaging 10.8 percent over the 8-year period, with a high of 12.3 percent.

---

[6] Brian Bremmer, "Can Maytag Clean Up Around the World?" *Business Week*, 30 January 1989, p. 89.

other appliances with $1.4 billion in sales. As a result, Maytag was burdened with $500 million in new debt. Krumm defended the acquisition as giving Maytag a strong foothold in a growing overseas market. CPC was best known for the Hoover vacuums it sold in the United States and Europe. Indeed, so dominant was the Hoover brand in England that many people did not vacuum their carpets, but "hoovered the carpet." CPC also made washers, dryers, and other appliances under the Hoover brand, selling them exclusively in Europe and Australia. In addition, it had six furniture companies, but Maytag sold these shortly after the acquisition.

Krumm had been instrumental in transforming Maytag, the number-four U.S. appliance manufacturer—behind General Electric, Whirlpool, and Electrolux—from a niche laundry-equipment maker into a full-line manufacturer. He had led an earlier acquisition spree in which Maytag had expanded into microwave ovens, electric ranges, refrigerators, and freezers. Its brands now included Magic Chef, Jenn-Air, Norge, and Admiral. The last years of Krumm's reign, however, were not marked by great operating results. As shown in Table 13.2, revenues showed no gain in the 1989–1992 period, while income steadily declined.

Trouble

Although the rationale for internationalizing seemed inescapable, especially in view of a recent wave of joint ventures between U.S. and European appliance makers, still the Hoover acquisition was troublesome. While it was a major brand in England and in Australia, Hoover had only a small presence in Europe. Yet, this was where the bulk of the market was, with some 320 million potential appliance buyers.

The probabilities of the Hoover subsidiary being able to capture much of the European market were hardly promising. Whirlpool was strong, having ten plants there in contrast to Hoover's two plants. Furthermore, Maytag faced entrenched European competitors such as Sweden's Electrolux, the world's largest appliance maker; Germany's Bosch-Siemens; and Italy's Merloni Group. General Electric had also entered the market with joint ventures. The fierce loyalty of Europeans to

TABLE 13.2. **Maytag Operating Results, 1989–1992**

	Revenue (000,000)	Net Income	% of Revenue
1989	$3,089	131.0	4.3%
1990	3,057	98.9	3.2
1991	2,971	79.0	2.7
1992	3,041	(315.4)	(10.4)

Source: Company annual reports.

Commentary: Note the steady erosion of profitability, while sales remained virtually static. For a comparison with profit performance of earlier years, see Table 13.1 and the net income to sales percentage of this more "golden" period.

domestic brands raised further questions as to the ability of Maytag's Hoover to penetrate the European market without massive promotional expenditures, and maybe not even then.

Australia was something else. Hoover had a good competitive position there, and its refrigerator plant in Melbourne could easily be expanded to include Maytag's washers and dryers. Unfortunately, the small population of Australia limited the market to only about $250 million for major appliances.

Britain accounted for half of Hoover's European sales. But at the time of the acquisition its major appliance business was only marginally profitable. This was to change: after the acquisition it became downright unprofitable, as shown in Table 13.3 for the years 1990 through 1992, as it struggled to expand in a recession-plagued Europe. The results for 1993, of course, will reflect the huge loss for the promotional debacle. Hardly an acquisition made in heaven.

Maytag's earlier acquisitions also were becoming soured. Its acquisitions of Magic Chef and Admiral were diversifications into lower-priced appliances, and these did not meet expectations. But they left Maytag's balance sheet and its cash flow weakened (see Table 13.4). Perhaps more serious, Maytag's reputation as the nation's premier appliance maker became tarnished. Meanwhile, General Electric and Whirlpool were attacking the top end of its product line. As a result, Maytag found itself in the number-three or -four position in most of its brand lines.

TABLE 13.3. Operating Results of Maytag's Principal Business Components 1990–1992

	Revenue (000,000)	Income[a] (000)
1990		
North American Appliances	$2,212	$221,165
Vending	191	25,018
European Sales	497	(22,863)
1991		
North American Appliances	2,183	186,322
Vending	150	4,498
European Sales	486	(865)
1992		
North American Appliances	2,242	129,680
Vending	165	16,311
European Sales	502	(67,061)

Source: Company annual reports.

Commentary: While these years had not been particularly good for Maytag in growth of revenues and income, the continuing, and even intensifying, losses in the Hoover European operation had to be troublesome. And this is before the ill-fated early 1993 promotional results.

[a] This is operating income, that is, income before depreciation and other adjustments.

TABLE 13.4. Long-Term Debt as a Percent of Capital from Maytag's Balance Sheets, 1986–1991

Year	Long-Term Debt/Capital
1986	7.2%
1987	23.3
1988	48.3
1989	46.8
1990	44.1
1991	42.7

Source: Company annual reports.

Commentary: The effect of acquisitions, in particular that of the Chicago Pacific Corporation, can be clearly seen in the buildup of long-term debt: in 1986, Maytag was virtually free of such commitments; two years later its long-term debt ratio had increased almost seven-fold.

ANALYSIS

Flawed Acquisition Decisions

The long decline in profits after 1989 should have triggered strong concern and corrective action. Perhaps it did, but the action was not effectual as the decline continued, culminating in a large deficit in 1992 and serious problems in 1993. As shown in Table 13.2, the acquisitions brought neither revenue gains nor profitability. One suspects that in the rush to fend off potential raiders in the late 1980s, the company bought businesses it might never have under more sober times, and that it also paid too much for these businesses. Further, they cheapened the proud image of quality for Maytag.

Who Can We Blame in the U.K. Promotional Debacle?

Corporate Maytag management was guilty of a common fault in their acquisitions: it gave newly acquired divisions a loose rein, letting them continue to operate independently with few constraints: "After all, these executives should be more knowledgeable about their operations than corporate headquarters would be." Such confidence is sometimes misguided. In the U.K. promotion, Maytag management would seem as derelict as management in England. Planning guidelines or parameters were far too loose and under-controlled. The idea of subsidiary management being able to burden the parent with $50 million of unexpected charges, and to have such erupt with no warning, borders on the absurd.

Finally, the planning of the U.K. executives for this ill-conceived travel production defies all logic. They vastly underestimated the demand for the promotional offer and they greatly overestimated paybacks from travel agencies on the package deals. Yet, it took no brilliant insight to realize that the value of the travel offer exceeded the price of the appliance—indeed, 200,000 customers rapidly arrived at this conclusion—and that such a sweetheart of a deal would be irresistible to many, and that it could prove to be costly in the extreme to the company. A miscalculation, or complete naivete on the part of executives and their staffs who should have known better?

How Could the Promotion Have Avoided the Problem?

The great problem resulting from an offer too good could have been avoided, and this without scrapping the whole idea. A cost-benefit analysis would have provided at least a perspective as to how much the company should spend to achieve certain benefits, such as increased sales, greater consumer interest, and favorable publicity. See the following information box for a more detailed discussion of the important planning tool of a cost-benefit analysis.

A cost-benefit analysis should certainly have alerted management to the possible consequences of various acceptance levels, and of the significant risks of high acceptance. However, the company could have set limits on the number of eligibles: perhaps the first 1,000, or the first 5,000. Doing this would have held or capped the costs to reasonably defined levels, and avoided the greater risks. Or the company could have made the offer less generous, perhaps by upping the requirements, or by lessening the premiums. Such more moderate alternatives would still have made an attractive promotion, but not the major uncontrolled catastrophe that happened.

INFORMATION BOX

COST-BENEFIT ANALYSIS

A cost-benefit analysis is a systematic comparison of the costs and benefits of a proposed action. Only if the benefits exceed the costs would we normally have a "go" decision. The normal way to make such an analysis is to assign dollar values to all costs and benefits, thus providing a common basis for comparison.

Cost-benefit analyses have been widely used by the Defense Department in evaluating alternative weapons systems. In recent years, such analyses have been sporadically applied to environmental regulation and even to workplace safety standards. As an example of the former, a cost-benefit analysis can be used to determine if it is socially worthwhile to spend X million dollars to meet a certain standard of clean air or water.

Many business decisions lend themselves to a cost-benefit analysis. It provides a systematic way of analyzing the inputs and the probable outputs of particular major alternatives. While in the business setting some of the costs and benefits can be very quantitative, they often should be tempered by nonquantitative inputs to reach the broadest perspective. Schermerhorn suggests considering the following criteria in evaluating alternatives:[7]

[7] John R. Schermerhorn, Jr., *Management for Productivity*, 6th ed. (New York: Wiley, 1999), p. 61.

(continues)

INFORMATION BOX (continued)

Benefits: What are the "benefits" of using the alternatives to solve a performance deficiency or take advantage of an opportunity?

Costs: What are the "costs" to implement the alternatives, including direct resource investments as well as any potential negative side effects?

Timeliness: How fast will the benefits occur and a positive impact be achieved?

Acceptability: To what extent will the alternatives be accepted and supported by those who must work with them?

Ethical soundness: How well do the alternatives meet acceptable ethical criteria in the eyes of multiple stakeholders?

What numbers would you assign to a cost-benefit analysis for Maytag Hoover's plan to offer the free airline tickets, under an assumption of 5,000 takers? 20,000 takers? 100,000 takers? 500,000 takers? (Make any assumptions needed as to costs.) What would be your conclusions for these various acceptance rates?

FINAL RESOLUTION?

Maytag's invasion of Europe proved a costly failure. In the summer of 1995, Maytag gave up. It sold its European operations to an Italian appliance maker, recording a $135 million loss.

Even by the end of 1996, the Hoover mess was still not cleaned up. Hoover had spent $72 million flying some 220,000 people and had hoped to end the matter. But the fight continues four years later with disgruntled customers who never flew taking Hoover to court. A Liverpool lawyer chortled: "There's about 365,000 people who haven't flown," said Denis Whalley. "I hope lots of other people who have been cheated by Hoover will come forward."[8] Even though Maytag had sold this troubled division, it still could not escape emerging lawsuits.

Update—Leonard Hadley

In the summer of 1998, Leonard Hadley could look forward and backward with some satisfaction. He would retire the next summer when he turned 65, and he had already picked his successor. Since assuming the top position in Maytag in January 1993, and confronting the mess with the U.K. subsidiary his first few months on the job, he had turned Maytag completely around.

He knew no one expected much change from him, an accountant who had joined Maytag right out of college. He was known as a loyal but unimaginative lieutenant of his boss, Daniel Krumm, who died of cancer shortly after naming Hadley his successor.

---

[8] "Hoover Can't Clean Up Mess from Free Flights," *Cleveland Plain Dealer,* 12 December 1996, p. 1-C; and Dirk Beveridge, "Hoover Loses Two Lawsuits Tied to Promotion," *Gannett Newspapers,* 21 February 1997, p. 4-F.

After all, he reflected, no one thought that major change could come to an organization from someone who had spent his whole life there, who was a clone so to speak, and an accountant to boot. Everyone thought that changemakers had to come from outside, like Al Dunlap of Scott Paper and Sunbeam. Well, he had shown them, and given hope to all number-two executives who resented Wall Street's love affair with outsiders.

Within a few weeks of taking over, he'd fired a bunch of managers, especially those rascals in the U.K. who'd masterminded the great Hoover promotion that cost the company dearly. He determined to get rid of foreign operations, most of them newly acquired and unprofitable. He just did not see that appliances could be profitably made for every corner of the world, because of the variety of regional customs. Still, he knew that many disagreed with him about this, including some of the board members who thought globalization was the only way to go. Still, over the next 18 months he had prevailed.

He chuckled to himself as he reminisced. He had also overturned the decades-long corporate mindset not to be first to market with new technology because they would "rather be right than be first." His "Galaxy Initiative" of nine top-secret new products was a repudiation of this old mindset. One of them, the Neptune, a front-loading washer retailing at $1,100, certainly proved him right. Maytag had increased its production three times and raised its suggested retail price twice, and still it was selling like gangbusters. Perhaps the thing he was proudest of was getting Maytag products in Sears stores, the seller of one-third of all appliances in the United States. Sears' desire to have the Neptune is what swung the deal.

As an accountant, he probably should be focusing first on the numbers. Well, 1997 was certainly a banner year with sales up 10.9 percent over the previous year, while profitability as measured by return on capital was 16.7 percent, both sales and profit gains leading the industry. And 1998 so far was proving to be even better, with sales jumping 31 percent and earnings 88 percent.

He remembered the remarks of Lester Crown, a Maytag director: "Len Hadley has—quietly, softly—done a spectacular job. Obviously, we just lacked the ability to evaluate him [at the beginning]."[9]

Leonard Hadley retired August 12, 1999. He knew he had surprised everybody in the organization by going outside Maytag for his successor. He was Lloyd Ward, 50, Maytag's first black executive, a marketing expert from PepsiCo, and before that Procter & Gamble, who had joined Maytag in 1996 and was currently president and chief operating officer.

UPDATE—2002

Hadley's choice of successor proved to be flawed, or maybe Ward was just a victim of circumstances mostly beyond his control. After fifteen months Ward left, citing differences with Maytag's directors amid sorry operating results. Hadley came out of retirement to be interim president and CEO in November 2000. Some 3,400

[9] Carl Quintanilla, "Maytag's Top Officer, Expected to Do Little, Surprises His Board," *Wall Street Journal*, 23 June 1998, pp. A1, A8.

Maytag workers, a quarter of Newton's population, roared when they heard the news. They had feared the company would be moved to either Chicago or Dallas, or that it would be sold to Sweden's Electrolux. Hadley assured them that such things would never happen as long as he was at the helm. He retired again in June 2001 when Ralph F. Hake became his successor.

Hake came to Maytag from Fluor Corporation, an engineering and construction firm, where he had been executive vice president. Before that he spent twelve years in various executive positions with Maytag's chief rival, appliance manufacturer Whirlpool.

The company was still in the little town of Newton, Iowa, and the "lonely Maytag repairman" now had an apprentice.

Source: Maytag 2001 Annual Report; Emily Gersema, "Maytag Re-hires Former CEO After Time of Internal Turmoil," *Wall Street Journal,* 15 January 2001, p. 311.

WHAT CAN BE LEARNED?

Beware Overpaying for an Acquisition

Hoping to diversify its product line and gain market share overseas, Maytag paid $1 billion for Chicago Pacific in 1989. As it turned out, this was far too much, and the debt burden was an albatross. Chief Executive Leonard Hadley conceded as much: "In the long view, it was correct to invest in these businesses. But the timing of the deal, and the price of the deal, made the debt a heavy load to carry."[10]

Zeal to expand, and/or the desire to reduce the attractiveness of a firm's balance sheet and thus fend off potential raiders, do not excuse foolhardy management. The consequences of such bad decisions remain to haunt a company, and the ill-advised purchases often have to be eventually sold off at substantial losses. The analysis of potential acquisition candidates must be soberly and thoroughly done, and rosy projections questioned, even if this means the deal may be soured.

Beware Giving Too Loose a Rein, thus Sacrificing Controls, Especially of Unproven Foreign Subsidiaries

Although decentralizing authority down to lower ranks is often desirable and results in better motivation and management development than centralization, it can be overdone. At the extreme, where divisional and subsidiary executives have almost unlimited decision-making authority and can run their operations as virtual dynasties, then corporate management essentially abdicates its authority. Such looseness in an organization endangers cohesiveness; it tends to obscure common standards and objectives; and it can even dilute unified ethical practices.

---

[10] Kenneth Labich, "What Companies Fail," *Fortune,* 14 November 1994, p. 60.

Such extreme looseness of controls is not uncommon with acquisitions, especially foreign ones. It is easy to make the assumption that these executives were operating successfully before the acquisition and have more firsthand knowledge of the environment than the corporate executives.

Still, there should be limits on how much freedom these executives should be permitted—especially when their operations have not been notably successful. In Maytag's case, the U.K. subsidiary had lost money every year since it was acquired. Accordingly, one would expect prudent corporate management to have condoned less decentralization and insisted on tighter controls than it might otherwise.

In Decision Planning, Consider a Worst-case Scenario

There are those who preach the desirability of positive thinking, confidence, and optimism, whether it be in personal lives, athletics, or business practices. But expecting and preparing for the worst has much to commend it, since a person or a firm is then better able to cope with adversity, avoid being overwhelmed, and more likely to make prudent rather than rash decisions.

Apparently the avid acceptance of the promotional offer was a complete surprise; no one dreamed of such demand. Yet, was it so unreasonable to think that a very attractive offer would meet wild acceptance?

In Using Loss Leaders, Put a Cap on Potential Losses

Loss leaders, as we noted earlier, are items promoted at such attractive prices that the firm loses money on every sale. The expectation, of course, is that the customer traffic generated by such attractive promotions will increase sales of regular profit items so that total profits will be increased.

The risks of uncontrolled or uncapped loss leader promotions are vividly shown in this case. For a retailer who uses loss leaders, the loss is ultimately capped as the inventory is sold off. With UK Hoover there was no cap. The solution is clear: Attractive loss leader promotions should be capped, such as the first 100 or the first 1,000 or for one week only. Otherwise, the promotion should be made less attractive.

The Power of a Cost-benefit Analysis

For major decisions, executives have much to gain from a cost-benefit analysis. It forces them to systematically tabulate and analyze the costs and benefits of particular courses of action. They may find that likely benefits are so uncertain as to not be worth the risk. If so, now is the time to realize this, rather than after substantial commitments have already been made.

Without doubt, regular use of cost-benefit analyses for major decisions improves executives' batting averages for good decisions. Even though some numbers may have to be judgmental, especially as to probable benefits, the process of making this analysis forces a careful look at alternatives and most likely consequences. For more important decisions, input from diverse staff people and executives will bring greater power to the analysis.

CONSIDER

What additional learning insights can you add?

QUESTIONS

1. How could the promotion of UK Hoover have been better designed? Be as specific as you can.
2. Given the fiasco that did occur, how do you think Maytag should have responded?
3. "Firing the three top executives of UK Hoover is unconscionable. It smacks of a vendetta against European managers by an American parent. After all, their only 'crime' was a promotion that was too successful." Comment on this statement.
4. Do you think Leonard Hadley, the Maytag CEO for only two months, should be soundly criticized for the U.K. situation? Why or why not?
5. Please speculate: Why do you think this UK Hoover fiasco happened in the first place? What went wrong?
6. Evaluate the decision to acquire Chicago Pacific Corporation (CPC). Do this both for the time of the decision and for now—after the fact—as a post-mortem. Defend your overall conclusions.

HANDS-ON EXERCISES

1. You have been placed in charge of a task force sent by headquarters to England to coordinate the fire-fighting efforts in the aftermath of the ill-fated promotion. There is neither enough productive capacity nor enough airline seats available to handle the demand. How do you propose to handle this situation? Be as specific as you can, and defend your recommendations.
2. As a staff vice president at corporate headquarters, you have been charged to develop companywide policies and procedures that will prevent such a situation from ever occurring again. What do you recommend?

TEAM DEBATE EXERCISE

Two schools of thought are emerging after the promotional debacle. One position advocates repudiating the offer, citing the impossibility of fulfilling all the demand. The other position maintains that the promise must be met at all costs, even if private planes have to be leased. Debate the options.

INVITATION TO RESEARCH

How is Ralph Hake doing as CEO? Has Maytag entered overseas markets again? How is the Neptune washer doing? Has Maytag brought out any other innovative products?

CHAPTER FOURTEEN

McDonald's— A Titan Falters

*F*ew business firms anywhere in the world have been able to match the sustained growth of McDonald's. Initially, it grew with one simple product, a hamburger, and while it has broadened its product mix today, it still remains uniquely undiversified.

The foundation for success had always been the most rigid standards and controls to be found anywhere. McDonald's insisted these be adhered to by all outlets, company-owned as well as franchised, and therein was an enduring marketing strategy.

For decades, no competitor could match the standards of quality, service, and cleanliness that made McDonald's unique. In recent years, however, these standards have slipped while competitors are countering its former advantage. And, after decades of seemingly unlimited demand for hamburgers, suddenly the market has become saturated. The ball game has changed. But before we get into that, let's see how McDonald's got started and the glory years that were to come.

RAY KROC'S DREAM

Ray Kroc faced a serious dilemma. He was fifty-seven years old, and all his life he had dreamed of becoming rich—and worked hard at it—but real success eluded him. He had played piano with dance bands, then turned to selling paper cups for a firm called Lily-Tulip. He also moonlighted by working for a Chicago radio station, accompanying singers and arranging the music programs. Then he thought he might make his fortune by selling land in a Florida land boom. But that did not work out, and a year later he returned to Chicago almost broke. Lily-Tulip gave him back his old job, and he stayed there more than ten years.

In 1937 Kroc became intrigued with a new gadget, a simple electrical appliance that could mix six milk shakes at the same time. He quit Lily-Tulip again and made a deal with the inventor. He soon became the world's exclusive agent for the Prince Castle Multi-Mixer and for the next twenty years traveled all over the country peddling it. Though he didn't yet know it, at long last he was on the threshold of his dream.

In 1954 Kroc received an order for eight of the Multi-Mixers from a small hamburger stand in San Bernardino, California. He wondered what wild kind of business sold so many milk shakes. So he decided to go out and see for himself this operation of Maurice and Richard McDonald that needed to make forty-five milk shakes at the same time.

When Ray Kroc arrived, he was amazed. It was a self-service hamburger stand, and he saw crowds of people waiting in line under golden arches. He was even more impressed with the speed of service and the cleanliness. Kroc badly wanted in on this business, and hounded the McDonald brothers until they allowed him to start selling franchises. By 1960 he had sold some two hundred franchises.

Kroc bought out the McDonald brothers, though he kept their name, and they took their money and quietly retired to their hometown of Bedford, New Hampshire. Once in control, it took Kroc only seventeen years to reach the billion-dollar milestone. It gave him great satisfaction to think that IBM had needed forty years to do this. Kroc would boast in his autobiography that the company was responsible for making more than a thousand millionaires—the franchise holders.[1]

When Kroc retired in 1968, the company had more than 1,200 restaurants, and sales were $400 million. He had laid the groundwork for great growth; by 1972 the number of outlets had climbed to 2,272 and sales were accelerating beyond $1 billion.

THE MCDONALD'S GROWTH MACHINE

In its *1995 Annual Report,* McDonald's management was justifiably proud. Sales and profits had continued the long trend upward, and even seemed to be accelerating. See Table 14.1 for sales and profits through 1998. Far from reaching a saturation point, the firm was opening more restaurants than ever, some 2,400 around the world in 1995, up from 1,800 the year before. "We plan to add between 2,500 and 3,200 restaurants in both 1996 and 1997, with about two thirds outside of the United States. In other words, we opened more than six restaurants per day in 1995; over the next two years, we plan to open eight a day."[2] And, "Our growth opportunities remain significant: on any given day, 99 percent of the world's population does not eat at McDonald's ... yet."[3]

Company management extolled the power of the McDonald's brand overseas, and how on opening days lines were sometimes "miles" long. "Often our challenge is to keep up with demand. In China, for example, there are only 62 McDonald's to serve a population of 1.2 billion."[4] By the end of 1995, the company had 7,012 outlets in 89 countries of the world, with Japan alone having 1,482. Table 14.2 shows the top ten countries in 1998 in number of McDonald's units.

Sometimes in marketing its products in different cultures, adjustments had to be made. Nowhere was this more necessary than in Yugoslavia during the NATO

[1] Ray Kroc and Robert Anderson, *Grinding It Out: The Making of McDonald's* (New York: Berkley Publishing, 1977), 200.
[2] *McDonald's 1995 Annual Report,* p. 8.
[3] Ibid., p. 7.
[4] Ibid.

TABLE 14.1.   Growth in McDonald's Sales and Profits, 1985–1998

	Sales (millions)	Percent Gain	Income (millions)	Percent Gain
1985	$11,011		$ 433	
1986	12,432	12.9	480	12.2
1987	14,330	15.3	549	14.4
1988	16,064	12.1	646	17.7
1989	17,333	7.9	727	12.5
1990	18,759	8.2	802	10.3
1991	19,928	6.2	860	7.2
1992	21,885	9.8	959	11.5
1993	23,587	7.8	1,083	12.9
1994	25,987	10.2	1,224	13.0
1995	29,914	15.1	1,427	16.6
1996	31,812	6.3	1,573	10.2
1997	33,638	5.7	1,642	4.3
1998	35,979	6.9	1,550	−5.6

Source: 1998 Annual Report.

Commentary: Of particular interest is how the new expansion policies brought a burst of revenues and profits in the mid-1990s. But after 1995, growth in sales and earnings slowed. Still, statistically this is a healthy company, and 1999 results should show improving growth.

TABLE 14.2.   Top Ten Foreign Markets in Number of McDonald's Units at Year End, 1998

	Restaurants
Japan	2,852
Canada	1,085
Germany	931
England	810
France	708
Brazil	672
Australia	666
Taiwan	292
China	220
Italy	201

Source: 1998 Annual Report.

Commentary: Is the popularity of McDonald's in Japan a surprise?

bombings in the Kosovo confrontation. The Information Box: McDonald's Successful Adventures in Serbia, 1999 describes the changes McDonald's made there for these turbulent times.

Growth Prospects in the United States

In 1995, with 11,368 of its restaurants in the United States, wasn't McDonald's reaching saturation in its domestic market? Top management vehemently disputed

---

INFORMATION BOX

McDONALD'S SUCCESSFUL ADVENTURES IN SERBIA, 1999

The NATO air war against Yugoslavia lasted 78 days. At first the fifteen McDonald's restaurants in Yugoslavia were closed due to angry mobs bent on vandalizing. Fanned by media attacks on "NATO criminals and aggressors," mobs of youth smashed windows and painted insults. But the restaurants soon reopened, downplaying the U.S. citizenship and presenting McDonald's as a Yugoslav company.

They promoted the McCountry, a domestic pork burger with paprika garnish. (Pork is considered the most Serbian of meats.) To cater to Serbian identity and pride, they brought out posters and lapel buttons showing the golden arches topped with a traditional Serbian cap called the sajkaca. Dragoljub Jakic, the 47-year-old managing director of McDonald's in Yugoslavia, noted that the cap "is a strong, unique Serbian symbol. By adding this symbol of our cultural heritage, we hoped to denote our pride in being a local company."[5] They also handed out free cheeseburgers at anti-NATO rallies. One restaurant's basement in Belgrade even became a bomb shelter.

The result? In spite of falling wages, rising prices, and lingering anger at the United States, the McDonald's restaurants were thronged with Serbs.

Still, McDonald's globally is a prominent symbol of American culture and attracts outbursts of anti-American sentiment. For example, in August 1999, a McDonald's in Belgium was burned down by suspected animal-rights activists. And India has seen militant critics: "They (McDonald's) are the chief killers of cows in the world. We don't need cow killers in India."[6]

Do you think McDonald's in Yugoslavia went too far in downplaying—some would say even denying—its American roots? Did it have any other reasonable option if it were to keep operating?

Should militant activists become more violent about McDonald's "conducting a global conspiracy against cows," do you think McDonald's should abandon the India market? Why or why not?

---

[5] Robert Block, "How Big Mac Kept From Becoming a Serb Archenemy," *Wall Street Journal*, 3 September 1999, p. B3.
[6] "Delhi Delights in McMutton Burgers," *Cleveland Plain Dealer*, 6 November 1999, p. 3-D.

this conclusion. Rather, it offered a startling statistical phenomenon to support accelerating expansion. Called Greenberg's law, after newly appointed McDonald's U.S. chairman Jack Greenberg, it maintained that the more stores McDonald's put in a city the more per capita transactions would result. Thus, with two stores in a city there might be 16 transactions per capita per year. Add two or four more stores and the transactions will not only double, or quadruple, but may even do better than that. The hypothesized explanation for this amazing phenomenon seemingly rested on two factors: convenience and market share. With more outlets, McDonald's increased its convenience to consumers, and added to its market share at the expense of competitors. Hence, the justification for the expansion binge.

Aiding this domestic expansion the company had been able to reduce the cost of building a new U.S. traditional restaurant by 26 percent by standardizing building materials and equipment and global sourcing, as well as improving construction methods and building designs. It had also found abundant market opportunities in building satellite restaurants. These were smaller, had lower sales volume, and served simplified menus. This format proved cost efficient in such nontraditional places as zoos, hospitals, airports, museums, and military bases as well as in retail stores such as Wal-Mart, Home Depot, and other major stores. For example, such satellite restaurants were in some 800 Wal-Mart stores by the end of 1995, with more planned. In October 1996, a McDonald's Express opened in an office building in Lansing, Michigan, a harbinger of more such sites to come.

In its eager search for more outlets, McDonald's did something it had never done before. It took over stores from weak competitors. In late summer 1996, it bought 184 company-owned Roy Rogers outlets. "Here was an opportunity that was maybe once in a lifetime," Greenberg stated.[7] Earlier the same year, it acquired Burghy's, an 80-store fast-food chain in Italy. And in New Zealand, it added 17 restaurants from the Georgie Pie chain.

The new stores were seldom like the old ones. The drive-through windows generated 55 percent of U.S. sales, and made fewer seats needed inside. This left more space available for gas stations or for indoor playgrounds—"Ronald's Playplaces"—to attract families. McDonald's made joint ventures with Chevron and Amoco to code-velop properties. It also signed an exclusive marketing deal with Disney for promoting each other's brands.

McDonald's has always spent big for advertising, and this has been effective. Even back in the 1970s, a survey of school children found 96 percent able to identify Ronald McDonald, ranking him second only to Santa Claus.[8] In 1995, advertising and promotional expenditures totaled $1.8 billion, or 6 percent of sales.[9]

[7] Gary Samuels, "Golden Arches Galore," *Forbes*, 4 November 1996, p. 48.

[8] "The Burger That Conquered the Country," *Time*, 17 September 1973, pp. 84–92.

[9] *McDonald's 1995 Annual Report*, p. 9.

Factors in the Invincibility of McDonald's

Through the third quarter of 1996, McDonald's could proudly claim 126 consecutive quarters of record earnings. Since its earliest days, the ingredients of success were simple, but few competitors were able to effectively emulate them. The basic aspects were:

- A brief menu, but having consistent quality over thousands of outlets.
- Strictly enforced and rigorous operational standards controlling service, cleanliness, and all other aspects of the operation.
- Friendly employees, despite a high turnover of personnel because of the monotony of automated food handling.
- Heavy mass media advertising directed mostly at families and children.
- Identification of a fertile target market—the family—and directing the marketing strategy to satisfying it with product, price, promotional efforts, and site locations. (At least in the early years this meant the suburban locations with their high density of families.)

However, by the end of 1996, international operations were the real vehicle of growth, providing 47 percent of the company's $30 billion sales and 54 percent of profits. Of no small concern, the domestic operation had not blossomed accordingly.

STORM CLOUDS FOR THE DOMESTIC OPERATION

Souring Franchisee Relations

In the market-share game, in which McDonald's dominated all its competitors, corporate management concluded that the firm with the most outlets in a given community wins. But as McDonald's unprecedented expansion continued, many franchisees were skeptical of headquarters' claim that no one loses when the company opens more outlets in a community since market share rises proportionately. Many a franchise holder wondered how much his sales would diminish when another McDonald's opened down the street.

The 7,000-member American Franchisee Association, an organization formed to look after franchisees' rights, claimed that McDonald's operators were joining in record numbers.[10] Other franchisees formed a clandestine group called the Consortium, representing dissidents who felt present management was unresponsive to their concerns. They remembered a kinder and gentler company. See the Information Box: The Contentment of Two McDonald's Franchisees for contrasting franchisee views on the high-growth market-share policy.

Other concerns of franchisees were a new set of business practices developed by corporate headquarters, known as Franchising 2000. The company claimed it instituted this as a way to improve standards for quality, service, cleanliness, and value by giving franchisees better "tools." But some saw this as a blatant attempt to gain more power over the franchised operations. One provision revived a controversial A, B, C,

[10] Richard Gibson, "Some Franchisees Say Moves by McDonald's Hurt their Operations," *Wall Street Journal*, 17 April 1996, pp. A1 and A8.

INFORMATION BOX

THE CONTENTMENT OF TWO McDONALD'S FRANCHISEES

In 1980, Wayne Kilburn and his wife, Mary Jane, took over the only McDonald's in Ridgecrest, California, a town of 26,000. The Kilburns prospered in the years to come. Then McDonald's instituted its "market-share plan" for Ridgecrest. Late in 1995 it put a company-owned restaurant inside the Wal-Mart. A few months later it built another outlet inside the China Lake Naval Weapons Center. A third company-owned store went up just outside the naval base. "Basically, they killed me," *Forbes* reported Kilburn saying, and he claimed his volume dropped 30 percent.[11]

In its *1995 Annual Report,* corporate headquarters offered another view concerning franchisee contentment. Tom Wolf was a McDonald's franchisee with 15 restaurants in the Huntington, West Virginia, and Ashland, Kentucky, markets. He opened his first McDonald's in 1974, had eight by the end of 1993, and opened seven more in the last two years, including two McDonald's in Wal-Mart stores and another in an alliance with an oil company; in addition he added indoor Playplaces to two existing restaurants.

Has all this investment in growth made a difference? The *Annual Report* quotes Tom: "I wouldn't change a thing. Sales are up. I'm serving more customers, my market share is up and I'm confident about the future. Customers say that the Playplaces and Wal-Mart units are 'a great idea.' The business is out there. We've got to take these opportunities now, or leave them for someone else to take."[12]

"The high growth, market-share policy should not bother any franchisee. It simply creates opportunities to invest in more restaurants." Evaluate this statement.

---

[11] Samuels, p. 48.
[12] *McDonald's 1995 Annual Report,* p. 32.

and F grading system, with only franchisees who received A's and B's eligible for more restaurants. Furthermore, McDonald's began using Franchising 2000 to enforce a single pricing strategy throughout the chain, so that a Big Mac, for example, would cost the same everywhere. The corporation maintained that such uniformity was necessary for the discounting needed to build market share. Those not complying risked losing their franchise.

Franchise relations should not be a matter of small concern to McDonald's. Table 14.3 shows the ratio of franchised restaurants to total restaurants both within and outside the United States. As can be seen, franchises comprise by far the largest proportion of restaurants.

Menu Problems

In 1993, domestic per-store sales were increasing at a 4 percent annual rate. By the third quarter of 1996, sales had slumped to a 3 percent decrease, this being the fifth quarter in a row of declining sales. In part this decline was thought to be attributable

TABLE 14.3. Percent of Franchised to Total Traditional McDonald's Restaurants, Selected Years, 1985–1998

	1985	1992	1995	1998
Traditional restaurants				
Total	8,901	13,093	16,809	24,800
Operated by franchisees	6,150	9,237	11,240	15,281
Percent franchised to total	69.1%	70.5%	66.9%	61.3%

Source: Calculated from *1998 Annual Report.*

Commentary: Whereas by 1998, the ratio of franchised to total restaurants had dropped, still more than 60 percent are still operated by franchisees. Perhaps this suggests that franchisee concerns ought to receive full consideration by corporate headquarters.

to older customers drifting away: "Huge numbers of baby-boomers … want less of the cheap, fattening foods at places like McDonald's. As soon as their kids are old enough, they go elsewhere."[13]

In an attempt to win more business from this customer segment, McDonald's with a $200 million promotional blitz launched its first "grownup taste" sandwich, the Arch Deluxe line of beef, fish, and chicken burgers. It forecast that this would become a $1 billion brand in only its first year. But before long, some were calling this a McFlop. In September 1996, Edward Rensi, head of U.S. operations, tried to minimize the stake in the new sandwich, and sent a memo to 2,700 concerned franchisees, "the Arch Deluxe was never intended to be a silver bullet."[14] On October 8, Rensi was replaced by Jack Greenberg.

McDonald's domestic troubles were not entirely new. As far back as the late 1980s, competitors, including Pizza Hut and Taco Bell, were nibbling at McDonald's market share, and Burger King was more than holding its own. Even the great traditional strength of McDonald's of unsurpassed controlled standards over food, service, and cleanliness seemed to be waning: A 1995 *Restaurants and Institutions Choice in Chains* survey of 2,849 adults gave McDonald's low marks on food quality, value, service, and cleanliness. Top honors instead went to Wendy's.[15]

In 1991, McDonald's reluctantly tried discounting, with "Extra Value Meals," largely to keep up with Taco Bell's value pricing. But by 1995, price promotions were no longer attracting customers, and per-store sales began slumping. The new, adult-oriented Deluxe line was not only aimed at older adults, but with its prices 20 percent more than regular items, it was expected to parry the discounting.

The company had previously had problems in expanding its menu. The McDLT was notably unsuccessful despite heavy promotion. More recently, the low-fat McLean, an effort to attract weight-conscious adults, was a complete disaster. In fact, this beef-and-seaweed concoction sold so badly that some operators kept only a few frozen patties on hand, while others, as revealed in an embarrassing TV expose, sold fully fatted burgers in McLean boxes to the few customers asking for them.

[13] Shelly Branch, "McDonald's Strikes Out With Grownups," *Fortune,* 11 November 1996, p. 158.
[14] Ibid.
[15] Ibid.

Some years before, the company had tried but failed to develop an acceptable pizza product. It also was unable to create a dinner menu that would attract evening-hour traffic. Two other experiments were also abandoned: a 1950s-style cafe and a family-type concept called Hearth Express that served chicken, ham, and meatloaf.

THE SITUATION IN THE NEW MILLENNIUM

Jack Greenberg was promoted to CEO of McDonald's in August 1998, and then to chairman of the board in May 1999. There was hope that he would improve the alienation felt by many franchisees. He began more diversifying within the fast-food industry, buying Donatos Pizza, a Midwestern chain of 143 restaurants, proclaiming: "We would like to make this a growth opportunity for our franchisees."[16] McDonald's also installed a new cooking system to deliver sandwiches to order, "Made for You," which meant fresher with less waste compared with the old system of holding bins. "You don't grow this business by having clean washrooms," Greenberg said. "We will grow this business through food."[17]

Despite Greenberg's leadership, McDonald's domestic operations continued to falter. By 2001, it was averaging only 1 percent same-store sales growth, far behind the 4 percent average of Burger King and Wendy's. After forty-four years as one of America's premier growth companies, market saturation seemed imminent. The main reason was thought to be a stale menu, but this was hardly a new insight.

Of perhaps just as much concern was the deterioration of the stringent controls that for decades had marked McDonald's as the paragon among all firms. A 2001 University of Michigan study on customer satisfaction showed conditions had gotten even worse since a 1995 survey that gave McDonald's low marks on food, service, and cleanliness. This 2001 study also ranked McDonald's among the poorest-performing fast-food chains, with 11 percent of customers dissatisfied because of slow service, wrong orders, dirty stores, and rude and uncaring employees. Estimates were that unhappy customers could mean an average of $60,000 in lost sales per year per store. In efforts to improve customer satisfaction, "customer recovery teams" were planned, along with better education of store managers and franchisees in handling complaints.[18]

Undoubtedly such problems reflected the difficulty many businesses had in hiring good help due to the low unemployment rates of the late 1990s. But other fast-food chains were doing better in this regard than McDonald's. Perhaps another factor contributed to the control problems. In recognition of franchisee complaints, Greenberg threw out the *Franchise 2000* rulebook with its eighty pages of onerous regulations and gave franchisees more say in their local menus.

---

[16] James P. Miller and Richard Gibson," Did Somebody Say Pizza?" *Wall Street Journal*, 1 May 1999, p. A4.

[17] Kevin Helliker and Richard Gibson, "The New Chief Is Ordering Up Changes at McDonald's," *Wall Street Journal*, 24 August 1998, p. B4.

[18] Richard Gibson, Dow Jones News, as reported in "McDonald's Leaders Finding Rudeness, Slowness Are Costing Company Business," *Cleveland Plain Dealer*, 16 July 2001, p. C6.

The frenetic growth in outlets of the mid-1990s was over, as many angry franchisees saw their sales decline as much as 20 percent due to cannibalization by nearby McDonald's outlets. In 1999, only 150 new outlets were added, down sharply from the 1,100 of a few years before.

Increasingly, Greenberg turned his attention to judicious food diversifications. He planned to grow the 143-store Donatos Pizza regional chain to a national one of a thousand stores. He bought into Chipotle Mexican Grill, a popular Denver-based chain of Mexican restaurants. The purchase of Aroma, a coffee-and-sandwich bar in London, England, showed perhaps the most promise. In the UK, the cold-sandwich market was almost double the size of the burger market and growing twice as fast, appealing to a mostly single, health-conscious, and female customer base that had practically no overlap with the burger crowd—therefore, no cannibalization. Some 150 stores were planned by 2002. In another major acquisition, McDonald's acquired the faltering Boston Market chain on May 26, 2000. About one hundred underperforming Boston Market restaurants were closed, and others were converted to McDonald's, Chipotle Mexican Grill, and Donatos Pizza. This still left more than 750 Boston Market restaurants that could challenge McDonald's management in achieving profitability.

In the major menu thrust beyond burgers, more new products were coming out of McDonald's test kitchens than ever before, many of these appealing regionally rather than nationally: for example, the McBrat, a $1.99 sandwich with sauerkraut and onion on the bratwurst, a big hit in Minnesota and Wisconsin; a McLobster Roll in New England; Homestyle Burger with hot mustard in Texas; the Brutus Buckeye Burger for Ohioans; and even bagel breakfast sandwiches, already doing well in six thousand stores.[19]

Still, U.S. sales grew just 3 percent in 2000, while fourth-quarter net earnings declined 7 percent. McDonald's responded with a "New Tastes Menu," a collection of forty-four items to be rotated four at a time. An analyst noted, however, that these were mostly "tired old products with such startling innovations like a strip of bacon or a dollop of ranch dressing."[20]

The Attractiveness of McDonald's Franchises

Despite concerns about future promise and publicity about franchisee concerns, franchise applications in the United States totaled more than ten times the number of outlets available. McDonald's could still be very choosy in selecting franchisees. This popularity of franchises meant that retiring franchisees could count on buyers for their stores, and the difficulty of gaining a franchise assured that only highly motivated people would be finalists.

Financial requirements were not for the marginal investor. Total price tag to start a typical full-size McDonald's was around $500,000 in 1998, with labor, at 8 percent of sales, and rent the major expenses after opening. A prospective franchisee trained

[19] Bruce Upbin, "Beyond Burgers," *Forbes*, 1 November 1999, pp. 218–223.
[20] Brandon Copple, "Same Old, Same Old," *Forbes*, 19 February 2001, p. 60.

at least a year, working in restaurants without pay, even performing such tasks as scrubbing bathrooms. When an opportunity finally came, it usually involved pulling up stakes and moving.[21]

The Situation in the Rest of the World

In Europe, mad-cow hysteria and currency woes were playing havoc, and McDonald's stock was at a two-year low. But non-U.S. restaurants continued to offer the best opportunities, and by the end of 2000 foreign restaurants outnumbered U.S. outlets by 15,900 to 12,408. International business contributed 52 percent of total operating income by 2000.[22] The success of the international operations partly reflected McDonald's adaptation to foreign environments. (We saw an example of this earlier, in the information box describing adaptations in Serbia.) Let us look at two more examples of adaptation—Egypt and Japan.

Egypt

In 2001 McDonald's franchises introduced the traditional Arab snack—deep-fried patties of ground beans flavored with spices—on an American-style hamburger bun with tomato, lettuce, pickles, and a spicy tahini sauce. At about 38 cents, this McFalafel was one of the cheapest items on the menu, but it was more than three times what a falafel sandwich cost in thousands of shops around the country. The company also sought an authentic touch for its advertising, hiring Egyptian pop star Shaaban Abdel-Rahim to sing its praises with the jingle, "If you eat a bite, you can't stop before finishing the whole roll." Only months before, Abdel-Rahim had helped fuel an anti-Israeli and anti-American campaign during Israeli-Palestinian battles, with the hit song, *I Hate Israel.*[23]

Japan Inroads

McDonald's has been in Japan for thirty years. By the end of 1995 it had 1,482 restaurants there, by far its largest penetration in any foreign market (see Table 14.2). By the end of 1998 there were 2,852 restaurants in Japan, and by 2001 nearly 3,600. McDonald's changed the eating habits of the nation, making fast food a part of everyday life and marking the birth of a business empire. McDonald's—"Maku" in Japanese shorthand—controlled about 65 percent of the fast-food burger market, with $3.5 billion in sales, while serving 1.3 billion customers a year. The mad cow disease scare that had so severely affected demand in Europe was largely averted in Japan, which used beef from Australia, where there had been no disease.

Through the years, McDonald's had walloped most of its competitors, including even Burger King, which pulled out of Japan. Price-cutting was found to be an effective strategy amid a decade-long economic slowdown. Part of the success came from

---

[21] Richard Gibson, "McDonald's Problems in Kitchen Don't Dim the Lure of Franchises," *Wall Street Journal,* 3 June 1998, pp. A1, A6.

[22] Company public information.

[23] From the Associated Press, "McDonald's Puts Arab Snack on a Bun," *Tri-City Herald,* 24 June 2001, p. B5.

adapting hamburgers to the Japanese palate. For example, the Teriyaki Mac Burger was cooked in an Oriental-flavored sauce, and the Calbee Burger featured a Korean-style taste.

On July 26, 2001, McDonald's Japan Co. became publicly listed with an initial public offering of $35 a share that raised $405 million. Then it raised its sights to another ten thousand outlets by 2010, and was gearing to tackle all rivals for eating out, such as shops offering beef-over-rice bowls, buckwheat noodles, and sushi.[24]

POSTSCRIPT

On December 12, 2002, the announcement came that CEO Jack Greenberg, now sixty, was stepping down at the end of the year, well ahead of his planned 2005 retirement. This marked the end of his four-year effort to reinvent the firm.

Greenberg's reinvention efforts included starting a fierce price war by selling two of McDonald's biggest sandwiches for $1 each, introducing some forty new menu items, and spending $181 million to overhaul the company's U.S. kitchens in order to make food hotter and fresher, as well as acquiring other restaurant chains. In November 2002, customers were even given the option of paying with credit cards and earning frequent-flyer miles. Still, sales had remained lackluster, and profits fell in seven of the past eight quarters, while the stock price had sunk to a seven-year low.

Aside from the acquisitions, customer response to most of these changes was poor (the verdict is still out on the credit-card option). The price war mostly resulted in all burger chains facing lower profits with little increase in sales. The new "Made for You" kitchen sacrificed speed and service. And Greenberg could never bring customer service up to historic levels, despite sending mystery shoppers to evaluate service. The mad cow scare in Europe in 2000 dragged down profits as well, but profitability was not regained with the end of mad cow concerns.[25]

ANALYSIS

After decades of uninterrupted growth in sales, profits, and number of stores opened, the domestic operation's growth in the latter 1990s seemed endangered. Admittedly, there were good gains in revenues and income, but these reflected a sharp increase in number of stores. For example, in 1996 McDonald's opened 2,500 new stores, four times the number opened just four years before. However, same-store sales dropped 2.5 percent from 1994 to 1995 for U.S. restaurants—all this despite vigorous discounting and promotional efforts. The situation was hardly improved by 2001, except that the number of new stores had slowed drastically. This was partly in deference to franchisees, who cringed at the increased competition—not so much from Wendy's, Burger King, and Taco Bell as from other McDonald's outlets.

---

[24] Yuri Kageyama, Associated Press, as appearing in "McDonald's Shakes Up Japan with IPO Plan," *Cleveland Plain Dealer*, 25 July 2001, p. C4.

[25] Compiled from Shirley Leung and Ron Lieber, "The New Menu Option at McDonald's: Plastic," *Wall Street Journal*, 26 November 2002, pp. D1, D2; and Shirley Leung, "McDonald's Chief Plans to Leave," *Wall Street Journal*, 6 December 2002, pp. A3, A6.

Relations with franchisees, formerly best in the industry, deteriorated in the mid-1990s as corporate management pursued policies that were more dictatorial and self-ish than ever before, policies that signaled the end of the kinder and gentler stance franchisees remembered. In particular, the new expansion policy—aimed at increased market share, regardless of its effect on established franchisees—portended worsening relations and the start of an adversarial instead of supportive climate.

Top management saw the cost-benefit consequences of the aggressive expansion policy as in the company's best interests, especially with greater cost efficiencies of new construction. If total market share could be substantially increased, despite same-store sales declining, the accounting analysis could support more stores. But was the trade-off with unhappy franchisees worth it?

A major domestic challenge for a growth-minded McDonald's was the menu—how to appeal to adults and expand market potential. If the dinner market could be tapped, this offered a major growth opportunity. But the last successful menu expansion had been the breakfast menu, and that was decades ago.

What menu changes should be made? With a history of failures, expectations could hardly be robust. Yet, McDonald's—like any chain organization, fast food or otherwise—can test different prices and strategies, or different menus and different atmospheres, in just a few outlets; and then, only if results are favorable, expand further. By the new millennium, acquisitions of other restaurant chains seemed the best bet for menu diversification, but the assimilation of some of these—such as the Boston Market acquisition—offered no profit guarantees.

The latter half of the 1990s and the beginning of the millennium saw lagging enforcement of the highest standards and controls in the world over product quality and service, those imposed since the days of founder Ray Kroc. Even chairman Greenberg was guilty of saying, "You don't grow this business with clean restrooms. You grow it with food." In consumer satisfaction surveys, the cornerstone of the mighty McDonald's was being surpassed by its competitors.

The international market may save the growth of McDonald's. Albeit with some menu adaptations, people in many countries of the world seem enamored with the hamburger, the symbol of the American way of life. As the *1995 Annual Report* noted, "Our growth opportunities remain significant: on any given day, 99 percent of the world's population does not eat at McDonald's … yet." Nevertheless, the poor recovery from the mad cow scare lessens the optimism.

UPDATE—2003

By 2003 McDonald's faced intensified competitive pressure. One firm in particular, Yum Brands, had become a major factor in the fast-food industry. PepsiCo had spun this organization off in 1997, and it was now the world's largest restaurant operator in units, with 33,000 restaurants in five major chains: Pizza Hut, Taco Bell, KFC (Kentucky Fried Chicken), Long John Silver's, and A&W All-American Food. CEO David Novak blamed the problems that led to the spin-off on PepsiCo's management and the emphasis on marketing to the neglect of quality, service, and atmosphere.

In 2003 as McDonald's, Burger King, and Wendy's keep trying to boost sales through 99-cent unprofitable leaders, Novak is trying to gain an edge by upgrading menus, service, and ambience. Since 1997, revenue has sagged from $9.7 billion to $7.8 billion in 2002 (mostly due to selling a number of company units to franchisees), but operating income more than tripled to $891 million in 2001, and debt was reduced from $4.6 billion to $2.1 billion.

Still, it takes time and money to renovate thousands of units.

Source: Melanie Wells, "Happier Meals," *Forbes,* 20 January 2003, pp. 77–78.

WHAT CAN BE LEARNED?

It Is Possible to Have Strong and Enduring Growth without Diversification?

For more than four decades, since 1955, McDonald's has grown continuously and substantially. In all that time, the product was essentially the hamburger with its various trimmings and accompaniments. Almost all other firms in their quest for growth have diversified, sometimes wisely and synergistically, at other times imprudently and even recklessly.

For such an undeviating focus, the product should have universal appeal, be frequently consumed, and have almost unlimited potential. The hamburger probably meets these criteria better than practically any other product, along with beer, soft drinks, and tobacco. And soft drinks, of course, are a natural accompaniment to the hamburger.

Eventually even the hamburger may not be enough for continued strong growth as the international market reaches saturation and the domestic market oversaturation. Then McDonald's may be forced to seek judicious diversifications or lose the growth mode.

The insight to be gained, however, is that firms in pursuit of growth often jump into acquisitions far too hastily when the better course of action would be to more fully develop market penetration of their existing products.

Beware the Reckless Drive for Market Share

A firm can usually "buy" market share, if it is willing to sacrifice profits in so doing. It can step up advertising and sales promotion. It can lower prices, assuming that lower prices would bring more demand. It can increase sales staff and motivate them to be more aggressive. Sales and competitive position then will usually rise. But costs may increase disproportionately. In other words, the benefits to be gained may not be worth the costs.

McDonald's, as we saw in its domestic operation in the mid-1990s, aggressively increased market share by opening thousands of new units. As long as development costs could be kept sufficiently low for these new units to be profitable and not cannibalize or take too much business away from other McDonald's restaurants, then the strategy was defensible. Still, the costs of damaged franchisee relations resulting in lowered morale, cooperation, and festering resentments could be real indeed. Interestingly, this market-share growth strategy was toned down by early 2000.

Maintaining the Highest Standards Requires Constant Monitoring

McDonald's heritage and its competitive advantage have long been associated with the highest standards and controls for cleanliness, fast service, dependable food quality, and friendly, well-groomed employees. The Information Box: Matching a Competitor's Strategy discusses strategy countering by competitors and the great difficulty in matching non-price strengths.

Alas, in the last few years even McDonald's has apparently let its control of operational standards slip. We have seen that surveys of customer satisfaction in 1995 and 2001 gave McDonald's low marks on food quality, value, service, and cleanliness, with its competitors showing up considerably better. Why this lapse? Without doubt, maintaining high standards among thousands of units, company-owned as well as franchised, requires constant monitoring and exhortation. But this was successfully done for over four decades.

Can Controls Be too Stringent?

In a belated attempt to improve standards and tighten corporate control, McDonald's instituted the controversial *Franchise 2000.* Among other things, this rulebook called for grading franchisees and penalizing those receiving the lower grades. McDonald's also wanted to take away any pricing flexibility for its

INFORMATION BOX

MATCHING A COMPETITOR'S STRATEGY

Some strategies are easily countered or duplicated by competitors. Price-cutting is the most easily countered. A price cut can often be matched within minutes. Similarly, a different package or a warranty is easily imitated by competitors.

But some strategies are not so easily duplicated. Most of these involve service, a strong and positive company image, or both. A reputation for quality and dependability is not easily countered, at least in the short run. A good company or brand image is hard to match because it usually results from years of good service and satisfied customers. The great controls of McDonald's with its high standards would seem to be easily imitated; but they proved not to be, as no other firm fully matched them until recently.

The strategies and operations most difficult to imitate often are not wildly innovative, nor are they complex and well researched. Rather, they seem to be simple, like doing a better job in servicing and satisfying customers and in performing even mundane operations cheerfully and efficiently.

What explanation can you give for competitors' long-standing inability to match the standards of McDonald's?

franchisees: All restaurants now had to charge the same prices, or risk losing their franchise. Not surprisingly, some franchisees were concerned about this new get-tough management style.

Can controls be too stringent? As with most things, extreme measures of control are seldom desirable. All firms need tight controls over far-flung outlets to keep corporate management alert to emerging problems and opportunities and maintain a desired image and standard of performance. In a franchise operation this is all the more necessary, since we are dealing with independent entrepreneurs rather than hired managers. However, controls can be so rigid that no room is left for special circumstances and opportunities. If the enforcement is too punitive, the climate becomes more like that of a police state than a teamwork relationship with both parties cooperating to their mutual advantage.

This brings us to the next insight for discussion.

Is There Room for a Kinder, Gentler Firm in Today's Hotly Competitive Environment?

Many longtime McDonald's franchisees remembered with sadness a kinder, gentler company, an atmosphere nurtured by founder Ray Kroc. To be sure, Kroc insisted that customers be assured of a clean, family atmosphere with quick and cheerful service. To Kroc, this meant strict standards, not only in food preparation but also in care and maintenance of facilities, including toilets. Company auditors closely checked that the standards were adhered to, under Kroc's belief that a weakness in one restaurant could have a detrimental effect on other units in the system. Still, the atmosphere was helpful—the inspectors were "consultants"—rather than adversarial. Kroc was proud that he was responsible for making more than a thousand millionaires—the franchise holders.

Many franchisees traced the deterioration of franchiser–franchisee relations to the 1992 death of Gerald Newman, McDonald's chief accounting officer. He spent much time interacting with franchisees, sometimes encouraging—he had a reputation for a sympathetic ear—sometimes even giving them a financial break.[26]

So, is it possible and desirable to be a kind and gentle company? With franchisees? Employees? Suppliers? Customers? Of course it is. Organizations, and the people who run them, often forget this in the arrogance of power. They blame their get-tough mind-set on the exigencies of competition and the need to be faithful to their stockholders.

Kind and gentle—is this an anachronism, a throwback to a quieter time, a relic long past its usefulness? Let us hope not.

CONSIDER

Can you add other learning insights?

---

[26] Gibson, "Franchisees Say McDonald's Hurt their Operations," p. A8.

QUESTIONS

1. How do you account for the reluctance of competitors to imitate the successful efforts of another firm in their industry? Under what circumstances is imitation likely to be embraced?

2. To date McDonald's has shunned diversification into unrelated food-retailing operations as well as nonfood options. Discuss the desirability of such diversifications.

3. "Eventually—and this may come sooner than most think—there will no longer be any choice locations anywhere in the world for new hamburger outlets. As a McDonald's stockholder, I'm getting worried." Discuss.

4. Does the size of McDonald's give it a powerful advantage over its competitors? How about Burger King in Japan? Why or why not?

5. What do you think is McDonald's near-term and long-term potential? What makes you think this?

6. Is it likely that McDonald's will ever find a saturated market for its hamburgers?

7. Discuss the importance of market share in the fast-food industry.

8. Discuss the desirability of McDonald's efforts to insist on the same price in all domestic restaurants.

9. Do you think McDonald's "adaptability" in such countries as Yugoslavia and Egypt went too far in repudiating U.S. values? Why or why not?

HANDS-ON EXERCISES

1. You have been given the assignment by Edward Rensi in 1993 to instill a recommitment to improved customer service in all domestic operations. Discuss in as much detail as you can how you would go about fostering this commitment among the ten thousand domestic outlets.

2. As a McDonald's senior executive, what long-term expansion mode would you recommend for your company?

3. As a Burger King senior executive, what long-term expansion mode would you recommend for your company to combat a McDonald's maybe grown a bit vulnerable?

TEAM DEBATE EXERCISE

1. Debate this issue: McDonald's is reaching the limits of its growth without drastic change. (Note: The side that espouses drastic change should give some attention to the most likely directions for such change, and be prepared to defend these expansion possibilities.)

2. Debate the issue of corporate management adopting a get-tough attitude toward franchisees, even if it riles some of them, versus involving them more in future directions of the company. In particular, be prepared to address the challenge of bringing customer satisfaction up to traditional standards.

3. Debate this contention: Market share is overemphasized in this industry. (Both sides, in their debate, may want to consider whether or not this assertion applies to other industries.)

INVITATION TO RESEARCH

Is McDonald's becoming more vulnerable to competitors today? Does it have any emerging problems? Has it attempted any major diversifications yet? Is the international operation still overshadowing the domestic?

Disney—Euro Disney and Other Stumbles

Disney continues to boast of one of the great brands in the world. Its appeal to kids, and to those who are kids at heart, seems everlasting. Yet, in the decade of the 1990s it stumbled, at first in Euro Disney, and then near the end of the millennium, in perhaps too aggressive an expansion program. Adding to the woes was an acrimonious lawsuit between Jeffrey Katzenberg, former studio chief who left the company in 1994, and Disney CEO Michael Eisner, whose compensation of $631 million topped the list of highest-paid executives in 1998.

EURO DISNEY

Prelude

With high expectations Euro Disney opened just outside Paris in April 1992. Success seemed ensured. After all, the Disney parks in Florida, California, and, most recently, Japan, were all spectacular successes. But somehow all the rosy expectations were revealed to be a delusion. The opening results cast even the future continuance of Euro Disney into doubt. How could what seemed so right be so wrong?

Optimism

Perhaps a few early omens should have raised some cautions. Between 1987 and 1991, three $150 million amusement parks had opened in France with great fanfare. All had fallen flat, and by 1991 two were in bankruptcy. Now Walt Disney Company was finalizing its plans to open Europe's first Disneyland early in 1992. This would turn out to be a $4.4 billion enterprise sprawling over 5,000 acres 20 miles east of Paris. Initially it would have six hotels and 5,200 rooms, more rooms than the entire city of Cannes, and lodging was expected to triple in a few years as Disney opened a second theme park to keep visitors at the resort longer.

Disney also expected to develop a growing office complex, one only slightly smaller than France's biggest, La Defense, in Paris. Plans also called for shopping malls, apartments, golf courses, and vacation homes. Euro Disney would tightly control all this ancillary development, designing and building nearly everything itself, and eventually selling off the commercial properties at a huge profit.

Disney executives had no qualms about the huge enterprise, which would cover an area one-fifth the size of Paris itself. They were more worried that the park might not be big enough to handle the crowds:

> "My biggest fear is that we will be too successful." "I don't think it can miss. They are masters of marketing. When the place opens it will be perfect. And they know how to make people smile—even the French."[1]

Company executives initially predicted that 11 million Europeans would visit the extravaganza in the first year alone. After all, Europeans accounted for 2.7 million visits to the U.S. Disney parks and spent $1.6 billion on Disney merchandise. Surely a park closer would draw many thousands more. As Disney executives thought more about it, the forecast of 11 million seemed most conservative. They reasoned that since Disney parks in the United States (population of 250 million) attract 41 million visitors a year, then if Euro Disney attracted visitors in the same proportion, attendance could reach 60 million with Western Europe's 370 million people. Table 15.1 shows the 1990 attendance/population ratios at the two U.S. Disney parks and the newest Japanese Disneyland, as well as the attendance-population ratios.

Adding fuel to the optimism was the fact that Europeans typically have more vacation time than do U.S. workers. For example, five-week vacations are commonplace for French and German employees, compared with two to three weeks for U.S. workers.

TABLE 15.1. Attendance and Attendance/Population Ratios, Disney Parks, 1990

	Visitors	Population	Ratio
		(millions)	
United States			
Disneyland (Southern California)	12.9	250	5.2%
Disney World/Epcot Center (Florida)	28.5	250	11.4%
Total United States	41.4		16.6%
Japan			
Tokyo Disneyland	16.0	124	13.5%
Euro Disney	?	310[a]	?

[a] Within a two-hour flight.

Source: Euro Disney, *Amusement Business Magazine.*

Commentary: Even if the attendance/population ratio for Euro Disney is only 10 percent, which is far below that of some other theme parks, still 31 million visitors could be expected. Euro Disney "conservatively" predicted 11 million the first year.

[1] Steven Greenhouse, "Playing Disney in the Parisian Fields," *New York Times,* 17 February 1991, Section 3: 1, 6.

The failure of the three earlier French parks was seen as irrelevant. Robert Fitzpatrick, Euro Disneyland's chairman, stated, "We are spending 22 billion French francs before we open the door, while the other places spent 700 million. This means we can pay infinitely more attention to details—to costumes, hotels, shops, trash baskets—to create a fantastic place. There's just too great a response to Disney for us to fail."[2]

Nonetheless, a few scattered signs indicated that not everyone was happy with the coming of Disney. Leftist demonstrators at Euro Disney's stock offering greeted company executives with eggs, ketchup, and "Mickey Go Home" signs. Some French intellectuals decried the pollution of the country's cultural ambiance with the coming of Mickey Mouse and company: They called the park an American cultural abomination. The mainstream press also seemed contrary, describing every Disney setback "with glee." French officials in negotiating with Disney sought less American and more European culture at France's Magic Kingdom. Still, such protests and bad press seemed contrived, unrepresentative, and certainly not predictive. Company officials dismissed the early criticism as "the ravings of an insignificant elite."[3]

The Location Decision

In the search for a site for Euro Disney, Disney executives examined 200 locations in Europe. The other finalist was Barcelona, Spain. Its major attraction was warmer weather, but its transportation system was not as good as that around Paris, and it lacked level tracts of land of sufficient size. The clincher for the Paris decision was its more central location. Table 15.2 shows the number of people within 2 to 6 hours of the Paris site.

The beet fields of the Marne-la-Vallee area was the choice. Being near Paris seemed a major advantage, since Paris was Europe's biggest tourist draw. And France was eager to win the project to help lower its jobless rate and also to enhance its role as the center of tourist activity in Europe. The French government expected the project to create at least 30,000 jobs and to contribute $1 billion a year from foreign visitors.

TABLE 15.2. Number of People within 2–6 Hours of the Paris Site

Within a 2-hour drive	17 million people
Within a 4-hour drive	41 million people
Within a 6-hour drive	109 million people
Within a 2-hour flight	310 million people

Source: Euro Disney, *Amusement Business Magazine.*
Commentary: The much more densely populated and geographically compact European continent makes access to Euro Disney much more convenient that it is in the United States.

[2] Greenhouse, p. 6.

[3] Peter Gumbel and Richard Turner, "Fans Like Euro Disney But Its Parent's Goofs Weigh the Park Down," *Wall Street Journal,* 10 March 1994, p. A12.

To entice the project, the French government allowed Disney to buy up huge tracts of land at 1971 prices. It provided $750 million in loans at below-market rates, and it spent hundreds of millions of dollars on subway and other capital improvements for the park. For example, Paris's express subway was extended out to the park; a 35-minute ride from downtown cost about $2.50. A new railroad station for the high-speed Train à Grande Vitesse was built only 150 yards from the entrance gate. This enabled visitors from Brussels to arrive in only 90 minutes. Once the English Channel tunnel opened in 1994, even London would be only 3 hours and 10 minutes away. Actually, Euro Disney was the second largest construction project in Europe, second only to construction of the English Channel tunnel.

Financing

Euro Disney cost $4.4 billion. Table 15.3 shows the sources of financing, in percentages. The Disney Company had a 49 percent stake in the project, which was the most that the French government would allow. For this stake it invested $160 million, while other investors contributed $1.2 billion in equity. The rest was financed by loans from the government, banks, and special partnerships formed to buy properties and lease them back.

The payoff for Disney began after the park opened. The company receives 10 percent of Euro Disney's admission fees and 5 percent of the food and merchandise revenues. This is the same arrangement as Disney has with the Japanese park. But in the Tokyo Disneyland, the company took no ownership interest, opting instead only for the licensing fees and a percentage of the revenues. The reason for the conservative position with Tokyo Disneyland was that Disney money was heavily committed to building the Epcot Center in Florida. Furthermore, Disney had some concerns about the Tokyo enterprise. This was the first non-American and the first cold-weather Disneyland. It seemed prudent to minimize the risks. But this turned out to be a significant blunder of conservatism, because Tokyo became a huge success, as the Information Box: The Tokyo Disneyland Success discusses in more detail.

TABLE 15.3. Sources of Financing for Euro Disney (percent)

Total to Finance: $4.4 billion	100%
Shareholders equity, including $160 million from Walt Disney Company	32
Loan from French government	22
Loan from group of 45 banks	21
Bank loans to Disney hotels	16
Real estate partnerships	9

Source: Euro Disney.

Commentary: The full flavor of the leverage is shown here, with equity comprising only 32 percent of the total expenditure.

INFORMATION BOX

THE TOKYO DISNEYLAND SUCCESS

Tokyo Disneyland opened in 1983 on 201 acres in the eastern suburb of Urazasu. It was arranged that an ownership group, Oriental Land, would build, own, and operate the theme park with advice from Disney. The owners borrowed most of the $650 million needed to bring the project to fruition. Disney invested no money but receives 10 percent of the revenues from admission and rides and 5 percent of sales of food, drink, souvenirs.

Although the start was slow, Japanese soon began flocking to the park in great numbers. By 1990 some 16 million a year passed through the turnstiles, about one-fourth more than visited Disneyland in California. In fiscal year 1990, revenues reached $988 million with profits of $150 million. Indicative of the Japanese preoccupation with things American, the park serves almost no Japanese food, and the live entertainers are mostly American. Japanese management even apologizes for the presence of a single Japanese restaurant inside the park: "A lot of elderly Japanese came here from outlying parts of Japan, and they were not very familiar with hot dogs and hamburgers."[4]

Disney executives were soon to realize the great mistake they made in not taking substantial ownership in Tokyo Disneyland. They did not want to make the same mistake with Euro Disney.

Would you expect the acceptance of the genuine American experience in Tokyo to be indicative of the reaction of the French and Europeans? Why or why not?

---

[4] James Sterngold, "Cinderella Hits Her Stride in Tokyo," *New York Times,* 17 February 1991, p. 6.

Special Modifications

With the experiences of the previous theme parks, and particularly that of the first cold-weather park in Tokyo, Disney construction executives were able to bring state-of-the-art refinements to Euro Disney. Exacting demands were placed on French construction companies, and a higher level of performance and compliance resulted than many thought possible to achieve. The result was a major project on time, if not completely on budget. In contrast, the Channel tunnel was plagued by delays and severe cost overruns.

One of the things learned from the cold-weather project in Japan was that more needed to be done to protect visitors from such weather problems as wind, rain, and cold. Consequently, Euro Disney's ticket booths were protected from the elements, as were the lines waiting for attractions, and even the moving sidewalk from the 12,000-car parking area.

Certain French accents—and British, German, and Italian accents as well—were added to the American flavor. The park has two official languages, English and

French, but multilingual guides are available for Dutch, Spanish, German, and Italian visitors. Discoveryland, based on the science fiction of France's Jules Verne, is a new attraction. A theater with a full 360-degree screen acquaints visitors with a sweep of European history. And, not the least modification for cultural diversity, Snow White speaks German, and the Belle Notte Pizzeria and Pasticceria are right next to Pinocchio.

Disney had foreseen that it might encounter some cultural problems. This was one of the reasons for choosing Robert Fitzpatrick as Euro Disney's president. He is American but speaks French, knows Europe well, and has a French wife. However, he was unable to establish the rapport needed and was replaced in 1993 by a French native. Still, some of his admonitions that France should not be approached as if it were Florida fell on deaf ears.

RESULTS

As the April 1992 opening approached, the company launched a massive communications blitz aimed at publicizing the fact that the fabled Disney experience was now accessible to all Europeans. Some 2,500 people from various print and broadcast media were lavishly entertained while being introduced to the new facilities. Most media people were positively impressed with the inauguration and with the enthusiastic spirit of the staffers. These public relations efforts, however, were criticized by some for being heavy-handed and for not providing access to Disney executives.

As 1992 wound down after the opening, it became clear that revenue projections were, unbelievably, not being met. But the opening turned out to be in the middle of a severe recession in Europe. European visitors, perhaps as a consequence, were far more frugal than their American counterparts. Many packed their own lunches and shunned the Disney hotels. For example, a visitor named Corine from southern France typified the "no spend" attitude of many: "It's a bottomless pit," she said as she, her husband, and their three children toured Euro Disney on a 3-day visit. "Every time we turn around, one of the kids wants to buy something."[5] Perhaps investor expectations, despite the logic and rationale, were simply unrealistic.

Indeed, Disney had initially priced the park and the hotels to meet revenue targets and had assumed demand was there at any price. Park admission was $42.25 for adults—higher than at the American parks. A room at the flagship Disneyland Hotel at the park's entrance cost about $340 a night, the equivalent of a top hotel in Paris. It was soon averaging only a 50 percent occupancy. Guests were not staying as long or spending as much on the fairly high-priced food and merchandise. We can label the initial pricing strategy at Euro Disney as *skimming pricing*. The Information Box: Skimming and Penetration Pricing discusses these strategies.

Disney executives soon realized they had made a major miscalculation. Whereas visitors to Florida's Disney World often stayed more than 4 days, Euro Disney—with one theme park compared to Florida's three—was proving to be a 2-day experience

[5] "Ailing Euro Disney May Face Closure," *Cleveland Plain Dealer*, 1 January 1994, p. E1.

INFORMATION BOX

SKIMMING AND PENETRATION PRICING

A firm with a new product or service may be in a temporary monopolistic situation. If there is little or no present and potential competition, more latitude in pricing is possible. In such a situation (and, of course, Euro Disney was in this situation), one of two basic and opposite approaches may be taken in the pricing strategy: skimming or penetration.

Skimming is a relatively high-price strategy. It is the most tempting where the product or service is highly differentiated because it yields high per-unit profits. It is compatible with a quality image. But it has limitations. It assumes a rather inelastic demand curve, in which sales will not be appreciably affected by price. And if the product or service is easily imitated (which was hardly the case with Euro Disney), then competitors are encouraged because of the high profit margins.

The penetration strategy of low prices assumes an elastic demand curve, with sales increasing substantially if prices can be lowered. It is compatible with economies of scale, and it discourages competitive entry. The classic example of penetration pricing was the Model T Ford. Henry Ford lowered his prices to make the car within the means of the general public, expanded production into the millions, and in so doing realized new horizons of economies of scale.

Euro Disney correctly saw itself in a monopoly position; it correctly judged that it had a relatively inelastic demand curve with customers flocking to the park regardless of rather high prices. What it did not reckon with was the shrewdness of European visitors: Because of the high prices they shortened their stay, avoided the hotels, brought their own food and drink, and bought only sparingly the Disney merchandise.

What advantages would a lower price penetration strategy have offered Euro Disney? Do you see any drawbacks?

at best. Many visitors arrived early in the morning, rushed to the park, staying late at night, then checked out of the hotel the next morning before heading back to the park for one final exploration.

The problems of Euro Disney were not public acceptance (despite the earlier critics). Europeans loved the place. Since the opening it attracted just under 1 million visitors a month, thus easily achieving the original projections. Such patronage made it Europe's biggest paid tourist attraction. But the large numbers of frugal patrons did not come close to enabling Disney to meet revenue and profit projections and cover a bloated overhead.

Other operational errors and miscalculations, most of these cultural, hurt the enterprise. A policy of serving no alcohol in the park caused consternation in a country where wine is customary for lunch and dinner. (This policy has since been reversed.) Disney thought Monday would be a light day and Friday a heavy one and allocated staff accordingly, but the reverse was true. It found great peaks and valleys in attendance: The number of visitors per day in the high season could be ten times the number in slack times. The need to lay off employees during quiet periods came up against France's inflexible labor schedules.

One unpleasant surprise concerned breakfast. "We were told that Europeans don't take breakfast, so we downsized the restaurants," recalled one executive. "And guess what? Everybody showed up for breakfast. We were trying to serve 2,500 breakfasts at 350-seat restaurants. The lines were horrendous."[6]

Disney failed to anticipate another demand, this time from tour bus drivers. Restrooms were built for 50 drivers, but on peak days 2,000 drivers were seeking the facilities. "From impatient drivers to grumbling bankers, Disney stepped on toe after European toe."[7]

For the fiscal year ending September 30, 1993, the amusement park had lost $960 million, and the future of the park was in doubt. (As of December 31, 1993, the cumulative loss was 6.04 billion francs, or $1.03 billion). Walt Disney made $175 million available to tide Euro Disney over until the next spring. Adding to the problems of the struggling park were heavy interest costs. As depicted in Table 15.3, against a total cost of $4.4 billion, only 32 percent of the project was financed by equity investment. Some $2.9 billion was borrowed primarily from 60 creditor banks, at interest rates running as high as 11 percent. Thus, the enterprise began heavily leveraged, and the hefty interest charges greatly increased the overhead to be covered from operations. Serious negotiations began with the banks to restructure and refinance.

ATTEMPTS TO RECOVER

The $921 million lost in the first fiscal year represented a shortfall of more than $2.5 million a day. The situation was not quite as dire as these statistics would seem to indicate. Actually, the park was generating an operating profit, but nonoperating costs were bringing it deeply into the red.

Still, operations were far from satisfactory although they were becoming better. It had taken 20 months to smooth out the wrinkles and adjust to the miscalculations about demand for hotel rooms and the willingness of Europeans to pay substantial prices for lodging, meals, and merchandise. Operational efficiencies were slowly improving.

By the beginning of 1994, Euro Disney had been made more affordable. Prices of some hotel rooms were cut—for example, at the low end, from $76 per night to $51. Expensive jewelry was replaced by $10 T-shirts and $5 crayon sets. Luxury sit-down restaurants were converted to self-service. Off-season admission prices were reduced from $38 to $30. And operating costs were reduced 7 percent by streamlining operations and eliminating over 900 jobs.

Efficiency and *economy* became the new watchwords. Merchandise in stores was pared from 30,000 items to 17,000, with more of the remaining goods being pure

---

[6] Gumbel and Turner, p. A12.

[7] Ibid.

U.S. Disney products. (The company had thought that European tastes might prefer more subtle items than the garish Mickey and Minnie souvenirs, but this was found not so.) The number of different food items offered by park services was reduced more than 50 percent. New training programs were designed to remotivate the 9,000 full-time permanent employees, to make them more responsive to customers and more flexible in their job assignments. Employees in contact with the public were given crash courses in German and Spanish.

Still, as we have seen, the problem had not been attendance, although the recession and the high prices had reduced it. Still, some 18 million people passed through the turnstiles in the first 20 months of operation. But they were not spending money as people did in the U.S. parks. Furthermore, Disney had alienated some European tour operators with its high prices, and it diligently sought to win them back.

Management had hoped to reduce the heavy interest overhead by selling the hotels to private investors. But the hotels had an occupancy rate of only 55 percent, making them unattractive to investors. Although the recession was a factor in such low occupancy rates, a significant part of the problem lay in the calculation of lodging demands. With the park just 35 minutes from the center of Paris, many visitors stayed in town. About the same time as the opening, the real estate market in France collapsed, making the hotels unsalable in the short term. This added to the overhead burden and confounded the business plan forecasts.

While some analysts were relegating Euro Disney to the cemetery, few remembered that Orlando's Disney World showed early symptoms of being a disappointment. Costs were heavier than expected, and attendance was below expectations. But Orlando's Disney World turned out to be one of the most profitable resorts in North America.

ANALYSIS

Euro Disney, as we have seen, fell far short of expectations in the first 20 months of its operation, so far short that its continued existence was even questioned. What went wrong?

External Factors

A serious economic recession that affected all of Europe undoubtedly was a major impediment to meeting expectations. As noted before, it adversely affected attendance—although still not all that much—but drastically affected spending patterns. Frugality was the order of the day for many visitors. The recession also affected real estate demand and prices, thus saddling Disney with hotels it had hoped to sell at profitable prices to eager investors to take the strain off its hefty interest payments.

The company assumed that European visitors would not be greatly different from those visitors, foreign and domestic, of U.S. Disney parks. Yet, at least in the first few years of operation, visitors were much more price conscious. This suggested that those within a 2- to 4-hour drive of Euro Disney were considerably different from the ones who traveled overseas, at least in spending ability and willingness.

Internal Factors

Despite the decades of experience with the U.S. Disney parks and the successful experience with the new Japan park, Disney still made serious blunders in its operational planning, such as the demand for breakfasts, the insistence on wine at meals, the severe peaks and valleys in scheduling, and even such mundane things as sufficient restrooms for tour bus drivers. It had problems in motivating and training its French employees in efficiency and customer orientation. Did all these mistakes reflect an intractable French mindset or a deficiency of Disney management? Perhaps both. But Disney management should have researched all cultural differences more thoroughly. Further, the park needed major streamlining of inventories and operations after the opening. The mistakes suggested an arrogant mindset by Disney management: "We were arrogant," concedes one executive. "It was like 'We're building the Taj Mahal and people will come—on our terms.'"[8]

The miscalculations in hotel rooms and in pricing of many products, including food services, showed an insensitivity to the harsh economic conditions. But the greatest mistake was taking on too much debt for the park. The highly leveraged situation burdened Euro Disney with such hefty interest payments and overhead that the breakeven point was impossibly high, and it even threatened the viability of the enterprise. See the Information Box: The Breakeven Point for a discussion of the important inputs and implications affecting breakeven, and how these should play a role in strategic planning.

Were such mistakes and miscalculations beyond what we would expect of reasonable executives? Probably not, with the probable exception of the crushing burden of debt. Any new venture is susceptible to surprises and the need to streamline and weed out its inefficiencies. While we would have expected such to have been done faster and more effectively from a well-tried Disney operation, European, and particularly French and Parisian, consumers and employees showed different behavior and attitude patterns than expected.

The worst sin that Disney management and investors could make would be to give up on Euro Disney and not to look ahead 2 to 5 years. A hint of the future promise was Christmas week of 1993. Despite the first year's $920 million in red ink, some 35,000 packed the park most days. A week later on a cold January day, some of the rides still had 40-minute waits.

POSTSCRIPT

On March 15, 1994, an agreement was struck aimed at making Euro Disney profitable by September 30, 1995. The European banks would fund another $500 million and make concessions such as forgiving 18 months' interest and deferring all principal payments for three years. In return, Walt Disney Company agreed to spend about $750 million to bail out its Euro Disney affiliate.[9] Thus, the debt would

---

[8] Gumbel and Turner, p. A12.

[9] Brian Coleman and Thomas R. King, "Euro Disney Rescue Package Wins Approval," *Wall Street Journal*, 15 March 1994, pp. A3, A5.

INFORMATION BOX

THE BREAKEVEN POINT

A breakeven analysis is a vital tool in making go/no go decisions about new ventures and alternative business strategies. This can be shown graphically as follows:

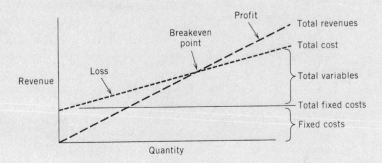

Below the breakeven point, the venture suffers losses; above it, the venture becomes profitable.

Let us make a hypothetical comparison of Euro Disney with its $1.6 billion in high interest loans (some of these as high as 11 percent) from the banks, and what the situation might be with more equity and less borrowed funds.

For this example, let us assume that other fixed costs are $240 million, that the average interest rate on the debt is 10 percent, and that average profit margin (contribution to overhead) from each visitor is $32. Now let us consider two scenarios: (a) the $1.6 billion of debt; and (b) only $0.5 billion of debt.

The number of visitors needed to break even are determined as follows:

$$\text{Breakeven} = \frac{\text{Total fixed costs}}{\text{Contribution to overhead}}$$

Scenario (a): Interest = 10% ($1,600,000,000) = $160,000,000
Fixed costs = Interest + $240,000,000
= 160,000,000 + 240,000,000
= $400,000,000

$$\text{Breakeven} = \frac{\$400,000,000}{\$32} = 12,500,000 \text{ visitors needed to break even}$$

Scenario (b) Interest = 10% (500,000,000) = $50,000,000
Fixed costs = 50,000,000 + 240,000,000
= $290,000,000

$$\text{Breakeven} = \frac{\$290,000,000}{\$32} = 9,062,500 \text{ visitors needed to break even}$$

(continues)

THE BREAKEVEN POINT *(continued)*

Because Euro Disney expected 11 million visitors the first year, it obviously was not going to breakeven while servicing $1.6 billion in debt with $160 million in interest charges per year. The average visitor would have to be induced to spend more, thereby increasing the average profit or contribution to overhead.

In making go/no go decisions, many costs can be estimated quite closely. What cannot be determined as surely are the sales figures. Certain things can be done to affect the breakeven point. Obviously it can be lowered if the overhead is reduced, as we saw in scenario b. Higher prices also result in a lower breakeven because of greater per customer profits (but would probably affect total sales quite adversely). Promotion expenses can be either increased or decreased and affect the breakeven point, but they probably also have an impact on sales. Some costs of operation can be reduced, thus lowering the breakeven. But the hefty interest charges act as a lodestone over an enterprise, greatly increasing the overhead and requiring what may be an unattainable breakeven point.

Does a new venture have to break even or make a profit the first year to be worth going into? Why or why not?

be halved, with interest payments greatly reduced. Disney also agreed to eliminate for five years the lucrative management fees and royalties it received on the sale of tickets and merchandise.

Still, the problems of Euro Disney were not resolved. However, a new source for financing emerged. A member of the Saudi royal family agreed to invest up to $500 million for a 24 percent stake. Prince Alwaleed had invested in troubled enterprises in the past; now his commitment to Euro Disney showed a belief in its ultimate success.

Finally, in the third quarter of 1995, Euro Disney posted its first profit, some $35 million for the period versus a year-earlier loss of $113 million. By now, Euro Disney was only 39 percent owned by Disney. The turnaround was attributed partly to lower prices and the new "Space Mountain" ride that mimicked a trip to the moon. Cheaper transportation to the park also helped, with cross-channel price wars pushing down the costs of traveling to Europe.

In August 1995 news broke of Walt Disney Company's proposed $10 billion acquisition of Capital Cities/ABC Inc. Experts saw this as creating an entertainment behemoth into the next century. Although many growth avenues were now possible, including great international growth in television programming and distribution such as ESPN and the Disney Channel, theme parks were considered very promising. CEO Michael Eisner announced possibilities of new theme parks in South America as well as in Asia.[10]

---

[10] Lisa Bannon, "Expanded Disney to Look Overseas for Fastest Growth," *Wall Street Journal*, 2 August 1999, p. A3.

In November 1997, *Forbes* magazine updated the situation with Euro Disney— it had been renamed Disneyland Paris—under the provocative title, "Mickey's Last Laugh." The article noted that it had 11.7 million visitors in 1996, up from 8.8 million three years before, and the cash-flow margins even exceeded those of Tokyo Disneyland, the world's most popular park.[11]

Later Problems for Walt Disney Company

Critical investor attention focused on Walt Disney Company in 1999. In April the firm reported a 41 percent drop in earnings for its fourth consecutive quarter of weak earnings. Analysts were pessimistic about Disney quickly having a turnaround, despite what most recognized as its underlying strength.

Over the previous two years, Disney had invested heavily in new enterprises, most of which were slow in generating any profits, and might even be years away from doing this. For example, there was Disney Cruise Line, an operation that lost $80 million in fiscal 1998, as serious delays were encountered in launching the first ship, the *Disney Magic*. But in 2001, with two ships in service, hopefully this venture would earn a profit.

Disney had started a chain of high-tech arcades called Disney Quest. It had begun a series of ESPN restaurants. It had expanded its Disney Channel and other cable operations. It was constructing a new theme park in Anaheim, California. The company also expanded vigorously on the Internet, both through its Disney Online unit and through the company's 43 percent investment in Infoseek. These all gobbled up funds.

Even some existing businesses were now faltering. Since the acquisition in 1995, Disney had struggled with its ABC network and its low ratings. Now ratings were improving, but Disney had saddled itself with a prodigious $1.1-billion-a-year contract with the National Football League to broadcast its games. Another key business, home videos of Disney animated films and old classics, was not meeting expectations.

The most sensational of Disney's problems involved the legal dispute with Jeffrey Katzenberg over whether he was owed $250 million in bonuses for his work at Disney. Ramifications go beyond the $250 million. Disney and CEO Eisner were accused of underreporting earnings and exaggerating expenses. This could stimulate lawsuits from finance companies, actors, writers, and unions whose pay was tied to a percentage of the take on movies and TV shows. Furthermore, Katzenberg's lucrative contracts with Disney—involving, for example, a $5 million home, $100,000 in home video equipment, private planes, and butler service—could inspire other executives and talents to up their demands. Surprisingly, few criticisms surfaced about Eisner's $631 million in 1998 compensation.[12]

---

[11] "Mickey's Last Laugh," *Forbes*, 3 November 1997, p. 16.

[12] This section has been compiled from various sources, including Keith Alexander, "Disney Case Grows Ominous," *USA Today*, 4 May 1999, p. 3B; Robert McGough and Bruce Orwall, "Disney: Lion King's Roar Stays Hoarse," *Wall Street Journal*, 29 April 1999, pp. C1 and C2; "Compensation Fit for a King," *Forbes*, 17 May 1999, pp. 202–203.

UPDATE—2002

To the delight of the French government, plans were announced in 1999 to build a movie theme park—Disney Studios, next to the Magic Kingdom—to open in 2002. It was estimated that this expansion would attract an additional 4.2 million visitors annually, drawing people from farther afield in Europe. Also late in 1999, Disney and Hong Kong agreed to build a major Disney theme park there, with Disney investing $314 million for 43 percent ownership while Hong Kong contributed nearly $3 billion. Hong Kong's leaders expected the new park would generate 16,000 jobs when it opened in 2005, certainly a motivation for the unequal investment contribution.

The Walt Disney Studios theme park opened in March 2002, as planned. It blended Disney entertainment with the history and culture of European film. Marketing efforts reflected a newfound cultural awareness, and efforts were focused largely on selling the new park through travel agents, whom Disney had initially neglected in promoting Disneyland Paris. The timing could have been better, since theme parks were reeling from the recession and the threat of terrorist attacks. A second Disney park opened in Tokyo in 2001 and was a smash hit. But the new California Adventure park in Anaheim, California, has been a bust.

Sources: "Hong Kong Betting $3 Billion on Success of New Disneyland," *Cleveland Plain Dealer,* 3 November 1999, p. 2C; Charles Fleming, "Euro Disney to Build Movie Theme Park Outside Paris," *Wall Street Journal,* 30 September 1999, pp. A15, A21; Bruce Orwall, "Euro Disney CEO Named to Head Parks Worldwide," *Wall Street Journal,* 30 September 2002, p. B8; Paulo Prada and Bruce Orwall, "A Certain 'Je Ne Sais Quoi' at Disney's New Park," *Wall Street Journal,* 12 March 2002, pp. Bl, B4.

WHAT CAN BE LEARNED?

Beware the Arrogant Mindset, Especially When Dealing with New Situations and New Cultures

French sensitivities were offended by Disney corporate executives who often turned out to be brash, insensitive, and overbearing. A contentious attitude by Disney personnel alienated people and aggravated planning and operational difficulties. "The answer to doubts or suggestions invariably was, Do as we say, because we know best."

Such a mindset is a natural concomitant with success. It is said that success breeds arrogance, but this inclination must be fought against by those who would spurn the ideas and concerns of others. For a proud and touchy people, the French, this almost contemptuous attitude by the Americans fueled resentment and glee at Disney miscues. It did not foster cooperation, understanding, or the willingness to smooth the process. One might almost speculate that had not the potential economic benefits to France been so great, the Euro Disney project might never have been approved.

Great Success May Be Ephemeral

We often find that great successes are not lasting, that they have no staying power. Somehow the success pattern gets lost or forgotten or is not well rounded. Other times an operation grows beyond the capability of the originators. Hungry competitors are always in the wings, ready to take advantage of any lapse. As we saw with Euro Disney, having a closed mind to new ideas or to needed revisions of an old success pattern—the arrogance of success—makes expansion into different environments more difficult and even risky.

While corporate Disney has continued to have strong success with its other theme parks and its diversifications, competitors are moving in with their own theme parks in the United States and elsewhere. We may question whether this industry is approaching saturation, and we may wonder whether Disney has learned from its mistakes in Europe.

Highly Leveraged Situations Are Extremely Vulnerable

During most of the 1980s, many managers, including corporate raiders, pursued a strategy of debt financing in contrast to equity (stock ownership) financing. Funds for such borrowing were usually readily available, heavy debt had income tax advantages, and profits could be distributed among fewer shares so that return on equity was enhanced. During this time a few voices decried the overleveraged situations of many companies. They predicted that when the eventual economic downturn came, such firms would find themselves unable to meet the heavy interest burden. Most lenders paid little heed to such lonesome voices and encouraged greater borrowing.

The widely publicized problems of some of the raiders in the late 1980s, such as Robert Campeau, who had acquired major department store corporations only to find himself overextended and unable to continue, suddenly changed some expansionist lending sentiments. The hard reality dawned that these arrangements were often fragile indeed, especially when they rested on optimistic projections for asset sales, for revenues, and for cost savings to cover the interest payments. An economic slowdown hastened the demise of some of these ill-advised speculations.

Disney was guilty of the same speculative excesses with Euro Disney, relying far too much on borrowed funds and assuming that assets, such as hotels, could be easily sold off at higher prices to other investors. As we saw in the breakeven box, hefty interest charges from such overleveraged conditions can jeopardize the viability of the enterprise if revenue and profit projections fail to meet the rosy expectations.

Be Judicious with the Skimming Price Strategy

Euro Disney faced the classical situation favorable for a skimming price strategy. It was in a monopoly position, with no equivalent competitors likely. It faced a somewhat inelastic demand curve, which indicated that people would come almost regardless of price. So why not price to maximize per-unit profits? Unfortunately for Disney, the wily Europeans circumvented the high prices by frugality. Of course, a severe recession exacerbated the situation.

The learning insight from this example is that a skimming price assumes that customers are willing and able to pay the higher prices and have no lower-priced competitive alternatives. It is a faulty strategy when many customers are unable, or else unwilling, to pay the high prices and can find a way to experience the product or service in a modest way.

CONSIDER

Can you think of other learning insights from this case?

QUESTIONS

1. How could the company have erred so badly in its estimates of the spending patterns of European customers?

2. How could a better reading of the impact of cultural differences on revenues have been achieved?

3. What suggestions do you have for fostering a climate of sensitivity and goodwill in corporate dealings with the French?

4. How do you account for the great success of Tokyo Disneyland and the problems of Euro Disney? What are the key contributory differences?

5. Do you believe that Euro Disney might have done better if located elsewhere in Europe rather than just outside Paris? Why or why not?

6. "Mickey Mouse and the Disney park are an American cultural abomination." Evaluate this critical statement.

7. Consider how a strong marketing approach might be made to both European consumers and agents, such as travel agents, tour guides, even bus drivers.

8. A major Disney stockholder angrily comments upon seeing the latest *Forbes* rankings of executive compensation: "It's an insult to us shareholders to pay Michael Eisner $631 million last year (1998), more than any other executive of any other firm, when Disney profits have been steadily declining under his leadership. I'm selling my Disney stock." Discuss.

HANDS-ON EXERCISES

Before

1. It is three months before the grand opening. As a staff assistant to the president of Euro Disney, you sense that the plans for high price and luxury accommodations are ill advised. What arguments would you marshall to persuade the company to offer lower prices and more moderate accommodations? Be as persuasive as you can.

After

2. It is six months after opening. Revenues are not meeting target, and a number of problems have surfaced and are being worked on. The major problem remains, however, that the venture needs more visitors and/or higher expenditures per visitor. Develop plans to improve the situation.

TEAM DEBATE EXERCISE

It is two years after the opening. Euro Disney is a monumental mistake, profitwise. Two schools of thought are emerging for improving the situation.

One is to pour money into the project, build one or two more theme parks and really make this another Disney World. The other camp believes more investment would be wasted at this time, that the need is to pare expenses to the bone and wait for an eventual upturn. Debate the two positions.

INVITATION TO RESEARCH

Has the recent profitability of Euro Disney continued? Has the declining profitability of the Disney Corporation been turned around? Is the Disney Cruise Line a success? Has the lawsuit by Jeffrey Katzenberg been settled, and if so, who won? Any other problems?

CHAPTER SIXTEEN

Borden—Letting Brands Wither

*E*lsie the cow has long been the symbol of Borden, the largest producer of dairy products. But Borden grew well beyond dairy products to become a diversified food processor and marketer. Decades of children cherished its Cracker Jack candied popcorn with a gift in every box; its Creamette pasta was the leading national brand, and it had strong regional brands as well. Lady Borden ice cream, milk, and frozen yogurt were well known, as were other dairy brands, national and regional. Even Elmer's glue belonged to the Borden family. With its well-known brands, Borden experienced solid growth in sales and profits for years and became a $7 billion company. Then in 1991, fortunes took a turn for the worse, and dark days were upon Borden. Top management had somehow allowed its brand franchises—the public recognition and acceptance of its brands—to deteriorate. Regaining lost ground was to prove no easy matter.

PRELUDE TO THE DARK DAYS

Borden was founded in 1857 by Gail Borden, Jr., a former Texas newspaperman. It sold condensed milk during the Civil War and later diversified into chemicals. In the 1960s Borden acquired such food brands as Cracker Jack and ReaLemon. Because of the wide earnings swings of cyclical chemical prices, Eugene J. Sullivan, the CEO, intensified the shift into consumer products in the 1970s.

In November 1991 Anthony S. D'Amato took the helm at Borden. He succeeded Romeo J. Ventres, a good friend, who convinced the board when he retired in 1991 that his protege, D'Amato, was the ideal successor. The two men, however, had sharply different management styles. Ventres was an idea man who had great faith in his top managers and gave them free rein. D'Amato was blunt, profane, and believed in personally becoming deeply involved in operations. D'Amato's different management approach was not well received by some Borden top managers, and the company went downhill fast under D'Amato's chairmanship.

But the seeds of Borden's problems were sowed before D'Amato took the helm. Ventres had dreamed of transforming Borden from a rather unexciting conglomerate into a major food marketer. Between 1986 and 1991, Ventres spent nearly $2 billion on 91 acquisitions. "We were hurriedly buying companies for the sake of buying companies," said one Borden executive. In its rush to move quickly on its acquisition program, the company sometimes spent as little as two weeks researching an acquisition candidate before making a decision.[1]

Some acquisitions turned out to be real losers. For example, in 1987 Borden purchased Laura Scudder potato chips for nearly $100 million. Unfortunately, major union problems led Borden to close all of Laura Scudder's California plants only a year after the purchase. Borden then shifted production to a plant in Salt Lake City, only to encounter high costs and quality control problems it could not correct. In 1993 it sold Laura Scudder for less than $20 million. All told, this fiasco cost Borden nearly $150 million.

Most acquisitions were small and medium-sized regional food and industrial companies. Ventres' strategy was to obtain growth by marketing these regional brands beyond their regular market areas. By consolidating manufacturing and distribution, he thought Borden could become the low-cost producer of a variety of product lines, thereby gaining more clout in the marketplace.

In the late 1980s this strategy seemed to work well. With its acquisitions, company sales grew 54 percent between 1985 and 1988. Earnings climbed even sharper to 61 percent, the most rapid growth in the company's history. (See Table 16.1.) Regional marketing and tailoring products to local tastes seemed a potent strategy.

In 1987, *Fortune* magazine featured Borden as a model of corporate performance. It termed the company "a consumer products brute" and extolled "some 40 acquisitions over two years that have made Borden, already the world's largest dairy company, the nationwide king of pasta and the second-largest seller of snack foods behind PepsiCo's Frito-Lay." The regional brand strategy was praised as motivating regionals to create new products as well as borrow from one another. For example, in just 6 weeks, Snacktime, one of Borden's new regional brands, developed Krunchers!, a kettle-cooked potato chip differentiated from those made the conventional way through continuous frying. The chip became an instant success, generating $17 million in annual sales.[2]

In 1987, the milk business was among the most profitable in the industry. Borden, with its Elsie the cow symbol, was able to charge more than competitors could, which was surprising for a commodity such as milk, which is virtually the same product whatever cow it comes from. The company insisted that its high quality and service standards made the "Borden difference." But when asked exactly what that difference was, a veteran dairyman in a succinct quote said, "About a buck a gallon."[3] Perhaps this was a portent of what was to come.

Premonitions

Flaws in the execution of the strategy were beginning to emerge by the end of the 1980s. In the race to expand the food portfolio, the company had ignored some of the

[1] Kathleen Deveny and Suein L. Hwang, "A Defective Strategy of Heated Acquisitions Spoils Borden Name," *Wall Street Journal*, 18 January 1994, p. A4.
[2] Bill Saporito, "How Borden Milks Packaged Goods," *Fortune*, 21 December 1987, pp. 139–144.
[3] Ibid., p. 142.

TABLE 16.1. Revenues and Net Income, 1983–1989

	Revenues ($millions)	% Change	Net Income ($millions)	% Change
1989	7,593	4.8	(61)	
1988	7,244	11.2	312	16.9
1987	6,514	30.2	267	19.7
1986	5,002	6.1	223	14.9
1985	4,716	3.2	194	1.5
1984	4,568	7.1	191	1.1
1983	4,265	—	189	—

Source: Company reports.

Commentary: Growth was steady during most of these years, but it really accelerated in 1987 and 1988. No wonder the 1987 *Fortune* article spoke in glowing terms about Borden.

well-known and successful brands it already had. For example, it had sold ice cream under the Lady Borden label for decades, but it ignored the golden opportunity in the 1980s to extend the line into superpremium ice cream, which was becoming highly popular. Borden showed the same negligence in not aggressively developing new products for many of its other strongest brand names. (See the Information Box: Brand Extension for a discussion of the effective brand extension strategy.) And one could wonder how much longer the price premium charged for milk and Lady Borden ice cream could hold up as the company moved into the skeptical 1990s.

INFORMATION BOX

BRAND EXTENSION

Brand extension can be a particularly effective use of branding. It is a strategy of applying an established brand name to new products. As a result, customer acceptance of the new products is more likely because of customer familiarity and satisfaction with the existing products bearing the same name. This reduces the risk of new-product failure. Today about one-half of new consumer products use some form of brand extension, such as the same product in a different form, a companion product, or a different product for the same target market.

The more highly regarded a brand is by customers, the better candidate it is for brand extension—provided that a new product will not hurt its reputation and has some relevance to it. The strong favorable image of the Lady Borden brand made it ideal for such brand extension. A favorable image should be zealously protected from being cheapened or having its perception of good value undermined.

Discuss why brand extension may not always work.

Borden was now finding difficulty in digesting its hodgepodge of acquisitions. (Table 16.2 shows the broad range of food and nonfood products and the business segment contributions to total sales and profits as of 1992.) It continued to operate as a conglomeration of unintegrated businesses and thereby proved to be neither as efficient as major competitors nor as able to amass marketing clout.

By the time D'Amato took over, the company was clearly ailing. By the end of 1991, sales had declined 5 percent from the previous year, and net income had fallen 19 percent. D'Amato quickly tried to consolidate the loosely structured organization, but all his efforts seemed only to make matters worse.

D'AMATO'S FUTILITY

Shortly after becoming CEO, D'Amato tried to better integrate the morass of consumer food businesses. He wanted to tighten up and centralize the widely decentralized company, with its "dozens of independent fiefdoms." Even corporate offices were scattered between New York City and the hub of the company's operations in Columbus, Ohio. Such geographical distance suited the hands-off management style of Ventres, who rarely got involved in day-to-day operations and spent most of his time at Borden's small Park Avenue offices in New York. D'Amato moved to centralize far-flung operations in Columbus. There he involved himself deeply in day-to-day operations. He increasingly saw the need to eliminate or sell many of Borden's small regional businesses while focusing most efforts on building national brands: a reversal of the strategy of Ventres.

TABLE 16.2. **Business Segment Contributions to Total Company Sales and Earnings, 1992**

	Sales	Operating Profits
Grocery[a]	26%	42%
Snacks and International Consumer[b]	26	18
Dairy[c]	20	5
Packaging and Industrial[d]	28	35

[a] Grocery products include North American pasta and sauces (Creamette, Prince, Dutch Maid, Goodman's, Classico, Aunt Millie's); niche grocery products (Eagle-brand condensed milk, Campfire marshmallows, Cracker Jack candied popcorn); refrigerated products (Borden cheese); and food service operations.

[b] Snacks and International Consumer products include Borden's worldwide sweet and salty snacks (Borden, Wise, Snack Time!); other food products outside the United States and Canada (Weber sweet snacks, KLIM milk powder, Lady Borden ice cream); and films and adhesives in the Far East.

[c] Dairy products, including milk, ice cream, and frozen yogurt, are sold under national and branded labels, which include Borden, Lady Borden, Meadow Gold, Viva, and Eagle.

[d] Packaging and Industrial products include consumer adhesives (Elmer's glue); wallcoverings; plastic films and packaging products (Proponite food packaging film, Resinite and Sealwrap vinyl food-wrap films); and foundry, industrial, and specialty resins.

Source: Company public information.

Analysts initially applauded D'Amato's strategy for turning Borden around, but their praise was short-lived. Results failed to meet expectations and even brought new problems.

D'Amato was especially wedded to the notion that the brand recognition of certain brands should allow the company to charge a premium price. For example, Borden's own research had shown that 97 percent of consumers recognized Borden as a leading milk brand.[4] D'Amato saw this as supporting such a premium price. Then, in early 1992, raw milk prices dropped by about one-third. Borden doggedly held its prices while competitors lowered theirs to reflect the drop in commodity prices. Before long, Borden began losing customers, who were realizing that milk is milk. Good brand recognition did not insulate a national brand from lower priced competition of other national brands and private brands. See the Information Box: The Battle of the Brands: Private versus National.

INFORMATION BOX

THE BATTLE OF THE BRANDS: PRIVATE VERSUS NATIONAL

Wholesalers and retailers often use their own brands—commonly referred to as private brands—in place of or in addition to the national brands of manufacturers. Private brands usually are offered at lower selling prices than nationally advertised brands, yet they typically give dealers more per-unit profit since they can be bought on more favorable terms, partly reflecting the promotional savings involved. Some firms, such as Sears and Penney, used to stock mostly their own brands. Thus, they had better control over repeat business since satisfied customers could repurchase the brand only through the particular store or chain.

With private brands directly competing with manufacturers' brands, often at a more attractive price, you may ask why manufacturers sell some of their output to retailers under a private brand. A major reason is to minimize idle plant capacity. Manufacturers can always rationalize that if they refuse private-label business, someone else will not, and competition with private brands will continue. Other manufacturers welcome private-brand business because they lack the resources and know-how to enter the marketplace effectively with their own brands.

By the 1990s, more knowledgeable and frugal consumers were realizing that private brands often offered the best value. National consumer brands were being hurt. Recognizing this new intense competition, some manufacturers of branded goods, led by makers of cigarettes and disposable diapers, in 1993 rolled back the price differentials over private brands of their national labels. Borden management had difficulty accepting the idea that the price premiums of its national brands were no longer sustainable if market share was to be maintained.

How do you personally feel about private brands?

---

[4] Elizabeth Lesly, "Why Things Are So Sour At Borden," *Business Week*, 22 November 1993, p. 82.

D'Amato opted to tough out the loss of market share, expecting that higher profit margins would offset somewhat lower sales. Only after almost a year of steadily declining sales did he abandon the premium-pricing policy. By then sales had fallen so drastically that the milk division was operating at a loss.

Another marketing mistake involved misuse of advertising. In his strategy to build up Borden's major brands, D'Amato had boosted marketing efforts for Creamette, the leading national pasta brand. With the sizable promotional expenditures, the brand's sales rose 1.6 percent in 1992. This may have seemed like a significant increase but for the fact that, nationally, pasta sales rose 5.5 percent.

How could the promotional efforts have been so ineffective? Unbelievably, most of the advertising featured recipes aimed at increasing pasta consumption, rather than at building selective demand for the Creamette brand.

Making the marketing efforts for Creamette even more misguided, Borden neglected its regional pasta brands, such as Anthony's in the West and Prince in the Northeast. These sales slumped, so that total division sales were down $600 million in the first nine months of 1993. D'Amato admitted the mistake: "There was a very strong desire to make Creamette the one bigger brand beyond anything else. That's a great objective, [but] when you do it at the expense of your strong regional brands, maybe it doesn't make any sense."[5]

The snack food division also bedeviled D'Amato. He planned to launch a national Borden brand of chips and pretzels in the expectation that this could replace many of the company's regional snack brands. Combining the regionals' manufacturing and distribution costs under a single brand should enable Borden both to cut costs and also gain marketing muscle. The company tested its new snack line in Michigan, but results were only mediocre. Unfortunately, Borden was going up against PepsiCo's Frito-Lay and Anheuser-Busch's Eagle Snacks—major entrenched national brands. It could not wedge its way in. The company finally refocused its efforts to attempt to build up regional brands such as Jay's and Wise. But they were ineffective or too late.

THE CHANGING OF THE GUARD

D'Amato's sweeping strategy to rejuvenate the ailing Borden left the company worse off than before. Two of its four divisions, dairy and snacks, were operating at losses. Its other two divisions, grocery products and chemicals, could not take up the slack. On October 27, 1993, Standard & Poor downgraded much of Borden's debt. Since the beginning of 1993, Borden's share price had plummeted 43 percent.

In June 1993 D'Amato hired Ervin R. Shames, 53, as president and heir apparent. Whereas D'Amato's background had been in chemical engineering for most of his 30 years with Borden, Shames was an experienced food marketer, having spent 22 years in the industry, holding top positions with General Foods USA

---

[5] Lesly, p. 84.

and Kraft USA. He most recently had been chair, president, and chief executive of Stride Rite Corporation. In making Shames president, D'Amato gave him a compensation package that exceeded those of Borden's other top executives, including himself.

Shames and D'Amato now attempted to correct Borden's problems together. They quickly stopped offering deals to retailers to encourage heavier end-of-quarter shipments. While these deals temporarily boosted sales, they hurt profits and also stole business from the next quarter.

Shames and D'Amato accelerated the examination of Borden's various businesses. Teams of management consultants and financial advisers helped with the evaluation. As a consequence, morale among managers, who feared drastic changes, plummeted almost to the point of paralysis.

In October 1993 the independent directors of the board considered the possibility of selling the entire company. But the efforts proved futile. Hanson PLC and RJR Nabisco briefly appeared interested, but talks broke down. Several other possible buyers, including Nestlé SA, also looked over Borden's portfolio of businesses but declined to negotiate. The weak condition of Borden was proving a major hindrance to any buyout. It likely would have to solve its own problems without outside help.

Shames and D'Amato believed that the biggest problem was the fact that the company was spread too thin in too many mediocre businesses. Although it was unlikely that the entire company could be sold at this time, still certain parts should be salable. They had to decide which should be sold if the company was to be streamlined enough to reverse the consequences of its haphazard and even confused former growth mentality. An early recognized candidate for pruning was the $1.4 billion chemical business. This had little relevance with the core food properties, but still it was a major profit generator, as shown in Table 16.2.

D'Amato was not to see the conclusions of his latest efforts to turn around Borden. On December 9, 1993, the board of directors fired him and left Shames in charge. At the same time, D'Amato's predecessor and former supporter, R.J. Ventres, resigned from his board seat. Operating results through 1993 were a disaster, as shown in Table 16.3.

TABLE 16.3. Operating Performance, 1990–1993

	Revenues		Net Income	
	($millions)	% Change	($millions)	% Change
1993	6,600[a]	(7.6)	(593)[a]	
1992	7,143	(1.3)	(253)	
1991	7,235	(5.2)	295	(19.0)
1990	7,633	—	364	—

[a] Estimates.

Source: Borden.

RECOVERY EFFORTS

Shames announced a $567 million restructuring plan on January 5, 1994. It included the sale of the salty snacks division and other niche grocery lines. The dividend was also slashed for the second time in 6 months. In a speech to security analysts, Shames identified four reasons for Borden's problems: lack of focus, insufficient emphasis on brand names, absence of first-rate executives and managers, and a tangled bureaucracy. He vowed to purge weak managers and increase advertising with much greater focus on core lines, notably pasta, the namesake dairy products, and industrial businesses such as adhesives and wallcoverings. For example, he planned to increase advertising for pasta from $2 million to $8 million for 1994 and to focus on the company's faded regional brands. The pasta would also be crossmarketed with Classico, the successful premium pasta sauce.

Shames also pledged to bring Borden from last place among food companies to the top 25 percent. See Table 16.4 for a ranking of Borden with other major competitors as of the beginning of 1994. He began bringing in a new management team, many of them his former colleagues. In a major shake-up, three senior managers announced their early retirement: the chief financial officer, the general counsel, and the former executive vice president in charge of the struggling snack food and international consumer products unit.[6]

Some security analysts were encouraged by Shames' speech. They believed that Borden's bringing in an experienced outsider—at the time, Shames had been with the company for only seven months—showed that the company was truly committed to the drastic changes needed for a turnaround. Other people were more skeptical. After all, Borden has been "restructuring" for five years. "Who's to say the latest plan will work any better than previous ones?" Joanna Scharf, an analyst with S. G. Warburg & Co., was among such skeptics: "I found some of [Shames] remarks heartening. However, this is not something that is going to turn around in six months." And she maintained she was not going to change her advice to investors to sell the stock.[7]

With so many brands in its portfolio stable, reflecting nearly 100 recent acquisitions, Borden lost focus. Key brands were often not sufficiently championed. Brand extensions, such as one for Lady Borden ice cream, were often overlooked or only half-heartedly attempted. One wonders how many opportunities were ignored by a management team whose attention was caught up in a frenzy for acquisitions.

A Sputtering Recovery

The troubles of Borden did not go away. At a $1 million cash salary plus mouthwatering stock options, Shames was unable to turn things around. His initial efforts were to build sales volume, but this adversely affected the bottom line of profitability. For example, with pasta, Borden held firm on prices despite a recent 75 percent

---

[6] Suein L. Hwang, "Borden Aides Leaving as Part of Shake-Up," *Wall Street Journal*, 15 February 1994, p. A4.

[7] Vindu P. Goel, "Putting Elsie Back on Track," *Cleveland Plain Dealer*, 23 January 1994, pp. 1-E, 5-E.

TABLE 16.4.   Comparison of Borden and Major Competitors, 5-year Average, 1988–1993

	Return on Equity	Sales Growth	Earnings per Share
General Mills	42.8%	10.0%	10.4%
Kellogg	31.8	10.2	11.6
H. J. Heinz	25.4	5.8	8.6
Quaker Oats	24.6	4.9	12.2
Sara Lee	21.1	6.2	16.1
Hershey Foods	18.4	7.1	8.3
Campbell Soup	16.5	5.3	NM[a]
Dole	11.7	11.7	–5.4
Borden	5.8	1.3	NM

[a] *NM*, not meaningful.

Source: Industry statistics as reported in *Forbes*, 3 January 1994, pp. 152–154.

Commentary: Borden's poor performance compared with that of its major peers is starkly indicated here, with Borden dead last in 5-year average return on equity, sales growth, and earnings per share.

increase in durum wheat prices, while competitors raised prices. The result: Borden gained less than a point of market share, but lost on the bottom line. So eager was Borden for volume that in November 1993 it paid an Oklahoma City-based supermarket chain $9.5 million for preferential treatment on grocer shelves.[8]

Shames failed to curb costs. Even though he shed 7,000 employees, payroll costs actually rose. Some of this was hardly Shames' fault. The board approved substantial salaries paid to former top executives. For example, D'Amato was paid $750,000 in cash severance, and $900,000 per year for four years plus $65,000 in secretarial and legal fee reimbursements. Borden still maintained a fleet of company jets to fly board members around the country. Country club memberships of executives hardly attested to a firm on the verge of bankruptcy. Consultant and advisory fees numbered in the millions. The fat could not be trimmed, it seemed.

Efforts to sell off some of the units to ease the crushing burden of creditor demands were also less than successful. For example, H. J. Heinz Company bought Borden's $225 million (sales) food service division for only 31 percent of annual revenues, a miserably low price for assets that should have brought $1 for every $1 in revenues.[9]

In late 1994, Borden was bought for $1.9 billion by Kohlberg Kravis Roberts and Co., a low figure for a $6 billion company but then it had been losing money. Robert Kidder, former top executive of Duracell, became CEO. Borden, once a top 20 public firm became the third largest private firm in the U.S. KKR directed hundreds of millions of dollars for updating plants, installing new systems, and developing new products. In May 1995, Borden underwent a complete restructuring, with

[8] Matthew Schifrin, "Last Legs," *Forbes*, 12 September 1994, pp. 150ff.

[9] Schifrin, pp. 150ff.

all marketing efforts split into 11 business units, each with its own board of directors, capital structure, and operational control, thus assuring 100 percent accountability.[10] Could Borden be on the verge of a turnaround?

ANALYSIS

Acquiring other businesses is a common growth strategy. Through acquisitions a company can quickly achieve a relatively large size, bypassing the time needed to develop such new ventures internally. By acquiring already proven businesses, the buyer can obtain personnel and management experienced to run such businesses effectively.

Several problems, however, can occur in such buyouts: First, a buying firm may pay too much and be saddled with heavy debt and interest overhead. Second, the acquisition may prove incompatible with the buyer's existing resources and strategy. In such a situation, it may find great difficulty in integrating the new enterprise with existing operations and making it a profit contributor.

In the 1980s Ventres, D'Amato's predecessor, took on $1.9 billion in debt to acquire 91 regional food and industrial companies. He had hoped to build these up to be regional powerhouses and to marry efficiencies of scale in manufacturing with the marketing nimbleness of regional operations. By centralizing production in the most efficient plants, costs should be lowered and profits enhanced. And there was always the potential for a regional brand to take off and be worthy of national distribution. This was the theory behind many of Borden's acquisitions in the 1980s.

Unfortunately, theory and practice did not meld well. The businesses were never integrated and continued to operate autonomously with diverse and often competing brands. Production never achieved the efficiency of most of the large competitors, and Borden still lacked their marketing clout. It also encountered great problems in allocating advertising among the diverse brands: Which should be given strong support, and why? And should the other brands be allowed to languish?

Compounding its problems with unwise and unassimilated acquisitions, Borden management grievously misjudged the mood of the market. It overestimated consumers' willingness to pay premium prices for its most popular brands. Borden's stubbornness in maintaining high prices for Lady Borden milk at the very time when raw milk prices were collapsing simply invited competitors to increase their market share at Borden's expense. Attempts to raise ice cream prices backfired as well.

The early 1990s, a period of recession and considerable unemployment and fear of layoffs, brought a new consumer recognition that many national brands were not much, if any, better than competing private brands. Many national-brand manufacturers, faced with declining sales in the face of strong private-label competition, began price rollbacks. So it was not surprising that Borden found difficulty with a changed marketing environment. What was surprising was its slowness to adapt to these changing conditions.

---

[10] "A New Life for Borden," *Prepared Foods*, July 1995, p. 35; and "Borden's CEO Finds Answers to How It's Been Losing Money," *Cleveland Plain Dealer*, 13 February 1996, p. 5-C.

WHAT CAN BE LEARNED?

Beware an Unfocused Strategy

An unfocused strategy often accompanies too much unrelated diversification. A firm has difficulty deciding what it is, other than being a conglomerate. Not many managements cope well with a lot of diversification, although many have tried to. Often such acquisitions become candidates for sale some years later, thus confirming flawed acquisition decisions.

In Borden's case most of the acquisitions were related to its major food business. But there were too many, and they were not integrated into the main corporate structure. Such diffusion of resources and uncoordinated marketing efforts made it difficult indeed to achieve either cost savings or a unified and powerful approach to the marketplace.

How Much Decentralization?

Here we are confronted with the negative consequences of too much decentralization or autonomy. Borden acquisitions' autonomy led to lack of coordination and great inefficiency.

Does this have to be true? Or can decentralization work without causing loss of control and efficiency? Can intrafirm competition among semi-independent units lead to greater performance incentive? The answer is yes, decentralization is often far more desirable than centralization. For example, we saw this in IBM's efforts to move away from its centralized bureaucratic organization toward more decentralization. Still, there are degrees of decentralization. Too much uncontrolled autonomy led to Borden's problems. There has to be some focus and common purpose along with sufficient controls to prevent unpleasant surprises. But in the final analysis, the issue depends on the competence of the managers. If they are highly competent, then an organization will likely thrive under decentralization. If they are incompetent, as appeared to be the case with Borden, then decentralization can be a disaster.

Run with Your Winners

Although any firm wants to develop new products and bring them to fruition as soon as possible, it must not neglect its older products and brands that are doing well, that are winners. Advertising and other marketing efforts, such as brand extension, should not be curtailed as long as the products are growing and profitable. Marketing commitments should perhaps even be increased for such winners, since favorable growth trends often can continue for a long time. Alas, Borden sometimes exercised the opposite strategy: It cut back on its winners and directed resources to futilely trying to build up weak regional brands.

But we should not completely condemn Borden for ignoring its winners. It threw all its advertising support behind Creamette, the leading national brand of pasta. But Creamette's sales failed to take off. Meantime, Borden's strong regional brands—in particular, Prince in the Northeast and Anthony's in the

West—stagnated with no support. D'Amato must have thought "damned if you do and damned if you don't." But there were reasons for the lack of success with the Creamette advertising, as we will examine next.

For Mature Products, Beware Using Primary-demand Advertising

Despite a strong boost in marketing efforts for Creamette in 1992, the brand's sales rose only 1.6 percent. At the same time total U.S. pasta sales rose 5.5 percent.[11] Was this poor showing the fault of the product? Hardly, since it was the leading national pasta brand. Rather, the advertising was at fault. Most of it was built around recipes that did more to promote pasta consumption than to promote the superior qualities of Creamette. In other words, a primary-demand theme was used rather than selective-demand theme stressing the merits of a particular brand. Because primary-demand advertising helps the industry and all competitors, it is best used with new products in a young growth industry. Primary-demand advertising is seldom appropriate in a mature industry. The results of the advertising efforts for Creamette confirm this. Shouldn't Borden managers have been more savvy? They should never have approved such a theme for an advertising campaign.

CONSIDER

Do you see any other learning insights coming from this case?

QUESTIONS

1. Do you think the problems in Borden's acquisition strategy stemmed from a flaw in the basic concept or in the execution? Support your position.

2. Is primary-demand advertising ever advisable for a mature product? If so, under what circumstances?

3. Prince is a strong regional pasta brand in the Northeast. What would it take to convert it into a national brand? Should Borden have attempted this?

4. Should Borden have made a strong effort to create a presence in the private brand market? Why or why not?

5. Critics have decried Borden's lack of focus. What does this mean? How can the criticisms best be resolved?

6. "After firing D'Amato, the board one month later adopted virtually the same restructuring plan he had proposed. What an injustice!" Discuss.

7. How much of a price premium do you think national brands ought to command over private brands? Justify your position.

---

[11] Lesly, p. 84.

HANDS-ON EXERCISES

1. It is 1984 and you are the assistant to the president. He has asked you to design a growth plan for the next decade. What are your recommendations? Take care to avoid the pitfalls that actually beset the company.

2. It is early 1994. You are the assistant to the new CEO, Ervin Shames. The company is in sorry straits. What do you propose to enable your boss to meet his pledge to boost Borden from the bottom of the food company heap to the top 25 percent?

TEAM DEBATE EXERCISE

Debate the issue of growth by acquisitions versus internal growth. Which of the pros and cons do you think are most compelling?

INVITATION TO RESEARCH

Since Borden is now a private company under the stable of Kohlberg Kravis Roberts and Co., it is difficult to find as much information as if it were publicly held. Still, you may be able to find something about the present fortunes of the firm and its brands.

CHAPTER SEVENTEEN

Snapple: A Sorry Acquisition

*I*n late 1994, Quaker Oats CEO William D. Smithburg bought Snapple Beverage Company for $1.7 billion. Many thought he had paid too much for this maker of non-carbonated fruit-flavored drinks and ice teas. But in a similar acquisition eleven years before he had outbid Pillsbury to buy Stokely–Van Camp, largely for its Gatorade, then a $90 million sports drink. Despite criticisms of that purchase, Gatorade went on to become a billion-dollar brand, and Smithburg was a hero. He was not to be a hero with Snapple.

THE COMPANY, QUAKER OATS

Quaker Oats had nearly $6.4 billion in fiscal 1995 sales, of which $1.7 billion was from foreign operations. Its brands were generally strong in particular grocery products and beverage areas. In hot cereals, generations had used Quaker oatmeal, and it was still the number-three selling brand in the overall cereal category. Quaker's ready-to-eat cereals included Cap'n Crunch and Life brands. The firm was a leading competitor in the fast-growing rice cake and granola bar categories, and also in rice and pasta with its Rice-A-Roni, Pasta Roni, and Near East brands. Other products included Aunt Jemima frozen products, French toast, pancake mixes, and syrups; Celeste frozen pizza; as well as grits, tortilla flour, and corn meal.

With the purchase of Snapple, sales of its beverage operation would approach $2 billion or about one-third of total corporate sales. Gatorade alone accounted for $1.3 billion worldwide in fiscal 1995 and growth continued with sales in the United States increasing 7 percent over the previous year, while overseas the gain was a whopping 51 percent. In order to help pay for the Snapple acquisition, several mature but still moneymaking units were divested, including pet foods and chocolates.

THE SNAPPLE ACQUISITION

The Snapple brand had a modest beginning in 1972 in Brooklyn, NY, and its beverages were initially sold to health-food stores. As the healthy lifestyle became popular among certain segments of the general public, Snapple's sales for a time increased as much as 60 to 70 percent a year, especially in the Northeast and West Coast. In 1992, it was purchased for $27.9 million by Boston-based Thomas H. Lee Co., which took the now-trendy brand public and built it up to almost $700 million in sales.

Unlike Gatorade, however, Snapple faced formidable competitors, including Coke's Fruitopia and Pepsi's joint venture with Lipton, which used low prices to capture 31 percent of the ice tea market. Snapple's growth rate had turned to declines by December 1994 when, in an outpouring of supreme confidence in his own judgment, Smithburg bought Snapple for $1.7 billion. Before long, many said he had paid about $1 billion too much. Table 17.1 shows the quarterly sales results of Snapple since June 1993 before the acquisition, and after the acquisition.

William Smithburg

At the time of the purchase, Smithburg was 56 years old, but looked younger. He liked to wear suspenders stretched tightly over muscular shoulders that he had developed from years of tournament handball. He had been CEO at Quaker Oats since 1981 and had evolved from a flashy boy wonder to a seasoned executive. He was also a fitness buff, and perhaps this colored his zeal for products like Gatorade and Snapple.

His interest in fitness developed as a result of a childhood bout with polio. While he recovered with no permanent damage, the experience shaped his life: "As soon as I started to walk and run again, I said, 'I have to stay healthy,' and it just became part of my life."[1] In his long tenure as CEO, that passion shaped Quaker, too. The company developed extensive fitness programs, including a heavily subsidized health club at headquarters. Quaker's product line, also, had increasingly emphasized low-fat foods compatible with the healthy lifestyle.

Indicative of Smithburg's personality, after graduating from DePaul University in 1960 with a BS degree in economics and marketing, he defied his

TABLE 17.1   Snapple's Sales Growth, 1993–1996

	Sales Growth (millions of dollars)							
	1993	%	1994	%	1995	%	1996	%
1st quarter			$134		$112	−12%		
2nd quarter	$130		243	+87%	200	−18%	180	−10%
3rd quarter	203		191	− 6%				−20%
4th quarter	118		105	−11%				

Source: 1995 Quaker Annual Report, and various 1996 updates.

Note: While we do not have complete information for all the quarters, still the negative sales since the second quarter of 1994—before the Snapple acquisition—can be readily seen: Every quarter since then has seen losses from the same quarter the preceding year.

[1] Greg Burns, "Crunch Time At Quaker Oats," *Business Week,* 23 September 1996, p. 72.

father by quitting his first job only three days later. He decided to enroll in Northwestern's business school.

With an MBA in hand he joined the Leo Burnett ad agency, and later, McCann Erickson. After five years of ad agency experience, he went to Quaker as brand manager for frozen waffles in 1966. There it took him ten years to become executive vice president of U.S. grocery products, Quaker's biggest division. Five years later in 1981 he became CEO, and was named chairman two years after that.

The same year he became chairman, he acquired Stokely–Van Camp, overbidding Pillsbury's $62-per-share bid with a $77 offer, which carried a price tag of $238 million. His own investment banker considered this too steep, and critics in the business press abounded. But Smithburg had done his homework, and his intuition was prescient. He recognized the potential in Stokely's Gatorade, a sport drink meant to replenish lost salts and fluids of athletes. "I'd been drinking Gatorade myself, and I knew the product worked."[2] A $90 million brand in 1983, by 1996 this was a $1.3 billion brand and held 80 percent of the growing sport-drink market.

Somehow, Smithburg did not do his homework well with Snapple, despite its seeming similarity to Gatorade.

Rationale for the Snapple Purchase

Snapple was the largest acquisition in Quaker's history. The *Quaker Oats 1995 Annual Report* discussed the rationale for this purchase and the "growth opportunity it offers to shareholders":

> Snapple appeals to all ages with its incomparable flavor variety in premium ice teas and juice drinks. Current sales are concentrated in the Northeast and West Coast. So, the rest of the country presents fertile territory for developing the brand. Because of its excellent cold-channel distribution, the Snapple brand has taught us a great deal about reaching consumers outside our traditional grocery channels. We can apply this knowledge to Gatorade thirst quencher, thereby enhancing its availability as well.[3]

So, Smithburg saw great opportunity to expand distribution of Snapple geographically from its present regional concentration. He thought it had wide appeal and that it could enhance sales of the already highly successful Gatorade.

Snapple beverages held good regional market positions in both the premium ready-to-drink tea and single-serve juice-drink categories. It was seemingly well positioned if consumer preferences continued to shift to all-natural beverages—and away from highly carbonated, artificially flavored, and chemically preserved soft drinks.

Apparently not the least of the reasons for Smithburg's infatuation with Snapple was that it had a "sexy aura," even though problems were already emerging when he bought it. He liked to contrast it with Quaker's pet food: Pet food "was a dead, flat business with five or six big companies beating their brains out in it."[4] So, it was not

[2] *Ibid.*, p. 74.
[3] *Quaker Oats 1995 Annual Report*, p. 6.
[4] Burns, p. 74.

surprising that the pet food business, which had been acquired less than nine years before, was sold a few months after Snapple was acquired.

Other speculations as to why Smithburg chased Snapple, besides misreading the growth potential, were that he wanted to make Quaker, which was a hotly rumored acquisition candidate, less vulnerable to a takeover. Some even speculated that Smithburg became bored with Quaker and sought the excitement of a splashy deal.[5]

PROBLEMS

One would think that Snapple's resemblance to Gatorade would bring instant compatibility and efficiencies in marketing the two brands. After all, with the proven success of Gatorade, Quaker had become the third-largest beverage company, after only Coca-Cola and Pepsi. And, like Gatorade, Snapple was a flavored, noncarbonated drink. Surely this was a compatible marriage.

But this was not the case. Only after it bought Snapple did Quaker fully realize that both Snapple's production and distribution systems were completely different from Gatorade's.

Quaker's production and distribution of Gatorade was state of the art. Its computers were closely integrated with those of its largest distributors and automatically kept these distributors well stocked, but not overstocked, with Gatorade.

The advertising of Gatorade was also markedly different. Several hundred million dollars a year was spent for Gatorade, with highly successful ads featuring Chicago Bulls star, Michael Jordan (Jordan was also a personal friend of Smithburg). Snapple's advertising, on the other hand, had run out of steam and was notably ineffective.

The production, distribution, and marketing efforts of Snapple at the time of the purchase were haphazard. Bottling was contracted to outsiders, and this resulted in expensive contracts for excess capacity when demand slowed. Snapple's 300 distributors delivered directly to stores; Gatorade's distributors delivered to warehouses. Quaker's efforts to consolidate the two distribution systems only created havoc. It tried to take the supermarket accounts away from Snapple distributors and give them to Gatorade, directing that the Snapple people concentrate on convenience stores and mom-and-pop retailers. Not surprising, Snapple distributors refused this downsizing of their operations. Eventually, Quaker backed down. But efforts at creating coordination and distribution efficiencies for 1995 were seriously delayed.

At the same time, Quaker failed to come up with a new business plan for Snapple in time for the peak 1995 season, which began in April. Tim Healy, president of a Snapple distributor in Chicago, noted, "there was no marketing plan, no initiatives, and no one to talk to [at Quaker]."[6]

The result was that 1995 sales of Snapple fell 9 percent, and there was a $100 million loss.

---

[5] *Ibid.*

[6] Scott McMurray, "Drumming Up New Business: Quaker Marches Double Time to Put Snap Back in its Snapple Drink Line," *U.S. News & World Report*, 22 April 1996, p. 59.

CORRECTIVE EFFORTS, 1996

As the dismal results of 1995 became widely publicized, Quaker faced the urgent need to vindicate the purchase of Snapple and somehow resurrect its failing fortunes. To aid the distributors, the company streamlined operations to reduce from two weeks to three days the time it took to get orders from bottlers to distributors. To do so, it coordinated its computers with the top 50 distributors, who represented 80 percent of Snapple's sales, so that it could replenish their inventory automatically, the way it was doing with Gatorade.

The company also introduced some packaging and product changes that it hoped would be more appealing both to dealers and to customers. It brought out 32- and 64-ounce plastic bottles of Snapple for families, along with 12-packs and 4-packs in glass bottles. It reduced the number of flavors from 50 to 35 and made taste improvements in some of the retained flavors. At the same time seasonal products were introduced, such as cider tea for Halloween.

To develop distributor enthusiasm, a two-day meeting had been held in San Diego. Quaker brought in comedian Bill Cosby to entertain and General Norman Schwarzkopf to motivate with a stirring speech on leadership. Then distributors were told that highly visible Snapple coolers would be placed in supermarkets, convenience stores, and schools—just like Coke and Pepsi.[7]

The weakness in the 1995 advertising also received, hopefully, corrective action. Quaker enlisted the creativity of Spike Lee, who had designed hyperkinetic TV commercials for Nike. While the campaign kept Snapple's "Made from the best stuff on earth," the new ads focused on Snapple's hope to become America's third choice in soft drinks, behind Coke and Pepsi, with such slogans as, "We want to be No. 3," and "Threedom = freedom." The goal of the advertising campaign, Smithburg explained, was to maintain Snapple's "funky" image while broadening its appeal beyond the East and West Coast markets.[8]

Still, sales languished. In late July, a huge nationwide sampling campaign was undertaken. In a $40 million effort, millions of bottles of the fruit-juice and ice tea lines were given away during the height of the selling season, hopefully to spur consumer interest regardless of cost.

RESULTS OF 1996 EFFORTS

Unfortunately, the results of the summer giveaways were dismal. Instead of gaining market share during the important summer selling months, Snapple lost ground.

Snapple tea sales fell 14 percent, and juice sales fell 15 percent. This compared poorly with industry tea sales, which also dropped, but only 4 percent, and industry juice sales, which fell 5 percent during a particularly cool summer in the Northeast.[9]

[7] Zina Moukheiber, "He Who Laughs Last," *Forbes,* 1 January 1996, p. 42.

[8] *Ibid.,* p. 60.

[9] "Snapple Continues to Lose Market Share Despite Big Giveaway," *Wall Street Journal,* 8 October 1996, p. B9.

Relentless media scrutiny even found fault with the way in which Snapple was being given away. One critic observed the sampling at a New Jersey concert in which 16-ounce cans were handed out only 20 feet from the entrance in front of signs prohibiting food or drink beyond the gate. Most people barely had time to taste the drink before throwing it away. Furthermore, "for its brand undermining efforts, Quaker gets no consumer research either. Solution: In exchange for the self-serve sample, ask a few short ... questions."[10]

The reputation of Smithburg was being eroded, his early success with Gatorade not enough to weather more current adversity. Online, cybercritics assailed him. In conference calls with financial analysts, he was peppered with barbed questions about this $600 million beverage for which he paid $1.7 million. "Even my dad," Smithburg laughed, "he says, 'What are you doing with Snapple?'"[11]

Under pressure, Smithburg cast off president and chief operating officer Philip Marineau, whom he had been grooming as heir apparent for many years. This departure was widely interpreted to be the result of Snapple's failure to justify its premium pricing, with Marineau the scapegoat. Nine months later, Donald Uzzi was replaced as president of Quaker's North America beverages unit. His successor was Michael Schott, former vice president of sales of Nantucket Nectars, a small, privately held drink maker.

Some critics assumed that Smithburg's job was in jeopardy, that he could not escape personal blame for the acquisition snafu. Still, the past success of Smithburg with Gatorade continued to sustain him. The board of directors remained supportive, although they denied him any bonus for 1995. What made the continued loyalty of the board more uncertain was Quaker's stock price, which had fallen 10 percent since just before the acquisition, even as the Standard & Poor's 500-stock index had climbed to new highs.

If Snapple could not be revitalized, Smithburg had several options regarding it. All of these, of course, would be admissions of defeat and that a major mistake was made in acquiring Snapple. Any one of them might cost Smithburg his job.

One option would be to spin off the ailing Snapple to shareholders, perhaps under the wing of the booming Gatorade. Smithburg was no stranger to such maneuverings since he had divested retail, toy, and pet-food operations in his years as CEO. An outright sale could probably only be made at bargain-basement prices and would certainly underscore the billion-dollar mistake of Smithburg's purchase. A less extreme option would be to draw back from attempts to make Snapple a national brand, and keep it as a regional brand in the Northeast and West Coast where it was well entrenched.

Perseverance

By early 1997 Smithburg still had not given up on Snapple. Quaker Oats announced it was pumping $15 million into a major four-month sweepstakes promotion for Snapple's

---

[10] Gabe Lowry, "They Can't Even Give Snapple Away Right," *Brandweek,* 30 September 1996, p. 16.

[11] Burns, p. 71.

diet drinks, this to start right after the new year when consumers might be more concerned with undoing the excesses of the holiday season and when competitors would be less likely to advertise chilled drinks in cold weather. The theme was to be "Escape with Taste," and among other winners would be 50 grand-prize trips to the refurbished Doral Resort and Spa in Miami. If the campaign developed any momentum, it should carry over to a retooled image campaign planned immediately afterward in the spring.

This promotion was the first from new president Mike Schott, and it built on one product category that managed to grow 16 percent in convenience stores during the previous summer, even as core juices and teas slid drastically. The promotion plan was well received by distributors: "This one [promotion] is wonderfully thought out," one distributor said. "Diet drinks in the first quarter? It's a no-brainer."[12]

Since being named the brand's president late in the year, Schott had been visiting distributors to build up relations, offer greater support, and dispel rumors that Snapple was going to retrench to a regional brand. Still, Snapple's sales and profits showed no rebound.

On March 27, 1997, Smithburg finally threw in the towel; he sold the ailing Snapple to Nelson Peltz, chief executive of the smallish Triarc Cos., owner of RC Cola and Arby's restaurants. The price was shockingly low, only $300 million, or just over half of Snapple's $550 million in sales—this for a brand for which Smithburg had paid $1.7 billion only three years before. The founder of Snapple, Leonard Marsh, who had previously sold his controlling interest, said that "they stole the company."[13]

Undoubtedly, Quaker was desperate to sell the money-draining Snapple, but at such a fire-sale price? As it turned out, the company had few options. Major suitors, such as PepsiCo, Coca-Cola, and Procter & Gamble, only wanted to consider a Snapple purchase along with Gatorade, Smithburg's crown jewel and most profitable brand.

On April 24, 1997, The *Wall Street Journal* reported that Quaker Oats had posted a $1.11 billion quarterly loss reflecting the final resolution of the Snapple affair, and that William Smithburg was stepping down. "Many investors have been asking for a long time why he hasn't stepped aside sooner," said one food-industry analyst.[14]

ANALYSIS

Beyond doubt the price paid for Snapple was wildly extravagant. Demand was slumping, distribution inefficiencies had surfaced, and the advertising had run out of steam. We can understand Smithburg's reasoning that he had bought Gatorade at a high price and turned it into a winner. Why shouldn't he do the same thing with Snapple? The price paid for Gatorade, $238 million for sales of $90 million at the time, was roughly comparable to the $1.7 billion for Snapple sales of almost $700 million.

[12] Gerry Khermouch, "Snapple Diet Line Gets $15 mil Push," *Brandweek*, 4 November 1996, p. 1.

[13] I. Jeanne Dugan, "Will Triarc Make Snapple Crackle?" *Business Week*, 28 April 1997, p. 64.

[14] Michael J. McCarthy, "Quaker Oats Posts $1.11 Billion Quarterly Loss," *Wall Street Journal*, 24 April 1997, pp. A3, A12.

But we can surely fault Smithburg for not demanding that his subordinates analyze more thoroughly the compatibility of the two operations. There should have been no surprises after the sale that the distribution systems of Gatorade and Snapple were not compatible and maybe could not be made so. Furthermore, it seems only reasonable to expect for a purchase of this magnitude that adequate research and planning would also have been done concerning the promotional efforts of Snapple, whether they were adequate for the coming year or whether changes needed to be made, and, if so, what changes. Should not stockholders expect that rather solid business plans would be in place before the acquisition was finalized by Quaker? Without such, the decision to let go of $1.7 billion seems rather like decision making by hunch and intuition. Perhaps it was.

The spinning of wheels in 1996, after the disastrous 1995, suggests that Smithburg had fallen prey to the decision-making error called *escalating commitment*. This is a resolution to increase efforts and resources to pursue a course of action that is *not* working, to be unable to "call it quits."[15]

See the Information Box: How to Avoid the Escalation Trap for advice by John Schermerhorn on not being trapped in an escalation commitment.

INFORMATION BOX

HOW TO AVOID THE ESCALATION TRAP

When should we call it quits, admit the mistake, and leave the scene as gracefully as possible, amid the cries of critics and the debris of sunk costs in a hopeless cause, and even embarrassment and shame and possible ouster by a board of directors tormented by irate investors? John Schermerhorn offers these guidelines to avoid staying in a lost cause too long:[16]

1. Set advance limits on your involvement in a particular course of action, and stick to them.
2. Make your own decisions; others may also be prone to escalation.
3. Carefully consider why you are continuing this course of action; unless there are sufficient reasons to continue, don't.
4. Consider the costs of continuing, and the savings in costs as a reason to discontinue.
5. Be on guard for escalation tendencies, especially where a big commitment has already been made.

Do you think Drucker's idea of an escalating commitment and Schermerhorn's suggestions for avoiding it have any downsides? In other words, when do you call it quits?

---

[16] John R. Schermerhorn, Jr., *Management*, 6th ed. (New York: Wiley, 1999), p. 67.

[15] Peter F. Drucker, "The Global Economy and the Nation-State," *Foreign Affairs*, vol. 76, September–October 1997, pp. 159–171.

You can imagine how the big commitment that had already been made for Snapple would have stimulated the escalating commitment to the fullest: "We have too much invested for this for fail."

If the product life cycle of Snapple had peaked before the Quaker purchase, this would account for the inability of Quaker management to reverse the downward trend of sales and profits. But such a possibility should surely have been considered before the acquisition decision. (See the Information Box: The Product Life Cycle.)

One would think that the best minds in a major corporation, and any outside consultants used, should have been able to bring Snapple to more healthy national and

---

INFORMATION BOX

THE PRODUCT LIFE CYCLE

Just as people and animals do, products go through stages of growth and maturity—that is, life cycles. They are affected by different competitive conditions at each stage, ranging often from no competition in the early stages to intense competition later on. We can recognize four stages in a product's life cycle: introduction, growth, maturity, and decline.

Figure 17.1 depicts three different product life cycles. Number 1 is that of a standard item in which sales take some time to develop and then eventually begin a slow decline. Number 2 shows a life cycle for a product in which a modification of the product or else the uncovering of a new market rejuvenates the product so that it takes off on a new cycle of growth (the classic examples of this are Listerine, originally sold as a mild external antiseptic, and Arm & Hammer Baking Soda, which was repositioned as a deodorizer). Number 3 shows the life cycle for a fad item or one experiencing rapid technological change and intense competition. Notice its sharp rise in sales and the abrupt downturn.

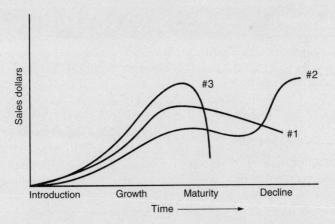

Figure 17.1 The product life cycle.

(continues)

THE PRODUCT LIFE CYCLE *(continued)*

Which life cycle most closely represented Snapple at the time of the acquisition? Snapple was definitely on a downward trend, which began the summer before Quaker purchased it, and this downward trend continued and even accelerated through 1995 and 1996. (See Table 17.1.) This suggests that Snapple had reached the maturity stage of its life cycle. As an admittedly trendy product, its curve in the worst scenario would resemble stage 3, the fad. An optimistic scenario would see a stage 2-curve, with strong efforts in 1997 bringing a rejuvenation. Perhaps the more likely life cycle is something akin to stage 1, with a slow downturn continuing for a lengthy period while aggressive efforts fail to stem the decline in an environment of more intense competition and less eager demand.

Do you agree with this prognosis? Why or why not?

international sales, or at least to a more profitable situation, even if the product life cycle had become less favorable. But in high-stake, near-crisis situations, prudent judgment may be abandoned as money is flung about in desperate efforts to turn things around. Often such merely aggravates the situation, as was the case with the expensive and poorly planned $40 million sampling effort and the $15 million sweepstakes program.

Finally, it is worth emphasizing again that in the acquisition quest, extensive homework should be done. These are *major* decisions. Hundreds of millions of dollars, even billions, are at stake if an unwise acquisition has to be divested a few years later. In addition, there is the management time taken up with a poorly performing product line at the expense of other responsibilities.

UPDATE—2001

Quaker's Gatorade remained a great strength of the company, having an estimated 78 percent of the sport-drink market. The success of this product made Quaker an attractive acquisition. In 2000, Coca-Cola expressed interest in buying Quaker, but faced a sticker price of $16 billion that its board of directors—among them Warren Buffett, one of the country's most astute investors—decided to reject.

Just a few months later, PepsiCo bid $14.02 billion, which Quaker accepted. The deal was expected to close by the end of June 2001, but federal antitrust enforcers continued to raise objections. The Federal Trade Commission (FTC) concern was that this merger would give Quaker's Gatorade brand even greater dominance once it became part of Pepsi's powerful distribution network. Coca-Cola's Powerade brand share was only 15 percent of the sport-drink market, while Pepsi's All-Sport, which the company agreed to sell, was a distant third. Opponents of the deal argued that it would enable Pepsi to gain too much clout with retailers—particularly convenience stores, where Gatorade and other Pepsi products such as Mountain Dew were already strong. FTC approval was difficult to obtain, although the deal had already been approved by several foreign regulators, including the European Union's antitrust authority. Then on August 2, 2001, in a rare deadlocked 2–2 vote, the FTC let PepsiCo proceed with the then $13.8 billion buyout of Quaker Oats Co.

Source: John R. Wilke and Betsy McKay, "PepsiCo Cites FTC for Further Delay of Quaker Deal," *Wall Street Journal*, 11 June 2001, p. B6; "FTC Allows PepsiCo to Buy Quaker Oats Despite Concerns," Associated Press as reported in *Cleveland Plain Dealer*, 2 August 2001, p. C5.

WHAT CAN BE LEARNED?

The Illusion of Compatibility

Bad acquisition decisions—in which the merger or acquisition turns out to be a mistake—often result from miscalculating the mutual compatibility of the two operations. Expectations are that consolidating various operations will result in significant cost savings. For example, instead of two headquarters' staffs, these can be reduced perhaps to a beefed-up single one. Sometimes even certain aspects of production can be combined, allowing some facilities to be closed for greater cost efficiencies. Computer operations, sales forces, and distribution channels might be combined. But for these combinations and consolidations to be feasible, the two operations essentially should be compatible.

As we saw in the case, the distribution channels of Snapple and Gatorade were not compatible, and efforts to consolidate brought serious rancor from those who would be affected. Quaker had failed to do its homework and probe deeply enough to determine the real depth of compatibility, not merely assuming compatibility because of product similarities.

Certainly we see many acquisitions and mergers of dissimilar operations: These are called *diversifications*. Some of these have little or no compatibility, and may not provide significant opportunities for reducing costs. Instead, they may be made because of perceived growth opportunities, to lessen dependence on mature products, to smooth out seasonality, and so on. Unfortunately, many of these dissimilar diversifications prove to be disappointing, and are candidates for divestiture some years later.

The Acquisition Contest

Once an acquisition candidate is identified, negotiations sometimes become akin to an athletic contest: Who will win? Not infrequently, several firms may be drawn to what they see as an attractive would-be acquisition, and a bidding war commences. Sometimes management of the takeover firm strongly resists. So, the whole situation evolves into a contest, almost a game. And aggressive executives get caught up in this game and sometimes overreach themselves in their struggle to win. No matter how attractive a takeover firm might be, if you pay way too much for it, this was a bad buy.

The Paradox of Perseverance: When Do We Give Up?

We admire people who persevere despite great odds: the student who continues with school even though family and work commitments may drag it out for ten years or more; the athlete who never gives up; the author who has a hundred rejection slips, but still keeps trying. So, how long should we persevere in what seems totally a losing cause? Isn't there such a thing as futility and unrealistic dreams, so that constructive efforts should be directed elsewhere? The enigma of futility has even been captured in classic literature with Don Quixote, the "Man from LaMancha," tilting his lance at windmills.

The line is blurred between perseverance and futile stubbornness, the escalating commitment of Peter Drucker. Circumstances vary too much to formulate guidelines. Still, if a direct assault continues to fail, perhaps it is time to make an end run.

When Should a Weak Product Be Axed?

Weak products tend to take up too much management, sales force, and advertising attention, efforts that could better be spent making healthy products better and/or developing replacements. Publicity about such products may even cause customer misgivings and tarnish the company's image. This suggests that weak and/or unprofitable products or divisions ought to be gotten rid of, provided that the problems are enduring and not a temporary aberration.

Not all weak products should be pruned, however; rationale for keeping them may be strong. In particular, the weak products may be necessary to complete a line to benefit sales of other products. They may be desirable for customer goodwill. Some weak products may enhance the company's image or prestige. Although such weak products make no money in themselves, still their intrinsic value to the firm may be substantial. Other weak products may merely be unproven, too new in their product life cycle to have become profitable; in their growth and maturity stage they may contribute satisfactory profits. Finally, possibly a new business strategy will rejuvenate the weak product. That is the hope, and the proffered justification for keeping a weak product when its demise is overdue.

So, where did Snapple fit into this theoretical discussion? The only justification for procrastination would seem to be that business strategy alternatives to turn around the brand had not been exhausted. In the meantime, the image of Quaker Oats in the eyes of investors, and the reflection of this in stock prices, was being savaged.

Be Cautious with Possible Fad Product Life Cycles

With hindsight, we can classify Snapple's popularity as a short-term phenomenon. But it was heady and contagious while it lasted. Snapple transformed ice tea into a new-age product by avoiding the need for preservatives and adding fruit flavors and introducing innovative wide-mouth, 16-ounce bottles. It also used Howard Stern, with his cult following, as its spokesman.

The public offering of stock in 1993 was sensational. The original offering price was to be $14, but this was raised to $20; in the first day of trading the stock closed at $29. Two years later, Quaker paid $1.7 billion for a company whose founders paid just $500 to acquire the name. But the euphoric life cycle was turning down, and the cult following was distracted by imitators, such as Arizona Iced Tea, Mystic, and Nantucket Nectars, as well as Coke and Pepsi through alliances with Nestea and Lipton.

Perhaps what can be learned is that product life cycles are unpredictable—especially where they involve fad or cult followers who may be as fickle as the wind, and where imitation is easy. To bet one's firm on such an acquisition can be risky indeed. But in truth, Smithburg had faced a similar situation with Gatorade, and won big. The moral: Decision making in the face of uncertainty can be a crapshoot. But prudence suggests a more cautious approach.

CONSIDER

Can you think of any other learning insights?

QUESTIONS

1. Why do you think the great Snapple giveaway was ineffective?
2. Do you think Snapple could have been turned around? Why or why not?
3. Do you think the premium retail price for Snapple was a serious impediment? Why or why not?
4. "Pouring more money into a lost cause is downright stupid. Smithburg has got to go." Discuss.
5. "This isn't a case where a guy has gone from a genius to a dummy. Who's better at running the company?" Discuss this statement.
6. "What's all the fuss about? Snapple is going great on our college campus. It's a success, man." Do you agree? Why or why not?
7. Do you drink Snapple? If not, why not? If so, how often—and how well do you like it?

HANDS-ON EXERCISES

Before

1. *Be a Devil's Advocate.* A major decision is at hand. You are a vice president of the beverage operation at Quaker. William Smithburg is proposing the acquisition of Snapple for some huge sum. Before this decision is made, you have been asked to array any contrary arguments to this expensive acquisition—in other words, to be a devil's advocate (one who takes a contrary position for the sake of argument and clarification of opposing views). What concerns would you raise, and how would you defend them?

After

1. It is late 1996. You are the assistant to Michael Schott, who has just been named president of Snapple. He asks you to formulate a strategic plan for resurrecting Snapple for 1997. What do you propose? Be as specific as you can, and be prepared to defend your recommendations.

2. *Be a Devil's Advocate.* The decision to sell Snapple for $300 million is on the table. What arguments would you array for not selling it at this low price? Be as persuasive as you can.

TEAM DEBATE EXERCISE

The acquisition of Snapple is accomplished. Now begins the assimilation. A major debate has ensued regarding whether Snapple should be consolidated with Gatorade, or whether it should remain an independent entity. Debate the two positions as persuasively as possible. Be sure to identify any assumptions you have made.

INVITATION TO RESEARCH

What is the situation with Snapple and with Smithburg today? Has Snapple prospered under its new ownership? Is Smithburg running any company?

CHAPTER EIGHTEEN

Newell Rubbermaid—Losing the Battle to Win Shelf Space

J ohn McDonough, CEO of Newell, specialized in buying small marginal firms and improving their operations. In ten years he had bought seventy-five such firms and polished them by eliminating poorer products, employees, factories, and stressing customer service. This format began to be called "Newellizing." It is hardly surprising that most of the acquisitions had strong brand names, but mediocre customer service. Rubbermaid fit this mode, though it was by far the biggest acquisition and would nearly double Newell's sales.

Rubbermaid, manufacturer and marketer of high-volume, branded plastic and rubber consumer products and toys, had been a darling of investors and academicians alike. For ten years in a row, it placed in the *Fortune* survey of "America's Most Admired Corporations," and it was No. 1 in both 1993 and 1994. It was ranked as the second most powerful brand in a Baylor University study of consumer goodwill, and received the "Thomas Edison Award" for developing products to make people's lives better. Under CEO Stanley Gault, Rubbermaid's emphasis on innovation often resulted in a new product every day, thereby helping the stock routinely to return 25 percent annually.

Surprisingly, by the middle 1990s Rubbermaid began faltering, partly because of inability to meet the service demands of Wal-Mart, a major customer. Rubbermaid stock plummeted 40 percent from the 1992 high, leaving it ripe for a takeover. Newell Company acquired Rubbermaid on March 24, 1999, expecting to turn it around. But then Newell had to wonder …

THE ACQUISITION AND WOLFGANG SCHMITT

Former Rubbermaid CEO Wolfgang Schmitt felt a cloak of apprehension settling over him in May 1999. It was only two months after the merger with Newell had been completed, and things were not going as he expected.

Schmitt had become CEO a year after the legendary Stanley Gault retired in 1991. Gault had returned in 1980 to his hometown of Wooster, Ohio (Rubbermaid headquarters) after more than thirty-one years with the General Electric Company. During Gault's tenure, Rubbermaid stock split four times, to the delight of stockholders. It was a tough act to follow.

Schmitt often thought about this, but he was certainly a worthy successor to Gault. He had spent all his working life with Rubbermaid, after graduating in 1966 from Otterbein College in Westerville, Ohio (about 60 miles from Wooster) with a degree in Economics and Business Administration. A recruiter visiting the campus convinced him to join Rubbermaid, a rapidly growing company. Schmitt started as a management trainee, and in twenty-seven years worked his way up the corporate ranks to become chairman of the board and chief executive officer in 1993. He was proud of this accomplishment, and thought his experience must be an inspiration to young people in the company: Any one of them could dream of becoming CEO, with hard work and loyalty. A significant highlight of his professional life came when he was invited back to Otterbein in November 1997 to inaugurate its Distinguished Executive Lecture Series.

During Schmitt's reign, Rubbermaid reached $2 billion in sales in 1994. When it celebrated its 75-year anniversary a year later, Schmitt set the company's sights on $4 billion in sales for the turn of the century. To do this, he knew it had to become a truly global company, and he instigated four foreign acquisitions that year.

He was an effective CEO; he knew he was. When the Newell Company, a slightly larger multinational firm, expressed an interest in merging, Schmitt thought he owed it to his stockholders, and to himself, to pursue this. After all, the two firms' housewares and hardware products and marketing efforts were compatible, and their combination would result in a $7-billion-a-year consumer products giant. Aiding Schmitt's decision to merge was a nice severance guarantee of $12 million after taxes in addition to his stock options. While Newell's CEO John McDonough would assume the CEO position of the merged corporation, Schmitt was to be a vice chairman and would work closely with McDonough to ensure the smooth merger and to help mold the new company.

Now, barely two months later, Schmitt had been shunted aside. He did not have an office at headquarters, his name was not listed on a new report of the seven highest-paid executives, and he was not even included in the list of directors reported to the Securities and Exchange Commission (SEC). He couldn't help feeling betrayed about no longer having a role in the operations of the company, after he had been so instrumental in bringing about the merger. At fifty-five years of age, he still had many productive years left. More than this, there was the principle of the thing: This was like a kick in the teeth.

But he was not alone. Three of Rubbermaid's five division presidents—the five divisions were Home Products, Little Tykes, Graco-Century, Curver, and Commercial Products—had already been replaced since the merger. Furthermore, in the Home Products division, only two of the top eight executives were still there.

NEWELL'S ASSESSMENT OF RUBBERMAID

If John McDonough of Newell was so unhappy with current Rubbermaid management and operations, why did he buy Rubbermaid in the first place—and for $6.3 billion dollars, more than two times current sales? At a shareholders' meeting a few months after the acquisition, McDonough tried to explain. He told them that Rubbermaid was a troubled company, but that once it's pulled into the revered operations of Newell, it can be great again.[1]

The shareholders were told that although jobs were being cut, operations would be stronger in the long run. As a strength, McDonough noted that Rubbermaid commanded 94 percent brand loyalty and generated great customer traffic in stores. But Rubbermaid executives needed to slash unnecessary costs, introduce robotics, and reduce product variety. For example, was it necessary to have dozens of the same type of wastebasket?

Still, McDonough saw poor customer service as the biggest deficiency of Rubbermaid, the most unacceptable aspect of its operation, and the one that Newell could most easily correct. After all, Newell had achieved a 98.5 percent on-time delivery rate in dealings with Wal-Mart. He would see that Rubbermaid was brought up to this same performance standard.

Rubbermaid's Customer Service Problems

Perhaps a declining commitment to customer service dated back to the retirement of Gault, though Schmitt would likely dispute that. Customer service can erode without being obvious to top management. While some customers complain, many others simply switch their business to competitors. Still, Rubbermaid's lapses in customer service should have been obvious for years. After all, Wal-Mart was not tolerant with vendors that did not meet its standards. When McDonough's people began digging deeper into Rubbermaid's operations, they found that the company wasn't even measuring customer service. This deficiency is almost the kiss of death when dealing with major retailers.

Up to the mid-1990s, about 15 percent of Rubbermaid's $2 billion-plus revenues came from Wal-Mart (see Chapter 21 for a complete case on Wal-Mart). Rubbermaid had had an impressive earnings growth of at least 15 percent a year to go along with 20 percent operating margins, much of this due to the generous space Wal-Mart gave its plastic and rubber products. This was to change abruptly.

In 1995 Wal-Mart refused to let Rubbermaid pass on much of its higher raw material costs, and began taking shelf space away and giving it to smaller competitors who undersold Rubbermaid. This resulted in a major earnings drop (see Table 18.1) that forced Rubbermaid to shut nine facilities and cut 9 percent of its 14,000 employees. "When you hitch your wagon to a star, you are at the mercy of that star."[2]

---

[1] Teresa Dixon Murray, "Newell Details Its Plans for Rubbermaid," *Cleveland Plain Dealer*, 27 May 1999, p. 1-C.

[2] Matthew Schifrin, "The Big Squeeze," *Forbes*, 11 March 1996, p. 46.

TABLE 18.1.   Rubbermaid Sales and Earnings, 1992–1997

	1992	1993	1994	1995	1996	1997
Sales (billions $)	$1.81	$1.96	$2.17	$2.34	$2.35	$2.40
Net earnings (millions $)	$184	$211	$228	$59	$152	$143
Percent of sales	10.2%	20.0%	18.9%	4.9%	14.2%	13.8%
Per Share	1.15	1.32	1.42	0.38	1.01	0.95

Source: Company reports.

Commentary: This six-year comparison of sales and the various profit indicators show rather starkly the decline in fortunes of Rubbermaid beginning in 1995. Sales remained practically static from 1995 on, although admittedly they were not growing very robustly in the three years before. The lack of growth occurred during a period of unprecedented economic prosperity.

The earnings comparisons show up worse. While acceptable earnings growth occurred up to 1995, they greatly worsened beginning in 1995. Not only were net earnings figures drastically reduced, but they showed little sign of recouping, even though there was some improvement from the bottom of 1995. Of course, net earnings as a percent of sales and per share also drastically declined from what they were in 1992-1994. Rubbermaid's major problems with Wal-Mart occurred in 1995.

Wal-Mart not only complained about poor deliveries but also began taking more drastic action. Each day Wal-Mart gives suppliers such as Newell a two-hour time slot in which their trucks can deliver orders placed twenty-four hours before. Should the supplier miss the deadline, it pays Wal-Mart for every dollar of lost margin. Now such a fast replenishment of orders required that factories be tied in with Wal-Mart's computers. Rubbermaid began installing software to do this in 1996 and had spent $62 million by 1999, but still was often not even achieving 80 percent on-time delivery service. This figure was unacceptable to Wal-Mart, and returns and fines for poor service rose to 4.4 percent of sales in 1998.[3] Finally, Wal-Mart purged most of its stores of Rubbermaid's Little Tikes toy line, giving the space to a competitor, Fisher Price. See the Information Box: The Demands of a Giant Retailer for a discussion of the power of a giant retailer and the demands it can make.

Wal-Mart had such high regard for the customer service of Newell that, upon hearing of the impending merger with Newell, Wal-Mart again began carrying Little Tykes toys. McDonough vowed to get Rubbermaid's on-time delivery rate of 80 percent up to Newell's 98.5 percent, and he began ripping out Rubbermaid's computer system and writing off the entire $62 million. In addition, McDonough claimed to be able to squeeze $350 million in costs out of Rubbermaid, which would double its operating income.[4]

AFTER THE MERGER

Newell did not quickly turn around and Newellize Rubbermaid, and stockholders were shocked and disappointed. In a time of rising stock prices, Newell Rubbermaid's shares plunged 20 percent in one day in September 1999 as the now-giant consumer

[3] Murray, "Newell Details Its Plans," p. 3-C.
[4] Michelle Conlin, "Newellizing Rubbermaid," *Forbes*, 31 May 1999, p. 118.

INFORMATION BOX

THE DEMANDS OF A GIANT RETAILER

Giant retailers, especially the big discount houses, stand in a power position today relative to their vendors. Part of this power lies in their providing efficient access to the marketplace; imagine the problems of a large consumer goods manufacturer in trying to deal with thousands of small retailers rather than the few big firms that dominate their markets. These giant firms can account for 50 percent and more of many manufacturers' sales. However, if such a major customer is lost or not completely satisfied, a vendor's viability could be in jeopardy.

Retailers like Wal-Mart make full use of their power position. Take paying of invoices, for example. Many vendors give a 2 percent discount if bills are paid within ten days instead of thirty. Wal-Mart routinely pays its bills closer to thirty days and still takes the 2 percent discount. Wal-Mart has also led in "partnering" with its vendors. This partnering really means that vendors have to pick up more of the inventory management and merchandising costs associated with Wal-Mart stores, with most of these costs involved in providing fast replenishment so that the stores can maintain lean stocks without losing customer sales through stockouts.

So-called slotting fees are common in the supermarket industry; that is, manufacturers pay to get things on store shelves. It is estimated that some $9 billion annually changes hands in private, unwritten deals between grocery retailers and food and consumer goods manufacturers.[5]

The following is an example of a slotting fee stipulation of a supermarket chain:

Effective January 1, 1996

Our slotting fee is ... $2,500

An item authorized, will remain authorized for a minimum of six months (as long as the basic cost does not go up substantially). Just as a reminder, many times it is the "slotting fee" that determines whether we authorize an item or not.

With the coercive power of a big retailer, a vendor is practically forced to meet their demands no matter what the cost.

Do you think a big manufacturer, such as Coca-Cola, can be coerced by a big retailer? Why or why not? What might determine the extent of retailer coercion? Can a manufacturer coerce a retailer?

---

[5] John S. Long, "Specialty Items to Drive New Market," *Cleveland Plain Dealer,* 6 October 1999, p. 4-F.

goods firm warned that third-quarter earnings would fall short of expectations. This was only the latest in a string of negatives, and Newell Rubbermaid's stock was to lose almost half of its value since the Rubbermaid acquisition in March. It blamed lower-than-expected sales of Rubbermaid's plastic containers and Little Tykes toys. Still, company officials maintained that "the integration process remains on plan."[6]

A month later, coinciding with a Wal-Mart announcement that it was expanding vigorously in Europe, Newell Rubbermaid said it would focus on expanding overseas to serve domestic retailers who are moving abroad. The company had been getting a quarter of its sales outside the United States. "Our customers are going international," McDonough said. "We have the opportunity to follow them. It's a once-in-a-lifetime opportunity."[7]

The company also maintained that it had sharply reduced the number of late shipments of Rubbermaid products and expected to have 98 percent of orders shipped on time either in the present quarter or next.[8]

Was this a wise merger? Did Newell pay too much for a faltering Rubbermaid? It was hardly likely in the first year of a merger that management would admit to maybe making a mistake. But stockholders were betting with their money. Meantime, Wolfgang Schmitt pondered his exile and the erosion of value of his stock options.

DISAPPOINTMENT

John McDonough resigned as CEO in November 2000, after Newell Rubbermaid cut profit forecasts three times in the year after the Rubbermaid acquisition. Joseph Galli—a "master marketer," as *Forbes* proclaimed him—and the first outsider in the company's ninety-nine-year history, became the chief executive in January 2001.

Newell needed a rescuer. McDonough, whose forte was buying underperforming companies and Newellizing them, had met his match. This was the third year of flat or falling profits. For 2001, sales were off 2.4 percent and net income down 42 percent, with share prices reflecting this. The $6 billion purchase of Rubbermaid, its biggest deal, had brought Newell to its knees, and Rubbermaid remained the sickest division.

Joseph Galli

The forty-three-year-old Galli in nineteen years at Black & Decker had built a reputation as a marketing wunderkind, a brand builder. He was running the company's crown jewel, the DeWalt brand, a high-margin line of power tools for skilled tradesmen and consumer do-it-yourselfers. Galli recruited teams of college graduates, dubbed "swarm teams," to be supermissionary salespeople hawking the DeWalt brand not only at store openings but at union halls and Nascar races as well. See the Information Box: Missionary Salespeople.

[6] James P. Miller, "Newell Rubbermaid Shares Fall 20% as an Earnings Short Fall Is Predicted," *Wall Street Journal*, 7 September 1999, p. A4.

[7] "Newell Rubbermaid to Resume Acquisitions, Expand Overseas," *Cleveland Plain Dealer*, 6 October 1999, p. 2-C.

[8] Ibid.

INFORMATION BOX

MISSIONARY SALESPEOPLE

Missionary or supporting salespeople do not normally try to secure orders. They are used by manufacturers to provide specialized services and create goodwill and more dealer push. They work with dealers, perhaps to develop point-of-service displays, train dealer salespeople to do a better job of selling the product, provide better communication and rapport between distributor and manufacturer, and in general, aggressively promote the brand. They are particularly important in selling to self-service outlets, such as supermarkets and discount stores, where with no retail clerks selling to customers, displays, shelf space, and in-stock conditions have to be the selling tools.

The supermissionaries or swarm teams of Galli are small armies of energetic college recruits who also work Nascar races, trade shows, new store openings, and the like. A typical supermissionary is given the use of a new Ford Explorer Sport Trac, a territory of fourteen Wal-Marts, and a mission: Make sure Newell's pens, bowls, buckets, and blinds are neatly displayed, priced right, and piled high in prominent spots.[9]

Evaluate this statement: "Good customer service doesn't do you much good, but poor customer service can kill you."

[9] Upbin, "Rebirth of a Salesman," 100.

Galli brought amazing growth to DeWalt, pushing $60 million in sales in 1992 to more than $1 billion by 1999, in the process providing 64 percent of the company's $4.6 billion sales. By age thirty-eight, Galli was the second-highest-paid executive at Black & Decker; he was in line for the top position, except that the CEO was not ready to step down anytime soon.

Galli left to be president of Amazon.com, staying only a year, then became chief of VerticalNet for 167 days. Some were calling him a tumbleweed, but conceded that if anybody could add sizzle to an unpretentious product line of such things as mop buckets, toilet brushes, and plastic containers, he might be the best.[10]

Galli spent his first three months at Newell Rubbermaid traveling the world and meeting every manager he could. His predecessor, John McDonough, was a diabetic whose leg had been amputated in 1999 and who spent almost all his time at company headquarters in Beloit, Wisconsin; in his first six months, Galli spent just thirty-six hours there.

Newell hadn't run a national ad campaign on television in three years. In 2000, the firm spent 0.7 percent on research and development. (Even the conservative Colgate spent 2 percent on the innovation of adding a new color of dish detergent.) Sales of the Rubbermaid unit had declined every year since 1998, and were now at $1.8 billion. No-name rivals were taking business away in major retailers such as Wal-Mart, Home Depot, Target, and Bed Bath & Beyond.

[10] Bruce Upbin, "Rebirth of a Salesman," *Forbes*, 1 October 2001, pp. 95–104.

Galli tripled spending on new product development for Rubbermaid. He promoted the brand on prime-time TV for the first time in three years with a budget of $15 million, more than was spent in the previous ten years combined. He also budgeted $40 million for swarm teams of well-paid college grads to push Newell Rubbermaid products at mass retailers, as they had done so successfully with power tools at Black & Decker.[11] Galli made his first acquisition in November 2002—buying American Saw and Manufacturing Co., thus expanding into the hand-tool and power-tool market that he knew so well.[12] Could it be that Newell Rubbermaid was on the verge of a turnaround?

ANALYSIS

This case illustrates not only the risks of dealing with behemoth customers but also the rewards if you can satisfy their demands. After all, in better days Newell Rubbermaid prepared to follow Wal-Mart to Europe and be a prime supplier of its stores there. But a vendor has to have the commitment and ability to meet stringent requirements. If a twenty-four-hour delivery cycle is demanded, the vendor must achieve this regardless of costs. If selling prices are to be pared to the bone, efficiency must somehow be jacked up and production costs pruned, or else profitability may have to be sacrificed even to the point of extreme concern. Otherwise, the vendor can be replaced.

The alternative? To be content with far less revenues and a host of smaller accounts, or else to have such a brand name as to be partly insulated from price competition. Rubbermaid thought it had this, due to its public accolades of past years. Perhaps this contributed to its apathy regarding its delivery service. But Wal-Mart was hardly impressed with the superiority of this brand's products that cost more than alternative suppliers and could not be delivered on time.

But note that improving service and shortening replenishment time is not easily or cheaply done. Rubbermaid spent $62 million on computer technology to enable it to meet Wal-Mart's demands, but it was not enough. Better control of warehouse inventories and production schedules is essential. The vendor will need to carry more of the inventory burden traditionally assumed by the retailer and incur additional expenses and investment for more manpower and trucks and other equipment. Perhaps the most damning indictment of Rubbermaid's service deficiencies was how long they continued without being corrected. The problem initially surfaced in 1995, but by 1999 on-time deliveries had still not improved appreciably. What was Rubbermaid top management doing all this time? Wolfgang Schmitt can hardly escape the blame that in almost five years he had not corrected this serious problem with the company's most important customer.

The eagerness to merge that we saw in this case, by both McDonough of Newell and Wolfgang Schmitt of Rubbermaid, may not always be in the best interests of shareholders, and certainly not of employees. It may even not be in the best interests of the executives involved, as Schmitt realized to his dismay—despite taking home a

[11] Ibid., 104.

[12] "Newell Rubbermaid to Buy American Saw in $450 Million Deal," *Wall Street Journal,* 25 November 2002, p. B6.

sizable severance package. But is this enough to make up for losing the power and prestige of a top management position, and all the perks that go with it?

In this era of merger mania, a more sober appraisal is needed by many firms. Not all mergers are in the best interests of both parties. Too many times a firm pays too much to acquire another firm, as we saw in Chapter 17 where Quaker Oats bought Snapple for $1.7 billion and three years later got rid of it for $300 million; also in Chapter 13, we saw Maytag paying $1 billion for Chicago Pacific and incurring a heavy debt burden. Frequently the glowing prospects of synergy do not work out. See the Information Box: Synergy for a discussion of the allure of synergy in a merger.

When an acquisition finally turns out to be unwise, especially where too much is paid for the acquired firm, the conclusion may be that someone fumbled the homework, that the research and investigation of the firm to be acquired was hasty, biased, or downright incompetent. Admittedly, in some cases several suitors may be bidding for the same acquisition candidate, and this then becomes a contest: Who will make the winning bid? The only beneficiaries to such a situation—besides the consultants, lawyers, and investment bankers—are the shareholders of the firm to be acquired.

INFORMATION BOX

SYNERGY

Synergy results from creating a whole that is greater than the sum of its parts, that can accomplish more than the total of the individual contributions. In an acquisition, synergy occurs if the two or more firms, when combined, are more efficient, productive, and profitable than they were as separate operations before the merger. Sometimes this concept is referred to as $2 + 2 = 5$.

How can such synergy occur? If duplication of efforts can be eliminated, if operations can be streamlined, if economies of scale are possible, if specialization can be enhanced, if greater financial and managerial resources can be tapped—then a synergistic situation is likely to occur. Such an expanded operation then should be a stronger force in the market than the individual single units that existed before.

The concept of synergism is the rationale for mergers and acquisitions. But sometimes combining causes the reverse: negative synergy, where the consequences are worse than the sum of individual efforts. If friction arises between the entities; if organizational missions are incompatible; if the new organizational climate creates fearful, resentful, and frustrated employees; then synergy is unlikely. And if greater managerial and financial resources are not realized—if indeed financial resources are depleted because of the interest overhead due to the acquisition—then synergy becomes negative. The whole, then, is less than the sum of its parts. Furthermore, if because of sheer optimism or an uncontrolled acquisitive drive, more is paid for the acquisition than it is really worth, then a grand blunder has occurred. Could that have been the case with the Rubbermaid acquisition?

Do you think a typical committee or group has more synergy than the same individuals working alone? Why or why not?

WHAT CAN BE LEARNED?

Customer Service Is Vital in Dealing with Big Customers

We saw in this case the consequences of not being able to meet the service demands of Wal-Mart. A vendor's very viability may depend on somehow gearing up to meet the service expectations. This should be a top priority if such a customer is not to be lost. Correcting the situation should be a matter of weeks or months, and not years.

The Well-known Brand Name Does not always Compensate for Higher Prices or Poor Service when Dealing with Big Retailers

Generally we think of a well-respected brand name as giving the vendor certain liberties, of insulating the vendor at least somewhat from vicious price competition, and even excusing the vendor from some service standards such as prompt and dependable delivery. After all, a respected brand name gives an image of quality, which lesser brands do not have, and an assured body of loyal customers.

Well, Wal-Mart's dealings with Rubbermaid before the merger certainly disprove that notion.

How can this be? It still becomes a matter of power position. Not having Rubbermaid, or Little Tykes toys, was hardly damaging to Wal-Mart with its eager alternative suppliers. But the loss of Wal-Mart, even if only partially through being given less shelf space, was serious for Rubbermaid.

The Positive Aspects of Organizational Restructuring for Acquisitions Are Mixed

The idea of restructuring generally means downsizing. Some assets or corporate divisions may be sold off or eliminated, and the remaining organization thereby streamlined. This usually means layoffs, plant closings, and headquarters relocations. In Rubbermaid's case, the small Ohio town of Wooster faced the loss of its headquarters and some three thousand jobs. Of course, management's defense always is that while jobs are being cut, the operations will be stronger in the long run. Perhaps, but not always.

Where an organization has become fat and inefficient with layers of bureaucracy, some pruning of personnel and operations is necessary. But how much is too much, and how much is not enough? Certainly those personnel who are not willing to accept change may have to be let go. Weak persons and operations that show little probability of improvement need to be cut, just as the athlete who can't perform up to expectations can hardly be carried. Still, it is usually better to wait for sufficient information as to the "why" of poor performance before assigning blame for unsatisfactory operational results. You may want to review Chapter 9 and the Scott Paper case for the worst scenario here.

Periodic Housecleaning Produces Competitive Health

To minimize the buildup of deadwood, all aspects of an organization periodically ought to be objectively appraised. Weak products and operations should be pruned, unless solid justification exists for keeping them. Such justification might include good growth prospects, or complementing other products and operations, or even providing a desired customer service. In particular, staff and headquarters personnel and functions should be scrutinized, perhaps every five years, with the objective of weeding out the superfluous. Most important, these evaluations should be done objectively, with decisive actions taken where needed. While some layoffs may result, they might not be necessary if suitable transfers are possible.

Going back to Rubbermaid, the five-year-long tolerance of little improvement in customer service was inexcusable, and one would think that heads should roll (as undoubtedly some did, and quickly, when Newell took over).

Is there Life without Wal-Mart for a Big Mass-Market Consumer Goods Manufacturer?

Can such a large manufacturer be strong and profitable without selling to the giant retailers? Certainly other distribution channels are available for reaching consumers—such as smaller retailers, different types of retailers, wholesalers, and perhaps even the Internet in coming years. For smaller manufacturers some of these are viable alternatives to Wal-Mart, Target, Home Depot, and the various large department store corporations.

Newell and Rubbermaid's products were diversified but still geared to rather pedestrian household and hardware consumer use—hardly the grist to create a fashion or fad demand. A limited distribution strategy, such as through boutiques, would hardly produce the sales volume needed. Only the megaretailers could provide the mass distribution and sales volume needed. Of course, Wal-Mart was not the only large retailer, but it was the biggest. Home Depot, Target, and the chain department stores were alternatives. But these tended to be just as demanding as Wal-Mart. This suggests that somehow the demands of giant retailers had to be catered to, regardless of the costs to or inclinations of firms like Newell and Rubbermaid.

Missionary Salespeople Can Be a Good Enhancement of Customer Service in Dealing with Large Retailers

Many vendors are realizing this today, and such sales-support staff are frequently used to provide the service, rapport, and feedback desirable in dealing with these most important clients. The vendor that provides the best such support may well win out over competitors. Furthermore, such missionaries may alert the vendor to emerging problems or competitive situations that need to be countered. When they are swarm teams like Galli's, they can be a powerful tool in winning the battle for shelf space.

CONSIDER

Can you add any additional learning insights?

QUESTIONS

1. "Periodic evaluations of personnel and departments aimed at pruning 'deadwood' cause far too much harm to the organization. Such 'axing' evaluations should themselves be pruned." Argue this position as persuasively as you can.

2. Now gather your most persuasive arguments *for* such "axing" evaluations.

3. How do you account for Rubbermaid's inability to improve its delivery service to Wal-Mart? What factors do you see as contributing to this ongoing deficiency?

4. Do you think Newell acted too hastily in discharging Schmitt and other top executives so soon after the merger? Why or why not?

5. Do you think Wal-Mart and the other large retailers are going too far in their demands on their suppliers? Where would you draw the line?

6. Stanley Gault's strategy of trying to introduce a new product every day was lauded as the mark of a successful firm permeated by innovative thinking. Do you agree with this?

7. Is it likely that a decades-old organization, such as Rubbermaid, would be bloated with excessive bureaucracy and overhead? Why or why not?

HANDS-ON EXERCISES

1. *Be a Devil's Advocate* (one who argues a contrary position). You have been asked by several concerned board members to argue against the avid Newellizing policy of John McDonough at the next board meeting. Marshal as many contrary or cautionary arguments as you can and present them as persuasively, yet as tactfully, as you can.

2. You are one of the three divisional presidents fired by McDonough in the first two months of the merger. Describe your feelings and your action plan at this point. (If you want to make some assumptions, state them specifically.)

3. You are a vice president of Rubbermaid, reporting to Wolfgang Schmitt in 1995. The first serious complaints have surfaced from Wal-Mart concerning unacceptable delivery problems. Schmitt has ordered you to look into the complaints and prepare a course of action. Be as specific as you can on how you would approach this problem and what recommendations you would make.

TEAM DEBATE EXERCISE

It is early 1998. The demands of Wal-Mart are intensifying, and Newell is making overtures to acquire Rubbermaid. Debate these two courses of action in this turnabout year for Rubbermaid: (1) We must gear up to meet Wal-Mart's demands, even though estimated costs of complying are investing $300 million dollars in a new computer network and other capital and operating costs; versus (2) It is better to sacrifice the increasingly dictatorial Wal-Mart account and seek alternative distribution.

INVITATION TO RESEARCH

What is Wolfgang Schmitt doing after being ousted from an active role with Newell Rubbermaid? Have Newell Rubbermaid's fortunes improved under Galli's management?

NOTABLE MARKETING
SUCCESSES

CHAPTER NINETEEN

Vanguard—Success with Minimal Marketing

Sometime, most likely in only a few years, Vanguard Group will become the largest mutual fund family in the world, besting Fidelity Investments. While Fidelity is still the biggest and increasing its fund assets about 20 percent a year, Vanguard is growing at 33 percent. The giant Fidelity advertises heavily, yet Vanguard does practically no advertising, spending a bare $8 million for a few ads to get people to ask for prospectuses. The Kaufmann Fund, one-hundredth Vanguard's size, spends that much for advertising, and General Mills spent twice as much just to introduce a new cereal, Sunrise.[1]

What is Vanguard's secret? How wise is it with such a consumer product to spurn marketing? The answer lies in the vision and steadfastness of John C. Bogle, the founder and recently retired chairman.

JOHN BOGLE AND THE CREATION OF VANGUARD

In 1950, as a junior at Princeton, Bogle was groping for a topic for his senior thesis. He wanted a topic that no one had written about in any serious academic paper. In December 1949 he read an article in *Fortune* on mutual funds. At that time, all mutual funds were sold with sales commissions often 8 percent of the amount invested, and this was taken off the top as a front end load. (This meant that if you invested $1,000, only $920 would be earning you money. Today we find no funds with a front end load more than 6.5 percent, so there has been some improvement.) In addition these funds had high yearly overheads or expense ratios. As Bogle thought about this, he wondered why funds couldn't be bought without salespeople or brokers and their steep commissions, and if growth could not be maximized by keeping overhead down.

Right after graduation he joined a tiny mutual fund, Wellington Management Company, and moved up rapidly. In 1965, at age 35, he became the chief executive.

---

[1] Thomas Easton, "The Gospel According to Vanguard," *Forbes*, 8 February 1999, p. 115.

Unwisely, he decided to merge with another firm, but the new partners turned out to be active managers, generating high overhead costs. The relationship was incompatible with Bogle's beliefs and in 1974 he was fired as chief executive.

He decided to go his own way and change the "very structure under which mutual funds operated" into a fund distribution company mutually owned by shareholders. The idea came from his Princeton thesis, and included such heresies as "reduction of sales loads and management fees," and "giving investors a fair shake" as the rock on which the new enterprise would be built. He chose the name "Vanguard" for his new company after the great victory of Lord Nelson over Napoleon's fleet with his flagship, HMS Vanguard. Bogle launched the Vanguard Group of Investment Companies on September 26, 1974, and he hoped "that just as Nelson's fleet had come to dominate the seas during the Napoleonic wars, our new flagship would come to dominate the mutual fund sea."[2]

But success was long in coming. Bogle brought out the first index fund the next year, a fund based on Standard & Poor's 500 Stock Price Index, and named it Vanguard 500 Index Fund. It was designed to mirror the market averages, and thus required minimal management decisions and costs. It flopped initially. Analysts publicly derided the idea, arguing that astute management could beat the averages every time, though they ignored the costs of high-priced money managers and frequent trading.

At the new millennium twenty-five years later, this Vanguard flagship fund that tracks the 500 stocks on Standard & Poor's Index had more than $75 billion in assets and had beat 86 percent of all actively managed stock funds in 1998, and an even higher percentage over the past decade. By early 2000 it would overtake Fidelity's famed Magellan Fund as the largest mutual fund of all. The relative growth between Magellan and Vanguard's 500 Index is shown in Table 19.1.

The Vanguard family of funds had become the world's largest no-load mutual fund group, with 12 million shareholders and $442 billion in assets as of the beginning of 1999. Fidelity, partly load and partly no-load, had nearly $700 billion, but the gap was closing fast.

TABLE 19.1. Relative Growth Comparisons of the Two Largest Mutual Funds

	Assets (millions $)		5-Year Gain
	6/30/94	6/30/99	(Percent)
Fidelity Magellan	$33,179	$97,594	194.2%
Vanguard 500 Index	8,443	92,644	997.3

Source: Company reports.

Commentary: Especially notable is the tremendous growth of Vanguard's 500 Index Fund in the last five years, growing from $8 billion in assets to over $92 billion.

[2] John C. Bogle, *Common Sense on Mutual Funds* (New York: Wiley, 1999), pp. 402–403.

Bogle, The Messiah

A feature article in *Forbes'* February 8, 1999 issue had this headline:

> The Gospel According to Vanguard
> How do you account for the explosive success of that strange business called Vanguard?
> Maybe it isn't really a business at all. It's a religion.[3]

Bogle's religion was low-cost investing and service to customers. He believed in funds being bought and not sold, thus, no loads or commissions to salespeople or brokers. Customers had to seek out and deal directly with Vanguard. The engine was frugality with the investor-owner's best interests paramount. This was not advertised, not pasted on billboards, but the gospel was preached in thousands of letters to shareholders, editors, Securities and Exchange Commission members, and congressmen. Bogle made many speeches, comments to the news media, and appearances on such TV channels as CNBC, and wrote two best-selling books. With his gaunt face and raspy voice, he became the zealot for low-cost investing, and the major critic of money managers who trade frenetically, in the process running up costs and tax burdens for their investors. As the legions of loyal and enthusiastic clients grew, word-of-mouth from past experiences and favorable mentions in business and consumer periodicals such as *Forbes,* the *Wall Street Journal, Money,* and numerous daily newspapers, as well as TV stations, brought a groundswell of new and repeat business to Vanguard.

Bogle turned 70 in May 1999, and was forced to retire from Vanguard's board. The new chairman, John J. Brennan, 44, seemed imbued with the Bogle philosophy, and with vision. He said, "We're a small company, and we haven't begun to explore our opportunities, yet." He noted that there's Europe and Asia, to say nothing of the trillions of dollars held in non-Vanguard funds. "It's humbling."[4]

GREAT APPEAL OF VANGUARD

Performance

Each year *Forbes* presents "Mutual Funds Ratings" and "Best Buys." The Ratings lists the hundreds of mutual funds that are open end, that is, can be bought and sold at current net asset prices.[5] The Best Buys are those select few that *Forbes* analysts judged to "invest wisely, spend frugally, and you get what you pay for," and that perform best in shareholder returns over both up and down markets. Vanguard equity and bond funds dominate *Forbes'* Best Buys:

> Of 43 U.S. *equity* funds listed in the various categories, 12 are Vanguard funds.
> Of 70 *bond* funds, 27 are Vanguard funds.[6]

---

[3] Easton, p. 115.

[4] Easton, p. 117.

[5] A far smaller number of mutuals are closed-end funds that have a fixed number of shares and are traded like stocks. These generally have higher annual expenses, yet sell at a discount from net asset value. We will disregard these in this case.

[6] *Forbes,* 23 August 1999, pp. 128, 136–137.

Forbes explains that "the preponderance of Vanguard funds in our Best Buy Tables is a testament to the firm's cost controls… Higher expenses, for most other fund families, are like lead weights. Why carry them?"[7] Table 19.2 shows representative examples of the substantially lower expenses of Vanguard funds relative to others on the Best Buy list.[8]

Looking at total averages, the typical mutual fund has an expense ratio of 1.24 percent of assets annually. The ratio for Vanguard's 101 funds is .28 percent, almost a full percentage point lower.[9]

How does Vanguard achieve such a low expense ratio? We noted before the reluctance to advertise at all; nor does it have any mass sales force. Its commitment

TABLE 19.2.   Comparative Expense Ratios of Representative Mutual Funds

	Annual Expenses per $100
Balanced Equity Funds:	
Vanguard Wellington Fund	0.31
Columbia Balanced Fund	0.67
Janus Balanced Fund	0.93
Ranier Balanced Portfolio	1.19
Index Equity Funds:	
Vanguard 500 Index	.18
T Rowe Price Equity Index 500	.40
Dreyfus S&P 500 Index	.50
Gateway Fund	1.02
Municipal Long-Term Bonds:	
Vanguard High Yield Tax Exempt	.20
Dreyfus Basic Muni Bond	.45
Strong High Yield Muni Bond	.66
High-Yield Corporate Bonds:	
Vanguard High Yield Corp.	.29
Fidelity High Income	.75
Value Line Aggressive Income	.81
Ivesco High Yield	.86

Source: Company records as reported in *Forbes Mutual Fund Guide,* 23 August 1999.

Commentary: The great cost advantage of Vanguard shows up very specifically here. It is not a slightly lower expense ratio, but one that is usually three or four times lower than similar funds. Take, for example, the category of Index Equity Funds, where the goal is to simply track the Index averages, which suggests passive management rather than free-wheeling buying and selling. Yet, Vanguard's costs are far below the other funds; in one case, the Gateway fund is five times higher.

[7] Ibid., p. 136.

[8] Ibid., pp. 128, 137.

[9] Easton, p. 116.

has been to pare marketing costs to the absolute minimum. But there have been other economies.

Fidelity and Charles Schwab have opened numerous walk-in sales outposts. Certainly these bring more sales exposure to prospective customers. But are such sales promotion efforts worth the cost? Vanguard decided not. It had one sales outpost in Philadelphia, but closed it to save money.

Vanguard discouraged day traders and other market timers from in-and-out trading of its funds. It even prohibited telephone switching on the Vanguard 500 Index; redemption orders had to come by mail. Why such market timing discouragement? Frequent redemptions run up transaction costs, and a flurry of sell orders might impose trading costs that would have to be borne by other shareholders as some holdings might have to be sold.

Not the least of the economies is what Bogle calls passive investing, tracking the market rather than trying to actively manage the funds by trying to beat the market. The funds with the highest expense ratios are hedge funds and these usually are the most active traders, with heavy buying and selling. Yet, they seldom beat the market but squander a lot of money in the effort and burden shareholders with sizable capital gains taxes because of the flurry of transactions. Still, the common notion prevails that more is better, that the more expensive car or service must be better than its less expensive alternative. See the Information Box for another discussion of the price-quality perception.

Another factor also contributes to the great cost advantage of Vanguard. It is a mutual firm, organized as a nonprofit owned by its customers. Almost all other financial institutions, except TIAA-CREF (and we will discuss this shortly), have stock ownership. The insurance industry used to be dominated by mutual firms, but somehow they did not stand out for their low costs and high performance, nor did they serve well their customer-owners. Most insurance firms, especially the large ones, have been demutualizing and in the process drawing up lucrative option packages for their executives. In the MetLife case, Chapter 22, the effort to demutualize was the major incentive to settle all the litigation pending against it.

Customer Service

Many firms espouse a commitment to customer service. It is the popular thing to do, rather like motherhood, apple pie, and the flag. Unfortunately, pious platitudes do not always match reality. Vanguard's commitment to service seems to be more tangible.

Service to customers is often composed of the simple things, such as just answering the phone promptly and courteously, or responding to mail quickly and completely, or giving complete and unbiased information. Vanguard's 2,000 phone reps are ready to answer the phone by the fourth ring. During a market panic or on April 15 when the tax deadline stimulates many inquiries, CEO John Brennan brings a brigade of executives with him to help answer the phones. Vanguard works to make its monthly statements to investors as complete and easy-to-understand as possible, and it leads the industry in this.

INFORMATION BOX

THE PRICE-QUALITY PERCEPTION

We had a similar box in Chapter 9 on Perrier, but the topic is worth further discussion. There we considered whether high-priced bottled water was that much better than regular tap water or lower-priced bottled water, and concluded that it usually was not. The same thing applies to perfume, to beer and liquor, and to many other consumer products. "You get what you pay for," is a common perception, and its corollary is that you judge quality by price: The higher the price, the higher the quality. But this notion leads many consumers to be taken advantage of, and for top-of-the-line brands and products to command a higher profit margin than lower-priced alternatives. Admittedly, sometimes we are led to the more expensive brand or item for the prestige factor.

When it comes to money management, by no means do high fees mean better quality; the reverse is usually true. And prestige should hardly be a factor since we are not inclined to show off our investments like we might a new car. Does a high-overhead index fund deliver better performance than a cheap one, than Vanguard? Not at all. And hedge funds as we noted before seldom even beat the averages despite running up some of the highest expenses in the mutual fund industry. Looking at Table 19.2, which shows typical expense ratios of Vanguard and its competitors, are the other funds doing a better job than Vanguard with their expenses three to five times as high? No, because their high expense ratios take away from any performance advantage, even if frequent trading resulted in somewhat better gains, and that seldom is achieved.

If Vanguard advertised its great expense advantage aggressively to really get the word out, do you think it would win many more customers? Why or why not?

The philosophy of a customer-service commitment was espoused by Bogle: "Our primary goal: to serve, to the best of our ability, the human beings who are our clients. To serve them with candor, with integrity, and with fair dealing. To be the stewards of the assets they have entrusted to us. To treat them as we would like the stewards of our own assets to treat us."

Bogle describes a talk he gave to Harvard Business School in December 1997 on how "our focus on human beings had enabled Vanguard to become what at Harvard is called a 'service breakthrough company.' I challenged the students to find the term *human beings* in any book they had read on corporate strategy. As far as I know, none could meet the challenge. But 'human beingness' has been one of the keys to our development."[10]

Not the least of the consumer best interests has been a commitment to holding down taxable transactions for shareholders. Vanguard has led the industry with tax-managed funds aimed at minimizing the capital gains that confront most mutual fund investors to their dismay at the end of the year.

[10] Bogle, pp. 423, 424.

COMPETITION

Why is Vanguard's low-expense approach not matched by competitors? All the other fund giants that sell primarily to the general public are for-profit companies. Are they willing to sacrifice profits to win back Vanguard converts? Hardly likely. Are they willing to reduce their hefty marketing and advertising expenditures? Again, hardly likely. Why? Because advertising is vital to their visibility and to seeking out customers.

TIAA-CREF

One potential competitor looms, another low-cost fund contender. TIAA-CREF, which manages retirement money for teachers and researchers, in 1997 launched six no-load mutual funds that are now open to all investors. The funds' annual expenses range from 0.29 percent to 0.49 percent, comparable with Vanguard's. A significant potential attraction over Vanguard is that each fund's investment minimum is just $250, compared with Vanguard's usual minimum of $3,000. As of late August 1999, the combined assets of the six TIAA-CREF funds was $1.5 billion, far less, of course, than the near $500 billion of Vanguard.

TIAA-CREF is also run solely for the benefit of its shareholders, being another mutual, with the long-term aim of providing fund-management services at cost. Still, there is some doubt that expense ratios can be kept low, should the new funds fail to attract enough investors.

Is this a gnat up against the giant Vanguard? Perhaps; however, the low investment requirement of only $250 should certainly attract cost-conscious investors who cannot come up with the $3,000 that Vanguard requires on most of its funds. Still, six fund choices versus the more than a hundred of Vanguard is not very attractive yet. Efforts to be as tax-efficient as Vanguard are also unknown.

ANALYSIS

The success of Vanguard with its disavowal of most traditional marketing techniques flies in the face of all that we have come to believe. It suggests that heavy advertising expenditures may at least be questioned as not always desirable—and what a heresy this is. It suggests that relying on word-of-mouth and whatever free publicity can be garnered may sometimes be better than advertising. All you need is a superior product or service. It supports the statement that marketing textbooks like to shoot down: "If you build a better mousetrap, people will come." Marketing wisdom says that without advertising to get the message out, this better mousetrap will fade away from lack of buyer knowledge and interest.

How do we reconcile Vanguard with the conventional thinking that marketing communication is essential to get products and services to customers (except perhaps when selling solely to the government or to a single customer)?

Maybe we should not try to fit Vanguard in with most of our traditional thoughts of marketing. Maybe it is the exception, the anomaly, in its seeming repudiation of marketing. Still, let us not be too hasty in this judgment.

I do not believe that Vanguard contradicts the traditional principles of market-ing. Rather, it has opened up rather intriguingly another approach to marketing and the advertising component: the effective use of word-of-mouth publicity. A superior and distinctive product as tangibly demonstrated in relative cost advantages, then effective word-of-mouth enhanced or developed through more formal publicity—from media, public appearances, and publications—can indeed replace the massive advertising expenditures of competitors. But there is a downside to all this.

But first, let us examine the role of word-of-mouth in more detail in the Information Box.

In one respect, however, Vanguard illustrates a commendable application of one important marketing principle: the desirability of uniqueness or product differentiation.

INFORMATION BOX

THE POTENTIAL OF WORD-OF-MOUTH AND UNPAID PUBLICITY

Word-of-mouth advertising, by itself, is almost always frowned on by the experts. It is the sign of the marginal firm, one without sufficient resources, so they say, to do what is needed to get established. Such a firm is bound to succumb to competitors who are bet-ter managed and better resourced. The best they can say for word-of-mouth advertising is that if the firm can survive for an unknown number of years, and if it really, really has a superior product or service, then it might finally attain some modest success.

Compared to spending for advertising, word-of-mouth takes far longer to have any impact, and most firms do not have the staying power to wait years, so the belief holds. The best strategy would be to have both, with healthy doses of advertising to jumpstart the enterprise, and let favorable word-of-mouth reinforce the advertising.

As we have seen, Bogle and his Vanguard repudiated the accepted strategy, yet became highly successful. But it took time, even decades. If you look at Table 19.1, in 1994 after 16 years the flagship Index 500 fund had reached $8 billion in assets; not bad, but far below the heavily advertised Magellan fund of Fidelity. Its growth has acceler-ated only in recent years. Would more advertising have shortened the period?

Bogle would maintain that such advertising would have destroyed the uniqueness of Vanguard by making its expenses like other funds. He would also likely contend that the favorable publicity enhanced the word-of-mouth influence of satisfied shareholders, and thus there was no need for expensive advertising. But in the early years of Vanguard it did not have much favorable publicity. On the contrary, it took experts a long time to admit that a low-expense fund with passive management could do as well or better than aggressively managed funds with a lot of buying and selling and big trading and mar-keting expenses.

So the success of Vanguard without much formal advertising attests to the success of word-of-mouth heavily seasoned with favorable free publicity. But was it too conserva-tive, especially in the early years?

Do you think Vanguard should have advertised more, especially in its early days? Why or why not? If yes, how much more do you think it should have spent?

It differentiated itself from competitors in two respects: (1) its resolve and ability to bring to market a low-priced product and at the same time one of good quality, and (2) its achievement of good customer service despite the low price.

Even today after several decades of competitors seeing this highly effective strategy, Vanguard still is virtually unmatched in its uniqueness, except for one newcomer that is hardly a contender, but could be a factor should Vanguard let down its guard and be tempted to seek more profits.

In Part V, we examine remarkably successful firms. In the next two chapters, we will find rather similar product differentiations of an airline and the world's largest retailer.

Prognosis—Can Vanguard Continue As Is?

Is it likely Vanguard can continue its success pattern without increasing advertising and other costs and becoming more like its competitors? Why should it change? It has become a giant with its low-cost strategy. The last decade saw a growing momentum created by favorable word-of-mouth and publicity that made the need for heavy advertising and selling efforts far less than in the early years. It took bravery, or audacity, in those early years not to succumb to the Lorelei beguilement that advertising and commission selling was the only viable strategy. Something would be lost if Vanguard were to change its strategy and uniqueness and become a higher-cost operation just like its competitors.

If Vanguard is so good, why are investors still in large numbers doing business with the higher-cost competitors? We can identify four groups or consumer segments who are noncustomers of Vanguard:

1. Those who have not studied the statistics and editorials of publications like *Forbes* and *The Wall Street Journal*, and are not aware of the Vanguard advantage.

2. Those who are naive in investing and content to let someone else—brokers or bankers—advise them and reap the commissions.

3. Those who are swayed by the massive advertisements of firms like Fidelity, Dreyfus, Rowe Price, and others.

4. Those who put their faith in the price-quality perception: The higher the price the higher the quality.

In addition to continued investments of its ardent customers, Vanguard should find potential in some flaking away or eroding of the commitment of these four consumer groups. Of course, the overseas markets also offer a huge and virtually untapped potential for Vanguard.

WHAT CAN BE LEARNED?

Marketing Can Be Overdone

The success of Vanguard shows that marketing can be overdone. Too much can be spent for advertising, without realizing congruent benefits. Sales expenses and branch office overhead may get out of line. Yet, few firms dare reduce such marketing costs lest they be competitively disadvantaged. For example, it is the brave executive who reduces advertising in the face of increases by competitors, though the results of the advertising may be impossible to measure with any accuracy. (See the first information box in Chapter 3 for a discussion of measuring the effectiveness of advertising.)

Still, despite the success of Vanguard in downplaying marketing, one has to wonder how much faster the growth might have been by budgeting more dollars for marketing at least in the early years.

Can Word-of-mouth Do the Job of Advertising by Itself?

In Vanguard's case, word-of-mouth combined with favorable unpaid publicity from the media brought it to the number-two, going on number-one, largest mutual fund family in the industry. However, the time it took for word-of-mouth, even eventually with good publicity, to build demand has to be a negative. Without such favorable publicity, word-of-mouth in the absence of advertising would have taken far longer.

The Benefits of Frugality

There is far too much waste in most institutions, business and nonbusiness. Some of the waste comes from undercontrolled costs and from a variety of extravagances, such as lavish expense accounts and entertainment, and expenditures that do little to benefit the bottom line. Other factors may be a top-heavy bureaucratic organization saddled with layers of staff personnel, and/or too many debt payments due to heavy investments in plant and equipment or mergers. Heavy use of advertising, as we saw in Chapter 3, when Coca Cola was outspending Pepsi by $100 million but was still losing market share, may not always pay off enough to justify the expenditures. In money management, trading costs may get far out of line.

Vanguard shows the benefit of austerity in greatly reduced expense ratios for its funds compared to competitors. At last, more and more astute investors are recognizing this unique cost advantage that not only gives a better return on their investment dollars but some of the best customer service in the industry.

The Power of Differentiation

Firms seek to differentiate themselves, to come up with products or ways of doing business that are unique in some respect from competitors. This is a paramount quest of marketing and accounts for the massive expenditures for advertising. Too often such attempts to find uniqueness are fragile, not very substantial, and easily lost or countered by competitors. Sometimes, though, they can be rather enduring, as for example the quality-image perception perpetrated by advertisements featuring the lonely Maytag repairman. If a firm can effectively differentiate itself from competitors, it gains a powerful advantage and may even be able to charge premium prices.

While Vanguard seemingly disregarded marketing, John Bogle found a powerful and enduring way to differentiate through low-cost quality products and superb customer service. For decades no competitor has been able to match this attractive uniqueness.

Beware Placing Too Much Faith in the Price-quality Relationship

We all are inclined to judge quality by its price relative to other choices. Often this is justified, although the better quality may not always match the higher price. In other words, the luxury item may not be worth the much higher price, except for the significant psychological value that some people see in the prestige of a fine brand name. Unfortunately, there are some products and services where the higher price does not really reflect higher quality, better workmanship, better service, and the like. Then we are taken advantage of with this price-quality perception. Beware of always judging quality by price.

CONSIDER

Can you think of additional learning insights?

QUESTIONS

1. "The success of Vanguard is due to media exploitation of what would otherwise be a very ordinary firm." Discuss.

2. Why do you think people continue to buy front-end load mutual funds with 5–6 percent commission fees when there are numerous no-load funds to be had?

3. Do you think Bogle's shunning advertising was really a success, or was it a mistake?

4. Was Vanguard's failure to open walk-in sales outposts a mistake and an example of misplaced frugality? Why or why not?

5. What are the differences in passive and active fund management? How significant are these?

6. "Vanguard seems too good. There must be a downside." Discuss.

7. What is a service-breakthrough company?

8. Can publicity ever take the place of massive advertising expenditures?

HANDS-ON EXERCISES

1. You are an executive assistant to John Brennan, the new CEO of Vanguard now that Bogle has retired. Brennan is thinking of judiciously adding some marketing and advertising expenditures to the paucity that Bogle had insisted on. He has directed you to draw up a position paper on the merits of adding some advertising and even some walk-in sales outposts such as other big competitors have already done.

2. You are John Brennan, CEO. It is 2005, and TIAA-CREF is turning out to be a formidable competitor and is gaining fast on your first-place position in the industry. What actions would you take, and why? Discuss all ramifications of these actions that you can think of.

TEAM DEBATE EXERCISES

1. You are a member of the board of directors of Vanguard. John Bogle is approaching the retirement age as set forth in the company policies. However, he wants to continue as chairman of the board, even though he is willing to let Brennan assume active management. Debate the issue of whether to force Bogle to step down or bow to his wishes.

2. Debate the no-advertising policy of Bogle.

INVITATION TO RESEARCH

Has Vanguard become number one in the mutual fund industry? Has it increased its advertising expenditures? Has Brennan made any substantial changes?

CHAPTER TWENTY

Southwest Airlines— "Try to Match Our Prices"

*I*n 1992 the airlines lost a combined $2 billion, matching a dismal 1991 and bringing their three-year red ink total to a disastrous $8 billion. Three carriers—TWA, Continental, and America West—were operating under Chapter 11 bankruptcy, and others were lining up to join them. But one airline, Southwest, was profitable as well as rapidly growing—with a 25 percent sales increase in 1992 alone. Interestingly enough, this was a low-price, bare bones operation run by a flamboyant CEO, Herb Kelleher. He had found a niche, a strategic window of opportunity, and oh, how he had milked it! See the Information Box: Strategic Window of Opportunity and SWOT Analysis for further discussion of a strategic window of opportunity and its desirable accompaniment, a SWOT analysis.

HERBERT D. KELLEHER

Herb Kelleher impresses one as an eccentric. He likes to tell stories, often with himself as the butt of the story, and many involve practical jokes. He admits he sometimes is a little scatterbrained. In his cluttered office, he displays a dozen ceramic wild turkeys as a testimonial to his favorite brand of whiskey. He smokes five packs of cigarettes a day. As an example of his zaniness, he painted one of his 737s to look like a killer whale in celebration of the opening of Sea World in San Antonio. Another time, during a flight he had flight attendants dress up as reindeer and elves, while the pilot sang Christmas carols over the loudspeaker and gently rocked the plane. Kelleher is a "real maniac," said Thomas J. Volz, vice president of marketing at Braniff Airlines. "But who can argue with his success?"[1]

Kelleher grew up in Haddon Heights, New Jersey, the son of a Campbell Soup Company executive. He graduated from Wesleyan University and New York University law school, then moved to San Antonio in 1961, where his father-in-law helped him set up a law firm. In 1968 he and a group of investors put up $560,000 to found Southwest; of this amount, Kelleher contributed $20,000.

---

[1] Kevin Kelly, "Southwest Airlines: Flying High with 'Uncle Herb'," *Business Week,* 3 July 1989, p. 53.

In the early years he was the general counsel and a director of the fledgling enterprise. But in 1978 he was named chairman, despite having no managerial experience, and in 1981 he became CEO. His flamboyance soon made him the most visible aspect of the airline. He starred in most of its TV commercials. A rival airline, America West, charged in ads that Southwest passengers should be embarrassed to fly such a no-frills airline, whereupon Kelleher appeared in a TV spot with a bag over his head. He offered the bag to anyone ashamed to fly Southwest, suggesting it could be used to hold "all the money you'll save flying us."[2]

He knew many of his employees by name, and they called him "Uncle Herb" or "Herbie." He held weekly parties for employees at corporate headquarters, and he encouraged such antics by his flight attendants as organizing trivia contests, delivering instructions in rap, and awarding prizes for the passengers with the largest holes in their socks. But such wackiness had a shrewd purpose: to generate a gung-ho spirit to boost productivity. "Herb's fun is infectious," said Kay Wallace, president of the

[2] Kelly, p. 53.

Flight Attendants Union Local 556. "Everyone enjoys what they're doing and realizes they've got to make an extra effort."[3]

THE BEGINNINGS

Southwest was conceived in 1967, folklore tells us, on a napkin. Rollin King, a client of Kelleher, then a lawyer, had an idea for a low-fare, no-frills airline to fly between major Texas cities. He doodled a triangle on the napkin, labeling the points Dallas, Houston, and San Antonio.

The two tried to go ahead with their plans but were stymied for more than three years by litigation, battling Braniff, Texas International, and Continental over the right to fly. In 1971 Southwest won, and it went public in 1975. At that time it had four planes flying between the three cities. Lamar Muse was president and CEO from 1971 until he was fired by Southwest's board in 1978. Then the board of directors tapped Kelleher.

At first Southwest was in the throes of life-and-death low-fare skirmishes with its giant competitors. Kelleher liked to recount how he came home one day "beat, tired, and worn out. So I'm just kind of sagging around the house when my youngest daughter comes up and asks what's wrong. I tell her, 'Well, Ruthie, it's these damned fare wars.' And she cuts me right off and says, 'Oh, Daddy, stop complaining. After all, you started 'em.'"[4]

For most small firms, competing on a price basis with much larger, well-endowed competitors is tantamount to disaster. The small firm simply cannot match the resources and staying power of such competitors. Yet Southwest somehow survived. Not only did it initiate the cut-throat price competition, but it achieved cost savings in its operation that the larger airlines could not. The question then became: How long would the big carriers be content to maintain their money-losing operations and match the low prices of Southwest? The big airlines eventually blinked.

In its early years, Southwest faced other legal battles. Take Dallas, and Love Field. The original airport, Love Field, is close to downtown Dallas, but it could not geographically expand at the very time when air traffic was increasing mightily. So a major new facility, Dallas/Fort Worth International, replaced it in 1974. This boasted state-of-the-art facilities and enough room for foreseeable demand, but it had one major drawback: It was 30 minutes farther from downtown Dallas. Southwest was able to avoid a forced move to the new airport and to continue at Love. But in 1978 competitors pressured Congress to bar flights from Love Field to anywhere outside Texas. Southwest was able to negotiate a compromise, now known as the Wright Amendment, that allowed flights from Love Field to the four states contiguous to Texas. In retrospect the Wright Amendment forced onto Southwest a key ingredient of its later success: the strategy of short flights.[5]

---

[3] Richard Woodbury, "Prince of Midair," *Time,* 25 January 1993, p. 55.

[4] Charles A. Jaffe, "Moving Fast by Standing Still," *Nation's Business,* October 1991, p. 58.

[5] Bridget O'Brian, "Southwest Airlines Is a Rare Air Carrier: It Still Makes Money," *Wall Street Journal,* 28 October 1992, p. A7.

GROWTH

Southwest grew steadily, but not spectacularly, through the 1970s. It dominated the Texas market by appealing to passengers who valued price and frequent departures. Its one-way fare between Dallas and Houston, for example, was $59 in 1987 versus $79 for unrestricted coach flights on other airlines.

In the 1980s Southwest's annual passenger traffic count tripled. At the end of 1989, its operating costs per revenue mile—the industry's standard measure of cost-effectiveness—was just under 10 cents, which was about 5 cents per mile below the industry average.[6] Although revenues and profits were rising steadily, especially compared with the other airlines, Kelleher took a conservative approach to expansion, financing it mostly from internal funds rather than taking on debt.

Perhaps the caution stemmed from an ill-fated acquisition in 1986. Kelleher bought a failing long-haul carrier, Muse Air Corporation, for $68 million and renamed it TransStar. (This carrier had been founded by Lamar Muse after he left Southwest.) But by 1987 TransStar was losing $2 million a month, and Kelleher shut down the operation.

By 1993 Southwest had spread to 34 cities in 15 states. It had 141 planes, and these each made 11 trips a day. It used only fuel-thrifty 737s and still concentrated on flying large numbers of passengers on high-frequency, one-hour hops at bargain fares (average $58). Southwest shunned the hub-and-spoke systems of its larger rivals and took its passengers directly from city to city, often to smaller satellite airfields rather than congested major metropolitan fields. With rock-bottom prices and no amenities, it quickly dominated most new markets it entered.

As an example of Southwest's impact on a new market, it came to Cleveland, Ohio, in February 1992, and by the end of the year was offering 11 daily flights. In 1992 Cleveland Hopkins Airport posted record passenger levels, up 9.74 percent from 1991. "A lot of the gain was traffic that Southwest Airlines generated," noted John Osmond, air trade development manager.[7]

In some markets Southwest found itself growing much faster than projected, as competitors either folded or else abandoned directly competing routes. For example, America West Airlines cut back service in Phoenix in order to conserve cash after a Chapter 11 bankruptcy filing. Of course, Southwest picked up the slack, as it did in Chicago when Midway Airlines folded in November 1992. And in California, Southwest's arrival led several large competitors to abandon the Los Angeles–San Francisco route, unable to meet Southwest's $59 one-way fare. Before Southwest's arrival, fares had been as high as $186 one way.[8]

Now cities that Southwest did not serve were petitioning for service. For example, Sacramento, California, sent two county commissioners, the president of the chamber of commerce, and the airport director to Dallas to petition for service. Kelleher consented a few months later. In 1991 the airline received 51 similar requests.[9]

---

[6] Jaffe, p. 58.

[7] "Passenger Flights Set Hopkins Record," *Cleveland Plain Dealer,* 30 January 1993, p. 3D.

[8] O'Brian, p. A7.

[9] Ibid.

A unique situation was developing. On many routes, Southwest's fares were so low they competed with buses, and even with private cars. By 1991 Kelleher did not even see other airlines as his principal competitors: "We're competing with the automobile, not the airlines. We're pricing ourselves against Ford, Chrysler, GM, Toyota, and Nissan. The traffic is already there, but it's on the ground. We take it off the highway and put it on the airplane."[10]

Following are several tables and graphs that depict various aspects of Southwest's growth and increasingly favorable competitive position. See Tables 20.1, 20.2, and 20.3, and Figure 20.1. Although Southwest's total revenues were still far less than those of the four major airlines in the industry (five if we count Continental, emerging from its second bankruptcy), its growth pattern indicated a major presence, and its profitability was second to none.

Tapping California

The formidable competitive power of Southwest was perhaps never better epitomized than in its 1990 invasion of populous California. By 1992 it had become the second largest player, after United, with 23 percent of intrastate traffic. Southwest achieved this position by pushing fares down as much as 60 percent on some routes. The big carriers, which had tended to surrender the short-haul niche to Southwest

TABLE 20.1. Growth of Southwest Airlines; Various Operating Statistics, 1982–1991

Year	Operating Revenues ($ millions)	Net Income ($ millions)	Passengers Carried (thousands)	Passenger Load Factor
1991	$1,314	$26.9	22,670	61.1%
1990	1,187	47.1	19,831	60.7
1989	1,015	71.6	17,958	62.7
1988	860	58.0	14,877	57.7
1987	778	20.2	13,503	58.4
1986	769	50.0	13,638	58.8
1985	680	47.3	12,651	60.4
1984	535	49.7	10,698	58.5
1983	448	40.9	9,511	61.6
1982	331	34.0	7,966	61.6

Source: Company annual reports.

Commentary: Note the steady increase in revenues and in number of passengers carried. While the net income and load factor statistics show no appreciable improvement, these statistics still are in the vanguard of an industry that has suffered badly in recent years. See Table 20.2 for a comparison of revenues and income with the major airlines.

[10] Subrata N. Chakravarty, "Hit 'Em Hardest with the Mostest," *Forbes*, 16 September 1991, p. 49.

TABLE 20.2. **Comparison of Southwest's Growth in Revenues and Net Income with Major Competitors, 1987–1991**

	1991	1990	1989	1988	1987	% 5-year Gain
Operating Revenue Comparisons ($ millions)						
American	$9,309	$9,203	$8,670	$7,548	$6,369	46.0
Delta	8,268	7,697	7,780	6,684	5,638	46.6
United	7,850	7,946	7,463	7,006	6,500	20.8
Northwest	4,330	4,298	3,944	3,395	3,328	30.1
Southwest	1,314	1,187	1,015	860	778	68.9
Net Income Comparisons ($ millions)						
American	(253)	(40)	412	450	225	
Delta	(216)	(119)	467	286	201	
United	(175)	73	246	426	22	
Northwest	10	(27)	116	49	64	
Southwest	27	47	72	58	20	

Source: Company annual reports.

Commentary: Southwest's revenue gains over these 5 years outstripped those of its largest competitors. While the percentage gains in profitability are hardly useful because of the erratic nature of airline profits during these years, Southwest stands out starkly as the only airline to be profitable each year.

TABLE 20.3. **Market Share Comparison of Southwest with Its Four Major Competitors, 1987–1991**

	1991	1990	1989	1988	1987
Total Revenues (millions):					
American, Delta, United, Northwest	$29,757	$29,144	$27,857	$24,633	$21,835
Southwest Revenues:	1,314	1,187	1,015	860	778
Percent of Big Four	4.4	4.1	3.6	3.5	3.6
Increase in Southwest's market share, 1987–1991: 22%					

Source: Company annual reports.

in other markets, suddenly faced a real quandary in competing in this "Golden State." Now Southwest was being described as a "500 pound cockroach, too big to stamp out."[11]

The California market was indeed enticing. Some 8 million passengers each year fly between the five airports in metropolitan Los Angeles and the three in the San Francisco Bay area, making it the busiest corridor in the United States. It was also one of the pricier routes, as the low fares of AirCal and Pacific Southwest Airlines had been eliminated when these two airlines were acquired by American and USAir.

[11] Wendy Zellner, "Striking Gold in the California Skies," *Business Week,* 30 March 1992, p. 48.

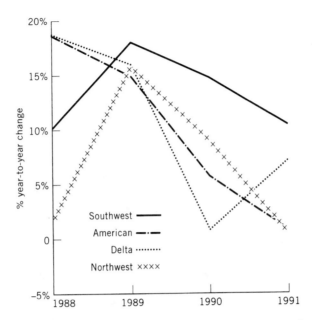

Figure 20.1. Year-to-year percentage changes in revenues, Southwest and its three major competitors, 1988–1991.

Southwest charged into this situation with its low fares and frequent flights. While airfares dropped, total air traffic soared 123 percent in the quarter Southwest entered the market. Competitors suffered: American lost nearly $80 million at its San Jose hub, and USAir still lost money even though it cut service drastically. United, the market leader, quit flying the San Diego–Sacramento and Ontario–Oakland routes where Southwest had rapidly built up service. The quandary of the major airlines was all the greater since this critical market fed traffic into the rest of their systems, especially the lucrative transcontinental and trans-Pacific routes. They could hardly abdicate California to Southwest. American, for one, considered creating its own no-frills shuttle for certain routes.[12] But the question remained: Could anyone stop Southwest, with its formula of lowest prices and lowest costs and frequent schedules? And, oh yes, good service and fun.

INGREDIENTS OF SUCCESS

Although Southwest's operation under Kelleher had a number of rather distinctive characteristics contributing to its success pattern and its seizing of a strategic window of opportunity, the key factors appear to be cost containment, employee commitment, and conservative growth.

[12] Ibid.

Cost Containment

Southwest has been the lowest cost carrier in its markets. Although its larger competitors might try to match its cut-rate prices, they could not do so without incurring sizable losses. Nor did they seem able to trim their costs to match Southwest's. For example, in the first quarter of 1991, Southwest's operating costs per available seat mile (i.e., the number of seats multiplied by the distance flown) were 15 percent lower than America West's, 29 percent lower than Delta's, 32 percent lower than United's, and 39 percent lower than USAir's.[13]

Many aspects of the operation contributed to these lower costs. With a single aircraft type, Boeing 737, for all its planes, costs of training, maintenance, and inventory were low. And since a plane earns revenues only when flying, Southwest was able to achieve a faster turnaround time on the ground than any other airline. Although competitors take upwards of an hour to load and unload passengers and then clean and service the planes, some 70 percent of Southwest's flights have a turnaround time of 15 minutes, and 10 percent have even pared the turnaround time to 10 minutes.

In areas of customer service, Southwest curbed costs as well. It offered peanuts and drinks, but no meals. Boarding passes were reusable plastic cards. Boarding time was minimal because there were no assigned seats. Southwest subscribed to no centralized reservation service. It did not even transfer baggage to other carriers; that was the passengers' responsibility. Admittedly, such customer service frugalities would be less acceptable on longer flights—and this helped to account for the difficulty competing airlines had in cutting their costs to match Southwest's. Still, if the price is right, many passengers might also opt for no frills on longer flights.

Employee Commitment

Kelleher was able to achieve an esprit de corps unmatched by other airlines despite the fact that Southwest employees were unionized. But there was no adversarial relationship with unions like Frank Lorenzo had at Eastern and Continental Airlines. Southwest was able to negotiate flexible work rules, with flight attendants and even pilots helping with plane cleanup. Employee productivity remained very high, permitting the airline to be leanly staffed. Kelleher resisted the inclination to hire extravagantly when times were good, necessitating layoffs during leaner times. This contributed to employee feelings of security and loyalty. The low-key attitude and sense of fun that Kelleher engendered helped, perhaps more than anyone could have foreseen. Kelleher declared, "Fun is a stimulant to people. They enjoy their work more and work more productively."[14]

Conservative Growth Efforts

Not the least of the ingredients of success was Kelleher's conservative approach to growth. He resisted the temptation to expand vigorously—for example, to seek to

---

[13] Chakravarty, p. 50.

[14] Ibid.

fly to Europe or get into head-to-head competition with larger airlines with long-distance routes. Even in its geographical expansion, conservatism prevailed. The philosophy of expansion was to do so only when enough resources could be committed to go into a city with 10 to 12 flights a day, rather than just 1 or 2. Kelleher called this "guerrilla warfare," concentrating efforts against stronger opponents in only a few areas, rather than dissipating strength by trying to compete everywhere.

Even with a conservative approach to expansion, the company showed vigorous but controlled growth. Its debt, at 49 percent of equity, was the lowest among U.S. carriers. Southwest also had the airline industry's highest Standard & Poor's credit rating, A minus.

GALLOPING TOWARD THE NEW MILLENNIUM

In its May 2, 1994 edition, prestigious *Fortune* magazine devoted its cover story to Herb Kelleher and Southwest Airlines. It raised an intriguing question: "Is Herb Kelleher America's Best CEO?" It called him a "people-wise manager who wins where others can't."[15] The operational effectiveness of Southwest continued to surpass all rivals, for example, in such productivity ratios as cost per available seat mile, passengers per employee, and employees per aircraft. Only Southwest remained consistently profitable among the big airlines, by the end of 1998 having been profitable for 26 consecutive years. Operating revenue had grown to $4.2 billion (it was $1.3 billion in 1991—see Table 20.2), and net income was $433 million, up from $27 million in 1991.

In 1999, Herb Kelleher was named CEO of the Year by *Chief Executive* magazine.

Geographical Expansion

Late in October 1996, Southwest launched a carefully planned battle for East Coast passengers that would drive down air fares and pressure competitors to back away from some lucrative markets. It chose Providence, Rhode Island, just 60 miles from Boston's Logan Airport, thus tapping the Boston–Washington corridor. The Providence airport escaped the congested New York and Boston air-traffic-control areas, and from the Boston suburbs was hardly a longer trip than to Logan Airport. Experience had shown that air travelers would drive considerable distance to fly with Southwest's cheaper fares.

As Southwest entered new markets, most competitors refused any longer to try to compete pricewise: They simply could not cut costs enough to compete. Their alternative then was either to pull out of these short-haul markets, or be content to let Southwest have its market share while they tried to hold on to other customers by stressing first-class seating, frequent-flyer programs, and other in-flight amenities.

---

[15] Kenneth Labich, "Is Herb Kelleher America's Best CEO?" *Fortune,* 2 May 1994, pp. 45–52.

In April 1997, Southwest quietly entered the transcontinental market. From its major connecting point of Nashville, Tennessee, it began nonstops both to Oakland, California and to Los Angeles. With Nashville's direct connections with Chicago, Detroit, Cleveland, Providence, and Baltimore–Washington, as well as points south, this afforded *one-stop,* coast-to-coast service, with fares about half as much as the other major airlines.

Two other significant moves were announced in late 1998. One was an experiment. On Thanksgiving Day, a Southwest 737–700 flew *nonstop* from Oakland, California to the Baltimore–Washington Airport, and back again. It provided its customary no-frills service, but a $99 one-way fare, the lowest in the business. The test was designed to see how pilots, flight attendants, and passengers would feel about spending five hours in a 737, with only peanuts and drinks served in flight. The older 737s lacked the fuel capacity to fly coast-to-coast nonstop, but with Boeing's new 737–700 series this was no problem. The Thanksgiving Day test was a precursor of more nonstop flights as Southwest had firm orders for 129 of the new planes to be delivered over the next seven years. This would enable it to compete with the major carriers on their moneymaking transcontinental flights.

In November 1998, plans were also announced for starting service to MacArthur Airport at Islip, Long Island, which would enable Southwest to tap into the New York City market. By late 1999 it was flying to 54 cities in 29 states. Table 20.4 lists these cities.

TABLE 20.4. Cities Served by Southwest, October 1999

Albuquerque	Ft. Lauderdale	Midland/Odessa	Rio Grande Valley (South Padre Island/Harlingen)
Amarillo	Hartford, CT°	Nashville	
Austin	Houston (Hobby & Bush Intercontinental)	New Orleans	Sacramento
Baltimore/Washington		Oakland	St. Louis
Birmingham	Indianapolis	Oklahoma City	Salt Lake City
Boise	Islip (Long Island)	Omaha	San Antonio
Burbank	Jackson, MS	Ontario, CA	San Diego
Chicago (Midway)	Jacksonville	Orange County	San Francisco
Cleveland	Kansas City	Orlando	San Jose
Columbus	Little Rock	Phoenix	Seattle
Corpus Christi	Los Angeles (LAX)	Portland	Spokane
Dallas (Love Field)	Louisville	Providence, RI	Tampa
Detroit (Metro)	Lubbock	Raleigh–Durham	Tucson
El Paso	Manchester, NH	Reno/Tahoe	Tulsa

° Service to Hartford, Connecticut began October 31, 1999.

UPDATE—2002

By mid-2002, with the 9/11 disaster still affecting airline travel, Southwest Airlines was the only major carrier that had been operating profitably over the past eighteen months. U.S. airlines were expected to post losses of as much as $8 billion in 2002—eclipsing the record in 2001 of $7.7 billion, with the loss in the more profitable business travel particularly acute. The high-cost airlines faced enormous pressure from low-fare carriers, most notably Southwest, but also from Internet sites that allowed bargain hunting. Southwest was now the nation's sixth largest airline, and it had been profitable for twenty-nine consecutive years.

In June 2001, just months before the September 11 attacks, Herb Kelleher retired. He was replaced by James Parker, who had joined Southwest in 1986 and admitted he was no Herb Kelleher. Parker's immediate challenge was to contain operating costs of soaring liability insurance and unionized workers agitating for raises to match rich contracts negotiated at other airlines before September 11. However, the bankruptcies of United Airlines and US Airways in late 2002 highlighted the need for other airlines to slash billions in operating costs, mostly by offering labor givebacks and this should subdue new labor demands. By 2002, Southwest had expanded to fifty-eight cities, although it entered no new cities for that year. Still, in 2002 it added more than thirty routes, exploiting the longer range of new Boeing 737-700 jets to fly transcontinental routes nonstop for the first time. For example, it could overlay its Chicago–Las Vegas–Los Angeles route with a nonstop flight. In 2003 Southwest planned to add cities again and had a backload of forty eager candidates.

Southwest was still following Kelleher's cautious growth strategy of adding just three cities a year, even if tempted by another carrier's demise—such as US Airways perhaps—to get quickly into other markets.

Be a Devil's Advocate (one who argues an opposing position to assure that all aspects of a course of action are considered). Argue against the slow-growth strategy of Southwest.

Sources: Scott McCartney, "Southwest Sets Standards on Costs," *Wall Street Journal*, 9 October 2002; Daniel Fisher, "Is There Such a Thing as Nonstop Growth?" *Forbes*, 8 July 2002, pp. 82, 84.

WHAT CAN BE LEARNED?

The Power of Low Prices and Simplicity of Operation

If a firm can maintain prices below those of its competitors, and do so profitably and without sacrificing expected quality of service, then it has a powerful advantage. We noted in the previous chapter the great advantage Vanguard had with its lowest expense ratio in the mutual fund industry. Here, Southwest also achieved this with its simplicity of operation and no-frills, but dependable, service.

Competition on the basis of price is seldom used in most mature industries (although the airline industry has been an exception), primarily because competitors can quickly match prices with no lasting advantage to anyone. As profits are destroyed, only customers benefit, and then only in the short run before the industry realizes the futility of price competition. (With new and rapidly changing industries, price competition is effective as productivity and technology improve and marginal competitors are driven from the market.)

The effectiveness of the cost controls of Southwest, however, shows the true competitive importance of low prices. Customers love the lowest price *if* the provider does not sacrifice too much quality, comfort, and service. While there was some sacrifice of service and amenities with Southwest, most customers found this acceptable because of the short-haul situation; friendly, dependable, and reasonable service was still maintained. Apparently the same no-frills service was found acceptable on longer flights too, as Southwest expanded these to meet demand.

An intriguing factor regarding the relationship of customer satisfaction and price is explored in the Information Box: The Key to Customer Satisfaction: Meeting Customer Expectations.

INFORMATION BOX

THE KEY TO CUSTOMER SATISFACTION: MEETING CUSTOMER EXPECTATIONS

Southwest consistently earns high ratings for its customer satisfaction, higher than those of its giant competitors. Yet, these major airlines all offer more than Southwest's food service; they also provide advance seat assignments, in-flight entertainment on longer flights, the opportunity to upgrade, and a comprehensive frequent-flyer program. Yet Southwest gets the highest points for customer satisfaction.

Could something else be involved here?

Let's call this *expectations*. If a customer has high expectations, perhaps because of a high price and/or the advertising promising high-quality, luxury accommodations, dependable service, or whatever, then if product or service does not live up to these expectations, customer satisfaction dives. Turning to the airlines, customers are not disappointed in the service of Southwest because they don't expect luxury; Southwest does not advertise this. They expect no frills, but pleasant and courteous treatment by employees, dependable and safe flights, and the low price. On the other hand, expectations are higher for the bigger carriers with their higher prices. This is well and good for the first- or business-class service. But for the many who fly coach …?

Do you think there is a point where a low-price/no-frills strategy would be detrimental to customer satisfaction? What might it depend on?

Source: This idea of expectations affecting customer satisfaction was suggested by Ed Perkins for Tribune Media Services and reported in "Hotels Must Live Up to Promises," *Cleveland Plain Dealer,* 1 November 1998, p. 11-K.

The Power of a Niche Strategy

Directing efforts toward a particular customer segment or niche can provide a powerful competitive advantage. This is especially true if no competitor is catering directly to such a niche, and if it is fairly sizable. Such an untapped niche then becomes a strategic window of opportunity.

Kelleher revealed the niche strategy of Southwest: While other airlines set up hub-and-spoke systems in which passengers are shunted to a few major hubs from which they are transferred to other planes going to their destination, "we wound up with a unique market niche: we are the world's only short-haul, high-frequency, low-fare, point-to-point carrier.... We wound up with a market segment that is peculiarly ours, and everything about the airline has been adapted to serving that market segment in the most efficient and economical way possible."[16] The Information Box: Criteria for Selecting Niches or Segments discusses this further.

Southwest has been undeviating in its pursuit of its niche. Although others have tried to copy it, none has fully duplicated it. Southwest still remains the nation's only high-frequency, short-distance, low-fare airline. As an example of its strong position, Southwest accounts for more than two-thirds of the passengers flying within Texas, and Texas is the second-largest market outside the West Coast. When Southwest invaded California, some San Jose residents drove an hour north to board Southwest's Oakland flights, skipping the local airport where American had a hub. In Georgia, so many people were bypassing Delta's huge hub in Atlanta and driving 150 miles to Birmingham, Alabama to fly Southwest that an entrepreneur started a van service between the two airports.[17]

Unlike many firms, Southwest did not permit success to dislodge its niche strategy. It has not attempted to fly to Europe or South America, or match the big carriers in offering amenities in coast-to-coast flights. In curbing such temptations it has not had to sacrifice growth potential: Its strategy still has many U.S. cities to embrace.

Seek Dedicated Employees

Stimulating employees to move beyond their individual concerns to a higher level of performance, a truly team approach, was by no means the least of Kelleher's accomplishments. Such an esprit de corps enabled planes to be turned around in 15 minutes instead of the hour or more of competitors; it brought a dedication to service far beyond what could ever have been expected of a bare-bones, cut-price operation; it brought a contagious excitement to the job obvious to customers and employees alike.

The nurturing of such dedicated employees was not due solely to Kelleher's extroverted, zany, and down-home personality—although this certainly helped. So did a legendary ability to remember employee names, and company parties, and a sincere interest in the employees. Flying in the face of conventional wisdom,

[16] Jaffe, p. 58.
[17] O'Brian, A7.

INFORMATION BOX

CRITERIA FOR SELECTING NICHES OR SEGMENTS

In deciding what specific niches to seek, these criteria should be considered:

1. *Identifiability.* Is the particular niche identifiable so that the persons who constitute it can be isolated and recognized? It was not difficult to identify the short-route travelers, and while their numbers may not have been readily estimated, this was soon to change as demand burgeoned for Southwest's short-haul services.

2. *Size.* The segment must be of sufficient size to be worth the efforts to tap. And again, the size factor proved to be significant: Southwest soon offered 83 flights daily between Dallas and Houston.

3. *Accessibility.* For a niche strategy to be practical, promotional media must be able to reach the segments without much wasted coverage. Southwest had little difficulty in reaching its target market through billboards and newspapers.

4. *Growth potential.* A niche is more attractive if it shows some growth characteristics. The growth potential of short-haul flyers proved to be considerably greater than for airline customers in general. Partly the growth reflected customers won from other higher cost and less convenient airlines. And some of the emerging growth reflected customers' willingness to give up their cars to take a flight that was almost as economical and certainly more comfortable.

5. *Absence of vulnerability to competition.* Competition, both present and potential, must certainly be considered in making specific niche decisions. By quickly becoming the low-cost operator in its early routes, and gradually expanding without diluting its cost advantage, Southwest became virtually unassailable in its niche. The bigger airlines with their greater overhead and less flexible operations could not match Southwest prices without going deeply into the red. And the more Southwest became entrenched in its markets, the more difficult it was to pry it loose.

Assume you are to give a lecture to your class on the desirability of a niche strategy, and you cite Southwest as a classic example. But suppose a classmate asks, "If a niche strategy is so great, why didn't the other airlines practice it?" How will you respond?

which says an adversarial relationship between management and labor is inevitable with the presence of a union, Southwest achieved its great teamwork while being 90 percent unionized. It helped, though, that Kelleher started the first profit-sharing plan in the U.S. airline industry in 1974. Now, employees own 13 percent of the company stock.

Whether such worker dedication can pass the test of time, and the test of increasing size, is uncertain. Kelleher has retired and his successor will be a different personality. Yet here is a model for an organization growing to large size and still maintaining employee commitment.

The attainment of dedicated employees is partly a product of the firm itself, and how it is growing. A rapidly growing firm—especially when such growth starts from humble beginnings, with the firm as an underdog—promotes a contagious excitement. Opportunities and advancements depend on growth. Where employees can acquire stock in the company and see the value of their shares rising, potential financial rewards seem almost infinite. Success tends to create a momentum that generates continued success.

CONSIDER

Can you identify additional learning insights that could be applicable to other firms in other situations?

QUESTIONS

1. In what ways might airline customers be segmented? Which segments or niches would you consider to be Southwest's prime targets? Which segments probably would not be?

2. Discuss the pros and cons for expansion of Southwest beyond short hauls. Which arguments do you see as most compelling?

3. Evaluate the effectiveness of Southwest's unions.

4. On August 18, 1993, a fare war erupted. To initiate its new service between Cleveland and Baltimore, Southwest announced a $49 fare (a sizable reduction from the then-standard rate of $300). Its rivals, Continental and USAir, retaliated. Before long the price was $19, not much more than the tank of gas it would take to drive between the two cities—and the airlines also supplied a free soft drink. Evaluate the implications of such a price war for the three airlines.

5. A price cut is the most easily matched marketing strategy, and it usually provides no lasting advantage to any competitor. Identify the circumstances where you see it as desirable to initiate a price cut and a potential price war.

6. Do you think it likely that Southwest's position will continue to remain unassailable by competitors? Why or why not?

7. In Chapter 6 we described another airline, Continental, and its employee-oriented leader, Gordon Bethune. Compare Bethune and Kelleher on as many traits as you can. Which do you think is the greater leader, and why?

HANDS-ON EXERCISES

1. Herb Kelleher has just retired, and you are his successor. Unfortunately, your personality is far different from his. You are an introvert and far from flamboyant, and your memory for names is not good. What is your course of action to try to preserve the great employee dedication of the Kelleher era? How successful do you think you will be? Did the board make a mistake in choosing you?

2. Herb Kelleher has not retired. He is going to continue beyond age 70. Somehow, his appetite for growth has increased as he has grown older, and he has charged you with developing plans for expanding into longer hauls— maybe to South and Central America, maybe even to Europe. Be as specific as you can in developing such expansion plans.

   Kelleher has also asked for your evaluation of these plans. Be as persuasive as you can in presenting this evaluation.

3. How would you feel personally about a five-hour transcontinental flight with only a few peanuts, and no other food or movies? Would you be willing to pay quite a bit more to have more amenities?

TEAM DEBATE EXERCISE

The Thanksgiving Day nonstop transcontinental experiment went fairly well, although customers and even flight attendants expressed some concern about the long, five-hour flight with no food and no entertainment. No one complained about the price.

Debate the two alternatives of going ahead slowly with the transcontinental plan with no frills, or adding a few amenities, such as some food, reading material, or whatever else might make the flight less tedious. You might even want to debate the third alternative of dropping this idea entirely at this time.

INVITATION TO RESEARCH

What is Southwest's current situation? What is its market share in the airline industry? Is it still maintaining a high growth rate? Has the decision been made to expand the nonstop transcontinental service, and have any changes been made in the no-frills service for this? How about international flights?

CHAPTER TWENTY-ONE

Wal-Mart—The Unstoppable

*I*n March 1992, Sam Walton passed away after a two-year battle with bone cancer. Perhaps the most admired businessman of his era, he had founded Wal-Mart Stores with the concept of discount stores in small towns, and had brought it to the lofty stature of the biggest retailer in the United States—ahead of the decades-long leaders, Sears and Penney—and in 1990 pushed ahead of an earlier great discount-store success, Kmart.

Walton's successors continued his legacy well. By the end of fiscal 1998, Wal-Mart's sales of $137.6 billion made it one of the largest corporations in the world; by 2002 sales were $217.8 billion, and it had knocked ExxonMobil out of first place.

THE EARLY YEARS OF SAM WALTON

Samuel Moore Walton was born in Kingfisher, Oklahoma, on March 29, 1917. He and his brother, James, born three years later, were reared in a family that valued hard work and thrift. They grew up in Missouri in the depths of the Great Depression.

By the time Walton entered eighth grade in Shebina, Oklahoma, he was already exhibiting the character traits that would dominate his future life: quiet and soft spoken, but a natural leader who became class president and captain of the football team. He even became the first Eagle Scout in Shebina's history.

At the University of Missouri, Walton excelled in academics and athletics. He worked his way through college by delivering newspapers, working in a five-and-dime store, lifeguarding, and waiting tables at the university.

After his graduation in 1940, Walton went to the J. C. Penney Company and became a management trainee at the Des Moines, Iowa, store. There he applied his work ethic, competed to become Penney's most promising new man, and became imbued with the Penney philosophy of catering to smaller towns and having "associates" instead of employees or clerks. He also met J. C. Penney himself and was intrigued with his habit of strolling around stores and personally meeting and observing customers and salespeople. After eighteen months, Walton left Penney's for the U.S. Army, but what he had learned in the Penney store in Des Moines was to shape his future ideas.

WAL-MART'S GROWTH TO THE BIGGEST RETAILER

Sam Walton was discharged from the Army in August 1945. By chance he stumbled on an opportunity to buy the franchise of a Ben Franklin variety store in Newport, Arkansas, and he opened it a month later. The lease arrangement with the building's owner did not work out, so Walton eventually relocated to Bentonville, Arkansas in 1950. During the 1950s and early 1960s, Walton increased his number of Ben Franklin franchises to fifteen. In the winter of 1962 he proposed at a Ben Franklin board meeting that the company should aggressively turn its efforts to discounting, citing the great potential of this emerging retail phenomenon. The company refused to consider such an innovative idea, so Walton and his brother went ahead anyway. They opened a Discount City in Rogers, Arkansas in 1962; and they opened a second store in Harrison, Arkansas in 1964. They incorporated the business as Wal-Mart Stores on October 31, 1969, and it became a publicly held company a year later. In 1970, Walton also opened his first distribution center and general office—a 72,000-square-foot complex in Bentonville, Arkansas. In 1972, Wal-Mart was listed on the New York Stock Exchange.

In 1976 Walton severed ties with Ben Franklin in order to concentrate on expanding Wal-Mart. His operations now extended to small towns in Arkansas, Missouri, Kansas, and Oklahoma. The essence of Walton's management philosophy during these building years was that of an old-fashioned entrepreneur; Walton personally roamed through his own stores, as well as those of competitors, always looking for new ideas in mass merchandising to maximize sales at attractive prices.

Rather than confronting the major retailers—department stores, chains such as Penney's and Sears, and the strong discounters such as Kmart—Walton confined his efforts to the smaller cities, ones major retailers shunned as having insufficient market potential. But he saw these small markets as a strategic window of opportunity, untapped by any aggressive firms. (You may want to review the Southwest Airlines case for a similar seizing of a strategic window.)

Growth accelerated. By the end of 1975 Walton had 104 stores with nearly six thousand employees and annual sales of $236 million, which generated $6 million net profit. The next year, the number of stores increased to 125, employees to 7,500, and sales to $340 million, with $11.5 million in profit, Table 21.1 compares the growth of sales and number of stores of Wal-Mart with Kmart, its major competitor, from 1980 to 1990, the decade that ended with Wal-Mart forging ahead to become the biggest retailer. By the end of 1990, Wal-Mart had 1,573 stores located in thirty-five states.

Some of these new stores were Wal-Mart SuperCenters, considerably larger than regular Wal-Marts, having a warehouse-style food outlet under the same roof as the discount store. While such food stores carried items comparable to products in a regular urban supermarket, the assortment and service were superior to most direct competitors in the smaller cities. The key advantage of adding food stores to general-merchandise discount stores was greater traffic: Because customers shop weekly for groceries, they are exposed far more to other merchandise in the stores than would otherwise be the case.

Wal-Mart was also opening another category of stores: Sam's Wholesale, also known as Sam's Clubs. These stores were first introduced in 1984, and by 1991 there

TABLE 21.1. Comparison of Growth in Sales and Number of Stores, Wal-Mart and Kmart, 1980–1990

	Kmart		Wal-Mart	
	Sales (millions)	Number of Stores	Sales (millions)	Number of Stores
1980	$14,204	1,772	$1,643	330
1981	16,527	2,055	2,445	491
1982	16,772	2,117	3,376	551
1983	18,597	2,160	4,667	642
1984	20,762	2,173	6,401	745
1985	22,035	2,332	8,451	859
1986	23,035	2,342	11,909	980
1987	25,627	2,273	15,959	1,114
1988	27,301	2,307	20,649	1,259
1989	29,533	2,361	25,810	1,402
1990	32,070	2,350	32,602	1,573

Source: Company annual reports.

Commentary: Several of these statistics are of particular interest. First, the comparison of the sales from 1980 to 1990, slightly more than one decade, of Wal-Mart and Kmart, show the tremendous growth rate of Wal-Mart, starting at little more than 10 percent of Kmart sales figures to forge ahead by 1990. And Kmart was no slouch during this period.

Second, Wal-Mart achieved its leadership in total sales with almost 800 fewer stores than Kmart had. This means that Wal-Mart's stores were achieving much higher sales volume than Kmart's, a fact that is further borne out by the statistics in Table 21.3.

were 148. This wholesale club concept came about as regular discount stores seemed to be reaching saturation in some locations. The wholesale warehouse went a step further in discounting.

Sam's Clubs were large, ranging up to 135,000 square feet. Each store was a membership-only operation, and qualified members included businesses and members of certain groups, such as government employees and credit union members. Although the stores were huge, they carried less than 5 percent of the total variety of items carried by regular discount stores. Assortments were limited to fast-moving home goods and apparel, generally name brands, with prices 8 to 10 percent over cost, well under those of discount stores and department and specialty stores. Sam's Clubs were the initial entry for Wal-Mart into the big metropolitan markets it had avoided in its early years.

In December 1987, Wal-Mart opened its newest merchandising concept, Hypermart USA, in Garland, Texas, a suburb of Dallas. The hypermart offered a combination of groceries and general merchandise in over 200,000 square feet of selling space. The stores also included a variety of fast-food and service shops, such as beauty shops, shoe repair, and dry cleaners. Thus, an atmosphere was created of one-stop shopping. But despite optimistic beginnings, the hypermarket idea proved unsuccessful; it was replaced with a scaled-down version, the SuperCenter.

For a comparison of sales and profitability of Wal-Mart with Kmart, Sears, and Penney from 1980 to 1990, see Table 21.2. Note that profitability comparisons include both operating profit as a percentage of sales, and the more valid measure of profitability, the return on equity, i.e., the return on the money invested in the enterprise. From this table we see that the awesome growth of Wal-Mart in sales and profitability compared with its nearest competitors. Table 21.3 shows another operational comparison, this time in the average sales per store for Wal-Mart and Kmart. And again, the comparison shows the great growth performance of Wal-Mart.

THE FUTURE WITHOUT SAM WALTON

On March 17, 1992, President Bush awarded Sam Walton the Medal of Freedom—a capstone among his other honors, which included Man of the Year, Horatio Alger Award in 1984, and "Retailer of the Decade" in 1989. Unfortunately, Walton did not live long to enjoy this high honor; he died of cancer nine days later, on March 26, 1992, just four days short of his seventy-fifth birthday and only months after guiding Wal-Mart to becoming the world's biggest retailer.

David Glass, fifty-three years old, assumed the role of president and chief executive officer. Glass was known for his hard-driving managerial style. He had gained his retail experience at a small supermarket chain in Springfield, Missouri, and joined Wal-Mart as executive vice president for finance in 1976. He had been president and chief operating officer since 1984, while Sam Walton kept the position of chief executive officer. About the transition, Glass said:

> There's no transition to make, because the principles and basic values he (Walton) used in founding this company were so sound and so universally accepted. … We'll be fine as long as we never lose our responsiveness to the customer.[1]

A new generation now was entrusted to continue the successful growth as Wal-Mart entered tougher competitive environments of U.S. metropolitan areas and then the world. By 1995, sales were $82 billion and only three Fortune 500 companies had higher sales: General Motors, Ford, and Exxon.

INTO THE NEW MILLENNIUM

In 2001 Wal-Mart knocked off ExxonMobil to become the biggest firm in revenues, with sales of $217.8 billion to ExxonMobil's $187.5 billion. General Motors sales were $177.3 billion, and Ford in fourth place had sales of $162.4 billion.[2] Table 21.4 shows selected statistics of Wal-Mart's operating performance at the beginning and end of

---

[1] Susan Caminiti, "What Ails Retailing," *Fortune*, 30 January 1989, p. 61.

[2] "Sales Super 500," *Forbes*, 15 April 2002, p. 168.

TABLE 21.2. 10-Year Comparison of Gross Revenues, Percentage of Operating Margin, and Return on Equity for Wal-Mart and its Competitors[a]

Year	Wal-Mart			Kmart			Sears			J.C. Penney		
	Gross Revenue	% Operating Profit Margin	Equity Return %	Gross Revenue	% Operating Profit Margin	Equity Return %	Gross Revenue	% Operating Profit Margin	Equity Return %	Gross Revenue	% Operating Profit Margin	Equity Return %
1981	$2,445.0	5.6	25.6	$16,527.0	2.2	9.0	$27,357	7.2	8.2	$11,860	7.5	13.2
1982	3,376.3	7.8	25.4	17,040.0	4.3	10.1	30,020	8.8	10.1	11,414	8.3	13.3
1983	4,666.9	8.3	26.6	18,878.9	6.0	16.7	35,883	9.7	14.4	12,078	8.7	13.1
1984	6,400.9	8.5	27.5	21,095.9	6.7	15.4	38,828	10.5	14.1	13,451	7.8	11.4
1985	8,451.5	7.2	25.6	22,420.0	6.2	14.4	40,715	9.5	11.5	13,747	7.7	9.8
1986	11,909.1	7.1	26.6	23,812.1	5.7	14.5	44,282	9.1	10.4	15,151	8.6	11.0
1987	15,959.3	6.8	27.8	25,626.6	5.8	15.7	48,439	8.5	12.1	15,747	9.1	14.6
1988	20,649.0	6.4	27.8	27,301.4	6.5	16.0	50,251	9.2	3.0	15,296	8.3	20.4
1989	25,810.7	6.5	27.1	29,532.7	5.8	6.5	53,794	9.2	10.6	16,405	9.2	18.4
1990	32,601.6	6.0	24.1	32,070.0	5.4	14.0	55,971	7.4	7.0	16,365	2.4	15.6

[a] Gross revenue is in $ billions.

Source: Company annual reports.

Commentary: The comparison with major competitors shows Wal-Mart far exceeding its rivals in revenue growth. The operating profit percentage exceeds Kmart's for most years, but Sears and Penney look better here. However, the true measure of profitability is return on equity, and here Wal-Mart shines: It indeed is a very profitable operation, while offering consumers attractive prices.

TABLE 21.3. **Average Sales per Store, Wal-Mart and Kmart, 1980–1990**

	Kmart	Wal-Mart
1980	$8,015,801	$4,978,788
1981	8,042,338	4,979,633
1982	7,922,532	6,127,042
1983	8,609,722	7,269,470
1984	9,554,533	8,591,946
1985	9,448,970	9,838,184
1986	9,835,611	12,152,040
1987	11,274,527	14,325,852
1988	11,833,983	16,401,111
1989	12,508,682	18,409,415
1990	13,646,808	20,726,001

Source: Computed from Table 21.1

Commentary: The great increase in sales per store for Wal-Mart is particularly noteworthy. In 1980 Wal-Mart's average store's sales was hardly one-half that of an average Kmart. By 1990 the average Wal-Mart store was generating more than 50% more sales than an average Kmart.

the decade 1992–2002. Wal-Mart's former closest retail rivals had been left in the dust by 2002, as can be starkly seen below:

	2002 Revenues ($billion)	% Change since 2001
Sears	$ 41.1	0.3
Target	39.9	8.1
Kmart	36.9	1.1
Penney	32.0	0.5
Wal-Mart	217.8	13.8

Its nearest rival up to 1990, the one that dominated the retail environment in the early days of Wal-Mart, was Kmart. But now Kmart was operating under Chapter 11 bankruptcy, with its very survival in doubt.

As it approached the millennium, and was only a short step away from becoming the world's largest firm, Wal-Mart turned to other growth opportunities. It bought Asda Group PLC, a large British supermarket chain, thereby greatly expanding its international presence. In the United States it not only accelerated the building of discount-grocery SuperCenters but also expanded its smallish (40,000 square foot) Neighborhood Markets, designed to fill the gaps between convenience stores and Wal-Mart's big SuperCenters. Wal-Mart also bought a small savings bank in Oklahoma that could pave the way for bringing to banking its low prices for such services as check cashing, credit cards, and loans.

TABLE 21.4.   Operating Performance, 1993–1995, Wal-Mart

(Dollar amounts in millions except per share data.)	1995	1994	1993
Operating Results			
Net sales	$82,494	$67,344	$55,484
Net sales increase	22%	21%	26%
Comparative store sales increase	7%	6%	11%
Other income—net	918	641	501
Cost of sales	65,586	53,444	44,175
Operating, selling, and general and administrative expenses	12,858	10,333	8,321
Interest costs:			
Debt	520	331	143
Capital leases	186	186	180
Provision for federal and state income taxes	1,581	1,358	1,171
Net income	2,681	2,333	1,995
Per share of common stock:			
Net income	1.17	1.02	.87
Dividends	.17	.13	.11

Source: 1995 Wal-Mart Annual Report.

Overseas expansion created the most waves. European merchants and labor unions ran scared, but consumers stood to benefit enormously: "Its low-pricing policies and customer-friendly attitude is likely to change the face of British retailing and its reputation for high prices and surly service," one scribe wrote.[3]

Threat of Wal-Mart led two rival French retailers to merge in a $16-billion-dollar deal, though the combined company would still be far smaller than Wal-Mart. The battle was perhaps fiercest in Germany, where Wal-Mart had ninety-five stores. Competitors began staying open longer and improving customer courtesy. However, regulators in Germany closely monitored whether prices were too low, while powerful trade unions worried that price wars would result in store closures and job losses.

To reduce costs, Wal-Mart began buying globally, negotiating one price for stores worldwide. In so doing, it changed the organization to combine some domestic and international operations including buying, new store planning, and marketing.[4]

[3] Ernest Beck, "The Wal-Mart Is Coming! And Shopping for the British May Never Be the Same," *Wall Street Journal*, 16 June 1999, p. A23.

[4] Emily Nelson, "Wal-Mart Revamps International Unit to Decrease Costs," *Wall Street Journal*, 10 August 1999, p. A6; David Woodruff and John Carreyrou, "French Retailers Create New Wal-Mart Rival," *Wall Street Journal*, 31 August 1999, p. A14; Ernest Beck and Emily Nelson, "As Wal-Mart Invades Europe, Rivals Rush to Match Its Formula," *Wall Street Journal*, 6 August 1999, pp. A1, A6; "European Retailers Brace for Wal-Mart," *Cleveland Plain Dealer*, 31 August 1999, pp. 1-C, 3-C.

INGREDIENTS OF SUCCESS

Management Style and Employee Orientation

Sam Walton cultivated a management style that emphasized individual initiative and autonomy over close supervision. He constantly reminded employees that they were vital to the success of the company, that they were essentially "running their own business," that they were "associates" or "partners" in the business, rather than simply employees.

In his employee relations philosophy, Walton borrowed from James Cash Penney, founder of the J. C. Penney Company, and his formulation of the "Penney idea" in 1913. The Penney idea also stressed the desirability of constantly improving the human factor, of rewarding associates through participation in what the business produces, and of appraising every policy and action to see whether it squares with what is right and just.

Walton emphasized bottoms-up communication, thereby providing a free flow of ideas throughout the company. For example, the "people greeter" concept (described in the Information Box: Greeters) was implemented in 1983 as a result of a suggestion received from an employee in a store in Louisiana. This idea proved so successful that it has been adopted by Kmart, some department stores, and even shopping malls.

Another example of listening to employees' ideas came when an assistant manager in an Alabama store ordered too many marshmallow sandwiches, or Moon Pies. The store manager told him to use his imagination to sell the excess, so John Love came up with an idea to create the first World Championship Moon Pie Eating Contest. It was held in the store's parking lot and became so successful that it became a yearly event, drawing spectators not only from the community but from all over Alabama, as well as surrounding states.[5]

INFORMATION BOX

GREETERS

All customers entering Wal-Mart stores encounter a store employee assigned to welcome them, give advice on where to find things, and help with exchanges or refunds. These "greeters" thank people exiting the store, while unobtrusively observing any indications of shoplifting.

Many retailers staff exits and entrances; what makes Wal-Mart's greeters unique is their friendliness and patience. Wal-Mart has found that retirees supplementing pensions usually make the best greeters and are most appreciated by customers. As noted earlier, the greeter idea originated as a suggestion from an employee (associate); Sam Walton liked the idea, and it became a company-wide practice.

Do you personally like the idea of a store employee greeting you as you enter and leave an establishment? On balance, do you think the greeter idea is a plus or a minus? Explain.

---

[5] Don Longo, "Associate Involvement Spurs Gains," *Discount Store News,* 18 December 1989, p. 83.

In 1972 Wal-Mart instituted a profit-sharing plan in which all associates share in the company's yearly profits. As one celebrated example of the benefits of such profit sharing, Shirley Cox had worked as an office cashier earning $7.10 an hour. When she retired after twenty-four years, her profit sharing amounted to $220,127.[6] In addition, associates may participate in a payroll stock purchase plan with Wal-Mart contributing part of the cost.

The Sam Walton philosophy was to create a friendly, down-home, family atmosphere in his stores. He described it as a "whistle while you work philosophy," one that stressed the importance of having fun while working because you can work better if you enjoy yourself. He was concerned about losing this atmosphere: "The bigger Wal-Mart gets, the more essential it is that we think small. Because that's exactly how we have become a huge corporation—by not acting like one."[7]

Another incentive spurred employees to reduce shrinkage (that is, the loss of merchandise due to shoplifting, carelessness, and employee theft). Employees were given $200 each per year if shrinkage limits were met, and they became detectives watching shoppers and each other. In 1989, Wal-Mart's shrinkage rate was 1 percent of sales, well below the industry average.[8]

A rather simple way to make employees feel part of the operation was regular sharing of statistics about the store's performance, including profits, purchases, sales, and markdowns. Many employees thought of Wal-Mart as their own company.

Not the least of the open and people-oriented management practices was what Walton called MBWA, Management by Walking Around. Managers, from store level to headquarters, walked around the stores to stay familiar with what was going on, to talk to the associates, and to encourage associates to share their ideas and concerns. Such interactions brought a personal touch usually lacking in large firms.

Not surprisingly, unions have not fared well at Wal-Mart. Walton argued that in his "family environment," associates had better wages, benefits, and bonuses than any union could get for them. In addition, the bonuses and profit sharing were inducements far better than those a union could negotiate.

State-of-the-Art Technology

The Wal-Mart decentralized management style led to a team approach to decision making. A huge telecommunications system permitted headquarters to easily communicate with stores. In addition, home-office management teams, using company airplanes, visited stores to assess their operations and any problems and to coordinate needed merchandise transfers among stores. A master computer tracked the company's complex distribution system.

[6] Example cited in Vance H. Trimble, *Sam Walton: The Inside Story of America's Richest Man* (New York: Dutton, 1990), 233.

[7] Ibid, pp. 104, 105.

[8] Charles Berstein, "How to Win Employee and Customer Friends," *Nation's Restaurant News*, 30 January 1989, p. F3.

Small-Town Invasion Strategy

Adopting a strategy similar to that used by the J. C. Penney Company more than half a century before, Wal-Mart for many years shunned big cities. Instead, the firm opened stores in smaller towns where competition consisted only of local merchants and small outlets of a few chains such as Woolworth, Gamble, and Penney.

These merchants typically offered only limited assortments of merchandise, had no Sunday or evening hours, and charged substantially higher prices than would be found in the more competitive environments of bigger cities. Larger retailers, especially discounters, had shunned such small towns as not affording enough potential to support the high sales volume needed for the low-price strategy.

But Wal-Mart found potential in abundance in these small-town markets, as customers flocked from all the surrounding towns and rural areas for the variety of goods and the prices. (In the process of captivating small-town and rural consumers, Wal-Mart wreaked havoc on the existing small-town merchants. See the Issue Box: Impact of Wal-Mart on Small Towns for a discussion of the sociological impact of Wal-Mart on small-town merchants.) The company honed its skills in such small towns, isolated from aggressive competitors, and then flexed its muscles and moved confidently into the big cities, whose retailers were as fearful of Wal-Mart as the thousands of small-town merchants had been.

Controlling Costs

Sam Walton was a stickler for holding down costs in order to offer customers the lowest prices. Cost control started with vendors, and Wal-Mart gained a reputation of being

---

ISSUE BOX

IMPACT OF WAL-MART ON SMALL TOWNS

During most of its growth years, Wal-Mart pursued a policy of opening stores on the outskirts of small rural towns, usually with populations between 25,000 and 50,000. Attractive both in prices and assortment of goods, a Wal-Mart store drew customers from miles around; and it was often the biggest employer in the town, with 200–300 local employees.

But the dominating presence of Wal-Mart was a mixed blessing for many communities. Small-town merchants were devastated and unable to compete. Downtowns became decaying vestiges of what perhaps a few months previously had been prosperous centers. But consumers benefited.

Wal-Mart brought trade-offs and controversy: Was rural America better or worse off with the arrival of Wal-Mart? On balance, most experts saw the economic development brought on by Wal-Mart as more than offsetting the business destruction it caused. But few could dispute the sociological trauma.

What is your assessment of the desirability of Wal-Mart coming into a rural small town? How might your assessment differ depending on your particular position or status in that community?

hard to please, of constantly pressuring suppliers to give additional price breaks and advertising money, and to provide prompt deliveries. (You may want to review Chapter 18, the Newell Rubbermaid case, for a vendor's problems in satisfying Wal-Mart.) In further efforts to buy goods at the lowest possible prices, Wal-Mart attempted to bypass middlemen and sales reps and buy all goods direct from manufacturers. In so doing, a factory presumably would save money on sales commissions of 2 to 6 percent, and was expected to pass this savings on to Wal-Mart. Understandably, this practice aroused a heated controversy from groups representing sales reps.

Wal-Mart achieved great savings with its sophisticated distribution centers and its own fleet of trucks that enabled it to buy in bulk directly from suppliers. Most goods were processed through one of the company's distribution centers. For example, take the distribution center in Cullman, Alabama, situated on twenty-eight acres with 1.2 million square feet. Some 1,042 employees loaded 150 outbound Wal-Mart trailers a day and unloaded 180. On a heavy day, laser scanners routed 190,000 cases of goods on an eleven-mile-long conveyor.[9]

Each warehouse used the latest in optical scanning devices, automated materials-handling equipment, bar coding, and computerized inventory. With a satellite network, messages could be quickly flashed between stores, distribution centers, and corporate headquarters in Bentonville, Arkansas. Handheld computers assisted store employees in ordering merchandise. These advanced technologies cut distribution expenses to half those of most chains.

Wal-Mart had previously been able to achieve great savings in advertising costs, compared to major competitors. While discount chains typically spent 2 to 3 percent of sales for advertising, Wal-Mart held it to less than 1 percent of sales. Some of this difference reflected low media rates in its small-town markets. But advertising costs were also kept low in larger markets by using very little local advertising, relying instead on national TV institutional commercials showing prices being slashed and Wal-Mart as a good and caring firm. See the Issue Box: Should We Use Institutional Advertising? for a discussion.

Wal-Mart's operating and administrative costs reflected a rigidly enforced, spartan operation. A lean headquarters organization and a minimum of staff assistants compared with most other retailers completed the cost-control philosophy and reflected the frugal thinking of Sam Walton that dated back to his early days.

"Buy American" and Environmental Programs

As foreign manufacturers increasingly took market share away from American producers—in the process, destroying some American jobs—public sentiment mounted for import restrictions to save jobs. In March 1985, Walton became concerned about what seemed to him a national problem. He ordered his buyers to find products that American manufacturers had stopped producing because they couldn't compete with foreign imports. Thus began Walton's "Buy American" program, which became a cooperative effort between retailers and domestic manufacturers to reestablish the

[9] John Huey, "America's Most Successful Merchant," *Fortune,* 23 September 1991, p. 54.

ISSUE BOX

SHOULD WE USE INSTITUTIONAL ADVERTISING?

Institutional advertising is nonproduct advertising designed to create goodwill for the firm rather than immediate and specific product sales. While the intent is laudable, the payoff is murky since it is difficult to measure goodwill and its effect on sales. With specific product advertising, of course, a retailer can determine the effectiveness of an ad by the specific sales it produces compared to previous periods when the product was not advertised. We suggest that most institutional advertising is based on faith—faith that enough people will see the ad or commercial and gain a favorable attitude toward the company, the assumption being that a favorable attitude translates into more sales.

Wal-Mart's heavy use of institutional commercials on TV was two pronged: (1) showing its employees as friendly and helpful people, not only to customers but to the community at large; and (2) showing prices enthusiastically being slashed. The objectives of presenting Wal-Mart in the most favorable light were in keeping with its Buy American campaign and environmental responsiveness efforts described in the next section. Such institutional advertising reinforced the image of Wal-Mart as a good citizen in the tradition of Sam Walton.

Be a Devil's Advocate (one who argues a contrary position for the sake of testing a decision). Argue as persuasively as you can that, while Wal-Mart's institutional advertising helped with a positive image, this did not conclusively translate into additional sales.

competitive position of American-made goods in price and quality. This program showcased the power of the huge retailer. Magic Chef, 3M, Farris Fashions, and many other manufacturers joined Walton's crusade, as Wal-Mart pledged to support domestic production for items ranging from film to microwave ovens to flannel shirts and other apparel.

Wal-Mart also became a leader in challenging manufacturers to improve their products and packaging in order to protect the environment. As a result, manufacturers made great improvements in eliminating excessive packaging, converting to recyclable materials, and getting rid of toxic inks and dyes.

Other environmental activities included participation in Earth Day events, with tree plantings, information booths, and videos to show customers how to improve their environment. Wal-Mart has also been active in fund-raising for local environmental and charitable groups, and in "adopt-a-highway" programs, in which store personnel volunteer at least one day every month to collect trash and clean up local highways and beaches.

THE ARROGANCE OF POWER

Wal-Mart is a powerful firm, one of the most powerful in the world because of its size and buying clout. While in many respects the relations with its various publics has been exemplary, one wonders if it has come close to crossing the line in its dealings with suppliers, and even in certain aspects of employee relations.

We saw in the Newell Rubbermaid case the price and service demands that the firm imposes on those vendors wishing to do business with it. For many of these vendors, the loss of Wal-Mart's business is life threatening; they have to accede to its dictates, or else. We saw Rubbermaid spending $62 million to install software so that its factories could be tied in with Wal-Mart's computers, and still this was not enough.

Wal-Mart led the retail industry in "partnering" with its vendors. If this were truly a two-way relationship it would be of mutual benefit and an example of a symbiotic relationship in which both parties gain from each other's success. However, Wal-Mart's partnering more often meant that vendors had to assume more of the inventory management and merchandising costs associated with their products in Wal-Mart stores; it also usually resulted in their having to guarantee fast replenishment so that the stores could maintain lean stocks. The power position of Wal-Mart made some of these demands on vendors a do-it-or-else situation: "If you can't do it, we'll find another vendor."

Regarding employee relations, I have received enough anecdotal complaints, particularly regarding unpaid overtime, to have some doubts about optimum employee relations with a maturing Wal-Mart.

UPDATE—2003

With few prime sites in the United States remaining untapped for stores, Wal-Mart aggressively sought to expand worldwide, but these efforts were not very successful. It has not done well in Argentina, Brazil, and Japan. Germany, in particular, was tough to crack; Wal-Mart still had losses five years after buying two local chains to gain entry into this market. German consumers were very price sensitive, and Wal-Mart failed to beat competitors who quickly undercut Wal-Mart and beefed up their private-label goods. Even Wal-Mart's use of greeters was met with disdain by German shoppers. These experiences cast doubt on the Wal-Mart model in all international markets.

Wal-Mart's most encouraging efforts were in the United Kingdom. In 1999 it acquired Asda, a U.K. supermarket chain, and this venture became a robust success as Wal-Mart's culture, buying power, and logistical and merchandising expertise propelled Asda to U.K.'s No. 2 retailer. Wal-Mart's U.K. sales of $15 billion in 2002 represented 43 percent of its total international revenue.

In January 2003, Wal-Mart bid to take over U.K.'s Safeway PLC, which would enable it to become the market leader in Britain. Local interests girded themselves against this threat to the status quo, and the success of Wal-Mart's effort was still in doubt.

Sources: Robin Sidel et al., "Wal-Mart Goes Shopping for Safeway," *Wall Street Journal,* 14 January 2003, p. B6; and Sara Calian et al., "Wal-Mart's Offer for Safeway Comes with the Risks Built In," *Wall Street Journal,* 15 January 2003, p. B12.

WHAT CAN BE LEARNED?

Take Good Care of People

Sam Walton was concerned with two groups of people—his employees and his customers. By motivating and even inspiring his employees, he found that customers also were well served. Somehow in the exigencies of business, especially big business, this emphasis on people tends to be pushed aside. Walton made caring for people common practice.

By listening to his employees, by involving them, by exhorting them, and by giving them a real share of the business—all the while stressing friendliness and concern for customers—Walton fostered a business climate almost unique in any large organization. In addition to providing customers with the friendliest of employees, his stores also offered honest values and great assortments and catered to the concerns of many middle-income Americans for the environment and American jobs.

Go for the Strategic Window of Opportunity

Strategic windows of opportunity sometimes come in strange guises. They represent areas of potential business overlooked or untapped by existing firms. But in the formative and early growth years of Wal-Mart, no window could ever have seemed less promising than the one Walton unlocked and threw open to great growth. Small towns and cities in many parts of rural America were losing population and economic strength, partly because of the decline in family farms and the accompanying infrastructure of small businesses. It was therefore not surprising that the major discount chains focused their growth efforts on large metropolitan areas. Although many small cities had Penney's and Sears outlets as well as Woolworth, Gamble, and Coast to Coast stores, they were usually small stores—often old, marginal, and rather in the backstream of corporate consciousness. This retail environment was one of small stores with limited assortments of merchandise and relatively high prices.

In this environment, Sam Walton seized his opportunity. He saw something that no other merchants had: that the limited total market potential meant a dearth of competition. He also saw that the potential was far greater than the population of the small town and its immediate surroundings. Indeed, a Wal-Mart store in a rather isolated rural community could draw customers from many miles away.

Do such windows of opportunity still exist today? You bet they do—for the entrepreneur with vision, an ability to look beyond the customary, and the courage to follow up on his or her vision.

Consider the Marriage of Old-Fashioned Ideas and Modern Technology

Walton embraced this strategy and made it work throughout his organization, even as it grew to large size. At the forefront of retailers in the use of communication technology and computerized distribution, Walton still was able to motivate his employees to offer friendly and helpful customer services to a degree that few large retailers have consistently achieved.

Other firms can benefit from the example of Wal-Mart in cultivating homespun friendliness with awesome technology, and competitors are trying to emulate it. The particular difficulty that many are finding, however, is in achieving consistency.

Showing Environmental Concern Can Pay Dividends

Today many people are concerned about the environment. It seems high time that we have such concern, while much of the environment can still be salvaged and protected. Given such sentiment, the firm that takes a leadership role for environmental protection stands to benefit in customer relations and, not the least, from positive media attention.

Another issue important to many Americans involves foreign inroads to the detriment of many U.S. manufacturers and jobs. Regardless of the great controversy over the desirability of free trade, many middle-class Americans have applauded the leadership of Wal-Mart in its widely publicized Buy American policy.

What is the moral for other businesses catering to consumers? Be alert to the increasing concerns of the public, and, where possible, act on them in a leadership role.

CONSIDER

Can you identify additional learning insights that could be applicable to firms in other situations?

QUESTIONS

1. How might you attempt to compete with Wal-Mart if you were: (a) a small hardware merchant? (b) a small clothing store for men? (c) a Woolworth?

2. Do you think Wal-Mart is vulnerable today, and if so, in what way? If you do not think it is vulnerable, do you see any limits to its growth?

3. When you shop at Wal-Mart, do you usually find the employees far superior in friendliness and knowledge to those of other retailers? If not, what are your conclusions regarding Wal-Mart's employee relations programs?

4. What weaknesses do you see Wal-Mart as having, either now or potentially? How can the company overcome them?

5. Can discounting go on forever? What are the limits to growth by price competition?

6. Discuss Wal-Mart's business practices (especially in regard to unions, invading small towns, and supplier relations) in view of their ethical ramifications for the industry and for society. Should students be encouraged to emulate these practices?

INVITATION TO ROLE PLAY

1. *Be a Devil's Advocate* (one who argues a contrary position). The decision is being made to phase out the hypermarkets. Argue as persuasively as you can that Wal-Mart is being too hasty and that the hypermarket concept should be continued, if necessary with some changes.

2. You are an ambitious Wal-Mart store manager. Describe how you might design your career path to achieve a high executive position. Be as creative as you can.

3. You are the principal adviser to David Glass, who replaced Sam Walton as chief executive. Even though Wal-Mart has expanded aggressively overseas in recent years, Glass still thinks the greatest potential lies in foreign markets. He has charged you to develop a strategy to make greater inroads. What do you advise, and why? (Hint: You may need to do some research on Wal-Mart's overseas presence at this time, i.e., how many stores and in which countries.)

TEAM DEBATE EXERCISES

1. Debate the notion of Wal-Mart aggressively seeking to enter small communities, such as in rural New England, where many people oppose this incursion. Should Wal-Mart bow to the public pressure (which the company deems to be from a small minority of vehement agitators), or should it carry on with "right on its side"?

2. Can the great growth of Wal-Mart continue indefinitely? Debate the pros and cons of this question.

INVITATION TO RESEARCH

Has Wal-Mart faltered since 2002? Are there any ominous signs on the horizon? Have the management style and employee relations changed since that described in the case? Are any stores unionized? Is the Buy American program still in effect?

PART SIX

ETHICAL MISTAKES

CHAPTER TWENTY-TWO

MetLife—
Deceptive Sales Tactics

*I*n August 1993, the state of Florida cracked down on the sales practices of giant Metropolitan Life, a company dating back to 1868 and the country's second largest insurance firm. MetLife agents based in Tampa, Florida, were alleged to have duped customers out of some $11 million. Thousands of these customers were nurses lured by the sales pitch to learn more about "something new, one of the most widely discussed retirement plans in the investment world today."[1] In reality, this was a life insurance policy in disguise, and what clients were led to think were savings deposits were actually insurance premiums.

The growing scandal rocked MetLife, eventually costing it several billion dollars in fines and restitutions. What was not clear for certain was the full culpability of the company: Was it guilty only of not monitoring agent performance sufficiently to detect unethical and illegal activities, or was it the great encourager of such practices? Regardless, MetLife did not react well to the legal and public relations stigma that enveloped it.

RICK URSO: THE VILLAIN?

The first premonitory rumble that something bad was about to happen came to Rick Urso on Christmas Eve 1993.

At home with his family, Urso received an unexpected call from his boss, the regional sales manager. In disbelief he heard there was a rumor going around the executive suites that he was about to be fired. Urso had known that the State of Florida had been investigating and that company auditors had also been looking into sales practices. On September 17, two corporate vice presidents had even shown up to conduct the fourth audit that year, but on leaving they had given him the impression that he was complying with company guidelines.

---

[1] Suzanne Woolley and Gail DeGeorge, "Policies of Deception?" *Business Week*, 17 January 1994, p. 24.

321

Urso often reveled in his good fortune and attributed it to his sheer dedication to his work and the company. He had grown up in a working-class neighborhood, the son of an electrician. He had started college, but dropped out before graduating.

His sales career started at a John Hancock agency in Tampa, in 1978. Four years later, he was promoted to manager and was credited with building up the agency to No. 2 in the whole company.

Urso left John Hancock in 1983 for Met Life's Tampa agency. His first job was as trainer. Only three months later, he was promoted to branch manager. Now his long hours and overwhelming commitment were beginning to pay off. In a truly inspiring success story, his dedication and his talent as a motivator of people swept the branch from a one-rep office to one of Met Life's largest and most profitable. By 1993 the agency employed 120 reps, seven sales managers, and thirty administrative employees. And he was the head. In 1990 and 1991, Urso's office won the company's Sales Office of the Year award. With such a performance history—the stuff of legends—he became the company's star, a person to look up to and to inspire trainees and other employees.

Urso's was the passion of a TV evangelist: "Most people go through life being told why they can't accomplish something. If they would just believe, then they would be halfway there. That's the way I dream and that's what I expect from my people."[2] He soon became known as the "Master Motivator," and increasingly was the guest speaker at MetLife conferences.

On the Monday after that Christmas, the dire prediction came to pass. Urso was summoned to the office of William Groggans, head of MetLife's Southeast territory, and there he was handed a letter by the sober-faced Groggans. With trembling hands he opened it and read that he was fired. The reason: engaging in improper conduct.

The Route to Stardom

Unfortunately, the growth of his Tampa office could not be credited to simple motivation of employees. Urso found his vehicle for great growth to be the whole-life insurance policy. This was part life insurance and part savings. As such it required high premiums, but only part earned interest and compounded on a tax-deferred basis; the rest went to pay for the life insurance policy. What made this so attractive to company sales reps was the commission: A whole-life policy paid a 55 percent first-year commission. In contrast, an annuity paid only a 2 percent first-year commission.

Urso found the nurses market to be particularly attractive. Perhaps because of their constant exposure to death, nurses were easily convinced of the need for economic security. He had his salespeople call themselves "nursing representatives," and his Tampa salespeople carried their fake retirement plan beyond Florida, eventually reaching thirty-seven states. A New York client, for example, thought she had bought a retirement annuity. But it turned out to be insurance even though as a single woman she didn't need such coverage.[3]

---

[2] Weld F. Royal, "Scapegoat or Scoundrel," *Sales & Marketing Management*, January 1995, p. 64.

[3] Jane Bryant Quinn, "Yes, They're Out to Get You," *Newsweek*, 24 January 1994, p. 51.

As the growth of the Tampa agency became phenomenal, Urso's budget for mailing brochures was upped to nearly $1 million in 1992, ten times that of any other MetLife office. This gave him national reach.

Urso's own finances increased proportionately as he earned a commission on each policy his reps sold. In 1989, he was paid $270,000. In 1993, as compensation exceeded $1 million, he moved his family to Bay Shore Boulevard—the most expensive area of Tampa.

Early Warnings

A few complaints began surfacing. In 1990, the Texas insurance commissioner warned MetLife to stop its nursing ploy. The company made a token compliance by sending out two rounds of admonitory letters. But apparently nothing changed. See the Information Box: The Vulnerability of Compliance that Is Only Token about the great deficiency of token compliance without follow-up.

An internal MetLife audit in 1991 also raised some questions about Urso's pre-approach letters. The term *nursing representative* was called a made-up title. The auditors also questioned the term *retirement savings policy* as not appropriate for the product. However, the report concluded by congratulating the Tampa office for its contribution to the company. Not surprisingly, such mixed signals did not end the use of misleading language at that time.

INFORMATION BOX

THE VULNERABILITY OF
COMPLIANCE THAT IS ONLY TOKEN

A token effort at compliance to a regulatory complaint or charge tends to have two consequences, neither good in the long run for the company involved:

1. Such tokenism gives a clear message to the organization: "Despite what outsiders say, this is acceptable conduct in this firm." Thus is set the climate for less-than-desirable practices.
2. Vulnerability to harsher measures in the future. As the malpractice continues, regulators who are convinced that the company is stalling and refusing to cooperate will eventually take more drastic action. Penalties will move beyond warnings to become punitive.

The firm may not have intended to stall, but that is the impression conveyed. If the cause of the seemingly token effort is faulty controls, one wonders how many other aspects of the operation are also ineptly controlled so that company policies are ignored.

Discuss the kinds of controls MetLife could have imposed in 1990 that would have made compliance actual and not token.

Allegations Intensify

In the summer of 1993, Florida state regulators began a more in-depth examination of the sales practices of the Urso agency. The crux of the investigation concerned promotional material Urso's office was sending to nurses nationwide. From 1989 to 1993, millions of direct mail pieces had been sent out. Charges finally were leveled that this material disguised the product agents were selling. For example, one brochure coming from Urso's office depicted the Peanuts character Lucy in a nurse's uniform. The headline described the product as "Retirement Savings and Security for the Future a Nurse Deserves." Nowhere was insurance even mentioned, and allegations were that nurses across the country unknowingly purchased life insurance when they had thought they were buying retirement savings plans.

As the investigation deepened, a former Urso agent, turned whistle-blower, claimed he had been instructed to place his hands over the words *life insurance* on applications during presentations.

As a result of this investigation, Florida Insurance Commissioner Tom Gallagher charged MetLife with serious violations.

METLIFE CORRECTIVE ACTIONS—FINALLY

Under investigation by Florida regulators, the company's attitudes changed. At first, MetLife had denied wrongdoing. But eventually it acknowledged problems. Under mounting public pressure, it agreed to pay $20 million in fines to more than forty states due to unethical sales practices of its agents. It further agreed to refund premiums to nearly 92,000 policyholders who had bought insurance based on misleading sales information between 1989 and 1993. These refunds were expected to reach $76 million.

MetLife fired or demoted five high-level executives as a result of the scandal. Urso's office was closed; all seven of his managers and several reps were also discharged. Life insurance sales to individuals were down 25 percent through September 1994 over the same nine-month period in 1993. Standard & Poor's downgraded MetLife's bond rating based on these alleged improprieties.

Shortly after the fines were announced, the Florida Department of Insurance filed charges against Urso and eighty-six other MetLife insurance agents, accusing them of fraudulent sales practices. The insurance commissioner said, "This was not a situation where a few agents decided to take advantage of their customers, but a concerted effort by many individuals to dupe customers into buying a life insurance policy disguised as a retirement savings plan."[4]

Now MetLife attempted to improve its public image by instituting a broad overhaul of its compliance procedures. It established a corporate ethics and compliance department to monitor behavior throughout the company and audit personal insurance sales offices. The department was also charged to report any compliance deficiencies to senior management and to follow up to ensure the implementation of corrective actions.

---

[4] Sean Armstrong, "The Good, the Bad and the Industry," *Best's Review, P/C,* June 1994, p. 36.

In MetLife's *1994 Annual Report*, Harry Kamen, CEO, and Ted Athanassiades, president, commented on their corrective actions regarding the scandal:

> We created what we think is the most effective compliance system in the industry. Not just for personal insurance, but for all components of the company. We installed systems to coordinate and track the quality and integrity of our sales activities, and we created a new system of sales office auditing.
>
> Also, there were organizational changes. And, for the first time in 22 years, we assembled all of our agency and district managers—about a thousand people—to discuss what we have done and need to do about the problems and where we were going.[5]

Meantime, Rick Urso started a suit against MetLife for defamation of character and for reneging on a $1 million severance agreement. He alleged that MetLife made him the fall guy in the nationwide sales scandal.

The personal ramifications on Urso's life were not inconsequential. More than a year later he was still unemployed. He had looked for another insurance job, but no one would even see him. "There are nights he can't sleep. He lies awake worrying about the impact this will have on his two teenagers." And he laments that his wife cannot go out without people gossiping.[6]

WHERE DOES THE BLAME LIE?

Is Urso really the unscrupulous monster who rose to a million-dollar-a-year man on the foundations of deceit? Or is MetLife mainly to blame for encouraging, and then ignoring for too long, practices aimed at misleading and even deceiving?

The Case against MetLife

Undeniably Urso did things that smacked of the illegal and unethical. But did the corporation knowingly provide the climate? Did his training promote the use of deceptive practices? Was MetLife completely unaware of his distortions and deceptions in promotional material and sales pitches? There seems to be substantial evidence that the company played a part; it was no innocent and unsuspecting bystander.

At best, MetLife top executives may not have been aware of the full extent of the hard-selling efforts emanating at first from Tampa and then spreading further in the organization. Perhaps they chose to ignore any inkling that things were not completely on the up and up, in the quest for exceptional bottom-line performance. "Don't argue with success" may have become the corporate mind-set.

At the worst, the company encouraged and even demanded hard selling and tried to pretend that such sales could still be accomplished with ethical standards of performance. If such ethical standards were not met, then company top executives could argue that they were not aware of wrongdoing.

---

[5] MetLife *1994 Annual Report*, p. 16.
[6] Royal, "Scapegoat or Scoundrel," p. 65.

There is evidence of company culpability. Take the training program for new agents. Much of it was designed to help new employees overcome the difficulties of selling life insurance. In so doing, they were taught to downplay the life insurance aspects of the product. Rather, the savings and tax-deferred growth benefits were to be stressed.

In training new agents to sell insurance over the phone, they were told that people prefer dealing with specialists. It seemed only a small temptation to use the title "nursing representative" rather than "insurance agent."

After the scandal, MetLife admitted that the training might be faulty. Training had been decentralized into five regional centers, and the company believed that this might have led to a less standardized and controlled curricula. MetLife has since reorganized so that many functions, including training and legal matters, are now done at one central location.[7]

The company's control or monitoring was certainly deficient and uncoordinated during the years of misconduct. For example, the marketing department promoted deceptive sales practices while the legal department warned of possible illegality, but took no further action to eliminate it.

AN INDUSTRY PROBLEM?

The MetLife revelations focused public and regulatory attention on the entire insurance industry. The insurance commissioner of Florida also turned attention to the sales and marketing practices of New York Life and Prudential. The industry itself seemed vulnerable to questionable practices. Millions of transactions, intense competition, and a widespread and rather autonomous sales force—all these afforded opportunity for misrepresentation and other unethical dealings.

For example, just a few months after the Tampa office publicity, MetLife settled an unrelated scandal. Regulators in Pennsylvania fined the company $1.5 million for "churning." This is a practice of agents replacing old policies with new ones, in which additional commissions are charged and policyholders are disadvantaged. Class-action suits alleging churning were also filed in Pennsylvania against Prudential, New York Life, and John Hancock.

But problems go beyond sales practices. Claims adjusters may attempt to withhold or reduce payments. General agents may place business with bogus or insolvent companies. Even actuaries may create unrealistic policy structures.

With a deteriorating public image, the industry faced further governmental regulation from both state and federal offices. But cynics, both within and outside the industry, wondered whether deception and fraud were so much a part of the business that nothing could be done about them.[8]

---

[7] "Trained to Mislead," *Sales & Marketing Management*, January 1995, p. 66.

[8] Armstrong, "The Good, the Bad and the Industry," p. 35.

ANALYSIS

Here we have an apparent lapse in complete feedback to top executives. But maybe they did not want to know. After all, nothing was life-threatening here; no product safety features were being ignored or disguised; nobody was in physical danger.

This raises a key management issue. Can top executives hide from less-than-ethical practices—and even illegal ones—under the guise that they did not know? The answer should be an emphatic no. See the Information Box: The Ultimate Responsibility for a discussion of management accountability.

So, we are left with top management of MetLife grappling with the temptation to tacitly approve the aggressive selling practices of a sales executive so successful as to be the model for the whole organization, even though faint cries from the legal staff suggested that such practices might be subject to regulatory scrutiny and disapproval.

The harsh appraisal of this situation is that top management cannot be exonerated for the deficiencies of subordinates. If controls and monitoring processes are defective, top management is still accountable. The pious platitudes of MetLife management,

INFORMATION BOX

THE ULTIMATE RESPONSIBILITY

In the Maytag case in Chapter 13 we examined a costly snafu brought about by giving executives of a foreign subsidiary too much rein. With MetLife the problem was gradually eroding ethical practices. In both instances, top management still had ultimate responsibility, and they cannot escape blame for whatever goes wrong in their organization. Decades ago, President Truman coined the phrase, "The buck stops here," meaning that in this highest position rests the ultimate seat of responsibility.

Any manager who delegates to someone else the authority to do something will undoubtedly hold them responsible for doing the job properly. Still, the manager must be aware that his or her own responsibility to higher management or to stockholders cannot be delegated away. If the subordinate does the job improperly, the manager is still responsible.

Going back to MetLife, or to any corporation involved with ethical and illegal practices, top executives can try to escape blame by denying that they knew anything about the misdeeds. This should not exonerate them. Even if they knew nothing directly, they still set the climate.

In Japan, the chief executive of an organization involved in a public scandal usually resigns in disgrace. In the United States, top executives often escape full retribution by blaming their subordinates and maintaining that they themselves knew nothing of the misdeed. Is it truly fair to hold a top executive culpable for the shortcomings of some unknown subordinate?

insisting that it had corrected the situation, hardly excuse them for permitting it to have happened in the first place.

Ah, but embracing the temptation is so easy to rationalize. Management can always maintain that there was no solid proof of misdeeds. After all, when do aggressive sales efforts cross the line? When do they become more than simply "puffing," and become outright deceptive? See the Information Box: Where Do We Draw the Line on Puffing regarding this admittedly gray area of the acceptable. Lacking indisputable evidence of misdeeds, why should these executives suspect the worst—especially since their legal departments, not centralized as they were to be later, were timid in their denunciations?

Turning to controls, a major caveat should be posed for all firms: In the presence of strong management demands for performance—with the sometimes imagined pressure to produce at all costs, or else—the ground is laid for less-than-desirable practices by subordinates. After all, career paths and even job longevity depend on meeting these demands.

In a climate of decentralization and laissez-faire, such abuses are more likely to occur. Such a results-oriented environment suggests that it's not how you achieve designated goals, but that you meet them. So, while decentralization on balance is usually desirable, in an environment of top management laxity toward good moral standards it can lead to undesirable practices.

At the least, it leads to opportunistic temptations by lower- and middle-level executives. Perhaps this is the final indictment of MetLife and Rick Urso. The climate was conducive to his ambitious opportunism. For a while it was wonderful. But the abuses of accepted behavior could not be disguised indefinitely.

And wherever possible, top management will repudiate its accountability.

INFORMATION BOX

WHERE DO WE DRAW THE LINE ON PUFFING?

Puffing is generally thought of as mild exaggeration in selling or advertising. It is generally accepted as simple exuberance toward what is being promoted. As such, it is acceptable business conduct. Still, most of us have come to regard promotional communications with some skepticism. "It's New! The Greatest! A Super Value! Gives Whiter Teeth! Whiter Laundry!" and so on.

We have become conditioned to viewing such blandishments with suspicion. But are they dishonest or deceptive? Probably not, as long as the exaggeration stays mild.

But it is a short step from mild exaggeration to outright falsehoods and deceptive claims. Did MetLife's "nursing representatives," "retirement plans," and hiding the reality of life insurance cross the line? Enough people thought so, including state insurance commissioners and the victims themselves.

Do you think all exaggerated claims, even the mild and vague ones known as puffing, should be banned? Why or why not?

The Handling of the Crisis

MetLife responded slowly to the allegations of misconduct. A classic mode for firms confronted with unethical and/or product liability charges is to deny everything, until evidence becomes overwhelming. Then they are forced to acknowledge problems under mounting public pressure—from regulatory bodies, attorneys, and the media—and have to scramble with damage control to try to undo the threats to public image and finances. In MetLife's case, fines and refunds approached $100 million early on. They would eventually reach almost $2 billion.

Being slow to act, failing to accept any responsibility, and for top executives, exhibiting aloofness until late in the game are actions tantamount to inflaming public opinion and regulatory zeal. We saw something similar in the Coca-Cola product-safety crisis in Europe: First there was denial, then grudging admission, then unco-ordinated remedial efforts, and only after the crisis had received alarming attention did top management become involved to finally lead massive restorative efforts.

How much better for all involved, victims as well as the organization itself, if initial complaints are promptly followed up. And, if complaints are serious, they should be given top management attention in a climate of cooperation with any agencies involved as well as the always-interested media.

LATER DEVELOPMENTS

On August 18, 1999, MetLife agreed to pay out at least $1.7 billion to settle final law-suits over its allegedly improper sales practices. In the agreement (in which MetLife admitted no wrongdoing), about six million life insurance policyholders and a million annuity contract holders were involved. Essentially, these customers were expected to get from one to five years of free term-life insurance coverage.

MetLife argued for years that it had done nothing wrong. It had previously dispensed with most of its litigation problems by settling rather than going to trial. The incentive for settling these final class-action suits, even at the cost of a massive charge, was to clear the way for MetLife's planned conversion to a stockholder-owned company from its current status as a policyholder-owned mutual company. "Clearly it's something they needed to put behind them before they demutualized," or went public.[9]

Harry Kamen, CEO of MetLife, brought Robert Benmosche, fifty-seven and an ex-Wall Streeter, on board in 1995 to turn things around. Benmosche solved many of MetLife's problems and became chairman when Kamen retired in 1998. In April 2000 Benmosche took the company public, and the stock offering raised $5.2 billion.

In his relentless restructuring, Benmosche axed poor performers—some 1,300, including 154 assistant vice presidents and higher in 2001—and demanded better results and ethical standards. He required agents to work full time instead of part time, as many had previously done: "I knew this was needed after I met someone who

---

[9] Deborah Lohse, "MetLife Agrees to Pay Out $1.7 Billion or More to Settle Policyholder Lawsuits," *Wall Street Journal*, 19 August 1999, p. B14.

complimented one of my agents for his plumbing skills," explained Benmosche. He also compelled all agents to get securities licenses so they could sell investments such as variable annuities. Bonuses were now tied into performance reviews and a division's financial results, and officer's bonuses were partly paid in stock that they were discouraged from selling: "If the top people . . . don't do what they have to do to make sure the company strongly survives, we should lose our shirts."[10] MetLife's revenues in 2001 were $32 billion, up 18 percent since Benmosche became chairman.

WHAT CAN BE LEARNED?

Beware the Head-in-the-Sand Approach to Looming Problems or Public Complaints

Ignoring or giving only token attention to suspected problems and regulatory complaints sets a firm up for a possible massive crisis. Covering one's eyes to malpractices and dangerous situations does not make them go away; they tend to fester and become more serious. Prompt attention, investigation, and action are needed to prevent these problem areas from getting out of hand. MetLife could have saved itself several billion dollars if it had acted on the early complaints of misrepresentation and misleading of customers.

Unethical and Illegal Actions Do not Go Undetected Forever

It may take months, it may take years, but a firm's dark side will eventually be uncovered. Its reputation may then be besmirched, it may face loss of customers and competitive position, and it may face heavy fines and increased regulation.

The eventual disclosure may come from a disgruntled employee (a whistleblower). It may originate from a regulatory body or an investigative reporter. Or it may come from revelations emanating from a lawsuit. Eventually, the deviation is uncovered, and retribution follows. Such a scenario should be—but is not always—enough to constrain those individuals tempted to commit unethical and illegal actions.

What made the MetLife deceptive practices particularly troubling is that they were so visible, and yet were so long tolerated. Much of the sales organization seemed to lack a clear definition of what was acceptable and what was not. Something was clearly amiss both in the training and in the controlling of agent personnel.

The Control Function Is Best Centralized in any Organization

Where the department or entity that monitors performance is decentralized, tolerance of bad practices is more likely than when centralized. The reason is

[10] Carrie Coolidge, "Snoopy's New Tricks," *Forbes*, 15 April 2002, pp. 100–102.

rather simple. Where legal or accounting controls are decentralized, the persons conducting them are more easily influenced. They are likely to be neither as objective nor as critical as when they are further from the situation. So, reviewers and evaluators should not be close to the people they are examining. And they should report only to top management.

A Strong Sales Incentive Program Invites Bad Practices

The lucrative commission incentive for the whole-life policies—55 percent first-year commission—was almost bound to stimulate abusive sales practices, especially when the rewards for this type of policy were so much greater than for any other. Firms often use various incentive programs and contests to motivate their employees to seek greater efforts. But if some are tempted to cross the line, the end result in public scrutiny and condemnation may not be worth whatever increases in sales might be gained.

Large Corporations Are Particularly Vulnerable to Public Scrutiny

Large firms, especially ones dealing with consumer products, are very visible. This visibility makes them attractive targets for critical scrutiny by activists, politicians, the media, regulatory bodies, and the legal establishment. Such firms ought to be particularly careful in any dealings that might be questioned, even if short-term profits have to be restrained. In MetLife's case, the fines and refunds eventually approached $2 billion. Although the firm in its 1994 annual report maintained that all the bad publicity was behind it, that there were no ill effects, some analysts wondered how quickly a besmirched reputation could truly be restored, especially with competitors eager to grab the opportunity presented.

Sometimes a Tarnished Reputation
Can Be Rather Quickly Restored

Contrary to some experts, there is compelling evidence that customers tend to quickly forget misdeeds, as they apparently did with MetLife under the new management of Benmosche. We saw a similar restoration of reputation with the unsafe tires of Firestone in Ford Explorers in Chapter 10. While the poor image of Continental Airlines was not due to product safety or deception, but rather to years of deteriorating service, this image was quickly turned around by enlightened, fresh management. Perhaps these experiences should be comforting to a firm that incurs image damage, perhaps through its own fault or maybe because of factors not directly under its control. It does help, however, if there is a change in top management. Still, in cases of unethical conduct, fines and perhaps a plethora of lawsuits are more immediate consequences of culpability.

CONSIDER

After reading the section "What Can Be Learned?" what additional learning insights do you see?

QUESTIONS

1. Do you think Rick Urso should have been fired? Why or why not?

2. Do you think the MetLife CEO and president should have been fired? Why or why not?

3. Why was the term *life insurance* seemingly so desirable to avoid? What is wrong with life insurance?

4. Given the widespread publicity about the MetLife scandal, do you think the firm could regain consumer trust in a short time?

5. "This whole critical publicity has been blown way out of proportion. After all, nobody was injured. Not even in their pocketbook. They were sold something they really needed. For their own good." Evaluate.

6. "You have to admire that guy, Urso. He was a real genius. No one else could motivate a sales organization as he did. They should have made him president of the company. Or else he should become an evangelist." Evaluate.

7. Do you think the arguments are compelling that the control function should be centralized rather than decentralized? Why or why not?

HANDS-ON EXERCISES

Before

1. It is early 1990. You are the assistant to the CEO of MetLife. Rumors have been surfacing that increasingly, life insurance sales efforts are not only too high pressure but also misleading. The CEO has ordered you to investigate. You find that the legal department in the Southeast Territory has some concerns about the efforts coming out of the highly successful Tampa office of Urso. Be as specific as you can about how you would investigate these unproven allegations, and explain how you would report this to your boss, assuming that some questionable practices seem apparent.

2. It is 1992. Internal investigations have confirmed that Urso and his "magnificent" Tampa office are using deceptive selling techniques in disguising the life insurance aspects of the policies they are selling. As the executive in charge in the Southeast, describe your actions and rationale at this point. (You have to assume that the later consequences are completely unknown at this point.)

After

3. The °@#% has hit the fan. The scandal has become well publicized, especially with such TV programs as *Dateline* and *20/20*. What would you do as top executive of MetLife at this point? How would you attempt to save the public image of the company?

TEAM DEBATE EXERCISE

The publicity is widespread about the "misdeeds" of MetLife. Debate how you would react. One position is to defend your company, rationalizing what happened and downplaying any ill effects. The other position is to meekly bow to the allegations, admit wrongdoing, and be as contrite as possible.

INVITATION TO RESEARCH

Is MetLife still prospering under Benmosche? Can you find any information contradicting the impression that the situation has virtually been forgotten by the general public? Can you find out whether Rick Urso has found another job? Could you develop the pros and cons of a mutual (policyholder-owned) firm and a public firm owned by stockholders?

CHAPTER TWENTY-THREE

ADM—Price-Fixing and Political Cronyism, and a Whistleblower

*I*n June 1995 a whistleblower informed federal investigators of the scheme of a giant multinational conglomerate, Archer-Daniels-Midland (ADM), to control sales of a widely demanded food additive and thus keep prices high worldwide. For three years, he had been secretly recording meetings of the firm's senior executives with Asian and European competitors. The whistleblower, Mark E. Whitacre, was revealed by an attorney who was supposedly conferring with him as a possible client.

Repercussions quickly followed. The company charged Whitacre with stealing from the firm and fired him. The plot became more complicated. But overhanging all was the role of the corporation and its 77 year-old top executive: Did they truly act unethically and illegally, or were the allegations exaggerated out of all proportion? What kind of a person was this whistleblower, a hero or a villain?

THE WHISTLEBLOWER, MARK E. WHITACRE

Mark Whitacre joined Archer-Daniels in 1989, and spent about half his career there helping antitrust investigators. He was a rising star, recruited to head the fledgling BioProducts division, where he rose to become a corporate vice-president and a leading candidate to become the company's next president while still in his thirties.

He had been recruited from Degussa AG, a German chemical company where he was manager in organic chemicals and feed additives. However, his resume inflated his credentials with the title executive vice-president; he was only a vice-president.

While at ADM, he earned a business degree from a home-study school in California. Later ADM issued biographical material crediting him with an MBA from Northwestern University and the prestigious J.L. Kellogg School of Management. In an interview, Whitacre admitted the claims about his MBA were inflated to impress Wall

Street analysts, but he blamed ADM: "I feel bad about it. I, along with other executives that speak at analysts' meetings, cooperated… it's a common practice."[1]

His ambition was to become president of ADM, which he claimed was promised him repeatedly.[2] How becoming a governmental informer would help him with this ambition seems murky.

Over three years he secretly helped investigators obtain videotapes revealing two senior executives meeting with Asian and European competitors in various places around the world. The executives were vice-chairman Michael D. Andreas, son and heir apparent of the 77-year-old Dwayne Andreas, chairman and chief executive; and vice-president Terrence Wilson, head of the corn-processing division. Sometimes Whitacre would wear a hidden microphone to obtain the incriminating evidence of price fixing. The Information Box discusses whistleblowing in general, but the travails of Whitacre graphically portray a worse scenario.

FBI agents on the night of June 27 entered the headquarters of the huge grain-processing company in Decatur, Illinois. They carted off files and delivered grand jury subpoenas seeking evidence of price collusion of ADM and competitors. Whitacre was one of the executives subpoenaed, and met with an attorney recommended by the company's general counsel office, a common practice when companies face governmental inquiries.

Shortly after this meeting, the attorney disclosed to ADM that Whitacre was the federal informant in their midst, thus imperiling Whitacre's position in the company. This seemed a clear ethical violation of the confidentiality of lawyer/client relations. But the attorney, John M. Dowd of a prominent law firm doing business with ADM, claimed that Whitacre authorized him to do so. Whitacre and his new attorney angrily denied any such authorization.

In any case, now the company had the knowledge to retaliate. They fired him, accused him of stealing $2.5 million, and reported these findings to the Justice Department. Later, the company increased the amount it claimed Whitacre had stolen to $9 million. They charged that he had been embezzling money by submitting phony invoices for capital expenditures, then channeling the payments into off-shore bank accounts.

The Justice Department saw the credibility of their key witness being weakened by such allegations, especially since Whitacre acknowledged that he had indeed participated in the bogus invoice schemes, although he said the payments were made with the full knowledge and encouragement of company higher-ups. Nevertheless, he and as many as 12 other ADM executives came under criminal investigation for evading taxes. The Justice Department's criminal fraud section further examined allegations that the off-the-books payments were approved by top management.[3]

A few days later, Whitacre tried to kill himself. At dawn, he drove his car into the garage of his new home, closed the door, and left the engine running. On this morning he was supposed to fly to Washington to meet with federal authorities. He had

[1] "ADM Informant Faces Widening Allegations; He Attempts Suicide," *Wall Street Journal*, 14 August 1995, p. A4.
[2] Ibid.
[3] Ronald Henkoff, "Checks, Lies and Videotape," *Fortune*, 30 October 1995, p. 110.

INFORMATION BOX
WHISTLEBLOWING

A whistleblower is an insider in an organization who publicizes alleged corporate misconduct. Such misconduct may involve unethical practices of all kinds, such as fraud, restraint of trade, price fixing, bribes, coercion, unsafe products and facilities, and violations of other laws and regulations. Presumably, the whistle blower has exhausted the possibilities for changing the questionable practices within the normal organizational channels and, as a last resort, has taken the matter to government officials and/or the press.

Since whistleblowing may result in contract cancellations, corporate fines, and lost jobs, those who become whistleblowers may be vilified by their fellow workers and fired and even framed by their firms. This makes whistleblowing a course of action only for the truly courageous, whose concern for societal best interest outweighs their concern for themselves.

However, there is sometimes a thin line between an employee who truly believes the public interest is jeopardized and the individual who has a gripe or is a fanatic. There are some who believe management is condoning misconduct when in fact such misconduct is isolated and without management awareness or acceptance. And some see whistleblowing as a means of furthering their own interests, such as gaining fame or even advancing their careers.

Ralph Nader, in a 1972 book on whistleblowing, suggested that corporate employees have a primary duty to protect society that exists over and above secondary obligations to the corporation. He gives examples of whistleblowing heroes, as well as a course of action for other would-be whistleblowers.[4]

Do you think you could ever be a whistleblower? Under what circumstances?

[4] Ralph Nader, Peter Petkas, and Nate Blackwell, *Whistleblowing* (New York: Bantam Books, 1972).

arranged for the gardener to come to work late that morning, but the gardener arrived shortly after seven and found Whitacre unconscious in his car.

Shortly before the suicide attempt, Whitacre had written a letter to the *Wall Street Journal,* acknowledging that he had received money from ADM through unusual means: "Regarding overseas accounts and kickbacks; and overseas payments to some employees, Dig Deep. It's there! They give it; then use it against you when you are their enemy."[5]

On September 13, 1995, F. Ross Johnson, an ADM board member, in a talk at Emory University's Goizueta Business School commented on Whitacre's suicide attempt: "You know, he tried to commit suicide. But he did it in a six-car garage, which, I think, if you're going to do it, that's the place to do it. [The audience laughed.] And the gardener just happened to come by. So now he is bouncing around."[6]

Whether the suicide attempt was genuine or contrived, Whitacre apparently faced a traumatic period in his life. He wound up in a suburban Chicago hospital with

[5] "ADM Informant Faces...", p. A1.
[6] "ADM and the FBI 'Scumbags'," *Fortune*, 30 October 1995, p. 116.

no job and no place to live. He had money problems, being unable to touch any of the funds in his overseas accounts. He and his wife had moved out of their $1.25 million estate near Decatur, Illinois, after contracting to buy a house near Nashville for $925,000. After the suicide attempt, they attempted to back out of the deal, only to be sued for breach of contract.

With all this, somehow Whitacre seemed to have landed on his feet by early October. True, he and his family were living in a rented house in the Chicago area, but he had become chief executive of Future Health Technologies, a startup biotechnology firm, at a six-figure salary comparable to what he earned legally at ADM.

THE ALLEGATIONS AGAINST THE COMPANY

By fall 1995, three grand juries were investigating whether ADM and some of its competitors conspired to fix prices. Three major product lines of ADM were allegedly involved: lysine, high-fructose corn syrup, and citric acid. Lysine is an amino-acid mixed with feed for hogs and chickens to hasten the growth of lean muscles in the animals. High-fructose corn syrup is a caloric sweetener used in soft drinks. Citric acid, like lysine, is a corn-derived product used in the detergent, food, and beverage industries.

The importance of these products in the total product mix of ADM is indisputable. For example, while lysine is virtually unknown to the public, it is a key ingredient in the feed industry. About 500 million pounds are produced annually. Prices since 1961 have been averaging more than $1 a pound. So millions of dollars are at stake to manufacturers. With modern facilities at its sprawling complex in Decatur, Illinois, ADM can produce about half the world's purchases of lysine annually. And this is one of the company's highest profit products.

The sweetener, high-fructose corn syrup, is a major product for ADM, with a $3 billion-a-year market worldwide. Soft drinks account for more than 75 percent of annual production.

ADM entered the citric-acid business in 1991 when it acquired a unit of Pfizer. Today it is the primary U.S. maker of this additive. One of the largest customers is Procter & Gamble, which uses it for detergents.

As one example of the seemingly incriminating evidence of price fixing uncovered in videotapes, Michael Andreas is shown during a meeting he attended with lysine competitors at the Hyatt Regency Hotel at Los Angeles International Airport. There the participants discussed sales targets for each company as a means of limiting supply. This would destroy the free supply/demand machinations of the market and would permit prices to be kept artificially high, thus increasing the profits of the participants.[7]

With the charges and countercharges of Whitacre and the company, investigations went beyond price fixing to tax evasion for high-level executives sanctioned by

---

[7] Reported in "Investigators Suspect a Global Conspiracy In Archer-Daniels Case," *Wall Street Journal,* 28 July 1995, pp. A1 and A5.

top management. Whitacre was the tip of the iceberg. The criminal-fraud division of the Justice Department began investigating whether the company illegally paid millions of dollars in off-the-books compensation to an array of company executives through foreign bank accounts.

It is worth noting the severity of the penalties if suits successfully come to pass. Fines for price fixing can range into the hundreds of millions of dollars, and some executives could even be given jail sentences. Furthermore, class-action suits by shareholders and customers can result in heavy damage awards. See the Information Box for a discussion of the famous price-fixing conspiracy of 1959 that set the precedent for jail sentences for executives involved.

ADM AND DWAYNE ANDREAS

The story of Archer-Daniels-Midland Co. is really the story of its chairman, Dwayne O. Andreas. In 1947, ADM chairman, Shreve Archer, died after choking on a chicken bone. Dwayne Andreas was a vice-president at Cargill, a rival firm. For the next 18 years he advanced steadily in the industry and became wealthy, while Archer-Daniels showed little growth. In 1966, at age 47, Andreas was asked to become a director at ADM. The founding families sold him a sizable amount of stock and proposed to groom him for the top spot. Four years later, he was named chief executive officer.

INFORMATION BOX

THE FAMOUS PRICE-FIXING CONSPIRACY OF 1959

In 1959, the biggest conspiracy of its kind in U.S. business history impacted the nation's thinking regarding business ethics.

Twenty-nine companies, including such giants as General Electric, Westinghouse, and Allis-Chalmers, were found guilty of conspiring to fix prices in deals involving about $7 billion of electrical equipment. The products involved in the conspiracy included power transformers, power switchgear assemblies, turbine generators, industrial control equipment, and circuit breakers. The companies were fined $1,924,500. Of particular note in this case, 52 executives (none of these top executives) were prosecuted and fined about $140,000. Even more startling, seven of the defendants received jail sentences. This was a first under federal antitrust laws.

On top of all that, almost 2,000 private-action, treble-damage cases were brought as a result of the court findings. In one of these alone, damages of $28,800,000 were awarded.

Incentives for the illegal actions stemmed from several sources. Without doubt, top management was exerting strong pressure on lower executives to improve their performance. Collusion with executives in other firms seemed to be a practical way to do this, especially in an environment rather blasé toward antitrust collusion. This attitude changed with the harsh penalties imposed by Judge J. Cullen Ganey.

Those executives who lost their jobs and went to jail were readily offered equivalent jobs in other corporations. The business community accepted them with open arms. Do you think they deserved such acceptance?

In 1995, Andreas was still firmly in command and running the publicly traded company almost as a personal dynasty. In 25 years he had built up the firm into the nation's biggest farm-commodity processor, with $12.7 billion in annual revenue. Table 23.1 shows the steady growth of revenues since 1986, while Table 23.2 shows the growth of earnings, not quite as steady but still almost two and a half times greater than in 1986.

POLITICAL MANEUVERING

Although company headquarters were at Decatur, Illinois, Andreas's influence in Washington was probably unparalleled by any other business leader. ADM led corporate America in political contributions; it contributed hundreds of thousands of dollars to both parties. Furthermore, Andreas supported Jimmy Carter's campaign—ADM even bought his struggling peanut farm in 1981. But Andreas also contributed generously to Ronald Reagan and George Bush. During the Reagan years, when U.S. firms were entering the Soviet market, ADM was in the vanguard. Andreas became close to then-Soviet president, Mikhail Gorbachev. But as a hedge, he also courted Boris Yeltsin, Gorbachev's emerging rival.

Perhaps his greatest political supporter became Senator Robert Dole, who is from the farm state of Kansas. When Dole's wife, Elizabeth, took over administration of the American Red Cross, Andreas donated $1 million to the cause. Dole also was given use of an ADM corporate plane, for which he paid the equivalent of a first-class ticket. An added factor in the friendship and rapport was the proximity of their vacation homes: Dole and his wife owned a unit in Sea View, Florida, as did David Brinkley, a renowned TV newsman, and Robert Strauss, an ADM board member, and, of course, Dwayne Andreas.[8] Interestingly, President Clinton also regarded Andreas as an ally.

TABLE 23.1. ADM Revenues, 1986–1995

Year Ending June 30	Sales (millions)	Year-to-Year Percent Increase
1986	$5,336	
1987	5,775	10.8%
1988	6,798	11.8
1989	7,929	11.6
1990	7,751	(2.2)
1991	8,468	9.3
1992	9,232	9.0
1993	9,811	6.5
1994	11,374	15.9
1995	12,672	11.4
Gain since 1986		137.5%

Source: Adapted from *1995 ADM Annual Report.*

---

[8] Reported in "How Dwayne Andreas Rules Archer-Daniels By Hedging His Bets," *Wall Street Journal,* 27 October 1995, p. A8.

TABLE 23.2. ADM Net Earnings 1986–1995

Year Ending June 30	Earnings (millions)	Year-to-Year Percent Increase
1986	$230	
1987	265	15.2%
1988	353	33.2
1989	425	20.3
1990	484	13.9
1991	467	(3.5)
1992	504	7.9
1993	568	12.7
1994	484	(14.8)
1995	796	64.5
Gain since 1986		246.1%

Source: Adapted from *1995 ADM Annual Report.*

Such political presence has brought great rewards to the company. ADM is a major beneficiary of federal price supports for sugar. Because such supports have kept sugar prices artificially high, ADM's sweetener, high-fructose corn syrup, has been attractive for giant companies such as Coca-Cola. Estimates are that fructose generates about 40 percent of ADM's earnings.[9]

Archer-Daniels also benefits from the 54-cent-a-gallon excise-tax break on ethanol, being the major producer of this corn-based fuel additive. Indeed, it is doubtful if the ethanol industry would exist without this tax break, and Bob Dole was its most ardent congressional supporter.

Despite all the campaign contributions and personal rapport with the seats of power in Washington, Andreas and ADM have done little direct lobbying. Rather, such efforts have been done indirectly through various commodity and trade associations. For example, the American Peanut Sellers Association, with ADM support, handles the lobbying on peanut price supports.[10]

The Board of Directors

The investigations and the charges and countercharges drew fire from some of the major institutional holders of ADM stock. For example, the California Public Employees Retirement System—Calpers, as it is known, and owner of 3.6 million shares of Archer-Daniels—complained, charging that the board was too closely tied to Chairman and CEO Dwayne Andreas. "The ADM board is dominated by insiders,

[9] Ibid.
[10] Ibid.

many of whom happen to be related to the CEO," Calpers complained. Calpers also criticized the ADM board for approving a 14 percent pay raise for Andreas, "rather than demand the CEO's resignation."[11] Other institutional investors also joined the criticisms: for example, the United Brotherhood of Carpenters, the Teamsters Union, and New York's major pension funds.

Shareholders had several other major criticisms of the board. It was supposed to authorize all capital expenditures above $250,000. The alleged claims for offshore pay were disguised as requests for spending on plant and equipment, and these the board passed with no hesitation. As to the charges of price-fixing and the allegations against major executives, the board was conspicuously uncritical, and finally made some token efforts to look further into the charges.

Brian Mulroney, former prime minister of Canada, co-chaired the special committee charged with coordinating the company's response to the federal investigations. One would think that part of his job was to safeguard the interests of shareholders. But major institutional shareholders doubted his objectivity, and noted his very close relations to Dwayne Andreas. Critics contended that what was needed was not a rubber-stamp special committee but "a team of experts to lead a full-blown, independent investigation."[12]

Regarding the composition of the board, critics seemed to have a case: The board was hardly objective and unbiased toward company top management; rather, it was highly supportive and dominated by insiders, many of whom were related to the CEO. For example, four of Archer-Daniels' 17 directors were members of the Andreas family. An additional six directors were retired executives or relatives of senior managers. The outside directors also had close connections to Andreas, such as Robert S. Strauss, the Washington lawyer whose firm represented ADM, and Mulroney, who was also with a law firm used by the company. Even Harvard University professor Ray Goldberg, a member of the board, had strong ties with Andreas, dating back to his dissertation.

While close bonds of boards with management are not unusual with many companies, such cozy relations can be detrimental to shareholders' best interests.

ANALYSIS

ADM's Conduct

ADM was found guilty of unethical conduct, and even illegalities regarding price fixing. Certain other activities of this giant company also posed ethical controversies even if they were not illegal—for example, packing the board with cronies dedicated to preserving the establishment at the expense of stockholders; the great quest for preferential treatment in the highest corridors of power; and just perhaps, the setting up of Whitacre. Let us examine these ethical issues.

---

[11] Joann S. Lublin, "Archer-Daniels-Midland Is Drawing Fire From Some Institutional Holders," *Wall Street Journal*, 11 October 1995, p. A8.

[12] Henkoff, p. 110.

Packing the board so that it is exceptionally supportive of the entrenched management may be condemned as not truly representing the rights of stockholders. But with Andreas at the helm, ADM's stock value rose at an annual average rate of 17 percent over the last decade. Few stockholders could dispute Andreas's contribution to the firm, even though they might fume at his riding roughshod over his critics—especially institutions holding large amounts of stock.

Some would maintain that the courting of favoritism and special treatment from high-level Washington politicians may have gone too far. But should not any organization have the right to do its best to push for beneficial legislation and regulation? Of course, some will be more effective than others in doing so. Is this so much different than competition in the marketplace?

Whitacre's Role

Why did Whitacre choose to be a government mole? As of this writing, nothing has been written about this. Still in his thirties, Whitacre had advanced to high position in the company, with corresponding substantial compensation (enough to afford an estate valued at more than a million dollars), and was at least one of the top candidates for the presidency of the firm. Yet he had been secretly taping supposedly illegal discussions. Why? What did he have to gain? There was so much to lose.

Added to this, he must have been a very capable executive, yet he was naive enough to leave himself vulnerable by accepting, and maybe even initiating, illegal scams through false invoices and overseas bank accounts. Then he apparently naively confessed to a company lawyer his involvement as an informant for the FBI, not just recently but for three years. It doesn't make much sense, does it?

LATER DEVELOPMENTS

In October 1996, ADM pleaded guilty to criminal price-fixing charges. The company paid a record $100 million fine and nearly that amount again to settle lawsuits brought by customers and investors. But its troubles were not over.

Early in December 1996, a federal grand jury charged Michael Andreas—who earned $1.3 million annually as the No. 2 executive at ADM and was heir apparent to his father to run the company—and Terrance Wilson, former head of ADM's corn-processing division, with conspiring with Asian lysine manufacturers to rig the price of lysine, a livestock feed additive. Andreas took a leave of absence with full pay, and Wilson retired. It was thought that any conviction or guilty plea by Michael Andreas would destroy his chances of continuing his family's three-decade-long reign over ADM. However, Dwayne Andreas could yet preserve the patrimony: His nephew, G. Allen Andreas, a fifty-three-year-old lawyer, was one of three executives named to share Dwayne Andreas's responsibility in a newly formed office of chief executive.

In a surprising twist to the case, Mark Whitacre—the whistleblower—was also indicted.

The Verdicts

The verdicts came in late 1998. After a week of deliberation in a two-month trial, the jury found Andreas, Wilson, and Whitacre guilty in a landmark price-fixing case, thereby giving the Justice Department its biggest convictions in a push against illegal global cartels. The federal prosecutors had been thwarted in attempts to rebuild the case after their mole, Whitacre, had been convicted of embezzlement and was already serving a nine-year prison sentence. The problem was solved by wringing confessions from Asian executives who were also involved in the conspiracy.

The bizarre behavior of Whitacre, after initially providing documentation of the birth of a price-fixing scheme, was unexpected and almost disastrous. It was also hard to explain, even given that he was a big spender who openly pined to become president of ADM.

WHAT CAN BE LEARNED?

Price Fixing Is One of the Easiest Cases to Prosecute

Conspiracies to fix prices are direct violations of the Sherman Act. The government does not need to prove that competition was injured or that trade was restrained. All that needs to be proven is that a meeting took place with agreements to fix prices, bids, or allocate market share.

The penalties for price conspiracies have greatly increased since the celebrated electrical equipment industry conspiracy of 1959. Given the ease of prosecution, one would think that no prudent executive would ever take such a risk. Yet, there have been sporadic instances of price-fixing since then, and we have it here with Michael Andreas, the son of Dwayne. Is there no learning experience?

Is Political Patronage Necessary?

We know that ADM sought political patronage and preferential treatment to an extraordinary degree—perhaps more than any other firm. Is this so bad?

Purists argue that this distorts the objectivity of our governmental institutions. Others say it is part of the democratic process in a pluralistic society. It might be so vital to our type of government that it cannot be eliminated—at best, can only be curbed.

On the other hand, it simply adds one more dimension to the competitive environment. Other firms can be encouraged to flex their muscles in the halls of government.

But when it comes to violations of the law, which supposedly reflects the wishes of society, then no firm is immune to the consequences. Even if its political patronage has been assiduously cultivated, it cannot escape the consequences of its illegal actions. The press, and the legal establishment, see to that.

Beware the "Shareholder Be Damned" Attitude

Some shareholders of ADM suspect that ADM had this attitude. As a consequence, the company faced at least two dozen shareholder lawsuits. As it approached the 1995 October annual meeting, nine big institutional investors announced plans to vote against reelecting ADM directors. But the move was largely symbolic, since their combined shares represented only 4.9 percent of the 505 million outstanding shares.[13] And their views received little attention in the meeting. Nor, apparently did those of other shareholders. the *Wall Street Journal* reported that at the meeting Andreas squelched criticisms of the issue of the antitrust probe and other allegations as he "summarily cut off a critic by turning off his microphone: 'I'm chairman. I'll make the rules as I go along,' Mr. Andreas said."[14]

A cozy relationship with the board encourages such attitudes. And when operating performance is continually improving, such shareholder criticisms may be seen as merely gnats striving for attention, and thus worthy of being ignored. If the top executive is inclined to be autocratic, then the environment is supportive.

But is this wise? Should adversity set in, sometime in the future, then such attitudes toward investors can be self-destructive, even with a supportive board. If performance deteriorates, no board can maintain its sheeplike support for incumbent management, not in the face of vehement shareholders (especially large institutional investors) or major creditors.

But does adversity have to come? Only the profoundest optimist can think that success is forever. In ADM's case, adversity is here and now.

An Organization's Ethical Tone Is Set By Top Management

If top management is unconcerned about ethical conduct, or if it is an active participant in less than desirable practices, this sets the tone throughout the organization. It promotes erosion of acceptable moral conduct in many areas of the operation. It becomes contagious as even those inclined to be more morally scrupulous join their colleagues. Then we have the "follow-the-leader" mindset.

In such an unhealthy environment, a few whistleblowers may arise and attempt to right the situation, often unsuccessfully and at great personal risk. Others who cannot tolerate the decline in moral standards, but don't have the courage to be whistleblowers, will leave the company. Almost inevitably, the misconduct will come to light, and repercussions of the severest kind result. Perhaps top management can escape the blame, though lower-level executives will be sacrificed. Occasionally, top management also comes under fire, and is forced to resign. Unfortunately, too often with healthy retirement benefits.

CONSIDER

Can you think of other learning insights?

[13] "Probe Tears Veil of Secrecy at Archer-Daniels-Midland," *Cleveland Plain Dealer*, 18 October 1995, p. 3C.
[14] "How Dwayne Andreas Rules," p. A1.

QUESTIONS

1. What is your position regarding top management's culpability for the misdeeds of their subordinates?

2. Do you think ADM's efforts at gaining political favoritism went too far? Why or why not?

3. "If Dwayne's son is found guilty of price-fixing, there's no way that the big man himself cannot be found guilty." Evaluate this statement.

4. "With all the false invoices and persons involved in these millions of dollars of payouts off-the-books, there's no way the company could not have known what was going on." Evaluate.

5. Speculate on what would lead Whitacre to "betray" his company. If a number of possibilities are mentioned, which do you think is most compelling?

6. With the severe penalties and ease of prosecution of price-fixing cases, why would any firm or any executive attempt it today?

7. Why do you suppose, with all its efforts to gain preferential treatment through courting the mighty in government, ADM has not resorted to direct lobbying? Has it missed a golden opportunity to further its causes?

HANDS-ON EXERCISES

Before

1. Assume that Dwayne Andreas wants to maintain high ethical standards in his organization. Describe how he should go about this.

After

2. Assume that several key executives have been found guilty of price-fixing; assume further that there are also indictments of illegal payments to certain executives. Further, the Senate ethics committee is investigating whether there have been improprieties in dealings with some members of Congress. How would you as CEO attempt damage control?

TEAM DEBATE EXERCISE

Debate the ethics of aggressively courting prominent politicians and government administrators. The two extreme positions would be: (1) going as far as you can short of being charged with outright bribery; (2) limiting relationship building to a few token contributions to trade association lobbying efforts.

INVITATION TO RESEARCH

Has ADM's public image been badly tarnished by all this publicity, or can you determine this? Has the firm continued to grow and prosper? Is the Andreas family still in control?

CHAPTER TWENTY-FOUR

Conclusions— What Can Be Learned?

*I*n considering mistakes, three things are worth noting:

- Even the most successful organizations make mistakes but survive as long as they maintain a good "batting average."
- Mistakes should be effective teaching tools for avoiding similar errors in the future.
- Firms can bounce back from adversity, and turn around.

We can make several generalizations from these mistakes and successes. Of course we recognize that marketing is a discipline that does not lend itself to laws or axioms. Examples of exceptions to every principle or generalization can be found. However, the decision maker does well to heed the following insights. For the most part they are based on specific corporate and entrepreneurial experiences and should be transferable to other situations and other times.

INSIGHTS REGARDING OVERALL ENTERPRISE PERSPECTIVES

Importance of Public Image

The impact, for good or bad, of an organization's public image was a common thread in many cases—for example, Nike, Continental, Southwest Airlines, Vanguard, Disney, Maytag, Perrier, United Way, and Harley-Davidson.

Nike shows the power of an image that was compatible with the product and attractive to the target market. The carefully nurtured association with some of the most esteemed male and female athletes in the world—many of whom its customers were eager to emulate—if only in their dreams—propelled Nike and its "swoosh" logo to dominance in the athletic apparel industry. Still, we saw a positive image become tarnished for Nike.

Continental Airlines is a case for hope. It shows that a reputation in the pits, not only with employees but also with the general public, can be resurrected and revitalized, even in just a short period of time. However, it takes inspired leadership to do so—and this Gordon Bethune, its new CEO, supplied.

Southwest's image of friendliness, great efficiency, and unbeatable prices propelled it to an unassailable position among short-haul airlines. Now it seeks to expand its image to longer hauls. Vanguard has also used its image of frugality and great customer service in the mutual fund industry to propel it to the top with relatively little advertising. Harley-Davidson was able to develop its image one step further—to a mystique with a devoted cult following. Gateway Computer tried to upgrade its Holstein cow image to a mystique, but without success.

Some images were less favorable. Disney found its image did not travel well to Paris, nor did Maytag's quality image succeed in the United Kingdom. Perrier responded aggressively to a contamination problem by making a major product recall, but lost its image of quality. The nonprofit, United Way, was brought to its knees by revelations about the excesses of its long-time chief executive, William Aramony. Donations dwindled and local chapters withheld funds from the national organization as the reputation of the largest charitable organization was sullied.

The importance of a firm's public image should be undeniable. Yet some continue to disregard their image and either act in ways detrimental or else ignore the constraints and opportunities that a reputation affords.

Power of the Media

We have seen or suspected the power of the media in numerous cases. Nike, Coca-Cola, United Way, IBM, Firestone and Ford, and Vanguard are obvious examples. This power is often used critically—to hurt a firm's public image. The media can fan a problem or exacerbate an embarrassing or imprudent action. In particular, this media focus can trigger the herd instinct, in which increasing numbers of people join in protests and public criticism. And the media in its zeal can sometimes cross the line, as in singling out Nike for all the employment abuses of Third World countries. But in Vanguard's case, positive media attention minimized the need for much advertising.

We can make these five generalizations regarding image and its relationship with the media:

- It is desirable to maintain a stable, clear-cut image and undeviating objectives.
- It is difficult and time-consuming to upgrade an image.
- An episode of poor quality risks a lasting stigma.
- A good image can be quickly lost if a firm relaxes in an environment of aggressive competition.
- Well-known firms, and not-for-profit firms dependent on voluntary contributions, are especially vulnerable to critical public scrutiny and must use great care in safeguarding their reputations.

Need for Growth Orientation—but Not Reckless Growth

The opposite of a growth commitment is a status quo mind-set, uninterested in expansion and the problems and work involved. Harley-Davidson's downfall in the 1950s was its contentment with the status quo; Sunbeam's lack of growth led to the ill-fated choice of "Chainsaw Al" Dunlap to get things moving again.

In general, how tenable is a low-growth or no-growth philosophy? Although at first glance it seems workable, it usually sows the seeds of its own destruction. Almost four decades ago the following caution was made:

> Vitality is required even for survival; but vitality is difficult to maintain without growth, at least in the American business climate. The vitality of a firm depends on the vigor and ambition of its members. The prospect of growth is one of the principal means by which a firm can attract able and vigorous recruits.[1]

Consequently, if a firm is perceived as not growth-minded, its ability to attract able people diminishes. Customers see a growing firm as reliable, eager to please, and constantly improving. Suppliers and creditors tend to give preferential treatment to a growing firm because they hope to retain it as a customer when it reaches large size.

In other cases firms had strong growth commitments, but somehow their growth in bureaucratic overhead let competitiveness slip and they fell back, sometimes after decades of market dominance. IBM readily comes to mind here, before its great comeback. So does Borden, reaping the consequences of reckless growth and unwise diversifications. Then we have the bungled growth efforts of Maytag's Hoover Division in the United Kingdom. Good financial judgment must not be sacrificed to the siren call of growth.

Therefore, an emphasis on growth can be carried too far. Somehow the growth must be kept within the abilities of the firm to handle it. Several examples—such as Southwest Airlines, Wal-Mart, and Dell Computer—showed how firms could grow rapidly without losing control.

We can make several generalizations about the most desirable growth perspectives:

- Growth targets should not exceed the abilities and resources of the organization. Growth at any cost—especially at the expense of profits and financial stability—must be shunned. In particular, tight controls over inventories and expenses should be established, and performance should be monitored closely.

- The most prudent approach to growth is to keep the organization and operation as simple and uniform as possible, to be flexible in case sales do not meet expectations, and to keep the breakeven point as low as possible, especially for new and untried ventures.

- Concentrating maximum efforts on the expansion opportunity is like an army exploiting a breakthrough. The concentration strategy—such as that of Southwest Airlines and McDonald's until recently—usually wins out over

---

[1] Wroe Alderson, *Marketing Behavior and Executive Action* (Homewood, Ill.: Irwin, 1957), 59.

more timid competitors who diffuse efforts and resources. But such concentration is riskier than spreading efforts.

- Rapidly expanding markets pose dangers from too conservative as well as overly optimistic sales forecasts. The latter may overextend resources and jeopardize viability should demand contract; the former opens the door to more aggressive competitors. There is no right answer to this dilemma, but management should be aware of the risks and the rewards of both extremes.

- A strategy emphasizing rapid growth should not neglect other aspects of the operation. For example, older stores should not be ignored in the quest to open new ones.

- Decentralized management is more compatible with rapid growth than centralized, because it puts less strain on home-office executives. However, delegation must have well-defined standards and controls as well as competent subordinates. Otherwise, the Maytag Hoover fiasco may be repeated.

- The safety and integrity of the product and firm's reputation must not be sacrificed in pursuit of growth and profits. This is especially important when customers' health and safety may be jeopardized, such as Ford and Firestone encountered with the Ford Explorer.

Strategic Windows of Opportunity

Several of the great successes we examined resulted from exploiting strategic windows of opportunity. Southwest found its opportunity by being so cost effective that it could offer both cut-rate fares and highly dependable short-haul service that no other airline could match. Similarly, Vanguard found its strategic niche with the lowest expense ratios and overhead in the mutual fund industry, as did Wal-Mart in retailing.

We make these generalizations regarding opportunities and strategic windows:

- Opportunities often exist when a traditional way of doing business has prevailed in the industry for a long time—maybe the climate is ripe for a change.

- Opportunities often exist when existing firms are not entirely satisfying customers' needs.

- Innovations are not limited to products but can involve customer services as well as such things as methods of distribution.

- For industries with rapidly changing technologies—usually new industries—heavy research and development expenditures are usually required if a firm is to avoid falling behind its competitors. But heavy R&D does not guarantee being in the forefront, as shown by the tribulations of IBM despite its huge expenditures.

Power of Judicious Imitation

Some firms are reluctant to copy successful practices of their competitors; they want to be leaders, not followers. But successful practices or innovations may need to be copied if a firm is not to be left behind. Sometimes the imitator outdoes the innovator. Success can lie in doing the ordinary better than competitors.

Nike achieved its initial success by imitating many of the successful practices of the entrenched German competitor, Adidas. Somehow the competitors of McDonald's for decades were unable to imitate its undeviating insistence on rigorous standards and controls over all aspects of the operation.

For fifty years, Boeing was the innovator in the commercial-jet industry, sometimes taking big risks to do so. It biggest risk was in the 1960s when it almost bankrupted itself to build the 747 that was twice the size of any other plane in commercial use. Now Airbus is the innovator with its huge plane, the 555-seat A-360. Boeing decided not to follow Airbus's lead.

We can make this generalization: It makes sense for a company to identify the characteristics of successful competitors (and even similar but noncompeting firms) that contributed to their success, and then adopt these characteristics if they are compatible with the imitator's resources. Let someone else do the experimenting and risk taking. The imitator faces some risk in waiting too long, but this usually is far less than the risk of being an innovator.

The Need for Prudent Crisis Management

Crises are unexpected happenings that pose threats, moderate to catastrophic, to the organization's well being. We described four cases in Part III: Scott Paper/Sunbeam, Firestone/Ford, Perrier, and United Way. Other cases that involved some crises were Boeing, Continental, Euro Disney, Coca-Cola, Maytag, ADM, MetLife, and Rubbermaid Newell. Some firms—such as United Way, Coca-Cola, and Euro Disney—handled their crisis reasonably well, although we can question how such crises were allowed to happen in the first place. However, Firestone/Ford, Maytag, ADM, Perrier, and MetLife either overreacted or underreacted and failed badly in salvaging the situation.

Most crises can be minimized if a company takes precautions. This suggests being alert to changing conditions, having contingency plans, and practicing risk avoidance. For example, it is prudent to prohibit key executives from traveling on the same air flight; it is prudent to insure key executives so that their incapacity will not endanger the organization; and it is prudent to set up contingency plans for a strike, an equipment failure or plant shutdown, the loss of a major distributor, unexpected economic conditions, or a serious lawsuit. Some risks, of course, can be covered by insurance, but others probably not. The mettle of any organization may be severely tested by an unexpected crisis. Such crises need not cause the demise of the company, however, if alternatives are weighed and actions taken only after calm deliberation.

Crises may necessitate some changes in the organization and the way of doing business. Firms should avoid making hasty or disruptive changes or, on the other extreme, making too few changes too late and too grudgingly. The middle ground is usually best. Careful planning can help a company minimize trauma and enact effective solutions. This planning should include worst-case scenarios.

Vulnerability to Competition and the Three Cs

Competitive advantage can be short-lived, success does not guarantee continued success, and innovators as well as long-dominant firms can be overtaken and surpassed.

With IBM, Boeing, Disney, and even United Way, we saw the three Cs syndrome of complacency, conservatism, and conceit that often characterizes the mind-set of leading organizations in their industries. We suggest that a constructive attitude of never underestimating competitors be fostered by:

- Bringing fresh blood into the organization for new ideas and different perspectives.
- Establishing a strong commitment with periodic feedback for customer service and satisfaction.
- Periodically making a corporate self-analysis designed to detect weaknesses as well as opportunities in their early stages.
- Continually monitoring the environment and being alert to any changes.

The environment is dynamic, often with subtle and hardly recognizable changes. Still, these changes may eventually have profound effects on ways of doing business, and a firm should be alert in order to protect its position as well as seize opportunities.

Environmental Monitoring

The dynamic business environment may involve changes in customer preferences and needs, in competition, and in the economy. It may involve changes even in international events—such as nationalism in Canada, NAFTA, OPEC machinations, changes in Eastern Europe and South Africa, and advances by Pacific Rim countries in productivity and quality control. IBM failed to detect and act upon significant changes in the computer industry. Borden misjudged the dynamics of its industry. Pepsi in South America failed to realize the intricacies of penetrating and protecting its several markets there. Even McDonald's did not recognize that the fast-food industry was at long last becoming saturated and facing a moderate groundswell toward healthy eating.

How can a firm stay alert to subtle and insidious or more obvious changes? It needs *sensors* to constantly monitor the environment. A marketing or economic research department may provide such sensors, but in many instances a formal organizational entity is not really necessary to provide primary monitoring. Executive alertness is essential. Most changes do not occur suddenly and without warning. Information can come from feedback by customers, sales representatives, and suppliers; news of relevant changes and projections in business journals; and even simple observations of what is happening in stores, advertising, prices, and new technologies. Unfortunately, in the urgency of dealing with day-to-day operating problems, executives can overlook or disregard changing environmental factors that may affect present and future business.

Consider the following generalizations regarding vulnerability to competition:

- Initial market advantage tends to be rather quickly countered by competitors.
- Countering by competitors is more likely to occur when an innovation is involved than when the advantage comes from more commonplace effective management and marketing techniques, such as superb customer service.

- An easy-entry industry is particularly vulnerable to new and aggressive competition, especially if the market is expanding. In new industries, severe price competition usually weeds out marginal firms.

- Long-dominant firms become vulnerable to upstart competitors because of their complacency, conservatism, and even conceit. They frequently are resistant to change and myopic about the environment.

- Careful monitoring performance trends of similar operating units at *strategic control points* can detect weakening positions before situations become serious. (This point is discussed further in the next section.)

- In expanding markets, increases in sales may hide a deteriorating competitive situation. Market-share data is more important.

- A no-growth policy, or a temporary absence from the marketplace, even if fully justified by extraordinary circumstances, invites competitive inroads. Example: Perrier.

Effective Organization

We can identify several organizational attributes that can help or hinder effectiveness.

Management by Exception

With diverse and far-flung operations, it becomes difficult to closely supervise all aspects. Successful managers therefore focus their attention on performances that deviate significantly from the expected norms at *strategic control points*. Such points should include market share, profitability measures, turnover ratios, various expense ratios, and the like, broken down by individual operational units. Trend information is important: Is performance getting better or worse? Subordinates can be left to handle ordinary operations and less significant deviations, so that the manager is not overburdened with details.

Management by exception failed, however, with Maytag and its overseas Hoover division. Seemingly, no budget restraints and approvals were needed for expenditures over a certain amount. The lack of such approval requirements can be directly blamed for the reprehensible promotional plans. By the time results came in, it was too late.

The Deadly Parallel

As an enterprise becomes larger, a particularly effective organizational structure is to have operating units of comparable characteristics. Sales, expenses, and profits can then be more readily compared, enabling both strong and weak performances to be identified so that appropriate action can be taken. Besides providing control and performance evaluation, this *deadly parallel* structure fosters intra-firm competition that can stimulate best efforts. For the deadly parallel to be used effectively, operating units must be fairly equalized, perhaps by size or through quotas or similar categories of sales potential. This is not difficult to achieve with retail units, since departments and stores can be divided into sales volume categories—often designated as A, B, and C units—and operating results compared within the category. The deadly parallel can also be used with sales territories and certain other operating units for which sales and applicable expenses and ratios can be directly measured and compared with similar units.

Lean and Mean

A new climate is sweeping our country's major corporations. In one sense it is good: It enhances their competitiveness. But it can be destructive. Vanguard, Southwest Airlines, and Wal-Mart have been in the forefront of the lean-and-mean movement; IBM has moved to it, but the downsizing had to be extreme and disruptive. Lean-and-mean firms develop flat organizations with few management layers, thus keeping overhead low, improving communication, involving employees in greater self-management, and fostering an innovative mind-set.

In contrast, we saw the organizational bloat of Borden and such behemoths as IBM before its turnaround, with their many management levels, entrenched bureaucracies, and massive overhead. A virtual cause-and-effect relationship exists between the proportion of total overhead committed to administration/staff and the ability to cope with change and innovate. It is like trying to maneuver a huge ship: Bureaucratic weight slows the response time.

The problem with the lemming-like pursuit of the lean-and-mean structure is in knowing how far to downsize without cutting into bone and muscle. As thousands of managers and staff specialists can attest, productivity gains have not always been worth the loss of jobs, the destruction of career paths, and the possible sacrifice of long-term potential. The extreme example of this was Dunlap's decimating of Scott Paper and Sunbeam.

Resistance to Change

People as well as organizations do not embrace change well. Change is disruptive; it destroys accepted ways of doing things and muddles familiar authority and responsibility patterns. Previously important positions may be downgraded or even eliminated, and people who view themselves as highly competent in a particular job may be forced to assume unfamiliar duties amid the fear that they cannot master the new assignments. When the change involves wholesale terminations in a major downsizing—as with IBM, Borden, Euro Disney, Scott/Sunbeam, and Boeing in its down cycles—the resistance and fear of change can become so great that efficiency is seriously jeopardized.

Normal resistance to change can be eased by good communication with participants about forthcoming changes, thus dampening rumors and fears. Acceptance of change is helped if employees are involved as fully as possible in planning the changes, if their participation is solicited and welcomed, and if assurances can be given that positions will not be impaired, only changed. Gradual rather than abrupt changes also make a transition smoother.

In the final analysis, however, making needed changes and embracing new opportunities should not be delayed or canceled because of possible negative repercussions on the organization. If change is desirable, as it often is with long-established bureaucratic organizations, then it should be done without delay. Individuals and organizations can adapt to change—it just takes some time.

SPECIFIC MARKETING STRATEGY INSIGHTS

Strengths and Limitations of Advertising

The cases provide several insights regarding the effectiveness of advertising, but they also present unanswered questions and contradictions. At the time of Coca-Cola's blunder with its New Coke, it was spending $100 million more for advertising than Pepsi, all the while losing market share. Vanguard became the star of the mutual fund industry—with virtually no advertising, unlike its competitors—relying instead on word-of-mouth and free publicity. Such outcomes raise doubts about the power of advertising.

However, the right theme can bring victory, as shown by Nike's great success with celebrity endorsements in creating an image irresistible to many of its customers. Dell's promotional efforts helped it best its closest competitors. Then we have two cases in which promotional efforts were too effective: Maytag Hoover's promotional campaign created more customer demand than it could handle; and the deceptive selling efforts of MetLife brought the wrath of regulators.

Thus the great challenge of advertising. We never know for sure how much should be spent to reach planned objectives, perhaps of increasing sales by a certain percentage or gaining market share. But, despite the inability to directly measure the effectiveness of advertising, only the brave—or foolhardy—executive stands pat in the face of increased promotional efforts by competitors.

We draw these conclusions: There is no assured correlation between expenditures for advertising and sales success. But the right theme or message can be powerful. In most cases, advertising can generate initial trial. But if the other elements of the marketing strategy are relatively unattractive, customers will not be won or retained.

Limitations of Marketing Research

Marketing research is touted as the key to better decision making, the mark of sophisticated professional management. The popular belief is that the more money spent for marketing research, the less chance for a bad decision. But there is no guarantee of that, as we saw with Coca-Cola.

At best, marketing research increases the batting average of good decisions—maybe by only a little, sometimes by quite a bit. To be effective, research must be current and unbiased. Customer attitudes can change significantly if months elapse between the research and the product introduction. The several million dollars spent in taste-test research for Coca-Cola hardly reassures us about the validity of even current marketing research. Admittedly, results of taste tests are difficult to rely on, simply due to the subjective nature of taste preferences. Still, the Coca-Cola research did not even uncover the latent and powerful loyalty toward tradition, and gave a false "go" signal for the new flavor.

We do not imply that marketing research has little value. Most flawed studies would have been worthwhile with better design and planning. Marketing research should have enabled Disney to better structure its pricing and other strategies to unique conditions facing its Euro Disney project.

Surprisingly, many successful new ventures initially used little formal research. Vanguard, Southwest Airlines, Wal-Mart—even McDonald's and Nike in their early days—apparently relied on entrepreneurial hunch rather than sophisticated research.

Why have we not seen more extensive use of marketing research for new ventures? Consider the following major reasons:

- Most of the founding entrepreneurs did not have marketing backgrounds and therefore were not familiar and confident with such research.
- Available tools and techniques are not always appropriate to handle some problems and opportunities. There may be too many variables to ascertain their full impact, and some of these variables will be intangible and impossible to measure precisely. Much research consists of collecting past and present data that, although helpful in predicting a stable future, are little help in charting revolutionary new ventures. If risks are higher without marketing research, these may be offset by the potential for great rewards.

The Importance of Price as an Offensive Weapon

Price promotions are the most aggressive marketing strategy and the one most desirable from the customer's viewpoint. We saw four notable marketing successes that based their major strategy on having lower prices than competitors: Dell Computer, Vanguard, Southwest Airlines, and Wal-Mart. But in another case, Euro Disney, high prices were a detriment in meeting performance goals. Now, low-price competition—a price war—is cutting into the profits of McDonald's as well as its competitors. Still, with Perrier a high-price strategy was the key to its marketing success before the crisis, as consumers perceived the high price as indicative of high quality.

The major disadvantage of low prices as an offensive weapon is that competitors are almost forced to meet the price-cutter's prices—in other words, such a marketing strategy is easy to match. Consequently, when prices for an entire industry fall, no firm may have any particular advantage and all suffer the effects in diminished profits. Thus, competitive advantage was thought to seldom be won by price-cutting. But we saw four major successes coming from greater operating efficiencies and lower overhead costs that permitted good profits, while most competitors could not meet their prices without losing money.

In general, other marketing strategies are more successful for most firms—strategies such as better quality, better product and brand image, better service, and improved warranties, all these aspects of non-price rather than price competition.

At the same time we have to recognize that in new industries, ones characterized by rapid technological change and production efficiencies, severe price competition is the norm, and it weeds out marginal operations. Even a substantial position in such an industry may not insulate a firm from price competition that can jeopardize its viability.

Analytical Tools for Marketing

We identified several of the most useful analytical tools for marketing decision making. In Disney we discussed breakeven analysis, a highly useful tool for making go/no-go decisions about new ventures and alternative business strategies. In Maytag, the cost-benefit analysis might have prevented the bungled promotion in England. The Southwest case introduced us to the SWOT (strengths, weaknesses, opportunities, threats) analysis. While these analyses do not guarantee the best decisions, they do bring order and systematic thinking into the art of marketing decision making.

Franchising

Franchising provides the vehicle for great growth in number of stores and other outlets. The growth comes from the lower investment needed for expansion by having independent franchisees put up much of the capital for new outlets. However, franchisee relations can present problems, as McDonald's recently found. In particular, problems are likely to be encountered in holding the line on prices and menus, as well as in meeting desired standards for service and cleanliness.

A Kinder, Gentler Stance?

In several cases, we could identify an arrogant mind-set as leading to difficulties. The French did not appreciate the arrogance of Disney, and the Euro Disney project was almost a disaster. Arrogance also eventually caught up with Aramony of United Way.

At the other extreme, is there room in today's competitive environment for a kinder, gentler stance by a business firm? While a firm normally comes into contact with numerous different parties, let us consider this question with regard to suppliers and distributors, customers, and employees.

Relations with Suppliers and Distributors

With the movement toward just-in-time deliveries in the search for more efficiency and cost containment, manufacturers and retailers are placing greater demands on suppliers. Those who cannot meet these demands will usually lose out to competitors able to do so. The big manufacturer or retailer can demand ever more from smaller suppliers, since it is in the power position and the loss of its business could be overwhelming. We saw the problems of Rubbermaid in being unable to meet the service demands of Wal-Mart. At the least, the big customer deserves priority attention since its business is so important to any supplier. Reebok's callousness in disregarding the new product concerns of Foot Locker led to its being supplanted by a hard-charging Nike in the sneaker wars of the early 1990s.

Some of the big retailers today, including Wal-Mart and Home Depot as well as supermarket chains, impose "slotting fees." A slotting fee essentially is a toll charged by the retailer for the use of its space; suppliers pay this up front if they wish to be represented in the retailer's stores. Other demands include driving cost prices down to rock bottom, even if this destroys the supplier's profits, and insisting that the supplier take responsibility for inventory control, even stocking shelves, as well as providing special promotional support. It is common for big customers, including such manufacturers as Dell, to make suppliers wait longer to be paid while the cash discount for prompt payment is routinely taken.

While organizations such as Wal-Mart argue that the use of clout leads to greater marketing efficiencies and lower consumer prices, it can be carried too far. The term *symbiotic relationship* describes the relationship between the various channel-of-distribution members: All benefit from the success of the product, and it should be to their mutual advantage to work together. The manufacturer and the distributor thus should represent a valued partnership.

The same idea applies for the dealers or distributors of a powerful manufacturer. They are on the same side; they are not in competition with one another. Yet, we have seen in several instances that a manufacturer created sour distributor–dealer relations. Pepsi was not closely attuned to the concerns of its longtime Venezuela bottler and lost distribution in that entire country. And McDonald's callously disregarded concerns of its domestic franchisees in its eager quest to open more and more outlets. Would a kinder, gentler approach to the other members of the channel-of-distribution team have prevented or resolved these problems?

Relations with Customers

Most firms pay lip service to customer satisfaction, but some go much further in this regard than others. The participation of Harley-Davidson at rallies and other events helped develop a cult following. While not exactly gaining a cult following, Vanguard has created a loyal and enthusiastic body of customers. A symbiotic relationship can also be seen as applying to manufacturer–customer relations: They both stand to win from highly satisfied customers. And again, isn't a kinder, gentler relationship a positive?

Giving Employees a Sense of Pride and a Caring Management

The great turnaround of Continental from the confrontational days of Frank Lorenzo had to be attributed mainly to the people-oriented environment fostered by Bethune. The marvel is how quickly it was done, starting with such a simple thing as an open-door policy to the executive suite and encouragement of full communication with employees.

Still, Continental was not unique in this enlisting of employees to the team. Kelleher of Southwest Airlines certainly developed this esprit de corps, which helped account for Southwest's great cost advantage. Ray Kroc of McDonald's fostered harmonious franchisee relations as McDonald's began its great growth, although such relations dimmed in recent years.

On the other hand, Boeing's problems with its peaks and valleys of layoffs and hiring destroyed any hope of widespread pride and esprit de corps among its employees, except perhaps for a nucleus. A sense of pride was certainly latent for a firm with such a national symbol, but management did not cultivate it in present-day Boeing.

ETHICAL CONSIDERATIONS

A firm tempted to walk the low road in search of greater short-run profits may eventually find that the risks far outweigh the rewards. We have examined more than a few cases dealing with ethical controversies, for example, ADM's indictment for price fixing and its more subtle efforts to gain special influence in the halls of government. Then there was MetLife's indictment for deceptive sales practices, and the exposés of undesirable practices by United Way. Not the least was Ford and Firestone's reluctance to admit and accept blame for product safety deficiencies that cost hundreds of lives. While we cannot delve very deeply into social and ethical issues, these insights are worth noting:[2]

- A firm can no longer disavow itself from the possibility of critical ethical scrutiny. Activist groups often publicize alleged misdeeds long before governmental regulators will.
- Trial lawyers are quick to pounce on anything that might bring big payoffs from deep-pocketed defendants.
- The media will help fan public scrutiny and criticism of alleged misdeeds.

Should a firm attempt to resist and defend itself? The overwhelming evidence is to the contrary. The bad press, the continued adversarial relations, and the effect on public image are hardly worth such a confrontation. The better course of action may be to back down as quietly as possible, repugnant though that may be to a management convinced of the reasonableness of its position. Better rapport with the media may be gained by corporate openness and cooperation, with company top executives readily available to the press.

GENERAL INSIGHTS

Impact of One Person

In many of the cases we examined, one person had a powerful impact on the organization. Sam Walton of Wal-Mart is perhaps the most outstanding example, but we also have Ray Kroc of McDonald's, who converted a small hamburger stand into the world's largest restaurant operation. Other examples are Herb Kelleher of Southwest Airlines, tormentor of the mighty airlines, and Phil Knight of Nike, who could never break the four-minute mile in college but went on to bring Nike world leadership in running and other athletic gear. Let us not forget John Bogle, founder and crusader of the Vanguard Fund Family, and his gospel of frugality.

For turnaround accomplishments, Gordon Bethune, who turned around a demoralized Continental Airlines, stands tall—as does Lou Gerstner of IBM. Virtually and undeservedly unknown is Leonard Hadly, who quietly turned around Maytag after the disaster with its United Kingdom subsidiary.

One person can also have a negative impact on an organization. William Aramony almost destroyed United Way by his high living and arrogance. Less well known is Dwayne Andreas, longtime CEO of ADM, who set the tone for illegalities both embarrassing and reprehensible. Frank Lorenzo with his confrontational labor relations almost destroyed Continental. And how can we forget "Chainsaw Al" Dunlap? The impact of one person, for good or ill, is one of the recurring marvels of history, whether business history or world history.

Prevalence of Opportunities for Entrepreneurship Today

Despite the maturing of our economy and the growing size and power of many firms in many industries, opportunities for entrepreneurship are more abundant than ever.

---

[2] For more depth of coverage, see R. F. Hartley, *Business Ethics* (New York: Wiley, 1993).